Endorsements
Renovating Your Mind

We highly recommend to you this well-written and scripturally sound Bible devotional. We suggest you start every day with a reading from it before you begin your regular daily Bible reading. There are many reminders in this book of God's great love for you, so much so, that it colors virtually every single devotional. We have come to expect nothing less than his best from this gifted young author as a longtime faithful member and Bible study leader in our Packinghouse Church family.

—**Pastor Ed Rea**
The Packinghouse
Redlands, CA

Renovating Your Mind does truly that. Patrick has such a gentle yet firm way of reminding us that we aren't to think, act or react to situations and circumstances in our lives as the world does; gently inviting and guiding us to think as God does. His words speak to you as a friend would over a cup of coffee, and in a way that while you may be receiving correction and discipline, you welcome it as from a friend. This devotional will speak to the hearts of many as we seek to think more and more like Jesus in this rapidly, ever-changing world.

—**Pastor Garrie Price**
Calvary Chapel Safe Harbor
Cabo San Lucas, Mexico

When I think of the author of this volume before you, I think of him in the context that I have known him in. In this sad world of spiritual consumerism, it's refreshing to find voices that have grown up within a single church. I remember Patrick in his earliest days as a Christian, and Michelle, his lovely wife, in just her earliest days! Both have spent the bulk of their lives as fixtures among the thousands that have crowded in to the Packinghouse in Redlands, California on any given weekend. Whether it was Bible studies, mission trips, or the prayer room ministry, these two have been known and appreciated as a trusted couple with a heart for the living God! I'm blessed to have been the one to perform their wedding! As you read this volume before you, if you have not had the privilege as I have, of growing in such a healthy church environment, you will hear the heartbeat of what such an environment produces. The phrases, the thought patterns, the heartbeat, and the love for scripture remind me of home. Patrick has not only captured the essence and flavor of what I have remembered from my home church, but he has also allowed the Lord's heart to beat through his words, not in the same way as one would consider the doctrine of inspiration, but in the way of a man that is kept by the Holy Spirit and determined as He is, to encourage and enlist men and women to love Christ more fervently, to live for God more passionately.

I thank the Lord for Patrick and Michelle. Their growth is a testimony to the Lord's faithfulness to stir up gifts for the equipping of the saints. I pray that as you read this devotional that your heart might "catch" a little more of what it means to belong to Him!

—**Pastor Frank Sanchez**
Calvary Christian Fellowship
Colton, CA

RENOVATING YOUR *Mind*

BY

PATRICK EGLE

Deep River BOOKS

Renovating Your Mind
Copyright © 2019 by Patrick Egle

Published by Deep River Books
Sisters, Oregon
www.deepriverbooks.com

ISBN – 13: 9781632695079
Library of Congress: 2019941302

Printed in the USA
2019—First Edition
28 27 26 25 24 23 22 21 20 19   10 9 8 7 6 5 4 3 2 1

Acknowledgments

When the Lord told me to write a devotional book, I had no idea just how difficult that would be. Thankfully, He knew, and that is why He placed some extraordinary people in my life to surround and support me through this incredible and very challenging adventure.

Michelle Egle, my wife and best friend: Without her daily grace, love, encouragement, support, and prayers, this book would never have seen the light of day. She continually lifted me up and refocused me when discouragement, depression, and fear would overwhelm me. No matter how hopeless it seemed, she never let me quit. Thanks love—you truly are the most amazing person I have ever met!

The Egle family—Paul, Linda, Chris, Julie, Sean, Pam, Kayla, Lex Borroto, and of course Mike(y) Sassmann: Their unfailing support and encouragement to press on and press through was invaluable to me during this process. Thank you guys so much for always listening, always providing input, and always praying me through this!

Bill and Deann Hanley, Mark and Jennifer Conley, Darrell and Barbara Luttrull, Walt and Cynthia Harrison: These people were my Aaron and Hur who continually lifted my arms as I grew weak and weary during the battle. Their diligent prayers, counsel, and love were always perfect in power and timing to keep me focused, refreshed, and purposed. Thank you guys so much for always being there for me!

Leah Moore-Evans: In the very early stages of this project, Michelle and I prayed that the Lord would bring alongside of us those who had experience in writing a book. The Lord answered those prayers by bringing Leah into our lives. She was an invaluable source of wisdom for me regarding copyright laws, editing, and publishing. She freely gave of her time to answer all of my questions and always let me bounce my crazy ideas off of her. And whenever I would get to that point where all I could say was "Ack!" (Moore-Evans, Leah. "Re: Devo Book," message to Patrick Egle, January 7, 2018 email), she would graciously talk me through it and ease my concerns. Thank you, Leah—you truly are an answer to prayer!

The prayer team: I wish I could list out all of the names of every single person who took the time to pray for us and with us, but I fear that I would leave someone out, so I thought it best to write a general acknowledgment to all of them. Thank you all so much for teaming up with us on this project and diligently praying for us through all of the seasons we faced. It was your prayers that carried us through and kept us going during the most difficult of times. Your great labor of love has and will reap much fruit!

Pastor Ed Rea: The first time I showed up at the Packinghouse in 2001, I was a brand-new Christian in search of a home. After attending a Wednesday night service, I left proclaiming I would never go back because the message "was too convicting." I decided to go back that Saturday night and give the Packinghouse one more try, to which I had the same exact same response. It was then that the Lord spoke to me and said, "Patrick, this is exactly where you need to be, because you need to hear the truth." Eighteen years later, I am still going to the Packinghouse because I am still hearing the truth, verse by verse. Thank you, Pastor Ed, for your great faithfulness to this congregation and for continually speaking truth into my life.

Publisher/editor: I want to thank Bill Carmichael, Andy Carmichael, Alexis Miller, Sean Tosello, Tamara Barnet, and the entire Deep River Books' staff, as well as my wonderful editor, Carl Simmons, who painstakingly endured all of the growing pains that a first-time author goes through. Thank you for the grace and patience you continually showed me, thank you for all of your hard work, and thank you for taking a chance on me, partnering with me on this incredible book.

And lastly, I want to acknowledge and thank all of the men and women who have contributed to this book by pouring into my life. To say I wrote this book on my own would be foolish at best. I realize and confess that everything I know and have written in this book came from someone somewhere who said, "This is truth, and this is what it means." Whether it was a sermon, a commentary, a book, a prayer, a song, a story, a conversation, a post, a text, a tweet, or an email, I received and I grew. My only regret, as I have come to realize, is that it is impossible for me to rightly cite every single person who has ever contributed to my growth. Through my best efforts, I have painstakingly searched and prayed and sought out every resource I have at my disposal so that credit for the intellectual property contained in this book may be given to whom it is due. But alas, I fear some have still gone without the recognition they deserve. To all of you, I say thank you, I will always be in your debt.

Dedication

To our beloved treasures, Kate and Joel,

The greatest inheritance we can ever leave you is not that of silver and gold, but that of Jesus Christ. We pray this book will help guide you in your walk with Him all the days of your lives, that you might live in the freedom and grace that He has so bountifully afforded us.

Never forget: The Lord is good, He is ready to forgive, and He has abundant mercy to all who call upon Him. So give thanks to the Lord, call upon His name, make known His deeds, and always, always, always, give yourselves to prayer.

We love you now and forever with all that we are,

Mom and Dad

Foreword

by Bill Hanley

"I will give you a new heart and put a new spirit within you; I will take the heart of stone out of your flesh and give you a heart of flesh."

(Ezekiel 36:26)

It started out as a part of an email chain—a collection of events that described Bible verses in the framework of what was going on while on this side of eternity. On several occasions before these emails were sent out, I'd heard Patrick teach from the Scriptures. He was a gifted teacher and leader in a weekly Bible study that we shared. Something about the emails was different. It quickly became apparent that the goal was to transform the way we approach this side of eternity. How do we take what Scripture tells us about how to love and follow Christ and apply it to the things that come up every day?

It was clear to me that Patrick wasn't on some philosophically motivated rant with an emphasis on our fallen way of thinking. To the contrary, the work contained in the devotionals came out of a heartfelt desire to serve Christ by applying His Word to our struggles, joys, and mediocrities. The goal was simply to share the rejuvenating promises of the Bible with everyone he knew.

Patrick's determined purpose has always been to magnify the glory of God by being a servant to the power of Christ's grace. Showing others the transformational authority that is only found in Christ's love, Patrick's efforts remind us of Paul's conviction: "For I am sure that neither death nor life, nor angels nor rulers, nor things present nor things to come, nor powers, nor height nor depth, nor anything else in all creation, will be able to separate us from the love of God in Christ Jesus our Lord" (Romans 8:38–39, ESV).

As you take the time to read this work, allow your heart of stone to be changed into a heart of flesh. Watch the way daily events are significant to our Lord when viewed through His Word. With a biblical perspective, understand better how to live with a heavenly purpose. Observe the beautiful way Patrick shares the spirit of the Lord moving in the lives of himself and others around him. Enjoy the power of Patrick's gift as he shares how to love our Lord with all your heart, mind, and soul.

JANUARY 1st

> Lamentations 3:22–23: "Through the LORD's mercies we are not consumed, because His compassions fail not. They are new every morning; great is Your faithfulness."

And so it begins . . . we are going to exercise more, eat better, lose weight, save more money, write a book, spend more time with God . . . on and on the list goes. What is it about January 1st that causes us to make new resolutions for our lives? What is it that stirs up these passions within us, where we are compelled to take the weak areas of our lives and make them better?

Simple—January 1st represents a new beginning for us; a fresh start . . . a clean slate. With it, we have hope for a better tomorrow, one in which we will be more disciplined, more grateful, more . . . better.

And yet according to Lamentations 3:22–23, we have this every morning with the Lord. "Through the LORD's mercies we are not consumed, because His compassions fail not. They are new every morning; great is Your faithfulness." Jeremiah wrote these verses after the Babylonians had destroyed Jerusalem because of Israel's constant rebellion and sin toward God. Yet even when they spit in God's face and told Him, "We neither want nor need You, God," the Lord, in His incredible mercy and grace, still had favor on them. It was only because of His abundant mercies and His unfailing compassion that they were not consumed, for God's faithfulness is great.

As believers in Jesus Christ, we should be overjoyed because the same exact truth applies to us as well. Imagine if we lived every morning with God like it was January 1st . . . a new beginning, a fresh start, a clean slate. Gone would be the guilt and condemnation from yesterday's failures, and instead we would have hope and joy for a better today—not because of something we can do or achieve, but because of God's great mercy and His unfailing compassion toward us. This is ultimately where we find our hope, our strength, and our joy to press on and walk worthy of the calling—to walk worthy of the great gift of salvation that we have been given.

Believer, it is very important to remember that we confess our sin, not because they need to be removed from us, but because we are already forgiven through the blood of Jesus Christ. We are forgiven, past tense, yet continually ongoing as if we have never sinned. If we were to take this to the ultimate reality of God's love and forgiveness, we would see that it's not just every morning that we have new mercies, but that it is every minute of every day, for the rest of our lives, that we are given new mercies.

When Jesus died on the cross, every single sin that we would ever commit was in full view, and yet He still said "It is finished" when He breathed His last breath. The Greek word there is *tetelestai*, which means paid in full. Historic receipts found in Greece had this word, *tetelestai*, written at the bottom where it showed the balance due. So we see that there is nothing left to do; all business has been concluded. That is what the cross means for the believer. It is finished and we are forgiven. So believer, let every moment be your January 1st because the truth is that there are new mercies for this day.

JANUARY 2nd

> Mark 9:23: "Jesus said to him, 'If you can believe, all things are possible to him who believes.'"

I often become discouraged and frustrated with myself when I don't simply believe God without having to make the choice to believe Him first. These are the times that I become vulnerable to the suggestion that there is something wrong with me for having to choose to believe, rather than just believing—like, if I have to choose to believe, then I really don't believe. Well, I am here to tell you, this is not true, so don't believe the lie.

We need to understand that God's truths are simply much bigger than the tiny spaces we have within us, and for us to believe His truths are for us, for our situation, for this time in our lives, our tiny, comfortable little spaces have to be stretched, and it is going to be uncomfortable for a little while. But this is how we grow our faith . . . this is how our trust in God is developed. Those tiny spaces become bigger spaces and we soon find it easier to take in those big truths when we need them.

There is an unwritten law of belief that says, when we continually make the choice to believe in something, and that belief is consistently affirmed, then our choice to believe transforms into belief without thought. For example, suppose you go to a friend's house and your friend offers you a seat in an old, broken-down chair. You think to yourself, "There is no way this chair is ever going to hold me." But you make the choice to believe it will, and as you slowly sit down in the chair, it holds. Time and time again you go to your friend's house and you sit in that same old, broken-down chair, each time choosing to believe it will not give out from under you. By continually doing this, you will soon begin to just sit in the chair without even thinking about it. When this happens, you have now graduated from making the choice to believe, to having belief without thought.

We find a great example of this in Mark 9 when a man brought his sick son to Jesus, unsure that Jesus could heal him. He said to Jesus, "'But if You can do anything, have compassion on us and help us.' Jesus said to him, 'If you can believe, all things are possible to him who believes'" (Mark 9:22–23). Notice the key word here from this man to Jesus—*if* You can do anything. This man had doubts. He did not believe without thought because the truth that Jesus could heal his son was too great for that tiny little space within him to receive. And so Jesus turns it back on him, "*If* you can believe, all things are possible to him who believes." Was Jesus saying to him, "You must believe without thought"? No, Jesus was saying, "You must choose to believe!"

"Immediately the father of the child cried out and said with tears, 'Lord, I believe; help my unbelief!'" (Mark 9:24). The father of the child made the choice to believe, and Jesus healed his son.

Though we may never have belief without thought in everything, we must remember that the more we choose to believe in God's character, His faithfulness, His love, His provision, His Word, etc., the easier the choice to believe will be for us in the future.

JANUARY 3rd

> Matthew 11:28: "Come to Me, all you who labor and are heavy laden, and I will give you rest."

I am tired—physically, mentally, spiritually . . . to the depths of my soul, tired. But if you were to look at my schedule recently, you wouldn't think so. Let's see . . . I went on a cruise to Ensenada the 23rd–26th, was off sick the 27th–28th, worked the 29th, and then was off again the 30th–3rd . . . what in the world do I have to be tired about?

It all started when I left for the cruise. I remember telling people before I left that all I wanted to do on the cruise was rest—just lie around the ship, relax, and do absolutely nothing. I justified this because I couldn't remember the last vacation that I had that wasn't a mission trip. So in the last days before the cruise, I checked out physically, mentally, and spiritually.

Well, as the cruise came to a close, I remember thinking to myself, "I haven't done anything substantial other than climb thousands of stairs and eat a ton of pizza, and yet I am not rested at all. In fact, I am even more exhausted now than

I was before I left." It was seriously weird; I found absolutely no rest at all on the cruise. I never once felt relaxed, never once felt a sense of peace . . . never once came to the point of just resting that I had so longed for. Then, over the next six days, I worked only one day, was out sick two days, and had three days off . . . yet here I was, still exhausted physically, mentally, and spiritually. So what gives?

It's simple, really—I tried resting *from* Jesus Christ instead of resting *in* Jesus Christ. When I boarded that ship, I left everything behind me, including God. I didn't want to think about work, church, Bible study, devotions . . . anything. I just wanted to "escape" and "get away from it all" because I was exhausted. Sure, we prayed at meals together and often talked about God, but I never once set time aside for me and God. . . . I never once rested in Him.

"Come to Me . . . and I will give you rest," Jesus says. Not, "Go on a cruise and you will find rest," "Sleep all day and you will find rest," or, "Stop serving and you will find rest." No, Jesus says, "Come to Me . . . and I will give you rest." He makes it clear that true rest can only be found in Him, because only He gives rest.

What is so amazing about this promise is the simplicity of it. We don't need to take a vacation, or go to some tropical paradise, or cut things out of our lives to receive this rest—we simply need to go to Jesus, and He will give us the rest that we are lacking. It is available to us anywhere, and at any time. In the midst of a hectic work day, while sitting in traffic, while the bills are piling up, while we are being wrongfully persecuted, while we are stricken with illness or disease, while our hearts are broken, while our lives are completely upside down and the world is against us, we can find rest in Jesus Christ.

Do you need rest? Don't make the same mistake I made and look to the world for it, because you aren't going to find it. Simply look to Jesus. Just spend time with Him, and you will find the rest for your soul that you so desperately long for.

JANUARY 4th

Psalm 119:50 (NIV): "My comfort in my suffering is this: Your promise preserves my life."

Every now and then I come across a scripture that is so simple and yet so deeply profound that I want to kick myself forever forgetting it. This is one of those scriptures. The psalmist reminds us that when our focus is on God's promises for us, we can find comfort despite our current sufferings: "I remember, Lord, your ancient laws, and I find comfort in them" (Psalm 119:52, NIV).

In Matthew 11:28–30 (NIV), Jesus gives us an invitation, "Come to me, all you who are weary and burdened and I will give you rest. Take my yoke upon you and learn from me, for I am gentle and humble in heart, and you will find rest for your souls. For my yoke is easy and my burden is light." When speaking on this verse, many people have used the illustration of a yoke that you place on an oxen when plowing a field; they explain that the "yoke" of Christ is perfectly suited for us so as to not chaff our shoulders or be too heavy for us to carry. His burden for us is therefore easy and light; this is very true indeed.

But there is another truth in this word "yoke" that is often overlooked. Back in the day, rabbis often used this word in reference to their teachings. So when Jesus says, "Take My yoke upon you and learn from Me . . . and you will find rest for your souls. For My yoke is easy and My burden is light," He is referring to His teaching. So what Jesus is telling us here is, "Listen to Me and learn from My teachings because it is there, in My words, that you will find rest for your souls. My teaching is very easy to understand and what it asks of you is very little."

One of the main reasons God has given us the Bible is to help us through the hardships we face in this life so that we would not give up, but rather will endure to everlasting life. Remember, God does not only promise us eternal life in Jesus Christ, but quality of life here on Earth as well. I am not speaking of riches or fame or health like a prosperity gospel, but rather hope, peace, and comfort in every situation; these are all ours whenever we need them.

But to receive them, we need to go to where these things reside. As Romans 15:4 says, "For everything that was written in the past was written to teach us, so that through endurance and the encouragement of the Scriptures we might have hope." This is what the psalmist is telling us here, "My comfort in my suffering is this: Your promise preserves my life." This is where he found hope, peace, comfort, and rest in the midst of his suffering; and this is where we will find them as well.

JANUARY 5th

Numbers 11:4: "Now the mixed multitude who were among them yielded to intense craving."

There will be many times in our lives that we will struggle with intense cravings from our past. Sometimes these cravings can be so intense that we are almost incapacitated from the pain of not fulfilling them. But isn't it interesting that when we long for the things of the past, we conveniently forget the horrors and pain of bondage that caused us to cry out to God in the first place? How easily we forget that even when we had these lusts fulfilled, we were still completely miserable because these things only brought destruction to our lives and could never satisfy us. Yet we often entertain the lie that if we just had those things now, our lives would be much better and we would be completely satisfied.

So why do we experience intense cravings from our past if we are new creations? Like a silversmith who removes the impurities from precious metals through the process of refining, we often find ourselves looking back and yearning for the things of the past because as we are continually being molded into the image of Christ through the process of sanctification, those old desires are being forced to the surface so that they might be permanently removed from our lives. And the closer those cravings get to being defeated, the more they will fervently fight to keep their grip on us. The danger in this process is that if we choose to yield to these intense cravings whenever they rise up to the surface, they will continue to rule over us as our lord and master, and we will never be rid of them.

So how do we stand firm when being tempted by these desires from our past? Notice that even though all of Israel was tempted, it was only the "mixed multitude" that yielded to their intense cravings. These are the ones who had a divided mind between God and the world; whose faith was not firmly established in the Lord because they struggled to decide who they truly wanted to serve. On the other hand, those who stood firm in the face of these temptations were the ones who firmly placed their faith in the Lord and trusted in what His Word said about what is good and what is evil.

For us to successfully combat the cravings from our past, we need to remember that the good old days are right now; in Jesus, our lives have never been as good as they are today, and tomorrow, they will be even better. The kingdom of God is not one that looks back, but one that looks forward to where God is leading us. Psalm 103:5 (NIV) promises us that God will "satisf[y] your desires with good things." In other words, the things that God has for us are far greater than anything we can ever have in this world. So believer, stand firm in the midst of temptation by looking forward to the things that the Lord has for us, pressing on toward the prize of the upward call of God in Jesus Christ (Philippians 3:13–14).

JANUARY 6th

Matthew 5:14: "You are the light of the world."

A while back, my wife Michelle gave me a bookmark that I have sitting on my desk at work, which says, "All the darkness in the world cannot extinguish the light of a single candle."[1] I have come to find out that this is a proven scientific fact; darkness cannot extinguish light. It doesn't matter how much darkness there is, it does not have the power to extinguish light, because darkness is simply the absence of light. As I thought about this, I realized that the darker it gets, the brighter the light from that single candle actually becomes, so in a very real way, darkness does not hinder light, but rather it magnifies it.

The Bible often contrasts light and darkness, with light being good and darkness being evil. As believers, we are to walk in the light because we are no longer of the darkness. First Thessalonians 5:5 reminds us of this: "You are all sons of the light and sons of the day. We are not of the night nor of darkness." As followers of Jesus Christ, we are lights in a world full of darkness. That is why Jesus told us, "You are the light of the world." No matter how dark this world gets—and it will get very dark—it cannot extinguish our light, which is the Holy Spirit living in and through us.

Years ago, a friend of mine in Belize opened a house of ministry in downtown Punta Gorda. Right across the street from her ministry, a strip club/bar/dance club/drug house was opening up. My friend did all that she could do to prevent it, but to no avail; it opened right on schedule. But then something strange happened: Her ministry took off and flourished, as many people who were living in that darkness were drawn to the light; and in a matter of weeks, the nightclub went out of business. As she prayed about all of this, the Lord spoke to her very clearly and said, "Light never runs from darkness, rather darkness runs from light."

Believer, as the lost stumble around in the darkness with no hope or security in life, we who have hope and security in and through Jesus Christ will be a shining beacon to them by how we live our lives in the midst of that darkness. This is what it means to be the light of the world, to shine in the midst of darkness, not to run from it. So when you see darkness abounding, and you will, don't lose hope; don't get caught up in the chaos and confusion that this life can often bring and begin living like you are a victim in all of this. Remember, you are the light of the world, and no matter how dark it gets, all the darkness in the world cannot extinguish the light of a single believer.

JANUARY 7th

Romans 12:2 (NIV): "Do not conform to the pattern of this world, but be transformed by the renewing of your mind."

One of the gifts that I believe God has given me is the ability to look at certain things from an entirely different point of view than most people. Maybe it's just the rebel in me, but oftentimes I challenge beliefs and points of view that most people just accept as the *status quo*.

For example, since Michelle and I got married, many people have come up to us and asked how married life is going; our responses usually range from "awesome" to "amazing," depending on what day it is. And almost like clockwork people respond to us with, "Just wait; that will all change," or "You're still in the honeymoon phase; that will wear off soon." It's almost like they are cursing us to have a stale marriage . . . how sad.

Here is my question to this type of thinking: Why? Why must it all change? Why must it wear off? Where in the Bible does it say that a marriage founded and centered on Jesus Christ cannot be awesome and amazing every day? Notice that I did not say "perfect." I know a retired couple that has been married for more than forty years, and they pinch themselves every night because they cannot believe just how awesome and amazing their marriage is. The scary part about having this type of negative thinking is that people willingly accept this as fact, and so they just allow it to happen because "it's going to happen anyway."

Michelle and I refuse to conform to this pattern of thinking, because it is a worldly thought pattern; there is nothing of God in this type of thinking. It is the same pattern that tells us when we are tempted, "You might as well sin, because you are going to sin anyway." The apostle Paul stated very clearly, "Do not conform to the pattern of this world, but be transformed by the renewing of your mind." We are to challenge these worldly thought patterns by standing firm and fighting against them, not just lie down and accept them as if we have no say in the matter.

Honestly, I have no idea what tomorrow will bring for Michelle and myself, but I know that today I will fight for awesome and amazing. I will serve my wife, I will pray for her, I will wash her in the Word of God, and I will love her as much as I possibly can—but one thing I will not do is just accept that things will change or wear off.

I challenge you to do the same, not just in your marriage but in all things— your walk with God, your job, your ministry, your life. One of my favorite sayings is "Be blessed, for He is God!" because being blessed is not a reactive thing that happens after something has occurred in our lives. Rather, it is a proactive choice that we make every minute of every day, because He is God and in Him we are blessed.

JANUARY 8th

John 4:34: "Jesus said to them, 'My food is to do the will of Him who sent Me, and to finish His work.'"

I have been feeling very hungry lately—not so much physically, but rather, spiritually. My desire for knowledge and wisdom has reached a point of frustration, as no matter how much I read or pray or study, I still feel unsatisfied. Michelle and I have been seeking the Lord a lot about this recently. I have also sought wisdom from my pastor and my spiritual big brothers, yet questions still remain . . . should I go to Bible college, seminary, or a school of ministry? How do I satisfy this hunger, Lord?

Yesterday at work, Michelle sent me a text saying, "Obedience is how we grow." That stirred in my heart all day long and eventually led me to remembering today's verse, "My food is to do the will of Him who sent Me, and to finish His work." These were the words that Jesus spoke to His disciples when they begged Him to go and eat some food. Jesus continued, "Do you not say, 'There are still four months and then comes the harvest'? Behold, I say to you, lift up your eyes and look at the fields, for they are already white for harvest!'" (John 4:35). Jesus, of course, was speaking about the harvest of lost souls—the very reason why He came to Earth.

So, the answer to my question, the solution to the hunger that I am feeling, will only be filled by doing the will of God and to finish the work He has called me to do. No amount of reading or praying or studying is going to fulfill this desire within me if I am not following God's will for my life. So the only question that remains is, what is God's will for me at this point in my life? That remains to be seen.

I do know one thing: Wherever we are, whatever we are doing, we are to serve God and make disciples. The harvest is ripe with people who are ready to find and accept Jesus as their Lord and Savior, for as He proclaimed to us, "I say to you, lift up your eyes and look at the fields, for they are already white for harvest!" Nothing will ever fulfill us as much as the food of following God's will for our lives. So, believer, are you feeling empty and unsatisfied with life? Preach the gospel and fulfill the ministry that the Lord has called you to, and you shall be satisfied.

JANUARY 9th

Luke 12:34: "For where your treasure is, there your heart will be also."

One day, a pig and a chicken were walking down the road when they saw a fundraiser taking place. The chicken said to the pig, "Hey, we should help them out and donate some bacon and eggs." The pig replied, "No way!" When the chicken asked him why not, the pig said, "Because for you it is a one-time donation; for me it is a lifetime commitment."

For many of us, making a commitment to something can be a very difficult thing to do. Yet the truth is, we are all fully committed to *something*. Luke 12:34 tells us, "For where your treasure is, there your heart will be also." Whatever we consider most significant and worthwhile is where we will find our complete commitment. The question is, where is your treasure?

As an avid football fan (Go Packers!), I am always tuned in to the happenings around the league. One year, as teams were shaping their rosters for the upcoming season, one team in particular broke open the bank to sign every big-name free agent possible. When the owner of this team was interviewed about the big splash in free agency, he simply stated, "We are going all in," meaning, we are committing every resource we have to winning the Super Bowl this year.

After that interview, I was speaking to a couple of missionary friends that Michelle and I visit quite often, and the pastor was telling me that because finances and support were low, they had to dip into their savings account to build a church; but no matter, he said: "We are all in." I was struck by the fact that the owner of the football team and the pastor had the same exact mindset—to go all in and fully commit all that they had to achieve their desired goal—yet the motives fueling their passion could not have been more different. One was trying to attain treasures in this world for himself; the other was trying to attain treasures in heaven for others.

I think it is a very wise thing for each one of us to step back and take a long look at our lives from time to time, so that we might rightly determine exactly where our treasure lies, because we are all committed to something. We should be asking questions like, where am I fully committed and what am I fully committed to? Jesus said it best when He said, "And what do you benefit if you gain the whole world but lose your own soul? Is anything worth more than your own soul?" (Matthew 16:26, NLT).

Funny thing about that football team: Even though they had built what they dubbed as "The Dream Team," they were one of the worst teams in the league that year. So, believer, what are you going all in to achieve? What are you investing your resources into? Choose wisely, for the returns are eternal.

JANUARY 10th

> Revelation 3:12: "He who overcomes, I will make him a pillar in the temple of My God, and he shall go out no more."

This phrase may not mean a lot to us, but to the Christians who lived in Philadelphia (in Asia Minor), this spoke volumes. You see, the region where Philadelphia was located had a lot of earthquakes; whenever there was an earthquake, the people living there would have to run out of the city to avoid all of the falling debris. This was a very chaotic life for these people as earthquakes would come at all times, day or night; and for me personally, there is nothing worse than being woken up at three a.m. by an earthquake.

When the people would return to the city after the earthquakes had stopped, oftentimes the only things left standing were the pillars. So when Jesus promised them, "He who overcomes, I will make him a pillar in the temple of My God, and he shall go out no more." He was essentially saying to them, "In Me, you will become a pillar in heaven; you will be unshakeable, immovable, and will always remain standing for all of eternity. You won't need to run anymore in fear of death, because you will be safe and secure in the temple of My God."

After Michelle and I got married, we decided through much prayer and counsel that we would step down from our respective ministries so that we could focus on our marriage. We originally set a time frame of two months before we would return to those ministries, but as we prayed more about what the Lord would have us do, I felt God say to me, "Patrick, you need to strengthen that which needs to remain strong." It was then that I remembered the people in Philadelphia and what Jesus had promised them. I believe God was telling me that our marriage needed to be a pillar that was firmly established in the Lord, so that when the storms of this life came, and everything else around us crashed, our marriage would be left standing . . . it would remain strong. Four months later, as we were seeking where the Lord would have us serve in ministry, He led us to our church's married couples' study, which just happened to be starting a book about strengthening your marriage and had a picture of a pillar on the cover.

The most important thing to note in all of this is that you need to have a solid foundation. You could have the strongest pillar in the world, but if it is built on a weak or shifting foundation, it is useless as it will just fall right over when the storms come. This is why we are told in Matthew 7:24–27 to establish everything in our lives on the Rock, Jesus Christ:

> Therefore whoever hears these sayings of Mine (Jesus), and does them, I will liken him to a wise man who built his house on the rock: and the rain descended, the floods came, and the winds blew and beat on that house; and it did not fall, for it was founded on the rock. But everyone who hears these sayings of Mine, and does not do them, will be like a foolish man who built his house on the sand: and the rain descended, the floods came, and the winds blew and beat on that house; and it fell. And great was its fall.

I think it is a very wise thing for all of us to take a step back and think about the things in our lives that we want to remain standing after the storms of life hit. Things like our marriages, our children, our businesses, our faith. And then we need to ask ourselves: What is the foundation that I have built these things on? Will they survive the storms that this life will bring?

So, believer, strengthen those things that need to remain strong starting with your faith; build everything in your life on God and make them pillars so that when the world around you crashes and crumbles, those things will remain standing.

JANUARY 11th

> Proverbs 27:7 (NCV): "When you are full, not even honey tastes good,
> but when you are hungry, even something bitter tastes sweet."

As we learn in the Bible, honey has many appealing qualities; it is a nutritious food, a useful medicine, a proper gift, and a valued possession. Because of this, honey was highly sought after and very desirable. So when Solomon wrote, "When you are full, not even honey tastes good," he was making a very powerful statement to the people back in his day. Essentially what Solomon is saying here is, "When you are full, even good things will not appeal to you."

I think Solomon is making a point to us about the things that we normally feast on. Think of it like this: If our diet consists mainly of junk food, chances are that when something nutritious is presented to us, it will not be appealing because our body will neither crave nor desire it. In spiritual terms, if we feast on the junk of this world, when the things of God are presented to us, they will not be appealing because we will neither crave nor desire them.

Solomon is warning us of the danger that comes with such a lifestyle because when we fill ourselves with the junk of this world, we will not have room for the things of God in our life. We see proof of this in the second half of this verse, "but when you are hungry, even something bitter tastes sweet."

Have you ever been so hungry that even something you did not like tasted good? Solomon cautions us, when we do not eat of the things of God, we become so hungry to fill that empty void in our lives that we will do just about anything to fill it. When this happens, we end up feasting on the junk of this world. When we do this, we end up living out Proverbs 26:11, "As a dog returns to his own vomit, so a fool repeats his folly." Every time we feast on the sin and junk of this world, that is exactly what we are doing—returning to our own vomit—because the things of this world are poison to our soul.

So, believer, when is the last time you took an account of what you feasting on? An easy way to find out is to ask yourself this question, "Do the things of God appeal to me? Do I have room for Him in my life, or have I filled my life with so much junk, that is all I really hunger for and desire?" Answer these questions and you will know exactly what your spiritual diet consists of. My prayer is that we all make room for God in our lives today, because when we taste of the things of God, we will see that He is good.

JANUARY 12th

> John 6:35: "And Jesus said to them, 'I am the bread of life. He who comes to Me shall never hunger, and he who believes in Me shall never thirst.'"

My wife Michelle called me at work this morning and shared with me the dream that she had last night. Apparently we were at dinner with another couple, when she became very thirsty. She ordered a diet cola, then another, then another. She said she remembered chugging the diet colas as fast as she could because she was so thirsty, but no matter how much drank, it would not quench her thirst.

As she told me her dream, the convictions I felt this morning in my time of prayer were confirmed to me, in that I have been lacking in my role as the spiritual leader of our home. Before Michelle called me and told me about her dream, I was meditating on Ephesians 5:26, which speaks to the role of the husband, "that He might sanctify and cleanse her with the washing of water by the word." I was thinking about this verse because it describes one of the ways that Jesus loves the church; and as Michelle's husband, I am to love her as Jesus loves the church.

This convicted me because lately I have been washing Michelle with TV shows, movies, video games, football, bike riding, fellowship, etc., but not the Word of God. Now there is nothing wrong with any of these activities per se; in fact, one of the great aspects of our marriage is that Michelle and I are best friends and we love doing a lot of the same things together. But as fun as these things can be, the simple truth is that none of them can ever take the place of being in the Word of God together; none of these things will ever truly fulfill, benefit, and cleanse us from this world.

This is one aspect of what Jesus is saying here, "I am the bread of life. He who comes to Me shall never hunger, and he who believes in Me shall never thirst." When Pastor Ed taught on this verse last week, he stated that when interviewed, a famous Hollywood star was asked if she had ever considered suicide. The star replied, "To tell you the truth, I don't know of anyone in this business that hasn't seriously thought about it." Many of the top stars in movies, music, and sports have openly stated that even though they have everything they could ever want or need, they still find themselves depressed and empty and have seriously considered suicide. Fame, fortune, riches, sex, drugs, alcohol, possessions, food, hobbies, etc., will never satisfy the hunger and thirst that we have inside of us. Those desires can only be met by having a personal relationship with Jesus Christ.

I imagine living in this world like being stuck on a raft in the ocean. If you drink the water from the ocean, you will just become thirstier; and no matter how many gallons of ocean water you drink, it will never satisfy the physical needs your body has, and eventually you will die of thirst. The same thing happens when we consume the things of this world; they only leave us hungry and thirsty for more; and no matter how much of them we consume, they will never satisfy the hunger and thirst that we have inside of us.

I pray that this challenges all of us to take an account of what we are consuming personally, and what we are consuming corporately as a family. To the all of the fathers and husbands reading this, stop for a minute and seriously consider what you are washing your wife and family with. Only One thing cleanses, only One thing benefits, and only One thing fulfills . . . and that is Jesus Christ, the bread of life.

JANUARY 13th

John 7:53: "And everyone went to his own house."

In 2007, when Michelle and I had just met and were quickly becoming friends, the Lord instructed us to stop communicating with one another and separate from each other. Though we did not understand why God would have us do this, we were obedient to what He had instructed us to do. As people around us saw this, some of them began giving us advice in the matter. More often than not it was, "What are you waiting for? You like her, she likes you, just start dating."

Then, once the Lord brought us together as boyfriend and girlfriend two years later, people soon began questioning why we weren't engaged yet. Again, the Lord had told us to wait, so we waited for two more years before we were married; and the longer we waited, the more intense the advice became.

Michelle and I always understood the good intentions of the people who were advising us with what they thought was best for us; in their hearts, they just wanted us to be happy. But what they did not consider was the fact that at the end of the day, Michelle and I would be the only ones who would have to come home and face our decisions.

As a society, we are great at giving people advice and telling them what we think they should do in just about every aspect of life. But when all is said and done, and we are all alone with our thoughts, each one of us must come home and face our decisions by ourselves. All of those people who are advising us are nowhere to be found; it's just us, God, and our decisions. This is what we see in the latter part of John 7.

On the last day of the Feast of Tabernacles, Jesus proclaimed that He was the Messiah as He cried out to all of Israel, "If anyone thirsts, let him come to Me and drink" (John 7:37). It was at this point that Israel became divided. Many said Jesus was the Prophet. Others said He was the Christ. Some doubted by saying, "Will the Christ come out of Galilee?" (John 7:41). Then the chief priests and Pharisees chimed in and rebuked all of those who believed in Jesus as the Messiah. But regardless what anyone thought or said, at the end of the day, "everyone went to his own house." Each person had to go home and face their own decisions that day. It didn't matter how many people were for or against their decision; each person had a choice to make and each person alone would be held accountable to that decision.

At the end of the movie *Indiana Jones and the Last Crusade*, the villain found himself in a room full of chalices. As he looked to his *expert* on what chalice to drink from to gain eternal life, she pointed him to one made of gold with jewels covering the outside. As he drank from this cup, he died rather horribly. It was then that the guardian of the chalice said, "He chose poorly." Notice that even though his expert had told him what chalice to drink from, only he paid the price for making that decision.

There are many "chalices" to drink from in this world, but there is only One who truly satisfies; there is only One who gives eternal life, and that is Jesus Christ. So seek for yourself and choose wisely, because when it all comes down to it, no one will have to face the decisions you make except for you.

JANUARY 14th

Hebrews 11:6: "But without faith it is impossible to please Him."

This is probably a very familiar verse for most of us, yet I have discovered that as we grow in the Lord, we continue to learn different aspects of His Word, even though we may know a verse by heart. This was the case a couple of weeks ago as I was serving in the prayer room with some brothers from church.

I remember we were discussing different aspects of faith when my good friend Darrell said, "God will never allow us to escape our need for faith." I asked him if he could repeat that again because I had never heard that before, and so he said it again: "God will never allow us to escape our need for faith." Upon listening to this the second time, I felt the door of my mind slowly creak open as a new truth was revealed to me.

If, according to Scripture, it is impossible to please God without faith, then we can rightly determine that everything we want to do for the Lord, and everything the Lord wants us to do for Him, will require a certain measure of faith. I think in the back of my mind I had always believed that there were *easy* things I could do for the Lord that didn't require faith; but as I thought about this more, I realized that there is nothing *easy* about serving God. Every single act of obedience, service, worship, and/or prayer will require a certain measure of faith from us.

This helps me a lot personally, because many times when I am asked to do something for the Lord, I make an excuse not to do it because that particular thing requires an act of faith. I say to myself, "I will just wait for the easy things to do." In "Patrick terms," this means things that I can do that won't require me to be challenged or stretched or to be uncomfortable . . . things that I *feel* ready for; basically, things that will not require an act of faith. This is not how the Lord would have us live our lives.

God wants us to grow and mature and be changed more and more into His image; and because of this, He will allow things into our lives that we do not understand. He will call us to do certain things that take us out of our comfort zone; He will orchestrate events that make us face our fears. Basically, God will never allow us to escape the need for faith in our lives, because acting on faith, living by faith, is what pleases the Lord. And as Paul well stated in Romans 1:17, "The just shall live by faith."

JANUARY 15th

1 Peter 1:7 (NIV1984): "These have come so that your faith—of greater worth than gold, which perishes even though refined by fire—may be proved genuine and may result in praise, glory and honor when Jesus Christ is revealed."

For the last two weeks, my wife Michelle and I have been hit with pretty heavy physical afflictions. We have had multiple doctor appointments, urgent care visits, and even an all-nighter in the emergency room at Redlands Community Hospital. Being that we were both sick, and had a lot of time off because the holidays were here, we spent almost the entire two weeks nursing one another back to health. And though this was not fun for either of us to go through, we understand that difficult times "come so that your faith—of greater worth than gold, which perishes even though refined by fire—may be proved genuine and may result in praise, glory and honor when Jesus Christ is revealed."

This was revealed to us Monday night as we were recapping what had happened over the last couple of weeks. It was interesting to us that we both looked very fondly on our time of affliction. In all honestly, it was actually kind of sad to me that we were getting better and things were going back to *normal* again. Please don't get me wrong—we both suffered and in no way was this enjoyable for us— but after reflecting on our difficult time together, it was apparent to us that our afflictions were actually an answer to prayer.

See, even before we got married, Michelle and I prayed that God would grow our love, our friendship, and would make us the man and woman that He wanted us to be. This has been, and is today, our greatest desire for our marriage. As we looked back over the last two weeks, we quickly realized that these prayers had been answered, because the whole time we were afflicted, our focus was only on seeking God and serving one another. That was it. There was nothing else in our lives to distract us from loving God and loving one another; and because of that, we grew closer together as we grew closer to God.

Understand, out of all the things God could make Michelle and I to be, the most important thing for us to be in His eyes is a man and a woman of faith, because without faith, it is impossible for us to please God (Hebrews 11:6). Faith in God is what will carry us through the adversity, the impossible situations, and the times of uncertainty that we will face in this life. Having an established faith in

God is what will compel us to do godly things in an ungodly world that will change lives for all eternity. And ultimately, Peter says, it is our faith during these times that will result in praise, glory, and honor when Jesus Christ is revealed. There is nothing more precious than this.

JANUARY 16th

> Acts 5:19–20: "But at night an angel of the Lord opened the prison doors and brought them out, and said, 'Go, stand in the temple and speak to the people all the words of this life.'"

As the Lord performed many signs and wonders among the people through the apostles, the high priest and his followers grabbed the apostles and threw them in jail. Much like Jesus, the apostles were persecuted because of their good works and their popularity among the people. They were a threat to the high priest, who wanted to keep the people in a system of religious works and bondage so they would continue looking to him and the Sadducees for their salvation.

"But at night an angel of the Lord opened the prison doors and brought them out, and said, 'Go, stand in the temple and speak to the people all the words of this life.'" Notice that the apostles were not just set free, but they were set free with a specific purpose in mind.[2] "Go, stand in the temple and speak to the people all the words of this life."

I think it is important to note that God did not just set them free so they could wander about aimlessly in their newfound freedom. Rather, He set them free with a very specific purpose in mind: to preach the gospel of life. It is the same reason we have been set free from our imprisonment as well. God did not free us from sin and bondage so that we may live comfortably in a Christian bubble, or indulge ourselves in the pleasures of this world; He set us free so that we might be used to set others free as well.[3]

But how that is carried out is very different. God has purposed some to write songs, some to play football, some to raise children through foster care, some to teach in public schools, and some to hand out tracts and feed the homeless. But regardless what it may be, there is a purpose built into each one of our hearts by the One who created us—a purpose that will fulfill our lives and always point to Him and His message of eternal life. Our responsibility is simply to go where He tells us to go and do what He tells us to do. So, believer, God has a purpose for you. Have you found it yet?

JANUARY 17th

Proverbs 15:1 (NIV): "A gentle answer turns away wrath, but a harsh word stirs up anger."

I have read this verse many times, and until this morning I have always thought that this proverb was only speaking in regard to dealing with others. For example, if someone is angry with me, and I respond to them with a gentle answer, then the situation will eventually be resolved peacefully. But what I noticed this morning was that the wisdom contained in this verse is not only about dealing with others; more importantly, it is about dealing with ourselves.

I believe Solomon was telling us to respond to others with a gentle answer, not so much for their sake, but more so for our sake. If we respond to a situation with a harsh word, we are merely allowing anger to have its way within us. But if we respond to a situation with a gentle answer, then we actually turn away wrath from coming in and gaining control over us. This is important for us to understand and implement, because "the wrath of man does not produce the righteousness of God" (James 1:20). And as believers, we are first and foremost witnesses of Christ.

The truth we need to remember about all of God's instructions to us is that we will always be the ones who are blessed first and foremost when we are obedient to them. We are instructed to forgive others because unforgiveness is poison to our souls; we are instructed to pray for our enemies so that our hearts will not become cold and calloused toward them; we are instructed to tithe and give joyfully because this will keep us from allowing greed and the love of money to establish a root in our heart. The end game in all of this is to make us more like Jesus, not more like the world. And when we are obedient to God's instructions, we are blessed and conformed more into His image.

JANUARY 18th

John 1:20: "I am not the Christ."

One of the first lessons I learned serving in the prayer room was that our role there is to pray for people, not to counsel them or try to fix their problems because, well, quite simply, we can't. There is only one name under heaven by which we are saved, healed, restored, freed, etc., and that is Jesus Christ (Acts 4:12). Our role is simply to point people to Jesus and help them surrender their problems to Him because He, and He alone, is the Christ.

Last night, a good friend of mine came into the prayer room for some much-needed prayer. As she sat down with me and poured out her heart about what was going on in her life, I quickly forgot the first lesson of serving in the prayer room; instead of pointing her to Jesus in prayer, I tried to be the Christ and save the day. I fervently searched my heart and mind to find those perfect words—that one insightful, profound thing that would just make it all better for her—but I couldn't. In doing this, I was praying for her in my strength and wisdom, and not in the power of the Holy Spirit. We are reminded in Zechariah 4:6 that it's "'Not by (our) might, nor by (our) power, but (always) by My Spirit' says the LORD." It's in these times that I need to remember, "I am not the Christ."

But it's not just in the prayer room that we need to remember this. How many times have we gone to work thinking that we can, or have to, do it all on our own? How many times have we lived with the belief that the fate of [fill in the blank] rests solely in our hands; that the outcome is completely reliant on us? Maybe we think that we are responsible for someone's happiness; maybe we think that we can make our marriage work with our insight and wisdom; maybe we think that we can raise our kids by drawing on our own experiences. What this type of thinking is really saying is that, "I am the Christ."

There is so much freedom and wisdom when we realize that "without Me (Jesus) you can do nothing" (John 15:5). True wisdom begins when we realize that we can do nothing good apart from God. So, believer, let yourself off of the hook today, for you are not the Christ.

JANUARY 19th

> James 5:16a: "Confess your trespasses to one another, and pray for one another, that you may be healed."

How many of us really like confessing those personal things that we struggle with to someone else? It is probably one of the more uncomfortable things to do as a Christian, because we have to destroy our "perfect Christian image" in order to do it. Yet in James 5:16 we are instructed to "Confess your trespasses to one another, and pray for one another, that you may be healed." James says that when we confess our sin to one another, and pray for one another, sin will lose its grip on us.[4]

We have to remember that sin is like an overpossessive lover—jealous, controlling, deceitful—and it does not want to share us with anyone else. It keeps us from confessing our sin to others by having us believe that no one else would understand our struggle, or that they would look at us differently because of that struggle. Yet the Bible tells us that all of our temptations are common to man (1 Corinthians 10:13), so no matter what we may struggle with, we are not alone in that struggle. David Guzik reminds us that "confession breaks the power of secret sin" because when we confess it, it is exposed and it loses all of its power over us.[5]

I know of many men who had struggled with porn addiction for years. And each man, to himself, will admit that they tried just about everything to break free from this bondage, yet they never could. But when they applied this verse and put it into practice, and found accountability with other men from church and continually confessed their sin and were prayed over, they were finally freed from that bondage.

It's also interesting to note that hidden sin not only hinders us spiritually, but it can also affect us physically as well. Many people have struggled with some kind of physical affliction or illness, only to be healed after they confessed some hidden sin and were prayed over. So we see that it is very important for us to have this type of fellowship regularly. We should all have one or two people in our lives that we can be brutally honest with and bare our souls to—people who will not judge us, but rather will listen to us and pray for us so that we might be healed from that sin. So, believer, do you have this type of fellowship in your life? If not, seek it out; pray that God would bring this type of accountability into your life, for as Ecclesiastes 4:9–10 says, "Two are better than one, because they have a good reward for their labor. For if they fall, one will lift up his companion. But woe to him who is alone when he falls, for he has no one to help him up."

JANUARY 20th

Luke 22:42 (NIV): "Father, if you are willing, take this cup from me; yet not my will, but yours be done."

As Jesus was praying in the garden of Gethsemane hours before His arrest and crucifixion, it was here, in an intimate time of prayer with the Father, that the cross—and everything that it represented spiritually, physically, and emotionally—was defeated. It was here that Jesus surrendered to God's will as He humbly stated, "not my will, but yours be done." This is the moment when Jesus made the choice to take our sin upon Himself—the moment when He decided He would drink our cup of God's wrath, defeating sin and death forever.

I was reminded of this as Michelle and I sat in the garden of Gethsemane with about forty others from our church in April of 2012. After a brief Bible study and some worship, we all separated and had some time to reflect on where we were and what this place meant for us. As Michelle and I prayed, I was reminded that some two thousand years ago, Jesus sat here, prostrate, and prayed this very prayer. And it was because He made the choice to take our sin and death, that we were there two thousand years later. We are literally fruit from the choice He made that day.

So as we continued to pray, I felt led to pray in the same spirit of submission that Jesus prayed—not for others, mind you, but for my own issues of life. "Father, heal me of my affliction; nevertheless, not my will, but Yours be done." Michelle and I continued to pray this prayer for all the things that we were carrying with us, always ending with "not my will, but Yours be done." It was so freeing to let go of these things into the scarred hands of the One who died for us, knowing that He is good, trusting that His will for us is perfect, and that His plans for us will bring about joy, purpose, and fulfillment even if it meant carrying around an affliction.

Does that mean I will stop praying for healing? No, not at all. But it does mean that I will stop worrying about it. Maybe this morning you find yourself in a similar situation. If so, believer, lift that thing up to God, submit it to Him in a time of intimate prayer, and surrender it to Him, knowing that there is no better place for that issue to be than in the hands of the very God who died for you.

JANUARY 21ˢᵗ

> Acts 14:22b: "We must through many tribulations enter the kingdom of God."

There are many misconceptions about the Christian walk. For example, when I got saved, I thought I was going to have to start wearing sweaters, part my hair on the side, and grow a mustache a la Ned Flanders, because that is what I thought being a Christian was. Another example is when a middle-aged woman came into the prayer room for the first time and asked us to pray for her; nervously she then asked if we were going to slap her on the forehead, causing her to fall backward. These misconceptions ended with much joy and relief when the truth was finally revealed, but not all misconceptions are like these.

Probably the most common misconception today is that the Christian walk is one without difficulty or tribulation. Thus, when new believers encounter hard times, they are unprepared and they stumble mightily as they believe that they must have done something wrong or that God has abandoned them. We must remember that we are "to be conformed to the image of His Son" (Romans 8:29). God's desire for us is not a temporary, physically comfortable life, but rather an eternal, everlasting spiritual faith that will carry us through this life.

The realization that "we must through many tribulations enter the kingdom of God" is a difficult one to accept; yet embracing this truth should strengthen and encourage us. When the apostle Paul said this to the believers in Lystra, Iconium, and Antioch, he was "strengthening the souls of the disciples, exhorting them to continue in the faith" as they were facing very difficult times (Acts 14:22b). Paul could rightly preach this message of endurance because he was still healing from a near-death experience that he had just days earlier when he was preaching the gospel in a nearby town. Jews from the surrounding cities had grabbed hold of him, dragged him outside the city gates, and stoned him, leaving him to die. But Paul "rose up and went (back) into the city" that they dragged him out of (Acts 14:20b), and continued the work of the ministry.

So, believer, as David Guzik reminds us, make no mistake about it: The life of one who walks with the Lord "year after year, trial after trial" is a hard one, as it takes a "strong soul and an encouraged faith" to endure the trials this life brings.[6] But know this, we are not overcome by tribulation; rather, we are overcomers of it in Christ Jesus. We are not conquered by suffering; we are more than conquerors of it through Him who saved us. For greater is He that is in you than he that is in the world (1 John 4:4). When we choose to endure the trials of this life, and not give up or lose faith, but rather press on, trusting in God's purposes and promises for us, standing firm in our faith, we will receive the crown of eternal life that is promised to all those who overcome. And that is definitely worth fighting for.

JANUARY 22nd

Hebrews 11:6: "But without faith it is impossible to please Him, for he who comes to God must believe that He is, and that He is a rewarder of those who diligently seek Him."

Yesterday, as some of us were praying in the prayer room during service, I was given a very powerful vision. This is what I saw . . . as people were sitting in church, each person had a gift gently placed in their lap. Each gift was packaged in beautiful white wrapping paper and was perfectly tied with a crimson red bow; the gifts were all the same size and shape, and they were all very light so as to not burden anyone under its weight.

The next part of the vision is what broke my heart: As I walked out into the sanctuary, I was saddened by the sheer number of people who had left their gifts behind, never even opening them. The more I thought about this, the more I began wondering what gift God had given each person the opportunity to receive. For some people it was salvation; for others it was healing, restoration, or maybe the freedom from the bondage of sin that they were suffering under; some gifts were answers to prayers, words of knowledge, instruction, and wisdom; while other gifts were exhortations of strength and endurance for the trials that they were going through. Regardless what the gift was, many had left church that day never receiving the blessing that God had for them.

The truth of the Christian life is that God wants to bless us; we see this portrayed throughout the Bible from Genesis to Revelation. The Bible clearly promises us in James 4:8 that if we draw near to God, He will draw near to us. So every time we worship God, open His Word, or pray individually or corporately, we have the opportunity to be blessed, because every time we do these things, we have an encounter with the living God.

But we need to come to God with the certain expectancy that somehow, in some way, God is going to bless us during this interaction. We need to be cognizant of this truth so that we are constantly searching and interacting with Him during these times of intimacy. For example, my brother often gets these free prize giveaways in the mail from local car dealerships. They promise him that if he comes down and test-drives a car, he will get a gift card, gas card, or another selected prize. So he goes down there with the expectancy that when he test drives a car, he is going to get a prize; and sure enough, every time he test-drives a car, he gets a prize just as promised. How much more will the God of all love and faithfulness bless us when He promises that He will? Yeah . . . abundantly more!

This is what the author of Hebrews 11:6 is instructing us to do; he says that when we come to God, we need to come to Him in faith, believing that He is (the living God; the giver of good and perfect gifts [James 1:17]; wanting to bless us with all we need) and that He is a rewarder of those who diligently seek Him. When we come to God with this focus and expectation, we will not miss out on the blessings that God has for us.

JANUARY 23rd

Daniel 3:18: "But if not, let it be known to you, O king, that we do not serve your gods, nor will we worship the gold image which you have set up."

King Nebuchadnezzar commanded Shadrach, Meshach and Abednego to bow down and worship his idol or be thrown into a fiery furnace. To this they responded, "Even if God does not save us O king, and we die, we will still worship Him." Without question, God is able to save, heal, free, bless in all things and at all times . . . but even if He doesn't, will we still serve Him? Even if we do not get what we desire the most, will we still praise God?

I have been dealing with a physical affliction of the skin for about two-and-a-half years now. I have been prayed over, gone to all of the doctors, done all of the tests, taken every treatment, and yet I still carry this with me. This affliction is by no means life-threatening, but it is uncomfortable and really limits what I can do physically, because being in the heat causes my affliction to spread.

A couple of years ago, as Michelle and I were preparing to go to Israel, I kept coming across the story of Naaman, the commander of the Syrian army who had leprosy. He was told to go see Elisha, the prophet of the God of Israel. Elisha instructed Naaman to wash in the Jordan River seven times and his skin would be restored to him. Naaman scoffed at Elisha's instructions at first, but after much raging and complaining, Naaman was finally obedient to what Elisha told him to do and his skin was completely restored to him, "like the flesh of a little child" (2 Kings 5:14). I kept thinking to myself, "This is it . . . the Lord has set all of this up so that I can be miraculously healed in the Jordan River."

I prayed about this for months, begging God to heal me at the Jordan. Well, the time finally came when we were having a baptism at the Jordan River. After being baptized with Michelle, we snuck off to the side and I began dipping in the Jordan seven times. It was a very emotional experience for me as I wanted to be healed more than anything; but as I was coming up from under the water for the seventh time, I felt God ask me, "Patrick, even if I do not heal you, will you still love Me?" I was overcome with emotion as tears were streaming down my face, "Lord, even if You do not heal me, I still love You." It was a very powerful moment for me as I found the peace of God in the midst of unfulfilled desire.

Being healed that day never would have brought me the peace, joy, and intimacy with God that I really needed, because these things are not found when everything is good and the sun is shining down on us. No, these things are only found during the storms of life, when things are crashing down around us, when our prayers are not answered to our liking, when our desires are not met, and yet we still say confidently, "I love You Lord, and I still trust You with my life." The peace of God is only found when we trust in who He is despite our circumstances.

JANUARY 24th

> Romans 8:13: "For if you live according to the flesh you will die; but if by the Spirit you put to death the deeds of the body, you will live."

Why do we often fail when confronted with a fleshly desire? Why does it seem like we are so powerless to stand firm against temptation and just say no when it calls on us to submit? The answer is simple: We try to use our flesh to defeat our flesh. As pastor Jim Cymbala explained, we try to fight our temptations with our own strength by building up a mindset that our willpower will keep us from giving in to that temptation; and if we are fortunate, it might actually work for a little while. But within a few days, that struggle is back and we find ourselves saying, "What's wrong with me?"[7]

The problem is not you per se; it's the flesh you carry around with you. The apostle Paul said that our flesh is a "body of death" (Romans 7:24) that we drag around with us until the day we die. We forget that our flesh is not for us; rather, it is totally and completely against us. It will always be given to the lusts of this world, and no matter how hard we try we will never be able to coerce it into helping us overcome the temptations that this life brings. We must understand that the flesh is directly opposed to the Holy Spirit and it only brings death to our lives, not life (Romans 8:6–7). Regardless if our struggle is with the lust of the flesh, the lust of the eyes, or the pride of life (1 John 2:16), our flesh will forever thirst, hunger, and scream out for these things until the day Jesus takes us home.

So what do we do until then? How do we endure the temptations of this life? Our passage in Romans tells us, "if (you live) by the Spirit, you put to death the deeds of the body." Galatians 5:16 echoes this very truth: "Walk in the Spirit, and you shall not fulfill the lust of the flesh." Cymbala wrote in his book *You Were Made for More*, "Nowhere in the New Testament does it say God will 'work with' our flesh. He only speaks about killing it. 'Therefore put to death your members which are on the earth; fornication, uncleanness, passion, evil desire, and covetousness, which is idolatry' (Colossians 3:5). The only hope for dealing with the inside enemy is to abandon ourselves to the leadership of the Holy Spirit."[8]

Since we can't separate ourselves physically from the flesh, we have to separate ourselves spiritually from the flesh. This is accomplished by walking in the Spirit through a daily, habitual lifestyle of abiding in Christ through prayer, His Word, and obedience to His instructions. This is not to say that when we walk in the Spirit we will be perfect, or that we will never be tempted; rather, it's saying that when we make wise choices as to how we spend our time and what we allow into our hearts and minds, the world and all of its lusts will fade into the background and its grip on us will be greatly diminished.

For example, I have been on many mission trips; and honestly, when I am on these trips, I do not struggle with the things that I struggle with at home. Why is that? Because on these trips, I am completely consumed with God . . . serving Him, seeking Him, submitting to His will. By doing this, my mind stays on Him; there's no place for the things of the world as the Holy Spirit fills my mind and occupies all my thoughts. The point is that when we walk in the Spirit, our flesh has no voice. It has been completely muted and has lost any influence it once had on us. So, believer, do not battle against the flesh with the flesh; rather, put on the whole armor of God so that you may stand firm in the day of adversity.

JANUARY 25th

> James 5:15: "And the prayer of faith will save the sick, and the Lord will raise him up."

The prayer of faith is not something that is due to worked up feelings, or even positive thinking. No, the prayer of faith is prayed when responding to the prompting of the Lord.[9] Now whether that faith is in response to His instructions, a la James 5:13–14, or in response to the moving of the Holy Spirit in someone's life, it is a prayer of faith. Does this mean that everyone will get healed when we pray for them? No, it doesn't, and only God can answer why. He has plans and purposes and timing that we cannot understand. Some people are healed immediately, some people are healed later, and some people are not healed until the Lord takes them home; regardless, all are healed.

So how do we know when to pray boldly in faith and when not to? Well, it's a trick question, as we are always to pray with the expectancy that the Lord is going to heal that person right then and there. As my dear friend Darrell often tells me,

"God is not going to be upset with us if we always pray in faith. He won't say to us, 'Stop that. Stop stepping out in faith like that. What's wrong with you?'"

God loves it when we pray in faith. I used to think to myself when praying for someone, "God, what if I pray in faith, and You don't heal that person? I don't want to misrepresent You to them." David Guzik reminds us, "God is big enough to handle His own reputation."[10] He doesn't need me to try to defend Him or His ways. Our job is to just pray for others in faith and leave the rest to God.

I would say this, though: Every time that we pray for someone, though their situation may not have changed right then and there, they have been changed. Their perspective is no longer one of hopelessness, or worry, or anxiety, but rather one of hope and promise. Prayer is not so much about fixing people's problems as it is about taking them into the presence of God and helping them surrender their issues to the loving God who died for them. When we pray for people, their focus is taken off of their problems and placed squarely on Him. They are reminded of who He is, what His Word says, and what He has promised us. The prayer of faith is not so much about results as it is about experiencing the One that we are praying to. Knowing that God hears our prayers and wants to help us should always stir us to pray in faith for others and for ourselves.

JANUARY 26th

> Psalm 68:19 (NIV): "Praise be to the Lord, to God our Savior, who daily bears our burdens."

Have you ever asked yourself why you feel overwhelmed when life gets heavy? I think for every person, the answer would be something to the effect of, "I have a lot on my shoulders." Now maybe those are not the exact words we use, but regardless, the point remains the same: We get overwhelmed when we try to carry life's burdens ourselves. This is not how it should be for us, as David reminds us: "Praise be to the Lord, to God our Savior, who daily bears our burdens."

David continues, "Our God is a God who saves; from the Sovereign LORD comes escape from death" (Psalm 68:20, NIV). What is David telling us, exactly? Basically, David is painting this picture that reminds us that God is in complete control of every single thing. He is Lord over all things, even the most overwhelming thing that we will ever face . . . death. From God, through Jesus Christ, comes the promise and guarantee of salvation, or in David's words, an "escape from death."

Jesus Christ has shouldered man's burden of sin and death, yet many people are still trying to carry those burdens themselves.

It is ludicrous for anyone to try and carry the burden for sin and death, because it is an impossible burden to carry. For anyone to try to do this, they would be completely overwhelmed by it and would be crushed under its enormous weight. In the same manner of thinking, it is just as foolish for us to try to carry our daily burdens as well, because they are not meant for us to carry.

Jesus made this very clear in Matthew 11:28 (NIV) when He stated, "Come to me, all you who are weary and burdened, and I will give you rest." Jesus knew that we would try to carry these burdens ourselves while still thinking we could find rest in it all; He makes it clear, "Come to Me and give Me that burden, I will carry it for you so that you can rest; it is not yours to carry." David affirms this statement in Psalm 55:22 (NIV), "Cast your cares on the LORD and he will sustain you; he will never let the righteous fall."

I think the underlying statement in all of this is that Jesus is already carrying all of our eternal and daily burdens for us as He "daily bears our burdens." To believe that we have to carry them, or that we are actually carrying them in any way, is undue stress and anxiety that is not meant for us. Think of it like two strong men carrying a large, heavy, solid oak desk and a five-year-old boy walking alongside them with his hands under it, thinking he is actually helping them carry it. Jesus says to all of us, "I got this! I am fully aware of what is going on in your life and I am fully in control, so release it to Me. Don't worry."

So, believer, whatever that burden is, realize that Christ is already carrying it for you. To worry about it is pointless and self-defeating. This is why we are told in Philippians 4:6–7 (NIV), "Do not be anxious about anything, but in every situation by prayer and petition, with thanksgiving, present your requests to God. And the peace of God, which transcends all understanding, will guard your hearts and your minds in Christ Jesus."

JANUARY 27th

John 21:3a: "Simon Peter said to them, 'I am going fishing.'"

Peter is at an interesting crossroad in his life. Even though he just had an encounter with the risen Christ, I believe his denial of Jesus in the courtyard was still fresh in his mind. The disciples had been instructed to go to a certain mountain in Galilee to meet with Jesus, yet here we find Peter back in his hometown of Bethsaida, fishing.

Hard to say what was going on in Peter's mind at this point, but I think we have all felt it before. It's that state of mind we get after we have failed in our walk with Jesus. We allow condemnation and self-loathing to be the dominant voice in our head and we refuse to believe that we can still be used by God, or that He would even want to use us anymore. This is when we quit on Jesus and say to ourselves, "I am done. I am a filthy, lowly failure and I deserve to die and rot forever all by myself." And then we go back to what was familiar, that which was once comfortable for us; where we were before Christ came into our lives. For Peter, it was fishing.

"And that night, they caught nothing" (John 21:3c).

But it's never the same, is it? Yeah, the sea still smells the same, the wind still comes from the same direction, the boat still floats, the nets still work, the people are the same . . . but in your heart, everything has changed. No longer is there the fulfillment and joy and purpose there once was; that familiar, comfortable place is now empty, void, hollow, tasteless, and fruitless. Once you have walked with Jesus and truly experienced life with Him, you can never go back to what was once familiar and comfortable because you have been changed.

We often compare being saved as going from a caterpillar to a butterfly. Well, can a butterfly go back to living the life of a caterpillar after it has experienced the beauty, wonder, and freedom of flight? I suppose it can, but that life would never truly fit the butterfly because the butterfly is made to fly, not walk in the muck and mire. It would completely go against its new nature. The same is true for us as we are brand new creations in Christ. We cannot go back to who we once were or what we once did; we must move forward: "but one thing I do, forgetting those things which are behind and reaching forward to those things which are ahead" (Philippians 3:13).

JANUARY 28th

Psalm 75:2: "When I choose the proper time, I will judge uprightly."

A couple of weeks ago in a Bible study I was attending, a discussion broke out regarding salvation. One person said that if you live in continual/habitual sin, then you have given away your salvation. Another person chimed in that once saved, always saved. Another person said that we are only forgiven seven times seventy. From an objective point of view, this was a fruitless and futile conversation because the Lord reminds us in many places throughout the Bible, "I will judge." Only God knows the heart of man and thus only He can judge rightly. Yet we still try, don't we?

I am not sure what it is within us that causes us to want to know the things that we are never going to know. Pride, ego, self-gratification . . . "I want to be the one to figure it out!" If we go back to the Garden of Eden, we are reminded that one of the reasons Eve disobeyed God was because she wanted to know all that the Lord knew. Look at how well that turned out. We see this today as people are constantly predicting the day that Jesus is going to come back for the church. Books have been written, seminars given, mathematicians have used numbers and theories and dates to create these massive detailed charts which supposedly predict the exact moment Jesus will come back, and yet we are told in the Bible that we will never know.

So what does Jesus say about salvation? "And when He [the Holy Spirit] has come, He will convict the world of sin, and of righteousness, and of judgment; of sin, because they do not believe in Me" (John 16:8–9). Notice that Jesus said the world will be convicted of sin "because they do not believe in Me." As pastor Chuck Smith pointed out, "(Salvation) boils down to a single issue: What have you done with Jesus?"[11] If we receive Him as our Lord and Savior, we are saved. If we don't, we're not. So how can I possibly know what you or anyone else has done with Jesus? How can I possibly know what happens in those last few seconds as someone takes their last breath and passes from this life to the next?

Many will respond and say that you will know a tree by its fruit, meaning that we will know if someone is saved by the fruit they produce in their lives. Yet here is the kicker: I can make the greatest, strongest, most iron-clad case as to why someone is not saved. I can prove it upside down and sideways from Scripture and list out all of the fruit from their life; I can publish it, document it, and have the entire world agree with me. And yet God still says, "I will judge"—not you, Patrick, or anyone else for that matter, "I will judge." "For the LORD does not see as man sees; man looks at the outward appearance, but the LORD looks at the heart" (1 Samuel 16:7).

So believer, let us stop getting "involved in foolish discussions . . . these things are useless and a waste of time" (Titus 3:9, NLT). Rather, let us walk circumspectly, redeeming the time, understanding what the will of the Lord is for us. Go forth and make disciples of all nations, and leave the judging to God.

JANUARY 29th

John 21:19: "He said to him, 'Follow Me.'"

There are many times in the Bible where Jesus instructs us to follow Him. The comforting aspect of this invitation to "Follow Me" is that in order for us to follow

Him, Jesus must first go before us (Deuteronomy 31:3). The reason I find this so comforting is because regardless what Jesus calls us to do, He will have already gone before us and prepared it for the work that He wants to accomplish. So whether Jesus tells us to follow Him to a foreign country as a missionary, a small town in Idaho as a pastor, our neighbor's house to share the gospel, a new job, or our parents' home to do a Bible study, Jesus has already gone ahead of us and has already prepared the way.

Read this excerpt from Psalm 78 in which the psalmist recalls how the Lord went before His people during the mass exodus from Egypt:

> But he brought his people out like a flock; he led them like sheep through the desert. He guided them safely, so they were unafraid; but the sea engulfed their enemies. Thus he brought them to the border of the Holy Land, to the hill country his right hand had taken. He drove out nations before them and allotted their lands to them as an inheritance; he settled the tribes of Israel in their homes. (Psalm 78:52–55, NIV1984)

Notice how the Lord went before His people and prepared every single thing for their arrival. Nothing has changed today, as the Lord continues to go before us and prepares everything for our arrival. Psalm 23:5 also captures this thought: "You prepare a table before me in the presence of my enemies." Deuteronomy 31:3 says it perfectly: "The Lord your God Himself will cross over before you." Notice that it is the Lord God Himself who goes before us and prepares the way for our arrival; that alone should bring peace and confidence in all that He calls us to do.

JANUARY 30th

Genesis 28:16: "Surely the Lord is in this place, and I did not know it."

In Genesis 28, we find Jacob running for his life after he had deceived his father Isaac into giving him his brother's blessing. Needless to say, Esau was not very pleased with Jacob and was planning to kill him once their father passed away. Upon learning of Esau's plan, Jacob decided to flee from his home and go stay with his Uncle Laban in Padan Aram until things cooled down.

One night, as Jacob was sleeping under the stars outside of the city of Luz, God came to him in a dream and promised him many blessings of land and descendants.

God reminded Jacob in the dream, "I am with you and will keep you wherever you go" (Genesis 28:15). When Jacob woke up the next morning he said, "Surely the LORD is in this place, and I did not know it."

David Guzik said, "Jacob was right in sensing the presence of the Lord there, but he was wrong in perhaps thinking God was in some places and not in others."[12] David understood this concept very well as he wrote, "Where can I go from Your Spirit? Or where can I flee from Your presence?" (Psalm 139:7). Believer, God is everywhere, all of the time. There is nowhere we can go where we can escape His presence. No matter if it is a place of location, or a place in life, God is in that place.

Oftentimes when we sin, we find ourselves running and hiding from God. We try isolating ourselves by going out into the desert places because we believe that God will not be in that place with us. Yet even there, in our place of brokenness and self-loathing, we too must realize, "The Lord is in this place." This amazing and comforting truth pertains to every place of life that we will ever face. In our places of sickness, brokenheartedness, suffering, mourning, fear, stress, loneliness, and eventually death, we can know for a fact that God is in that place with us. His promise to Jacob is His promise to us as well, "I am with you and will keep you wherever you go."

I once heard a great story about the missionary Gladys Aylward as she tried to escape war-torn Yang Chen in 1938. The region she was in was quickly invaded by Japanese forces and despite being wounded herself, she had to lead ninety-four orphans to safety over some very rugged terrain. As the story goes, one morning she found herself with no apparent hope of reaching safety. A thirteen-year-old girl walking with her tried to comfort her by saying, "Don't forget what you told us about Moses in the wilderness," to which Gladys replied, "Yes, my dear, but I am not Moses." The young girl wisely replied, "Yes, but God is still God."

JANUARY 31st

> Genesis 37:24: "Then they took him and cast him into a pit. And the pit was empty; there was no water in it."

Would you consider Joseph to be a victim? Maybe in a court of law he would be defined as a victim, but I would say no to this question simply because the Bible never proclaims us to be victims in any situation. Rather, it says in Romans 8:37, "Yet in all these things we are more than conquerors through Him who loved us." Awhile back, the Lord spoke to me very clearly about how many times we, as

Christians, live, act, and pray as though we are a defeated people—that we are victims because our circumstances, trials, temptations, and afflictions are too great for us to overcome and that there is seemingly no hope for victory. The apostle Paul destroyed this type of hopeless behavior and thinking by reminding us, "Yet in all things we are more than conquerors through Him who loved us."

Do you know what a conqueror is? It is someone who has victory after a battle has taken place. Well here, Paul emphatically points out to us that we are "*more than* conquerors," meaning that we have victory over all things before the battle even takes place. Paul says that when difficulties come, and they will come, we should not live as though our situation is hopeless and that we are helpless victims in it all. Rather, we should live in the full assurance of hope and victory because of the love and power that our Lord and Savior Jesus Christ has toward us.

There are many times in life where we will find ourselves in a waterless pit. We were hurt by the people we love, sin has so easily ensnared us, sickness has weighed us down, life's circumstances are seemingly against us . . . yet even there, even in the waterless pit, when we are seemingly all alone and in a hopeless situation, the Lord says, "As for you also, because of the blood of your covenant, I will set your prisoners free from the waterless pit. Return to the stronghold, you prisoners of hope. Even today I declare that I will restore double to you" (Zechariah 9:11–12).

Think about what it means to be a "prisoner of hope." It means we are held captive by hope; we are under its authority. This is how we are described in Zechariah when we find ourselves in the waterless pits of life; we are prisoners of hope, not hopeless victims. There is nothing we can do to escape the hope we have in Jesus Christ, as we are its prisoner. And remember, the definition of the word "hope," as it is used in the Bible, means to know for certain, to be absolutely sure of something. So we see that we are prisoners of God's assurances and promises, and that we can do nothing to escape them. Romans 5:5 (emphasis added) reminds us of this very thing, "Now hope *does not* disappoint, because the love of God has been poured out in our hearts by the Holy Spirit who was given to us."

FEBRUARY 1st

John 10:14 (NIV): "I am the good shepherd; I know my sheep and my sheep know me."

There is no doubt in my mind that God knows me. There is no doubt in my mind that God knows you. John 10:14 tells us as much, "I know my sheep." It truly is an amazing thing when we consider how well God knows us. He knows our comings and our goings; He knows when we are lying down and when we are sitting up; He knows what we think and what we desire; He knows the very number of hairs on our head, and He knows the exact number of days we have on this earth; He records in His journal what we say and what we do, and His thoughts toward us outnumber the grains of sand on the earth. God knows us unlike any other person knows us, even ourselves.

The second half of this verse is very similar: "my sheep know me." So what do we know about God? Have you ever thought about that? Take a minute and consider everything that you know about God. Obviously I cannot list everything we know about God, because there is simply too much to list. But in this, we see that there is a relationship between God and us—a relationship that is built almost like a marriage. Its purpose is so that we can know one another on a more intimate level.

I was convicted by this the other day as I was praying to God and realized that my relationship with God had turned into writing devotions, teaching, praying for others, leading worship, etc. I realized that my relationship was with serving God in ministry, and not with knowing God intimately. It is amazing how fast our focus can switch because I never even saw it change.

But it did change, because I had lost sight of what a relationship with God is. Sure, I was studying His Word for devotions and teachings, and I was seeking Him on behalf of others, but I got away from spending time just talking to Him. We need to remember that a relationship goes both ways. If it is only one-sided, is it really a relationship?

Imagine, as a husband, that I worked every day to support my family, did the dishes, cut the grass, took out the garbage, etc., but I never actually sat down and spent time with my family. Would I really have a relationship with them? No, I wouldn't. It is the same with God. We can spend our lives working and serving in ministry, but in no way does that mean we are building on our relationship with Him. So, believer, never mistake serving God as having a relationship with God; rather, take the time to get to know Him intimately and then allow His Spirit to compel you to serve. You will be glad you did.

FEBRUARY 2nd

Exodus 6:1: "Then the LORD said to Moses, 'Now you shall see what I will do to Pharaoh. For with a strong hand he will let them go, and with a strong hand he will drive them out of his land.'"

After God called Moses to go to Egypt and deliver God's people from the hands of Pharaoh, God gave Moses this promise, "Now you shall see what I will do to Pharaoh. For with a strong hand he will let them go, and with a strong hand he will drive them out of his land." And sure enough, just as God had promised Moses, Pharaoh drove out the nation of Israel from Egypt.

The thing I want you to notice is that this did not happen right away. There was much work to be done before this promise would ever come to pass, as Moses would have many encounters with Pharaoh before Pharaoh would eventually drive out the nation of Israel as God had promised. In this, we must remember that God's promises do not come in our timing; they come in His timing. Some happen right away, like the infilling of the Holy Spirit when we surrender our lives to Jesus Christ, or the forgiveness of our sins when we ask God for forgiveness (1 John 1:9). But for many promises, we must wait for them to come to pass as God desires. Does that mean that just because we have to wait for the promise, it will not come to pass as God said it would? It sure seems that way sometimes, doesn't it? But it's not true; God's promises will always come to pass just as He said they would.

Proverbs 13:12 reminds us, "Hope deferred makes the heart sick, but when the desire comes, it is a tree of life." When we have to wait for God's promises to come to pass, we will be tested greatly, as we will be tempted to lose hope. This is what Solomon meant when he wrote, "Hope deferred makes the heart sick." Our hearts will literally feel sick as our self-imposed deadlines for these promises pass. But look at the second half of this verse: "when the desire comes, it is a tree of life." Notice Solomon did not say "if" the desire comes, but rather, "*when* the desire comes." God's promises *always* come to pass. So, believer, even though you may be waiting for a promise to be fulfilled, and your heart may grow sick during this time of waiting, never lose hope, because God always keeps His promises.

FEBRUARY 3rd

Isaiah 58:9: "Then you shall call, and the LORD will answer."

One of the more challenging aspects of walking with the Lord is to trust that He always hears and answers our prayers. There have been many times where I have specifically prayed for something and there was seemingly no response from God. So I continued to ask, seek, and knock, and yet there was still no response. This is about the time when I usually get discouraged and depressed, as I begin to believe that God is either not listening, not answering, or that somehow I have drifted away from Him and did not even realize it.

The Bible reminds us about these times in Proverbs 13:12, "Hope deferred makes the heart sick." It is a natural progression for us to begin thinking these things. Yet the Bible promises that God does hear us, and that He will answer us. So what do we do in these times of seemingly unanswered prayer? What I have learned is that we need to step back from that prayer we are obsessed with, and begin praying for other things.

For example, I was in one of these times we are talking about and became obsessed with one specific prayer so much that I was not praying for anything else; and because God was not answering that one prayer, I believed all of the lies that Satan threw at me. Well, one morning, as I was driving to work, I found myself in very heavy traffic on the freeway and I couldn't change lanes to get off the freeway. I remember thinking to myself, "Why pray? God is not answering your prayers; just get off at the next off ramp and circle back." But I prayed anyway, "Father, please make room for me to get over so I can make my exit." Instantly, like the parting of the Red Sea, a huge space opened up for me and I was able to slide over and get off the freeway.

Now, you may be thinking to yourself, "What's the big deal?" The big deal was that as soon as that one little prayer was answered, I realized that God was still working in my life. It reassured me that God heard my prayers and that He was in fact answering them. My entire perspective regarding this one specific prayer was changed. I now knew that God was answering me, "Wait."

I am certain that there are specific prayers being lifted up in your life right now, and maybe you find yourself in the same situation that I was in. Believer, take a step back, pray for all things, and watch God work in your life. Rest assured, He hears you and He is answering.

FEBRUARY 4th

1 Timothy 1:16: "However, for this reason I obtained mercy, that in me first Jesus Christ might show all longsuffering, as a pattern to those who are going to believe on Him for everlasting life."

It is no secret who the apostle Paul was before Christ got a hold of him. He was a Pharisee named Saul who truly believed he was doing God's work by persecuting, imprisoning, and murdering Christians. For some reason, though, the magnitude of what Saul had done does not impact me very much; maybe it's because I wasn't around when he did all of those things, or maybe it's because I don't see him like that. I know him as Paul in Christ, not Saul in the world.

But back in those days, when Paul's actions were very well known to pretty much everyone around, these words carried a lot of weight. Paul told Timothy in this letter, "But God had mercy on me so that Christ Jesus could use me as a prime example of His great patience with even the worst sinners. Then others will realize that they, too, can believe in Him and receive eternal life" (1 Timothy 1:16, NLT).

Paul told Timothy that he was an example to everyone of Christ's longsuffering, an example of the amazing grace God has toward all of mankind. By being an example of God's grace, no one could say, "God can't forgive what I have done." As Paul well stated in 1 Timothy 1:15, "This is a faithful saying and worthy of all acceptance, that Christ Jesus came into the world to save sinners, of whom I am chief." Paul essentially affirms to us here, "If God can forgive me, the chief of all sinners, for what I have done, He can forgive anyone."

Often times when we hear stories about Ted Bundy or Jeffrey Dahmer coming to salvation—men who murdered many people—we cringe at the idea of seeing them in heaven. "God, how could you forgive them for what they have done?" Yet they, like Paul, are an example to us of Christ's longsuffering, a pattern of God's amazing grace for those who will be coming to salvation one day.

I admit that it was hard for me to accept the fact that I was completely forgiven when I came to the Lord, as I am sure it was for many of you as well. But once I finally accepted His forgiveness, and believed it to be true, it was then hard for me to share what I had done because I wanted to be this perfect Christian in other people's eyes. But we should never miss an opportunity to share where God has brought us from— not reveling in our debauchery as many do when they share their testimony, but rather reveling and boasting in the grace that has been afforded to us through Christ Jesus our Lord. We should be an example to others of Christ's longsuffering so that all may say to themselves, "If God can forgive that person, surely He can forgive me."

FEBRUARY 5th

> Matthew 11:28 (NLT): "Then Jesus said, 'Come to me, all of you who are weary and carry heavy burdens, and I will give you rest.'"

I love the fact that Jesus invites us to come to Him with all of the issues of life so that we might find rest in every situation. This should be common practice for every believer because only Jesus can truly carry our burdens and work them out for good (Romans 8:28). But this should not be the only reason why we come to Jesus.

Michelle and I were talking with a friend of ours the other day and she was telling us about one of her brothers. "He only calls when he needs something," she said. "He never calls just to say hello." It was then that Michelle and I looked at each other and kind of sighed because we know that we often do this very thing with the Lord.

Going to Jesus only when we need help is not the sort of relationship we are to have with Him. Listen to John 15:15 (NLT): "I no longer call you slaves, because a master doesn't confide in his slaves. Now you are my friends, since I have told you everything the Father told me." Not only does Jesus call us His friends, but He also states that He wants to confide in us as His friends.

When I think about the friendship that we are to have with Jesus, I often think about the friendship I have with Michelle. We have spent hours together talking about life, what we are feeling, thinking, desiring, struggling with . . . we travel together, go on long walks, watch movies, read the Bible, pray, serve together . . . we do all of these things because we love spending time with each other and because we want to know one another on a deeper, more intimate level.

This is how we should view our relationship with Jesus. Just as my friendship with Michelle did not stop the day we got married, our friendship with Jesus should not stop the day we are saved; rather, it should grow and mature more and more each day. We need to make a purposeful effort to spend time with Jesus with the sole intention to know Him more. This is what friends do, and this is when He will confide in us the things of the Father.

FEBRUARY 6th

Psalm 118:7 (NLT): "Yes, the LORD is for me; He will help me."

There is often a question we ask of the Lord when difficulties arise in our lives: "God, why won't You help me?" We may not use these same exact words, mind you; it may be more like, "God, why won't You answer me?" "God, why won't You heal me?" or "God, how could You let this happen?" Regardless what the question might be, the underlying theme is the same: We begin to question God's motives for our lives because we believe that God is somehow failing us. The psalmist seemingly answers all of our questions for us by essentially saying, "Yes, God is for you, and yes, He will help you!"

As I thought about all of the times that I have questioned God's motives for my life, I asked myself the same thing that Isaiah asked the people of Israel: "What else can God possibly do to show you that He is for you?" (see Isaiah 5:4). This is not to say that we should beat ourselves up over those moments of unbelief because, as the Bible reminds us, we are just flesh and it is the human condition to naturally doubt God. But just because it is the natural thing for us to do, it does not mean we should believe or even act on those natural tendencies.

The apostle Paul asked the same question in Romans 8:31–32: "What then shall we say to these things? If God is for us, who can be against us? He who did not spare His own Son, but delivered Him up [on the cross] for us all, how shall He not with Him also freely give us all things?" With everything that God has done to deliver us from sin and death, how could we possibly believe that God is not for us at any point or time in our lives? We doubt Him because deep down in our flawed experiences of imperfect love, we still believe that God's love is dependent on what we do and don't do.

The key to gaining peace and joy in these moments of turmoil and doubt is to know that God's Word is greater than our feelings. Though it might seem like He is against us, or has even abandoned us, we can be assured that "His faithful love [for us] endures forever" (Psalm 118:1, NLT). So, believer, repeat after me: Yes, the Lord is for me, and yes, He will help me.

FEBRUARY 7th

John 17:17: "Sanctify them by Your truth. Your word is truth."

Do you believe this Scripture? Honestly, deep down, do you believe that God's Word is absolute truth? The promises, the assurances, the instruction . . . is it truth, or just folklore? This is a question that I often find myself asking time and time again. Not because I don't believe God's Word per se, but because I often do things in the wrong order when difficulties come into my life.

There are many times when I will look at my situation, diagnose it, make a determination about it, speak it out, and *then* look at God's Word. The problem with this order of events is that we diagnose our situation first; then proclaim what it is and how it is going to play out second; and lastly, look at God's Word to try to somehow fit it into our situation. This is not what this verse says we should do. This verse rightly proclaims that God's Word alone is truth, and that by this truth we are sanctified (set apart).

We are told that God's Word sanctifies us from the world; in turn, we need to sanctify God's Word from the world as well. His Word should be set apart from our circumstances so that we can look at His truth in such a way that our circumstances, feelings, or doubts will not influence or diminish what His Word says. His Word, as truth, needs to stand alone in our lives without anything attached to it. In other words, we need to allow His truth to tell us about our situations, and not allow our situations to tell us about His truth.

This is how Jesus defeated Satan when Satan tempted Jesus in the wilderness. This is how the apostle Paul learned to be content in whatever situation he found himself in. And this is how we will stand strong and be steadfast during the storms of this life.

American hymn writer H. L. Hastings, in describing God's Word, wrote:

> Infidels for eighteen hundred years have been refuting and overthrowing this book (the Bible), and yet it stands today as solid as a rock. Its circulation increases, and it is more loved and cherished and read today than ever before. Infidels, with all their assaults, make about as much impression on this book as a man with a tack hammer would on the pyramids of Egypt. When the French monarch proposed the persecution of the Christians in his dominion, an old statesman and warrior said to him, "Sire, the Church of God is an anvil that has worn out many hammers." So the hammers of the infidels have been pecking away at this book for ages, but the hammers are worn out, and the anvil still endures. If this book had not been the book of God, men would have destroyed it long ago . . . rulers have all tried their hand at it; they die and the book still lives.[13]

So, Christian, what do you believe? Is His Word truth above all other truths?

FEBRUARY 8th

> Hebrews 6:19: "This hope we have as an anchor of the soul, both sure and steadfast, and which enters the Presence behind the veil."

A couple of weeks ago, Michelle and I and two other couples from our fellowship paid a visit to some dear friends who are struggling with some very serious physical afflictions. After Michelle led us in worship, I shared some thoughts that the

Lord had placed on my heart for them. One of those thoughts was contained in this verse, "This hope we have as an anchor of the soul, both sure and steadfast, and which enters the Presence behind the veil."

The hope that the writer of Hebrews is talking about is our hope in Jesus Christ. The word literally means to know for certain, to have no doubt. Our hope in Jesus Christ is well placed, because we know without a doubt that we are forever secure in Him. He is the anchor who keeps us from drifting away from God. When you consider all of the distractions and temptations that the world throws at us, and add our own sinful nature to that mix, we desperately need an anchor who is "both sure and steadfast," who will keep us from being swept away by the current of this world.

Notice that our hope entered "the Presence behind the veil." In the temple, the veil separated man from the very place where God's presence dwelt. When the high priest would make the sacrifice and take it into the Holy of Holies, he would then have to leave God's presence. But our eternal High Priest, Jesus Christ, entered into "the Presence behind the veil" when He sacrificed Himself on the cross, and did not have to leave God's presence; instead, He "sat down at the right hand of the Majesty on high" (Hebrews 1:3). So the anchor of our soul lies behind the veil, in the very presence of God Almighty, and is the Guardian of our souls forever.

When we were praying for our friends that night, our good friend Walt was given a vision of a tether coming down from heaven that was attached to this couple. The thought here was that they were not anchored to anything here on earth, but rather that they were anchored to Christ in heaven. And because they were anchored in heaven, the tether had lifted them up off of the ground, above their circumstances, carrying them through this very difficult time.

As I thought about this visual, I pictured two tethers—one coming down from heaven, and the other coming from up from the earth. Then I pictured a huge ship in the midst of a great storm, and I asked myself, "What would be better to have: an anchor that is tethered to the bottom of the ocean, weighing us down, or an anchor that is tethered to heaven, lifting us up?"

With that thought, I think it is important to understand that we all have a choice to make in regard to what we anchor our soul to. We can choose Jesus Christ and anchor our soul in heaven, or we can choose the world and anchor our soul to earth. We cannot, however, choose both. Understand this: Both anchors are sure and steadfast, but only one will lift you up; the other will pull you down. So let me ask you, where is your hope placed?

FEBRUARY 9th

> Exodus 16:4 (NIV): "Then the LORD said to Moses, 'I will rain down bread from heaven for you. The people are to go out each day and gather enough for that day. In this way I will test them and see whether they will follow my instructions.'"

After God delivered the Israelites from the Egyptians in miraculous fashion, the Israelites soon became worried as they found themselves in the desert with food and water reserves running low. "In the desert the whole community grumbled against Moses and Aaron. The Israelites said to them, 'If only we had died by the LORD's hand in Egypt! There we sat around pots of meat and ate all the food we wanted, but you have brought us out into this desert to starve this entire assembly to death'" (Exodus 16:2–3, NIV). From their point of view, the Israelites saw no hope for tomorrow, so they grumbled and complained about their situation today.

In response to their grumbling, God told Moses that He would provide for His people—but to test their faith in Him, God instructed His people to only gather enough food for that day so they would have to trust Him for tomorrow. And therein lies the challenge of faith for the people of Israel and for us today—to have faith that God will not just abandon us in the deserts of life, but that He will provide for all of our needs every single day. This must have been a very hard thing for the Israelites to do . . . to see so much food and yet only gather enough for one day, trusting that God would provide for tomorrow, and the next day, and the next day, and so on. How many of us would have gathered some extra food "just in case" God failed us tomorrow? Yeah, I would have, too.

It is actually our concern for tomorrow's needs that causes us to stumble today. We worry about things that have not even come to pass yet; all the while, we miss out on the blessings that we are given today. The Bible compels us over and over again not to worry about tomorrow, but rather, focus on how God has provided for this day. We are to leave tomorrow to God, knowing that He is the same God tomorrow that He was today. As the old saying goes, today is the tomorrow that we worried about yesterday, and all is well.

It's in these moments of testing that we need to ask ourselves, "Has God ever failed us? Has His goodness ever stopped? Has there ever been a time in our lives that He has not provided exactly what we needed and when we needed it?" The answer to all of these questions is a resounding no, yet we still worry about tomorrow, don't we? Michelle and I often talk about how the other shoe never drops with

God. Even though we expect an end to God's goodness after the immense blessings of today, it never comes. Truly God's faithfulness and His goodness toward us endure forever.

In Hebrews 13:5 (NIV), God says, "Never will I leave you; never will I forsake you." If you look at the Greek root words here, there are five negatives used. So this verse actually reads, "I will never, never, never, never, never leave you; I will never, never, never, never, never forsake you." What do you think God is trying to tell us?

FEBRUARY 10th

> Psalm 130:3 (NIV1984): "If you, O LORD, kept a record of sins, O Lord, who could stand?"

So many times, when I am wallowing in the after-effects of my sin, I am convinced that I am the worst sinner of all time. I am convinced that in no way are "real" Christians as bad as I am, and this time, there will be no forgiveness for me. If that is true, and there is no forgiveness for me, then there can also be no forgiveness for anyone else as well. With that being said though, if I believe others are forgiven for their sin, then I must also believe that I am forgiven for my sin.

"If you, O LORD, kept a record of sins, O Lord, who could stand?" Notice the psalmist did not say, "If you, O LORD, kept a record of *my* sins. . . ." No, he clearly stated, "If you, O LORD, kept a record *of sins*, O Lord, who could stand?" The psalmist is speaking only about sins here, not about those who committed the sin. I believe his point was that if God kept a record of just the sins that are committed, He would quickly see that every single person would have multiple sins assigned to them; and if we are all guilty of sin, then who could possibly stand against God's perfect judgment? No one. Thankfully for us, through the blood of Jesus Christ, we can all receive complete and total forgiveness for our sin. For "with you there is forgiveness" (Psalm 130:4, NIV).

In those moments of realizing our sin, it can be very difficult to believe we are forgiven when we confess that sin, especially if it is something that we continue to fall into. This is why the writer of Hebrews instructs us, "Let us therefore come boldly to the throne of grace, that we may obtain mercy and find grace to help in time of need" (Hebrews 4:16). Pastor John Blanchard wrote, "For daily need there is daily grace, and for sudden need there is sudden grace, and for overwhelming need there is overwhelming grace."[14] This is what James was talking about when he wrote in James 4:6a, "But He gives more grace."

So how do we receive this amazing grace? James 4:6b tells us, "God resists the proud, but gives grace to the humble." We receive grace when we humble ourselves before God. In 1 John 1:9 we are told, "If we confess our sins, He is faithful and just and will forgive us our sins and cleanse us from all unrighteousness." To confess our sins means to agree with God about what He says sin is. By confessing our sins to God through Jesus Christ, we are in fact humbling ourselves before God; in return, we receive His abundant grace.

We need to remember that when Jesus Christ died on the cross for our sin, He died knowing full well every sin we would ever commit. This is why there is a measure of grace given to each one of us daily, a measure that is more than enough for that day's needs. Many expositors have noted that grace is not simply our ticket through the door into heaven; it is also our fuel for the journey. D. L. Moody understood this very well. He once wrote, "A man can no more take in a supply of grace for the future, than he can eat enough for the next six months; or take sufficient air into his lungs at one time to sustain life for a week. We must draw upon God's boundless store of grace from day to day as we need it."[15] So, believer, regardless how much grace you need for this day, rest assured, His grace is sufficient.

FEBRUARY 11th

> Romans 12:2a: "And do not be conformed to this world, but be transformed by the renewing of your mind."

As we were serving in the prayer room a couple of weeks ago, the word "expose" was used by one of our brethren during a time of prayer. Immediately I reflected on what the word "expose" means: to lay open to the influence of something. I then thought of what happens to us when we expose ourselves to radiation. If we expose ourselves to small amounts of radiation, the impacts are minimal. But if we expose ourselves to large amounts of radiation, it can cause premature aging, cancer, even death. The more radiation we expose ourselves to, the more powerful the effect it has on our bodies. The thing that really hit me was the physical transformation that takes place in our bodies without us having to do anything. Radiation automatically changes us physically.

As I thought about this, I began to think about what happens when we expose ourselves to God. If we expose ourselves to small amounts of God, we can expect small changes in our lives spiritually. But if we expose ourselves to large amounts of God, we can expect much bigger changes in our lives spiritually. The more of God we expose ourselves to, the more powerful the effect He has on our lives. And similar to the effects of radiation, when we expose ourselves to God, there is automatically a transformation that takes place in our lives. God just supernaturally changes us spiritually. The difference is that radiation poisons us and God cleanses us.

The word "transformed" that is used in this verse means to change into another form, and speaks of a permanent kind of change. It carries the idea of an inward change that is essential for us as believers. What Paul was saying to us in this verse is that we should not allow ourselves to be changed on the outside by the things of the world, but rather that we should be changed inwardly by the things of God.

Please understand that we will be changed by whatever influence we expose ourselves to. In 2 Corinthians 4:4, Satan is called the god of this world, so you can imagine the changes that take place in our lives when we expose ourselves to the things of this world. We view them as harmless, but the reality that anything outside of God is evil should really compel us to consider what we are exposing ourselves to on a daily basis. As parents, this should motivate us to control what movies, TV shows, Internet sites, music, video games, and people our children are exposed to. If you think about it, the world is a spiritual radiation that poisons our soul.

Paul tells us that there has to be a renewing of our mind. No longer are we to think as the world thinks, but rather, we are to take on the way God thinks and approach the world and the things in it by what His Word says about them. A. W. Tozer once wrote, "Our thoughts not only reveal what we are, they predict what we will become. We will soon be the sum total of our thoughts."[16] And our thoughts will be determined by what we expose ourselves to.

FEBRUARY 12th

> Romans 5:1: "Therefore, having been justified by faith, we have peace with God through our Lord Jesus Christ."

As I was driving to work this morning, I was thinking about the "grace periods" that we have in life. For example, at the apartment complex Michelle and I live at, we have a grace period for our rent check. Though the rent is due on the first of every month, there is a grace period for all renters until the fourth of the month. So as long as we get our rent check in by the fourth of every month, it is not considered late and there are no penalties. Maybe you have a grace period at your job where as long as you are not more than ten minutes late, you don't have to call in and let someone know. Or maybe you have a grace period at school where if you can't turn in your homework in class the day it is due, you can still turn it in anytime later that day.

Regardless of what the grace period may be, if we drop off our rent check by the fourth of the month, or get to work within that ten-minute window, or turn in our homework before that day is over, we have peace because we are covered by the grace of another. Understand that we only find peace in these situations because the grace that is given to us is given freely by someone we are accountable to. It was their desire to give this grace to us, and when we meet the deadline that they set, and receive the grace that they have afforded us, we no longer have to worry or fear because we are covered by their grace.

Well there is a grace period in life that none of us can afford to miss. This grace period begins the second we are able to decide for ourselves if we want to surrender our lives to Jesus or not, and it ends the second we die. This is the amount of time we have to accept His free gift of salvation. The problem with this grace period is that none of us know the deadline for it. It could come at any second for any one of us, and once this deadline has passed, the offer of grace is rescinded and the penalty is eternal death.

But once we surrender our lives to Jesus Christ, we are justified, meaning that we are forgiven for all time. No more condemnation, no more doubt, no more fear, no more worry. We met the deadline for God's grace period on eternal life and we can be at complete peace because the only one we are accountable to for our sin is God; and by His own desire, He has freely given us grace that removes our sin through His Son Jesus Christ. There is nothing left for us to do but to receive and rejoice.

FEBRUARY 13th

1 Corinthians 2:10: "But God has revealed them to us through His Spirit. For the Spirit searches all things, yes, the deep things of God."

Many times when I am teaching or writing devotions, I try to play the role of the Holy Spirit in other people's lives by trying to cover every angle, every thought, and every application that could possibly come up in the material being covered. This is an impossible task to try and take on because the Word of God connects to every part of life; the sheer amount of information in trying to do this is overwhelming, to say the least. By me trying to play the role of the Holy Spirit, I am trying to fill a role that is not mine to fill.

"But God has revealed them to us through His Spirit." There is a level of faith required of us when we teach, write devotions, or share the gospel in that we are to have faith that the Holy Spirit will reveal truths to people as we share with them. Our job is simply to pray, search God's Word, and then speak as we are led by the Holy Spirit, knowing that He is working in others' lives and that He will reveal to them the things that they need to hear.

I have had people come up to me after a teaching and say, "When you said [this], it totally ministered to me." But I never said what they heard. It was the Holy Spirit working in them, speaking to them, and revealing the things to them that they needed to hear. There have been times when I have shared a specific truth with someone, and the Holy Spirit used that truth to trigger another truth within that person that was applicable to their needs. Only He has the power to do that, because only He "searches all things, yes, [even] the deep things of God," and knows exactly what people need to hear.

The challenge for us here is to be obedient to the prompting of the Holy Spirit and share only what He tells us to share—no more, and no less—for "[My word] shall accomplish that which I purpose, and shall succeed in the thing for which I sent it" (Isaiah 55:11, ESV). God has a specific purpose for every truth that is shared; ours is not to figure out that purpose, ours is just to have faith that He is working in that person's life and that He will meet their need in His time and in His way, according to His purpose.

FEBRUARY 14th

1 John 4:19: "We love Him because He first loved us."

There is something powerful about the words, "I love you." They are only three little words, yet they carry so much weight with them. For the one saying it, it is a declaration of the choice that they have made to love someone for who they are, not for what they do. Love is a choice, not a feeling. For the one receiving it, it brings comfort, joy, and security knowing that someone genuinely cares for them and wants to be in their life even when things get difficult.

But there is this whole other dynamic to saying "I love you," which comes in the form of the response. For example, I remember one time when Michelle and I were on the phone, and as we were saying goodbye, I told her, "I love you." She also said, "I love you." The troubling thing for me was that I did not hear her say, "I love you, too." And because I did not hear her say that last word "too," I thought she did not hear me, and so I immediately called her back to make sure that she had heard me. I needed her to acknowledge the fact that she heard it, that she received it, and that she believed it. That is what that "too" means when we add it in there—"I heard it, I receive it, and I believe it." It is amazing how leaving out that one little word affected me so much.

Last night, as Michelle and I were praying, I told Jesus, "I love you, too, Lord." It was then that I realized, I had never said that to Him before. I have told Him that I loved Him thousands of times, but never once have I ever said, "I love you, too, Lord." The more I thought about this, the more I was perplexed. Why don't we ever say to Jesus, "I love you, too"? After all, He said it to us first, for "We love Him because He first loved us." Every day, and in so many ways, God tells us that He loves us. He tells us through His creation, through His people, through His Word, and more importantly, through the cross. "God demonstrates His own love toward us, in that while we were yet sinners Christ died for us" (Romans 5:8, NASB). And yet I had never said to Him, "I love you, too, Lord."

There was something powerful about saying that to Him last night because when I did, I acknowledged the fact that He said it to me first. I acknowledged the fact that He loves *me*. This is very important for me personally, because even though I can tell anyone that Jesus loves them and really believe it, I often struggle with the belief that He loves me. Yet when I said "I love you, too, Lord," I not only acknowledged the fact that He loves me, but I also received it and believed it.

FEBRUARY 15th

> James 3:5–6: "Even so the tongue is a little member and boasts great things. See how great a forest a little fire kindles! And the tongue is a fire, a world of iniquity. The tongue is so set among our members that it defiles the whole body, and sets on fire the course of nature; and it is set on fire by hell."

Here in Southern California, we know all too well how one little spark can cause massive devastation. In October of 2007, wildfires destroyed more than 500,000 acres of land and more than 1,500 homes. The fires were triggered by sparks of downed power lines, a ten-year-old playing with matches, and an overturned semitruck that caught fire. At one point, the fires were so large that they were visible from outer space.

James likens the destruction a wildfire can cause to that of the tongue. In fact, he says that an uncontrolled tongue "is a fire, a world of iniquity," meaning that there is no end to its destruction; it can be an endless pit of sin and destruction if it is left uncontrolled. James also says that it is "so set among our members that it defiles the whole body." The word "defile" used here means to pollute or to contaminate. When our tongue is left uncontrolled, it fully contaminates us. Jesus spoke about this in Matthew 15:11, when He stated that it's "[n]ot what goes into the mouth that defiles a man; but what comes out of the mouth, this defiles a man."

James also says that an uncontrolled tongue "sets on fire the course of nature." John MacArthur stated that this phrase literally means "the circle of life," and emphasizes the fact that the damage the tongue can cause will extend well beyond the person speaking, as it will "affect everything in his or her sphere of influence."[17] That includes our spouse, our kids, our family, our friends, our job, our ministry, our witness, etc.

James' point here is a common theme throughout the Bible: What we do directly affects others. The thought that our sin only affects us, or that it can somehow be contained or controlled, is a lie from the pit of hell. Ron Daniel commented that we do not see the type of widespread destruction that a tongue can cause more plainly then we do with gossip. It is probably the most overlooked sin in the church today. This was such a serious issue in the early church that Paul warned both Timothy and Titus about gossipers in the church and how destructive they could be. The Greek word that Paul used for these gossipers in 1 Timothy 3:11 is *diabolos*. If this word is familiar to you, it is because it is the name given to the devil. In Spanish he is called *el Diablo*. When we gossip, James says our tongue "is set on fire by hell itself" (James 3:6, NLT), meaning that we are now under the influence of the devil and are basically doing his work for him.[18]

None of us want that—or even want to ever do that— but when we do not control our tongue, and just open up our mouths and let that beast out, that is exactly what happens as our tongue is set on fire and destroys; it destroys lives, marriages, reputations, children, innocence, confidence, etc. Only by the power of the Holy Spirit can the tongue ever be controlled, because the mouth speaks whatever is in the heart (Matthew 12:34). And only the Holy Spirit can change the heart of man.

FEBRUARY 16th

James 3:11–12: "Does a spring send forth fresh water and bitter from the same opening? Can a fig tree, my brethren, bear olives, or a grapevine bear figs? Thus no spring yields both salt water and fresh."

James continues his theme of the untamable tongue by using a couple analogies of nature. As David Guzik explained, "James points out the ultimate impossibility of such a contradiction. If bad fruit and bitter water continue to come forth, it means that there is no contradiction. The tree is bad and the spring is bad."[19] Jesus said in Matthew 12:33–34, "Either make the tree good and its fruit good, or else make the tree bad and its fruit bad; for a tree is known by its fruit. Brood of vipers! How can you, being evil, speak good things? For out of the abundance of the heart the mouth speaks."

So again, we don't have a tongue problem; we have a heart problem. We can't tame our tongues because we can't change our hearts; only the working of the Holy Spirit in our lives can bring such radical transformation. This is why Jesus said in John 16:7, "It is to your advantage that I go away; for if I do not go away, the Helper will not come to you. But if I go, I will send Him to you." As much as Jesus could do for us while He was here on Earth, He knew that teaching, healing, being an example, and loving us would never change the heart of man. Jesus had to leave so that the Holy Spirit could come and infill us with His presence. It's only the work of the Holy Spirit in our lives that changes us from the inside out. He is the One who cleanses our hearts.

Pastor Jim Cymbala wrote in his book *Spirit Rising*, "We know that Jesus the Son is seated at the right hand of the Father. So that means the Holy Spirit is God's only agent on earth. He is the only experience we can have of God Almighty, the only way we can have the work of Jesus Christ applied to our lives, and the only way we can understand God's Word."[20] The role of the Holy Spirit in our lives is to be the power that we need to live a life that is pleasing to God.

In Acts 1:8, Jesus said, "you shall receive power when the Holy Spirit has come upon you." The word "power" that Jesus uses here can be translated "ability"; so, in Christ, we have the ability of the Holy Spirit within us to control the tongue as we rely on Him as our source of power, for when we walk in the Spirit, we will not fulfill the lusts of the flesh (Galatians 5:16).

FEBRUARY 17th

> Exodus 31:2: "See, I have called by name Bezalel the son of Uri, the son of Hur, of the tribe of Judah."

Bezalel is not really a household name like Abraham and Moses, but that does not mean he is any less significant than the "rock stars" of the Bible we often talk about.

In fact, we see that God called Bezalel by name, meaning that God specifically called Bezalel to be set apart for a very special work. Just as God chose Abraham and Moses for very particular tasks, God also chose Bezalel.[21]

It's important to note that in the Old Testament, the Holy Spirit was not poured out on all those who believed; only those chosen by God for a specific purpose were anointed in such a way. So when we read in Exodus 31:3 that God filled Bezalel with His Holy Spirit, we must ask, "What was this man's calling to, where he needed an infilling of God's Spirit?" Bezalel was a craftsman. Now generally when we hear of someone being set apart for God's purposes and being filled with the Holy Spirit, we automatically think of missionaries or pastors or some "higher" calling than just the average job. Yet here is a man being filled with the Spirit of God and being set apart to be a craftsman for the Lord.

I think it's important to understand that God saw the work that Bezalel would be taking part in as a craftsman just as spiritually significant as the work that Abraham and Moses took part in.[22] The most important aspect to this work though, was that it was to be done unto God, not unto man. This is what Colossians 3:23 says: "Whatever you do, do it heartily, as to the Lord and not to men." The empowering and gifting of the Holy Spirit in our lives is never to be used for our purposes; rather, it is to be used for God's purposes.

For most of us, we are not called to be pastors of a megachurch or missionaries in a foreign land; we are called to work Monday through Friday at a job that seemingly has no spiritual significance at all. Some are called to be stay-at-home moms raising children, and some are already retired; does this mean that we are insignificant and not being used by God? Not at all. As believers, we are all gifted and filled with the same Holy Spirit; we are all called by name; and we are all set apart for the work that God has called us to. None of us are insignificant in the eyes of the Lord, regardless what job we may or may not have. Our role is to seek the Lord and find out where He wants us, and then work as directed by the Holy Spirit.

FEBRUARY 18th

Ecclesiastes 1:3: "What profit has a man from all his labor in which he toils under the sun?"

The question that Solomon posed to us in Ecclesiastes 1:3 is one that we should all continually consider throughout our days here on Earth. "What profit has a man from all his labor in which he toils under the sun?" In other words, "What does man gain from all of his activities in this life?" Solomon's conclusion to this question is written over and over again throughout the book of Ecclesiastes: It's all vanity. It's all empty, unfulfilling, and meaningless. This is what Solomon painfully discovered after a lifelong pursuit of searching out the activities of this life.

Understand that Solomon was not just a wise man; he was also a searcher of knowledge and truth. He documented in the book of Ecclesiastes how he searched out everything under the sun (in this life), and found that none of it fulfills. He tested all things, tried all things, and experienced all things; there is nothing we can have or experience in this life that Solomon did not already have or experience. This is what he meant when he wrote, "there is nothing new under the sun" (Ecclesiastes 1:9). It's all been done already. As Ray Stedman well said, "No thing, no pleasure, no relationship, nothing he found had enduring value in life. After man has sucked dry all the immediate delight, joy, or pleasure out of something, what is left over, what endures, what will remain to continually feed the hunger of his life for satisfaction?" [23] Nothing, Solomon says, not one thing.

I had a coworker come into my office one morning after he had just received his thirty-five-year service award. He said to me, "You know, I have been here thirty-five years. I have poured myself into my job and have received all the awards and achievements that my job has to offer. I have made a great name for myself here at the county. But it is so meaningless. I feel like I have wasted my life."

Jesus summed it up for us this way in Mark 8:36, "For what will it profit a man if he gains the whole world, and loses his own soul?" The questions I am continually challenged with are, "What am I doing with my time? What am I investing in? Am I seeking the will and purposes of God, or am I living for myself and wasting my life?" Jesus said in Revelation 22:12 (ESV), "Behold, I am coming soon, bringing my recompense with me, to repay each one for what he has done." So let me ask you, believer, what are you doing with your life?

FEBRUARY 19th

> Numbers 13:32a: "And they gave the children of Israel a bad report of the land."

As the children of Israel were nearing the Promised Land, Moses sent twelve spies to go search out the land and report back to him what they had found. Upon their return, the spies told Moses that the land was one that flowed with milk and honey, just as God had said. They also reported that the land was full of fortified cities and people who were much stronger than they were (Numbers 13:31). Well, we all know the story here: Israel allowed fear to make their decision for them, and they ended up wandering in the desert for forty years because they chose fear over faith.

In December of 2012, I had surgery on my right shoulder because of an ongoing injury that was getting worse over time. Prior to having surgery, I had to go to the hospital and fill out all of the paperwork and answer all of the questions that go along with the pre-op process. Throughout this time, the doctor, nurses, and hospital staff continually warned me of the pain that I was going to experience after surgery, so I needed to be sure to take the pain meds that I was going to be given. As I shared this with the brethren at church, and was being prayed over, my good friend Darrell reminded me of the "bad report" that was given to the children of Israel. I was immediately filled with peace about the whole situation.

As I was leaving the hospital after surgery, my doctor reminded me again to be sure to take the pain meds before I went to bed because when the nerve block wore off, the pain was going to come quickly. That night, as Michelle and I were talking with some friends about the surgery, they mentioned that they knew some people who had taken these particular pain meds and had broken out in a rash afterward. With my existing skin condition, this was the last thing that I needed. So Michelle and I prayed. And as we prayed, I kept thinking about the word that was given to me through prayer about the "bad report"; I kept thinking how the children of Israel let the fear of that bad report dictate their actions. And so, after much prayer, Michelle and I decided to just stick with Motrin and see what happened. Well, the "incredible" pain never came.

All of this to say, we will get many bad reports in this life about our health, our jobs, the economy, our pregnancy, our children, etc.—but only God really knows what is going to happen from one minute to the next. The truth is, any report given apart from God is going to be a bad report. And so with that, we need to take every report to God and ask Him if it holds any truth.

FEBRUARY 20th

> Proverbs 17:9: "He who covers a transgression seeks love, but he who repeats a matter separates friends."

I learned early on in my Christian walk that forgiveness is an essential part of having a pure heart and clear conscience in the sight of the Lord, because holding things against one another consumes our thoughts and poisons our hearts. When

Jesus instructed us to forgive one another in Matthew 6:14, He did not do this for the sake of the one who offended; rather, He did it for the sake of the one who was offended.

Harboring bitterness or unforgiveness is like drinking poison and expecting the other person to die; it only destroys the one holding onto it. But when we choose to forgive someone of a wrongdoing, we essentially show them the same love that Jesus shows us every single day. This is what the author of Proverbs is pointing out to us here: "He who covers a transgression seeks love." To forgive someone is to not only love them as Christ loves us, but it's also what which we seek to fill ourselves with. It is with this act of love that our hearts are cleansed and our perspective toward that person is changed, as we literally take on the very mind of Christ.

But there is another part of forgiveness that is often overlooked: "but he who repeats a matter separates friends." To truly forgive someone means that we are to never bring up that offense again. If it is forgiven, it is gone forever. Too many times we say we forgive someone, only to bring up that transgression over and over again to use against them when it suits us; this is not forgiveness. Imagine if Jesus continually brought up our wrongdoings—would we really ever feel like we were truly forgiven?

Forgiveness will never be something that we *feel* like doing, because it's not in our nature to forgive one another. Rather it is something we are commanded to do, a choice we must make because we trust and believe what God's Word says about forgiveness. The key is to forgive right away, before our heart grows hard and that poison is sealed within us. Waiting to forgive someone would be like getting bit by a snake and then waiting to take the antivenom—it doesn't make sense because you want to get rid of that poison as soon as possible, before it causes any damage. The same goes with unforgiveness. So, believer, remember that love cannot grow where unforgiveness is present, because love and hate cannot coexist.

FEBRUARY 21st

> Exodus 33:3: "Go up to a land flowing with milk and honey; for I [God] will not go up in your midst, lest I consume you on the way, for you are a stiff-necked people."

When Moses went up the mountain to meet with God for forty days, the children of Israel had Aaron make a golden calf that they could worship as their god. Yet even with that blatant rebellion and idolatry, God did not deny the children of

Israel the Promised Land or the protection that He had promised them.[24] In Exodus 33:1–2, God said to Moses, "Depart and go up from here, you and the people whom you have brought out of the land of Egypt, to the land of which I swore to Abraham, Isaac, and Jacob, saying, 'To your descendants I will give it.' And I will send My Angel before you, and I will drive out the Canaanite and the Amorite and the Hittite and the Perizzite and the Hivite and the Jebusite."

God promised the children of Israel that He would still drive out the inhabitants of the Promised Land and bless them with the land flowing with milk and honey; yet He also stated, "I will not go up in your midst . . . for you are a stiff-necked people." In other words, as David Guzik explained, God would still give them the land, but "He would deny Israel His presence" because they were a people who continually refused to humble themselves and surrender to Him and His commands. God was testing the children of Israel to see if they only desired the material things of the world, or if they really desired a close, intimate relationship with Him as their Father. Their response to God would determine if they only loved His blessings, or if they truly loved God Himself.[25]

Many people today want Jesus to be their Savior so they can have the assurance of eternal life in heaven, our Promised Land, but they want nothing to do with Jesus as their Lord. They want the blessings in this life and in the next, but they do not desire a personal, intimate relationship with God Himself. This is what I call drive-thru Christianity. We come to God and place our order, praying for exactly what we want or need, yet we have no desire to know the One who gives us all things. Of what value is this kind of life? Is there any fulfillment or joy in having every blessing this life can afford, and yet live without God?

Understand that God is the essence of fulfillment. Having a relationship with Him is what satisfies us, not receiving blessings. We could have everything in this world, and the next, yet without God, we would still have nothing. So, believer, is your desire simply for the blessings of God, or is it for God Himself?

FEBRUARY 22nd

> Psalm 2:3: "Let us break Their bonds in pieces and cast away Their cords from us."

Have you ever witnessed someone trying to help a wild animal that is hurt? It is quite the scene as the animal will fight feverishly against those who are trying to help it, simply because it does not understand the intent of the helpers. Maybe you have tried to catch a stray dog or cat that was wandering into the street, only to have it run away from you because it did not understand the danger it was in. In a very similar way, man incessantly rages against God when all that God wants to do is save him.

The psalmist ponders this very subject in Psalm 2:1–3, "Why do nations rage, and the people plot a vain thing? The kings of the earth set themselves, and the rulers take counsel together, against the LORD and against His Anointed, saying, 'Let us break Their bonds in pieces and cast away Their cords from us.'" God's intent is not to harm man, but rather to free him from the bondage of sin and death. Yet in our own self-willed, prideful ignorance, we feverishly fight God with all that we are just so we can get away from Him.

The problem is that man does not view God as someone who wants to help him, but rather as someone who wants to imprison him. "Let us break Their bonds in pieces and cast away Their cords from us." As Ron Daniel pointed out, we strive to break away from God's grasp "like a rebellious child" squirming and fighting to break away from a parent's loving embrace.[26] God's bonds are not bonds of imprisonment like a heavy yoke that is put on an animal to control it; rather God's bonds are bonds of love to protect us, guide us, and keep us from wandering into the waterless pits of this world. This is what Hosea 11:4 reminds us: "I drew them with gentle cords, with bands of love, and I was to them as those who take the yoke from their neck. I stooped and fed them." Until man realizes what God's intent really is, and how much danger he is in apart from God's free gift of salvation, he will fight God to the very end.

FEBRUARY 23rd

Proverbs 20:24: "A man's steps are of the LORD; how then can a man understand his own way?"

I recently watched the original *Karate Kid* with Pat Morita (Mr. Miyagi) and Ralph Macchio (Daniel). My favorite part of the movie was the confrontation between the two men after Mr. Miyagi had promised to train Daniel in karate. When Daniel showed up to start his training, Mr. Miyagi had Daniel wax cars, paint fences, and sand the floors. Daniel quickly grew frustrated and angry because he didn't understand how any of this helped him learn karate; but once Mr. Miyagi showed him how it all worked together, he was humbled and grateful for all that Mr. Miyagi had him do.

Walking with God can be a lot like this sometimes as we do not always understand why things happen the way they do. Yet when we see the finished product sometime later, we are so grateful and thankful for everything that God did and allowed that we usually end up asking Him for forgiveness because of our unbelief and our lack of faith through the process.

As believers, we must remember that we are called to walk by faith, not by sight. I don't know why we ever think this will be an easy thing for us to do, because it never is. No matter how many times God proves His faithfulness to us, we still struggle trusting Him in the midst of difficulties because our vision and understanding are based solely on what we see and feel. We cannot fathom how God will work it all out, and so we spend all of our time and energy trying to understand things that we are never going to understand, leaving us frustrated and angry.

Solomon reminds us, "A man's steps are of the LORD; how then can a man understand his own way?" He reminds us that we will never understand why God does certain things until we see them all come together. But just because we don't understand what is happening, it does not mean we cannot trust Him while we are going through it. Believer, God *is* faithful. He has never let us down and He will never let us down. His heart, in all of His ways, is for our very best. As Romans 8:28 promises us, God works all things together for the good of those who love Him. So even though you may be waxing cars, painting fences, and sanding floors right now, have faith in God and trust that He will use it all for your benefit.

FEBRUARY 24th

Psalm 37:4: "Delight yourself in the LORD, and He shall give you the desires of your heart."

A woman came into the prayer room one day, and as she shared with me about how I could pray for her, she told me that she never asks for God's wisdom and that she does not want to know His will for her life. Confounded by this, I had to ask her why. She told me that she was afraid of God's plan for her life and that if she asked for God's will, He would call her to be single for the rest of her life and would send her off to some place like Africa.

I understand this thinking to a certain degree. It can be a very scary thing to come to God and say, "Here I am Lord, Your will be done," because He just *might* send us off to Africa, or call us to do that which we are most afraid of doing. For this woman, the fear of being single for the rest of her life was too much for her to bear, and so rather than ask for God's will and His direction for her life, she made her own choices and did what she thought was best. The problem for her, as she expressed it, was that she was miserable and her life was a mess.

When she asked me what I thought about all of this, I told her that what she was doing was insane. I then shared with her the definition of insanity: to continually do the same thing over and over again and expect a different result. This woman had been repeating the same destructive cycle over and over again for years, and yet she still ran from the Lord in fear of His plans for her life. What she did not understand was that she was miserable and her life a mess because she did not want God's will for her life.

Proverbs 8:35 reminds us that God's wisdom brings life, "For whoever finds me [wisdom] finds life, and obtains favor from the Lord." And Psalm 37:4 assures us, "Delight yourself in the Lord, and He shall give you the desires of your heart." The truth is that we should never fear what God has planned for us, nor should we ever neglect seeking His will and wisdom for our lives. He is good; His ways are perfect; and He knows what is best for us. So, believer, delight yourself in the Lord, seek His face, find His will for your life, and fulfill the purpose you were created for.

FEBRUARY 25th

> Psalm 59:9: "I will wait for You, O You his Strength; for God is my defense."

As a young believer attending church, the Lord brought many couples into my life who took me in and became spiritual parents for me. Much like what Aquilla and Priscilla did for Apollos, these couples discipled me in the way of the Lord and helped to put feet to my faith. One of the couples that I was very fond of had a daughter who became good friends with an ex-girlfriend of mine. Soon, this couple distanced themselves from me because of some things my ex-girlfriend had told their daughter about me. The more I tried to explain myself and fix the situation, the more the wedge between us was driven in.

This is when God brought me to this verse, "I will wait for You, O You his Strength; for God is my defense." Knowing that people think badly of you—especially people you respect and care about—and not being able to defend yourself or fix the situation, is excruciating to say the least. But as I took my hands off of this situation and waited on God, my strength was made full.

About a year later, the wife of the couple came up to me on a Sunday morning crying. The first words out of her mouth were, "Please forgive us!" It turns out that my ex-girlfriend began saying the same things about their daughter that she had said about me. They realized the huge mistake they had made by not handling the situation properly, and were devastated by how they had treated me. As I witnessed all of this unfold, there was an immense joy in my heart because I knew that I had taken God at His word and stood firm in faith; and He proved, once again, that He would never, ever fail me. My relationship with that couple was restored and we all learned a very valuable lesson.

The thought that we can control what people say or think about us is vanity; as Solomon said, it is like chasing the wind (Ecclesiastes 1:14). The only control we have in this life is in the choices we make; outside of that, there is only the illusion of control. To try to make people believe us, or to defend ourselves when such matters arise, usually ends up making things worse, as the enemy will just twist our words around and use them as a wedge between us. But when we release control of that situation to God and wait on Him, He will be our defense, the truth shall come out, and there will be great victory.

FEBRUARY 26th

Psalm 25:8 (NLT): "The Lord is good and does what is right; He shows the proper path to those who go astray."

I would say the biggest concern for any believer is a loved one's salvation. Many who come into the prayer room ask prayer for a prodigal child who has turned their back on God or for a parent who is stubbornly bound in their pride, refusing to even discuss the subject of God and His plan for salvation. The psalmist reminds us that God is inherently good and always does what is right, for He "shows the proper path to those who go astray."

We must remember that it is the Lord's greatest desire that all men be saved (1 Timothy 2:4) and that He takes "no pleasure in the death of the wicked, but that the wicked turn from his way and live" (Ezekiel 33:11). God desires all men to repent and turn from their wicked ways so that He might be gracious to them. Regardless how hopeless it might seem for certain loved ones to come to Christ, we must remember that God is always working in and around their lives to draw them to Him, and He will not stop wooing them until they take their last breaths here on Earth.

To understand this better, we should look no further than ourselves. At some point in our rebellion to God, He showed us the proper path to take and eventually we took it. For some it happened when they were a small child; for others, like me, it took twenty-nine years. Regardless, God never stops drawing us closer to Him. Listen to what Charles Spurgeon once wrote about this: "Art thou praying for some beloved one? Oh, give not up thy prayers, for Christ is 'mighty to save.' You are powerless to reclaim the rebel, but your Lord is Almighty. Lay hold on that mighty arm, and rouse it to put forth its strength."[27]

Believer, never stop praying for the lost, and never give up hope for salvation. Our God is a good God, and He always does what is right. He will show that loved one the proper path to take; we just need to be diligent in prayer that when it is shown to them, they will take it.

FEBRUARY 27th

> James 5:13–14: "Is anyone among you suffering? Let him pray. Is anyone cheerful? Let him sing psalms. Is anyone among you sick? Let him call for the elders of the church, and let them pray over him, anointing him with oil in the name of the Lord."

Who is the "him" that James is talking about when he says, "Let him pray . . . let him sing . . . let him call"? Yeah . . . me, you, "anyone," James says. James uses the word "anyone" three times in these two verses to make the point that anyone, regardless who they are or what they have done, can call upon the Lord. Prayer is not reserved just for pastors or prayer warriors or elders in the church, and it is not only for the "big things" in life; prayer is for every believer and for every situation. We know this because God invites us to come to Him and pray. "Ask, and it will be given to you; seek, and you will find; knock, and it will be opened to you" (Matthew 7:7); "Let us therefore come boldly to the throne of grace that we may obtain mercy and find grace to help in our time of need" (Hebrews 4:16). So we see that God not only invites us to come to Him in prayer, but we also see that He wants to help us in our time of need as well.

"Rejoice always, pray without ceasing, in everything give thanks; for this is the will of God in Christ Jesus for you" (1 Thessalonians 5:16–18). Did you catch that? This is the will of God for *you*. How many times have you asked God what His will is for your life? Here it is: Rejoice always, pray without ceasing and in everything, give thanks. Philippians 4:6 also reminds us of this: "Be anxious for nothing, but in everything, by prayer and supplication, with thanksgiving, let your requests be made known to God." I love the NLT version of this verse: "Don't worry about anything; instead, pray about everything." The point is, God wants to hear from you about everything going on in your life, all the time. This is why James continually emphasizes in these verses, "Let him pray, let him sing . . . let him call," for "You do not have, because you do not ask" (James 4:2).

FEBRUARY 28th

James 5:13b: "Is anyone cheerful? Let him sing psalms."

I thought it was interesting that sandwiched between suffering and sickness is this thought of singing psalms. James 5:13–14 says, "Is anyone among you suffering? Let him pray. Is anyone cheerful? Let him sing psalms. Is anyone among you sick? Let him call for the elders of the church, and let them pray over him, anointing him with oil in the name of the Lord." There is much to be said about praising God in the midst of our trials and afflictions, as it is during these times that praise lifts our countenance, relieves our anxiety, and places our focus back on God where it belongs.

I believe that James is telling us that just as singing is natural for us to do when we are joyful, praying should be just as natural for us to do when we are sick or suffering. Prayer shouldn't be something that others have to remind us of, or even force us to do; and prayer should never be our last resort, rather it should be something that we automatically take part in because we believe in the power of prayer.

The Greek mathematician Archimedes once wrote, "Give me a place to stand and with a lever I will move the whole world." In a very real way, God has given us such a lever in prayer; with it, we can move the world because prayer can do everything that God can do. Pastor Ed Rea once said, "Prayer moves the hand that moves the universe, and [God] invites us to ask for that power today."[28] Do you believe that's true?

In Exodus 32, we read about how the children of Israel made a golden calf and then began to worship it, thus making God very angry. God told Moses that He was going to destroy the nation of Israel (Exodus 32:9–10), yet Moses interceded for his people; he prayed for them, he pleaded with God to spare their lives, and we are told that the "the LORD relented" and did not destroy them (Exodus 32:14).

The word "relented" used here is also the word "repented," meaning that God changed His mind. As David Guzik explained, "Moses' prayer did not change God, but rather it changed the standing of the people in God's sight—the people were now in a place of mercy, whereas before they were in a place of judgment."[29] So, believer, do you believe that there is power in prayer? Do you believe that prayer changes things? If you do, then pray. If you don't, then pray even more.

FEBRUARY 29th

> Isaiah 6:1: "In the year that King Uzziah died, I saw the Lord sitting on a throne, high and lifted up, and the train of His robe filled the temple."

I once asked my mom when she and my dad got married, and rather than say "November 23, 1963," she said, "We were married the day after John F. Kennedy was assassinated." For my mom to say that they were married the day after Kennedy was assassinated was to place a backdrop of what they were experiencing on that day. Everyone was sad and discouraged because Kennedy was such a loved man; for him to die in such a tragic way left many people feeling afraid and vulnerable. So when Isaiah wrote, "In the year that King Uzziah died, I saw the Lord sitting on a throne, high and lifted up, and the train of His robe filled the temple," Isaiah was placing a backdrop of what he was experiencing when he saw the Lord sitting on a throne.[30]

King Uzziah was a great king as he did what was right in the sight of the Lord (2 Kings 15:3). He led Judah to many victories over their enemies, and his fame spread far and wide as he was loved by all the people (2 Chronicles 26:8). Yet his life had a tragic ending to it as he transgressed against the Lord, became leprous, and spent the rest of his life in isolation. It was such a tragic end to such a great man that Isaiah became discouraged. Much like the question people asked when Kennedy was assassinated and when 9/11 took place, Isaiah was also asking, "Lord, where are You in all of this?"[31]

For Isaiah, hopelessness was building: Uzziah was dead, chaos was mounting, and Judah's enemies were stirring. It was then, in that moment, when it seemed darkest, when it seemed like the Lord was nowhere to be found, that Isaiah "saw the Lord sitting on a throne, high and lifted up, and the train of His robe filled the temple." Though it seemed like everything was out of control and was falling apart, the Lord made it abundantly clear to Isaiah that He was still on the throne and that He was still very much in control.

We will often have similar feelings and experiences in our lives that Isaiah had here, and in those moments of despair we need to remember and trust that the Lord is still sitting on the throne, high and lifted up above all other things. Though His ways are mysterious, His character is clearly revealed in and through the Bible. He is good, He is faithful, and He is fully in control of all things.

MARCH 1st

Matthew 14:30: "Lord, save me!"

In James 5:16b, James wrote, "The effective, fervent prayer of a righteous man avails much." So what does it mean to pray fervently? When Elijah prayed for rain, he bowed down on the ground, placed his head between his knees, and prayed for rain seven times. What's really interesting about the position that Elijah was in when he prayed was the same position a woman who was giving birth in that day would be in during labor. In a very real and powerful way, Elijah labored in prayer until the Lord answered him. This is an example of fervent prayer.

With that being said, though, fervent prayer can sometimes be very simple as well. You don't have to be in a specific position to pray fervently. I remember hearing a story about a pastor, a priest, and a rabbi, who were all sitting in an office one day discussing the most effective way to pray. The pastor started off by saying, "The most effective way to pray is to pray on your knees." Disagreeing with him, the priest said, "No, it is most effective to pray with your hands folded and your head bowed down." "You are both wrong," the rabbi stated, "the most effective way to pray is with your hands raised high in the air." Listening to their conversation was a telephone repairman who was working on the phone system in the office. "Excuse me," he said, "I don't know about any of that, but the most effective prayer I ever prayed was when I was hanging upside down from a telephone pole."

Prayer is always going to be about the heart, not the position. One of my all-time favorite fervent prayers is "Lord, save me!" This is the prayer that Peter cried out to Jesus after he climbed out of the boat and began walking on water. It wasn't long and drawn out, and it definitely wasn't eloquent, but man, it sure was fervent.

Charles Spurgeon once wrote this regarding prayer, "Short prayers are long enough. There were but three words in the petition, which Peter gasped out, but they were sufficient for his purpose. Not length but strength is desirable. A sense of need is a mighty teacher of brevity. If our prayers had less of the tail feathers of pride and more wing, they would be all the better."[32]

Believer, fervent prayer is never going to be about the position you are in or even the words you use. Fervent prayer will always be about opening up your heart and pouring it out to the Lord—not by way of a certain method, but by way of a certain relationship. Remember, fervent prayer is not so much about getting what we want as it is about birthing a deeper relationship with God.

MARCH 2nd

> Psalm 145:18 (NLT): "The LORD is close to all who call on Him, yes, to all who call on him in truth."

A couple of weeks ago in a Bible study I was attending, we were singing a song that expressed our deep hunger for God. As I was singing this song, I remember fully desiring more of God. It was then that the Holy Spirit impressed on my heart, "Patrick, if you really do want more of God, He is totally available for you . . . as much as you will ever want."

I became very convicted, as I was reminded how we often sing songs and pray prayers as if God is hard to reach; as if He is so far from us that we have to beg and plead just so we can reach Him. Yet this could not be further from the truth as the psalmist reminds us, "The Lord is close to all who call on Him, yes, to all who call on Him sincerely." It was in that moment that the words of that song were changed from us hungering for more of Him, to Him hungering for more of us.

Believer, please understand, it's not we who are hungry for God; it is He who is hungry for us. All day long He waits for us to call on Him and fellowship with Him, and yet we occupy our lives with just about everything but Him, and then we sing these songs as if He is the one who is hard to get a hold of. The truth is that God is always available to us. If we really want more of Him, He is ours to freely have, as much as we could ever want because He desires more of us.

MARCH 3rd

> Daniel 1:8: "But Daniel purposed in his heart that he would not defile himself."

While Daniel was in captivity, it would have been very easy for him to justify why it was OK to eat the delicacies of King Nebuchadnezzar. "But Daniel purposed in his heart that he would not defile himself." John MacArthur remarked that to indulge in these foods was "understood as honoring" the false gods that Nebuchadnezzar worshipped, and so Daniel refused to compromise his faith no matter how convenient it might have been.[33] Instead, he requested that he might eat only vegetables and drink only water; God honored Daniel's faithfulness and gave him favor with those in charge of him. I cannot help but think that if we, as believers, purposed in our hearts as Daniel did to not compromise, God would bless us tremendously just as He blessed Daniel. Truth be told, it takes a strong person with a strong faith to say no to convenience if it means compromising in their faith. Oh, how we need to be those people today.

I ran into an old friend of mine a couple of years back. When I asked her how things were going, she told me that she had gotten a divorce. Her husband was abusive and had been cheating on her, and after much counsel and prayer, it was decided that they should get a divorce because he refused to repent and change his ways. She told me that after the divorce, her husband was still living in the house with her and her daughter because she couldn't afford to live on her own; yet it was clear that God was telling her that she needed to have him move out.

For weeks she battled with this decision because for the life of her, she couldn't see how it would ever work out. Finally, she decided to obey the Lord's instructions, trusting that God would provide for her just as His Word promises, and she told her ex-husband that he had to leave. Within days after having him move out, my friend's landlord called her and said he was lowering her rent; the next day at work, her boss came to her and said he was giving her a raise. God rewarded my friend because she made the choice to be obedient to His instructions and not compromise in her faith . . . and He will do the same for us as well.

MARCH 4th

Deuteronomy 11:24 (NIV): "Every place where you set your foot will be yours."

There has been a pattern of learning in my life lately, and it goes something like this: I pray, "Lord, please (do this, give me that, change me, etc.)"; and the response I get from God is, "Patrick, if you really do want (whatever that prayer request is), then apply My Word to your life and put forth the effort to receive it, because it is completely available to you." The lesson that I am continually being reminded of is that in order to receive the things that I am praying for, there has to be an effort put forth on my part. These requests are not going to just magically come about through osmosis as I sit and play video games all day. If I truly want these things, I have to go and get them.

I liken this to when God spoke to the children of Israel regarding their inheritance of the Promised Land. God said to them, "Every place where you set your foot will be yours." God promised the children of Israel land in abundance; all they had to do was go and get it. Yet we know that the children of Israel never occupied more than ten percent of what God had for them, simply because they would not put forth the effort to go and get it.

Think of it like this: If we truly want God's will and are putting forth the effort to diligently seek Him, is He really going to hide it from us? Of course not, because it's God's desire for all of us to know His will for our lives. In fact, God promises us in His Word that if we seek Him, we will find Him (1 Chronicles 28:9). But we have to put forth the effort to seek, knock, and ask (Matthew 7:7).

As I consider all of these things, I cannot help but think that God wants so much more for us then what we have right now. His innate desire is to bless us abundantly, yet we often settle for so much less simply because we don't want to take the time or put forth the effort to apply His Word to our lives.

It reminded me of a story a friend once told me about Alexander the Great. One day, a beggar asked for a handout from Alexander, so Alexander threw the man several gold coins. Amazed at his generosity, one of Alexander's generals said to him, "Copper coins would have met the beggar's need. Why give him gold?" Alexander responded, "Copper coins might have met the beggar's need, but gold coins fit my mercy and generosity." And so it is with God, to a much greater and higher degree. So, believer, how much more does God have for you that you are missing out on, simply because you are not putting forth the effort to seek His face and apply His Word to your life?

MARCH 5th

John 3:16: "For God so loved the world . . ."

I began meditating on what true love really is, and it led me to think about video games. Let me explain. When video games first came out, there was a reset button on the console that would allow you to start the game over if you made a mistake or took a wrong path. As games became more in depth, and game consoles became more advanced, reset buttons were replaced with memory cards and hard drives that gave you the ability to save your progress as you went through the game. This technology has revolutionized gaming because it allows for gamers to make any choice that they want to make without consequence. Gamers know full well that if they make a mistake, they can simply go back to their last saved point, load it up, and avoid making that same mistake again.

This approach works great in gaming, but it doesn't translate too well into marriage. Many people go into marriage confessing that they love one another, yet they really have no idea what loving someone truly entails. To them, love is a feeling that is based on good times, what their spouse does for them, and how their spouse treats them. So when hard times come, and their spouse makes mistakes and hurts them, fails them, and the feelings of love are gone . . . they want to just hit the reset button and start all over with someone else. The world says that true love is a feeling based on what others do for you. The Bible says that true love is a choice that is based on what you do for others.

We see a perfect example of true love in the story of creation. At some point, in the beginning, God decided that He was going to create man. And as He thought about this new creation of His, God decided that He didn't want to make man to be like a robot, who would have to do whatever God said without choice. No, God wanted His new creation to be like Him and have the free will to make his own choices. More specifically though, God wanted man to be able to make the choice to love Him and obey Him freely. But, with that free will, God also knew that man would make the choice to sin, thus separating man from fellowship with God.

God knew that man would become evil, rebellious, and perverse, and that eventually man would deny Him and worship other gods. God knew that man would curse His name and raise his fist to Him in spite; God knew that He would have to become a man and die on the cross in order to save all of mankind from eternal death. God also knew that many would still reject Him and curse Him even after He died for them. God knew every selfish, sinful, perverse choice that you and I and everyone else in this world, past or present, would ever make. And yet God, knowing all of these things, still made the choice to create us, to love us, and to die for us. This is true love.

So, believer, remember: Love is not a feeling; it is a choice we make every day and in every situation. To say, "I have fallen out of love with my spouse," or "I cannot love this or that person" is to say that you no longer have free will; it is to say that you no longer are capable of making choices, and we all know this is not true. So choose to love today, and watch as your heart changes.

MARCH 6ᵗʰ

John 16:9: "of sin, because they do not believe in Me."

Jesus reminds us that one of the roles of the Holy Spirit is to convict the world of sin; more specifically, "of sin, because they do not believe in Me." Notice that sin is defined as having unbelief in Jesus. "In other words, it boils down to a single issue: What have you done with Jesus?"[34] Not our lying, stealing, cheating, adultery, murder, etc., but rather by our single decision to either accept or reject Jesus Christ as our Lord and Savior.

Too often we embrace condemnation after we stumble and fall by saying things like, "How in the world can I be saved?" And then we torture ourselves for days, all the while neglecting the promise of 1 John 1:9, "If we confess our sins, He is faithful and just to forgive us our sins and to cleanse us from all unrighteousness."

In doing this, we take on the false perspective that when we do good things, or when we don't do bad things, we are somehow more righteous in God's eyes. And by taking this perspective, we are essentially saying that what Jesus did on the cross was not enough for us; we must still earn our righteousness by works and deeds. Yet we must remember that on the cross Jesus said it is finished; there is nothing left to do; the debt of man's sin has been paid in full.

When we surrender our lives to Jesus Christ and call on Him as Lord and Savior, the Bible tells us that we are made righteous in God's sight. More specifically, as Jeremiah wrote, "The LORD is our Righteousness" (Jeremiah 23:6, ESV). Our righteousness in God's eyes has nothing at all to do with us, or what we do, or what we don't do; our righteousness is solely based on Jesus Christ. Second Corinthians 5:21 says, "For He [God] made Him [Jesus] who knew no sin to be sin for us, that we might become the righteousness of God in Him."

Please do not get me wrong; we should absolutely be broken when we sin because sin is very serious. But we should only be broken to the point where it leads us to repentance, back to God, not to where it becomes condemnation and drives us from God. So how do we balance the fact that we are sinners with the fact that we have total forgiveness in Christ? How do we keep from cheapening His grace and just running to sin because we have that forgiveness?

The key, I believe, is in Psalm 119:7 (NLT): "As I learn your righteous regulations, I will thank you by living as I should!" The psalmist realized that saying "thank You" to God wasn't enough for all that God had done for him. So he made a choice; he purposed in his heart to thank God by living as he should—by living as God had instructed him to live. This is the attitude and outlook that we are to have in regard to sin. We should be so thankful for what God has done for us that we will do everything in our power to avoid sin, not run to it, because we know we have forgiveness.

MARCH 7th

> Judges 16:20: "But he did not know that the LORD had departed from him."

Samson was a man who, from the time he was born, was blessed by God and empowered by the Holy Spirit (Judges 13:24–25). God purposed Samson to fight against the Philistines by gifting him with incredible strength and skill for battle. At one point, Samson killed one thousand Philistines with the jawbone of a donkey. But despite his amazing strength and incredible feats of bravery, Samson's life came to a sad end.

A woman named Delilah seduced Samson in order to find out what the source of his strength was. Eventually, after "his soul was annoyed to death" (Judges 16:16, NASB) by her constant prying, Samson told Delilah his secret, and while he was sleeping, she cut his hair. The next morning the Philistines attacked, and Samson went out to meet them as he had done many times before. This time, however, they captured him, bound him, and put out his eyes because Samson "did not know the Lord had departed from him." Though I'm sure Samson did not feel any different that morning, the Lord had in fact left Samson because of Samson's longstanding disobedience to God's commands, not because his hair was cut. Samson lived in compromise for so long that he just figured nothing would ever change.

We find a similar story with the church of Sardis in Revelation 3:1 (NASB) where Jesus said to them, "I know your deeds, that you have a name that you are alive, but you are dead." Though this church looked alive because it had a great reputation among men and was still performing good deeds, it was in fact a dead church.

John MacArthur said, "The church of Sardis was like a museum in which stuffed animals are exhibited in their natural habitats. Everything appears to be normal, but nothing is alive. Sin killed the Sardis church. What are the danger signs that a church is dying? A church is in danger when it is content to rest on its past laurels, when it is more concerned with liturgical forms than spiritual reality, when it focuses on curing social ills rather than changing people's hearts through preaching the life-giving gospel of Jesus Christ, when it is more concerned with material than spiritual things, when it is more concerned with what men think than what God said, when it is more enamored with doctrinal creeds and systems of theology than with the Word of God, or when it loses its conviction that every word of the Bible is the Word of God Himself."[35]

We should be so reliant on the presence and power of the Holy Spirit that we could do absolutely nothing without Him. So, believer, let me ask you something: If the Holy Spirit left your life, your church, your business, your marriage . . . would you notice?

MARCH 8th

> 1 Timothy 2:1: "Therefore I exhort first of all that supplications, prayers, intercessions, and giving of thanks be made for all men."

Why are we instructed to pray for others? We are told why in 1 Timothy 2:3: "For this is good and acceptable in the sight of God our Savior, who desires all men to be saved and to come to the knowledge of the truth." God desires that all men be saved and that they might come to the knowledge of truth, and prayer plays a vital role in these things coming to pass.

A brother at church came up to me last week and asked me how he should witness to his family. He told me that his family has some very strange beliefs and that whenever he shares the Word of God with them, they get into an argument because they do not want to hear it. I told him to pray, but not just pray *for* them—pray *with* them. I learned a long time ago that if you have the time to tell someone you will pray for them, then you should pray with them right then and there. Why, though? What is the big deal? Well, think about it—whenever we pray, we are brought into the very presence of God; so why not take someone with you, especially someone who does not know the Lord?

Understand that when we pray with someone, whether that person is a believer or not, he or she has an encounter with the living God. I picture it like us walking them right over to God and introducing them to Him. That alone is reason enough to pray with people when given the opportunity. I once heard a story about a pastor who was asked to preach a sermon to a large crowd one morning at sunrise. The pastor was so overwhelmed with emotion that all he could do was pray. As tears rolled down his face, he prayed his heart out to the Lord. Sometime later, when he revisited the area, the local pastor informed him that more than forty people had given their lives to the Lord that morning. The pastor said, "But all I did was pray."

"Yes," the other pastor replied, "but the more incredible thing is that none of them spoke English."

MARCH 9th

> Genesis 45:7: "And God sent me before you to preserve a posterity for you in the earth, and to save your lives by a great deliverance."

The story of Joseph is an amazing one. Here was a man who was thrown into a pit by his brothers, sold to slave traders, sold again to Egyptians, and then thrown into jail because of false accusation. But that is not the end of the story. Through perseverance and obedience to God, Joseph ultimately became the second most powerful man in Egypt. Why was all of this allowed, you ask? It was done "to preserve a posterity for you in the earth, and to save your lives by a great deliverance." The "you" mentioned here was not just Joseph's family, but the nation of Israel as well. Like Jesus, Joseph endured hard times for the sake of others.

I was thinking about this when one of the guys in the prayer room told me some recent news about our good friend Ted. About four years ago, Ted was in a dune buggy accident and fractured the C-2 vertebrae in his neck. Now, I am not a doctor, but even I know that Ted should have died or at least should have been paralyzed as the C-2 vertebrae are located just below the base of the skull. But after neck fusion surgery and a lot of physical therapy, Ted was back to work as a truck driver.

Recently, Ted was in a serious motorcycle accident when a truck clipped him on the freeway. The original diagnosis was that Ted was going to lose his entire leg, but now it looks like he may only lose his foot. As he was being transferred from the hospital to the convalescent rehab facility, Ted had an opportunity to talk to the guys in the ambulance about Jesus. By the time they reached the rehab facility a short time later, Ted had led both men to Christ. And now, having been at the facility for just over a week, Ted has led around twenty-five people to the Lord—not just patients, but doctors, nurses, hospital staff . . . basically whoever Ted ran into.

The kneejerk reaction when we hear a story like this is to assume that Ted has something we do not have—like his gifting is more powerful than ours, or something to that effect. Well, let me tell you, Ted is just a regular person just like you and me. The anointing he has received from God is the same anointing that we have all received as believers (1 John 2:20). When James wrote about Elijah in James 5:17, James made it clear that Elijah had "a nature like ours," even though God did amazing things in and through his life. Paul and Barnabas said the same thing to the Greeks and Jews in Acts 14 after they healed a paralytic and the people wanted to worship them. The real truth is that these men just made themselves available to God, and by doing that, God used them mightily. So, believer, when you face seasons of difficulty in your life—and you will—how will you respond? Will you view that situation as a curse, or as an opportunity to be used by the Lord?

MARCH 10th

> 1 John 2:15: "Do not love the world or the things in the world. If any-
> one loves the world, the love of the Father is not in him."

It's good to remember when reading the New Testament that although the English language has only one word for "love," the Greek language has many. So when I see a verse with the word "love" written in it this many times, I go to the Greek to find out which kind of love they are referring to.

The first two uses of the word "love" in this verse is the Greek word *agapao*, which means "to welcome." As David Guzik pointed out, the term "world" that is used here does not refer to people or creation, but rather has the idea of "the world's system or way of doing things."[36] So John tells us that we are not to welcome the world's way of doing things into our hearts, for if we do this, if we love the world's ways, then the "love of the Father is not in" us.

The word "love" that John uses in the second half of this Scripture is the Greek word *agape*, which has the idea of a self-giving love that gives without demanding repayment. This love completely contradicts the world's way of loving as it is the love that can only be had through a relationship with Jesus Christ. Something I found really interesting is the word "in" that John uses here. It is the same exact word in Greek, *en*, that is used to describe how the Holy Spirit comes *en* us when we surrender our lives to Jesus Christ.

The point is, there is only room in our heart for one thing. We either welcome the world into our heart, or we welcome the Holy Spirit into our heart; we cannot welcome both because darkness and light cannot coexist. That is what John is saying here: If you welcome the world's ways of doing things into your heart, then you are not going to have the love of the Father in you. "For all that is in the world—the lust of the flesh, the lust of the eyes, and the pride of life—is not of the Father but is of the world" (1 John 2:16).

When we come to Jesus Christ and surrender our lives to Him, there is a process that must take place within us. That is what Romans 12:2 talks about when it says we are to be "transformed by the renewing of our mind." We need to stop thinking like the world and we need to begin thinking like God. Our habit patterns need to change, words have to be redefined, filters have to be replaced, and problems need to have a different source of reliance when we are struggling. We must begin to reject the world's way of doing things and embrace God's way of doing things, for the love of the world brings death, while the love of the Father brings life. So, believer, what are you welcoming into your heart?

MARCH 11th

> Proverbs 3:12: "For the LORD corrects those he loves, just as a father corrects a child in whom he delights."

The other day, Michelle was talking with one of our best friends about their two-year-old daughter. Apparently, when our friends asked their daughter who her best friend was, she said, "Patchik." Our friends lovingly responded to their daughter, "Patrick is your very good friend, absolutely, but Jesus is your best friend."

I started thinking about why a two-year-old girl would choose me to be her best friend over, say, her mom or dad. It's actually pretty simple when you think about it: Whenever I am over there, she and I play and laugh and do all sorts of fun stuff. But I am never the one who disciplines her, corrects her, instructs her, makes her take a nap, go to bed, take a bath, eat, share . . . you know, all of those things that are essential to her development. In this scenario, spiritually speaking, I am representative of the world, while her parents are representative of God.

It's no secret that children hate discipline, because they want to be able to do whatever it is they want to do. They have a hard time understanding that not everything they want to do is a good thing. They have a hard time seeing the bigger picture of choices versus consequences, and so when discipline or correction comes, they look at it like a bad thing.

Are we any different, though? The world tells us to have fun and do whatever it is we want to do, whereas the Lord is the one who disciplines us and corrects us when we need it. He is the one who gives us the structure and balance that we so desperately need for our spiritual development. He does these things because He loves us and He has our best interests in mind. "For the Lord corrects those he loves, just as a father corrects a child in whom he delights."

The role of the parent in a child's life is not to be their best friend; it is to be the person who loves them enough to discipline and correct them, even though it may not be pleasant for the child or for the parent at the time. As I look back at my upbringing and remember the discipline I received from my parents, I hated every moment of it; but I am so thankful for it now.

The thing that I thought was really interesting about all of this was that even though our friend's daughter said that I was her best friend, when the terrors come in the middle of the night, or she gets sick, or scrapes her knee, she will not be calling or running to "Patchik"; she will be calling and running to her mom and dad because, ultimately, she trusts them and knows that they love her. Though it may sound strange, through proper discipline and correction, children begin to trust their parents; and as they grow in understanding, they discover just how much their parents truly do love them.

MARCH 12ᵗʰ

Matthew 5:45 (ESV): "For He makes His sun rise on the evil and on the good, and sends rain on the just and on the unjust."

Jesus reminds us in this verse that storms are a part of life whether you are a believer or not, because God "sends rain on the just and on the unjust." So what's the purpose behind the storms of life? We gain a little insight into this from Hebrews 6:7–8: "For the earth which drinks in the rain that often comes upon it, and bears herbs useful for those by whom it is cultivated, receives blessing from God; but if it bears thorns and briars, it is rejected and near to being cursed, whose end is to be burned."

Think of it like this: When a rainstorm comes, the land that receives that rain produces fresh vegetation which in turn bears fruit; thus, the need for the storm is justified and the purpose of the storm is fulfilled. The writer of Hebrews says that when storms are received in the proper way, they are a "blessing from God." But if the land does not produce fruit, then the purpose of the storm is wasted.[37]

As I thought about this, I began thinking about the valley that we live in. After a storm has come through and given us some much-needed rain, everything is green and lush and beautiful; flowers are blooming, plants are growing . . . you can literally see how rain has brought life to this valley. But when there are no storms and the sun is shining day after day, this valley becomes very ugly, as it turns into a dry, brown, fruitless land.

The same goes with us. If our lives were easy all of the time and we never faced any storms, our lives would be just like this valley—dry, brown, and fruitless. But because God loves us and wants us to grow and bear much fruit, He allows storms to come into our lives that nourish and enrich us. This is how the apostle Paul was able to say in Philippians 4:11, "I have learned in whatever state I am, to be content." Notice that being content was not something that was natural to Paul; he makes it very clear that he had to learn to be content. This was only possible because of the storms that he had endured. So, believer, when the storms of life come, do not run from them, but rather receive them with faith, knowing that with storms comes much fruit.

MARCH 13th

> Isaiah 26:3: "You will keep him in perfect peace, whose mind is stayed on You, because he trusts in You."

With a huge decision looming in our near future, Michelle and I thought it wise to fast, pray, and seek counsel from the Lord. As the day went on, and the hours passed, I started to become discouraged because I wasn't hearing anything from the Lord. In my mind I was thinking, "God, this isn't right. I am fasting and praying; why aren't You answering me?" The problem was that I was only seeking an answer; I was not seeking the Lord.

The whole purpose of fasting and praying is to draw near to God and experience Him in a more intimate way; it is not some ritual or work that we do in order to get what we want. I became frustrated because I had no peace about the situation. I had no peace about the situation because I had never truly surrendered it to God. I had never truly surrendered it to God because I did not trust Him with it.

Notice what Isaiah tells us in this verse, "You will keep him in perfect peace, whose mind is stayed on You, because he trusts in You." To understand what Isaiah is saying here, you need to reverse the order of the words: "Because he trusts in You, his mind will stay on You, and You will keep him in perfect peace." Though my mind had stayed on God all day, I had never really surrendered that decision to God, trusting that He would work it out.[38] In my mind, I had to have an answer right then and there so that I could work it out myself.

Later that night, I spent a couple of hours praying to God, surrendering this situation to Him, knowing that He would direct our paths (Proverbs 3:6). Once I did that, His perfect peace overwhelmed me.

As I write this devotion, a decision still needs to be made in this situation and the deadline is rapidly approaching; yet Michelle and I are at perfect peace because we trust that God knows and that He is in complete control. So, believer, "Be anxious for nothing, but in everything by prayer and supplication, with thanksgiving, let your requests be made known to God; and the peace of God, which surpasses all understanding, will guard your hearts and minds through Christ Jesus" (Philippians 4:6–7).

MARCH 14ᵗʰ

Matthew 8:26: "O ye of little faith . . ."

Michelle and I have begun house-hunting for the first time in our lives, and what an eye-opener it has been for us. The market right now is a seller's market, as there are simply more buyers than there are houses to buy; so when a house becomes available, people flock to it and fight over it like wild animals.

The other day a house came back on the market in a very desirable area. I quickly called my real estate agent, but I could not get a hold of her. As I sat there waiting for a callback, the level of anxiety was rapidly increasing in my heart and so I frantically called the listing agent, but I could not get a hold of her either. As time slowly, painfully, ticked by, I began to become very angry, because I believed that we were going to lose out on this house simply because I could not get a hold of anybody. All hope was lost.

The Lord quickly reminded me of Philippians 4:6–7, where we are told to be anxious for nothing and to make all of our requests made known to God through prayer and thanksgiving. As I sat there and meditated on this verse, I saw what I had become in the span of forty-five minutes . . . an anxious, irrational, faithless person. Instead of changing the worldly market system, I allowed the worldly market system to change me.

I was also reminded that though it's a seller's market, and though there are more buyers than there are homes, in all reality, it's God's market, not the world's. He is the One who is ultimately in control of all of it, and He dictates who gets what and when. As I shared my experience with a brother in the prayer room, he simply responded to me, "O ye of little faith." Truer words could not have been spoken.

But all of this brings to my mind a great question: When we come to the cross, what do we bring that actually contributes to the power of the cross? The answer is quite simple: absolutely nothing. We come to the cross guilty, lost, and hopeless; trembling with an aching heart in all of our perfect weaknesses. The only thing we bring to the cross is an abundance of sin, and yet we find complete forgiveness because of the perfect work that Jesus Christ did that day at Calvary. Not the work *we* did . . . the work *He* did.

So the question we must ask ourselves is this: If we can trust God with our eternal salvation, how can we not trust Him with the temporal things of this world like houses, cars, jobs, illnesses, relationships, etc.? Truth be told, we cannot rely on both ourselves and the Holy Spirit; it has to be one or the other. We must remember that it's "'Not by [our] might nor by [our] power, but by [His] Spirit,' says the LORD" (Zechariah 4:6).

MARCH 15th

Proverbs 2:10: "When wisdom enters your heart . . ."

Matthew Henry wrote that "When wisdom has possession of thee, it will 'keep thee.'"[39] We are not speaking of merely head knowledge here, but rather a heart knowledge that will transform us into the very image of wisdom. When this happens, our decisions, desires, words, actions, and lives will all reflect its character. Listen and pay close attention to what happens when we enthrone wisdom in our lives:

> When wisdom enters your heart, and knowledge is pleasant to your soul, discretion will preserve you; understanding will keep you, to deliver you from the way of evil; from the man who speaks perverse things; from those who leave the paths of uprightness to walk in the ways of darkness; who rejoice in doing evil and delight in the perversity of the wicked; whose ways are crooked and who are devious in their paths; to deliver you from the immoral woman. . . . For her house leads down to death. . . . [It will keep you so] that you may walk in the way of goodness and keep to the paths of righteousness. (Proverbs 2:10–16, 18, 20)

Solomon reemphasizes this truth in Proverbs 3:1–2, "But let your heart keep my commands; for length of days and long life and peace they will add to you." He also gives us a warning about wisdom, "Let not mercy and truth forsake you; my son . . . let them not depart from your eyes—keep sound wisdom and discretion" (Proverbs 3:3, 21).

I thought it was very profound that Solomon said truth (wisdom) can leave us. I liken this to riding a bike; as long as you are pedaling, you are moving forward. But when you stop pedaling, eventually your momentum will leave you and you will come to a complete stop. This is generally when we find ourselves in trouble because we have stopped walking in the counsel of the Spirit and we have begun walking in the counsel of our flesh.

The writer of Hebrews gives us some great advice that we would wise to listen to: "show the same diligence to the full assurance of hope until the end, that you do not become sluggish, but imitate those who through faith and patience inherit the promises" (Hebrews 6:11–12). So we must not only seek wisdom for a season; rather, we must be diligent in seeking it until the very end so that we might inherit the promises of eternal life. "For the upright will dwell in the land, and the blameless will remain in it" (Proverbs 2:21).

MARCH 16th

Psalm 89:33: "Nevertheless My lovingkindness I will not utterly take from him, nor allow My faithfulness to fail."

This morning I was reflecting on some of the decisions I have made in the last couple of months, and let's just say that I was not encouraged. "Did I make the wrong choice, Lord? Was I supposed to do this instead of that?" Quickly my mind began to trace back even further to decisions I had made years ago, "Lord, is this now because of that then?" I became increasingly discouraged and frustrated with myself, but then I was reminded of this amazing attribute of God: He . . . is . . . faithful.

As I stood on this principle of God's character, knowing that I could never change it, His peace washed over me and I was reminded that God's faithfulness is greater than any mistake I could ever make. God says to us even in times of discipline and correction, "My lovingkindness I will not utterly take from him, nor allow My faithfulness to fail." God is always faithful to us.

The challenge for us is to step outside of ourselves, what we are feeling, what we are thinking, and stand on who God says He is. "For if our heart condemns us,

God is greater than our heart" (1 John 3:20). God's faithfulness is greater than our feelings. Even when we are not faithful to God, and we give into fear and disobey Him, even then God remains faithful to us. "If we are faithless, He remains faithful; He cannot deny Himself" (2 Timothy 2:13).

Even when we do not believe God can save us, help us, heal us, provide for us, or free us, He is faithful. There is a great story about a father who brought his child to Jesus, desperately seeking healing for his son. And without faith, he asked Jesus, "'*if* You can do anything, have compassion on us and help us.' Jesus said to him, '*If* you can believe, all things are possible to him who believes.' Immediately the father of the child cried out and said with tears, 'Lord, I believe; help my unbelief'" (Mark 9:22–24). Jesus healed this man's child—not because of the man's faith, but because God is faithful.

More importantly, even when we sin, and we are certain that we have worn out God's grace this time; all we need to do is confess to Him our sin' for He is faithful and just to forgive us of our sin and cleanse us from all unrighteousness (1 John 1:9). So, believer, whenever you feel that you have finally exhausted God's grace, or your faith fails you because a prayer has not been answered, remember these words: "But the Lord is faithful" (2 Thessalonians 3:3).

MARCH 17th

Proverbs 9:10b: "and knowledge of the Holy One is understanding."

As I have been reading through the book of Proverbs this month, there has been one word that has continually jumped out to me: "understanding." We are told in many different places, "apply your heart to understanding," "lift up your voice for understanding," "understanding will keep you," "get understanding!" (Proverbs 2:2, 3, 11; 4:5). On and on Solomon speaks about understanding and how vital it is for us to have. So I began asking myself, "What exactly is understanding?"

One of the rules to studying the Bible that I have found most helpful is to allow Scripture to explain and define Scripture. Case in point, Proverbs 9:10 (emphasis added) tells us that "knowledge of the Holy One *is* understanding." So understanding is defined as having the knowledge of God. The more I thought about this, the more it made perfect sense to me. I do not know how many times I have said to God, "I don't understand why You did this, or allowed that, God." But the more I have grown in my knowledge of who God is, the more I trust Him in those situations that I do not understand.

We need to accept the fact that there are certain situations and things of this life that we will just never understand. But the more we know God, the more we will gain understanding of who He is in those situations. We may not understand the situation itself, but we will understand the God who is in control of that situation. It is there, and only there, that we will find the peace and rest that surpasses our need for understanding.

MARCH 18th

> Galatians 5:22–23: "[T]he fruit of the Spirit is love, joy, peace, long-suffering, kindness, goodness, faithfulness, gentleness, self-control. Against such there is no law."

It is often said that these are the fruits of the Holy Spirit as He works through our lives. But notice that the apostle Paul wrote "The *fruit* of the Spirit," not, "The *fruits* of the Spirit." The word "fruit" used here is singular, not plural. So what Paul is really saying in this verse is "The fruit of the Spirit is love." The eight characteristics that follow (joy, peace, longsuffering, kindness, goodness, faithfulness, gentleness, self-control) are all different byproducts of this love. David Guzik suggested that these eight characteristics are actually a description of "what love in action looks like."[40]

And really, at its very core, that is what love is, right? An action. First John 3:18 tells us as much: "[L]et us not love in word or in tongue, but in deed and truth." The love that is referred to in Galatians 5:22–23 is the love known as *agape*—a self-sacrificing love that gives its very best for the sake of others without demanding or expecting something in return. The word *agape* itself is a noun, but it comes from the root word *agapao,* which is a verb. This word speaks of a continual act of loving. So again, at its very core, love is an action.

We need to remember, "love can only truly be known by the action that it prompts."[41] For example, in John 3:16 we are told, "For God so loved the world that He gave His only begotten Son." We know of God's love for us because there was an action assigned to that love; He sent His Son Jesus Christ to die on the cross for us. If God had merely stated that He loved us over and over again, but there was never any action prompted by that love, then we wouldn't truly know God's love for us. The same can be said for us. The only way others will truly know we love them is when that love prompts us to act out that love in and around their lives.

MARCH 19th

1 John 4:7: "Beloved, let us love one another."

The term "beloved" used here comes from the same root word, *agapao*, that the word *agape* comes from, and it basically means "to be worthy of love." So let me ask you something: Do you believe that you are worthy of being loved? I ask this because those who struggle with the belief that they are worthy of love often end up struggling to love others the way that God wants them to.

God told me before I even met Michelle that I was never going to be able to truly love my wife until I accepted and believed His love for me first. It makes sense if you think about it, because how can you give something out that you have not first received?

We often ask the question, "Why do you love me?" because deep down we do not believe that we are worthy of being loved. We think that love is somehow based on what we do, what we don't do, what we look like, etc. If we do enough good things, or if we look like this, then we will be loved; but when we make mistakes, or are not in tip-top shape, then that love is gone. The truth is that none of this has anything to do with God's love for us and it should have nothing to do with how we love, or are loved by others.

To understand this, we must ask ourselves, "Why are we loved by God?" Is it because of who we are, what we do, or what we look like? No. We are loved by God because true love, the love that is of God, the *agape* love, is all about God choosing to love us in spite of who we are, what we do, and what we look like. It has nothing at all to do with us; we are loved by God simply because God has chosen to love us.

With that being said, take it one step further and ask yourself this: "What qualifies someone to be worthy of love?" The world says it is who they are, or what they do, or what they look like. But according to the Bible, you just need to be human: "For God so loved the world" (John 3:16). Knowing this, when I read the word "beloved" in the Bible, I see two different words combined into one word: "believe" and "loved." Thus we should read it as, "(Insert your name here), believe you are loved," because in essence, that is exactly what this word means.

You could even break the word down further and just say "be loved," as in be still, be blessed, be joyful, etc. The thought here is to just accept the fact that you are loved; stop fighting it, stop questioning it, stop analyzing it, and stop trying to understand it . . . just embrace it as truth, because God has chosen to love you.

MARCH 20th

1 John 4:9–10: "In this the love of God was manifested toward us, that God has sent His only begotten Son into the world, that we might live through Him. In this is love, not that we loved God, but that He loved us and sent His Son to be the propitiation for our sins."

The apostle John reminds us that God's perfect love was revealed when Jesus died on the cross for us. He loved us first, when we were unlovable, and because of that love, He became "the propitiation for our sins" so that "we might live through Him." The hidden theme in these verses is not what God did to show His love for us, but rather *when* He did it. Romans 5:8 tells us, "But God demonstrates His own love toward us, in that while we were still sinners, Christ died for us."

John makes it a point to remind us that Christ died for us when we were His enemies. That's what Romans 5:1 says: "Therefore, having been justified by faith, we have peace with God through our Lord Jesus Christ." David Guzik pointed out that Paul does not say that we now have the "peace *of* God," but rather we now have "peace *with* God."[42] No longer do we war with God as we once did as enemies of God; we now have been reconciled to God through the death and resurrection of Jesus Christ.

John brings this up to remind us of who we were before Christ. Do you remember? We all have a testimony to share of the abundant grace and love that God showed us by forgiving us of our sin. Shouldn't we then extend that same measure of grace and love to others? We need to remember that God did not just die for us. He died for every single person, because everyone is worthy of love. That includes the hypocrites, the legalists, the perverse, the abortionists, the murderers, the rapists, the drug dealers, the terrorists . . . Christ died for every single one of us so that we might all live through Him.

I would say that we do pretty well at loving the lovable; and on occasion we might even love those who annoy or even bother us; but rarely, if ever, will we love those who are our enemies. So John says to us, "Beloved, if God so loved us, we also ought to love one another" (1 John 4:11). In other words, if God loved you when you were at your very worst, then you should be able to take what you have received from Him and love one another. That is the challenge that is laid before us as believers, to love others just as we have been loved by God.

MARCH 21st

Acts 16:25: "But at midnight Paul and Silas were praying and singing hymns to God, and the prisoners were listening to them."

Last week, Michelle and I got up at 5:20 am to go running. This would not be such a big deal, except for the fact that I have not been able to run for more than two years because of some health issues. Needless to say, it was a huge struggle for me just to run up and down our street. The next day my legs were pretty sore; the day after that I could barely walk because my legs hurt so much. But it was a good pain. It was a pain that I gladly received because I knew the benefit that came from that pain.

Paul and Silas knew this truth all too well. Earlier in the day these two men had cast a demon out of a slave girl, and in return they were arrested, beaten, and imprisoned (Acts 16:16–24). Yet even after all that happened, "at midnight Paul and Silas were praying and singing hymns to God." It is an amazing thing when you consider the pain that these men were in. Their backs had been ripped open from being beaten, "their feet were fastened in stocks designed to induce painful cramping by spreading their legs, as wide as possible"[43] and yet here they were praying and singing hymns to God. For them, this was pain that they gladly received because they understood the benefit of it.

Isn't it interesting how much we abhor pain that is impressed on us by others, yet we gladly deal with self-inflicted pain because we know the benefit of it. For example, we exercise to burn fat and to sculpt and shape our bodies. Those adjectives alone describe a very painful process that we gladly put ourselves through because we know the good that comes from it. Yet when spiritual suffering, affliction, or persecution comes, we quickly take on the role of a victim and wallow in our suffering.

We need to ask ourselves, is it the pain that causes our suffering, or is it our outlook on that pain that causes suffering? As Paul would later write in Romans 8:18, "For I consider that the sufferings of this present time are not worthy to be compared with the glory which shall be revealed in us." It's all about perspective. So, believer, what is your perspective?

MARCH 22nd

1 John 4:12: "No man has seen God at any time. If we love one another, God abides in us, and His love has been perfected in us."

This is a very interesting passage of Scripture here. John tells us that no man has ever seen God, which is absolutely true. And yet, at the same time, we learn in the book of 1 John that God is visible for all men to see, which is also true . . . so what gives? Let me explain.

Throughout this book, John continually proclaims that God *is* love. With that, John also says that "His love has been perfected *in us* . . . *if* we love one another." So this, in a sense, is when God is made visible to all of mankind. God is manifested in our love (*agape*) for one another. He said that God cannot be seen when we love those who we like, those who are kind to us, and those whom we love; rather God is seen when we love those who are unlovable; those who are stubborn, selfish, mean, and rude. This is when God is truly manifested to the world.[44]

I would say most people who are unbelievers are thoroughly confused about who God is. There are so many cults and factions saying, "This is God" that most people simply don't know what to believe. But even though those around us may not know the Gospels of Matthew, Mark, Luke, or John, they know the gospel of (insert your name here), and when God is being revealed through your life by how you love them, the invisible God is clearly manifested in a real and powerful way.[45]

In the book of Acts we read about Paul and Silas being beaten, arrested, imprisoned, and shackled. At midnight they sang hymns and prayed to God causing all of those around them to listen intently. Then, after a giant earthquake had opened all of the cell doors and loosed all the chains, the jailer, who thought that all of the prisoners had escaped, was about to kill himself when Paul called out, "Do yourself no harm, for we are all here" (Acts 16:28).

Paul and Silas could have escaped, but they understood that if they did, the jailer would have been executed, and so they stayed simply because his life was more important to them than theirs. Upon hearing this, the jailer fell at their feet and said, "What must I do to be saved?" (Acts 16:30). This is God made visible. May it be so with us today.

MARCH 23rd

> 1 John 5:21 (NLT): "Dear children, keep away from anything that might take God's place in your hearts."

Many times when we read the "do's" and "do not's" of the Bible, we automatically assume that it is for God's benefit that we do, or do not, do those things. Yet we often forget that God's instructions are always for our benefit and betterment, not His. I was thinking about this as Michelle and I began budgeting for our household. One of the things we decided to do was to cancel our TV service and just keep our Internet. For weeks I battled with this decision as I admit, there was an aspect of fear involved. I have had TV for as long as I can remember, and so for me the idea of canceling it was a very scary thing to do. Finally, though, I made the choice to cancel our cable service, and as crazy as it is for me to say, my heart was kind of sad. It literally felt as if I were losing a friend. And the more I thought about it, the more it made sense to me as to why I was feeling this way.

Have you noticed that when we are sad, we often look to TV to cheer us up through a comedy; when we are lonely, we often look to TV to be our companion and to bring us hope through a love story; when we are burdened with our problems, we often look to TV to become an escape from reality? Though this methodology might provide a temporary relief for us, a distraction from what is really going on in our lives, in the long run it does not help us or our situation at all. Only God can bring the joy, hope, and deliverance that we so long for.

And it's not just TV that we do this with either; there are many things in this life we try to replace God with such as food, shopping, drugs, sports, possessions, exercise, etc. Yet we must remember that no matter how much we do, no matter how much we accumulate, and no matter how great the euphoria might be, nothing will ever fulfill that which we lack, because God is the only thing that can fill the void in our lives. So, believer, ask yourself: Has anything taken God's place in your heart?

MARCH 24th

> 1 John 5:14–15: "Now this is the confidence that we have in Him, that
> if we ask anything according to His will, He hears us. And if we know
> that He hears us, whatever we ask, we know that we have the petitions
> that we have asked of Him."

The word "confidence" that John uses here is an amazing word. It means to have such freedom in speaking that you cheerfully, courageously, and confidently divulge all things without fear. John says that this is the attitude that we should have when we come to God in prayer because "if we ask anything according to His will, He hears us. And if we know that He hears us, whatever we ask, we know that we have the petitions that we have asked of Him."

We gain a lot of insight here into the purpose of prayer. Prayer is not designed to get God to accomplish our will; rather, prayer is designed to find out what the will of God is for our lives. So John gives us assurance here by saying that if we ask anything according to God's will, it shall be done.

When Michelle and I were praying about marriage, I admit, I had a lot of fears; but my greatest fear was being outside of God's will, and so we prayed and waited for God to reveal His will for us. It wasn't until we both got to the point where we could honestly say to God with all of our heart, mind, and soul, "Not my will, but Your will be done" that our prayers were answered and God brought us together as husband and wife. And really, this should be our heart in every prayer that we pray to God: "Not my will, but Your will be done."

Now maybe you are sitting here thinking, "What a rip-off. We only get what's according to God's will—what about what I want and what I need?" Well, think about all of this logically for a second. We know that the will of God includes everything that we will ever need spiritually, physically, emotionally, and materialistically, right? I mean, God promises that for each one of His children. We also know that there is nothing we will ever need that is outside of God's will for us, because everything outside of God's will for us is not good. So we really need to ask ourselves, would we really want those prayers that are outside of God's will to be answered? Remember, God only says "no" to those things that are outside of His will for us. Now I admit, these are the times when our faith in who God is, is really put to the test. Is He really the good God that we say He is when everything is going right for us? Is He really trustworthy? Is His will really the best for us?

So many times we get angry at God because He doesn't answer our prayers according to what we want, or what we think we need, and yet the whole time God is merely protecting us from those things that would harm or hinder us. So, believer, have bold confidence when you come to God in prayer knowing that if it is in His will, the answer will always be "yes."

MARCH 25th

Matthew 12:13: "Then He [Jesus] said to the man, 'Stretch out your hand.' And he stretched it out, and it was restored as whole as the other."

I once heard a pastor teach on this section in Matthew and he said something really interesting about this verse. The pastor saw this man as having a hand that was paralyzed, kind of gnarled up into a fist. And when Jesus said to him, "Stretch out your hand," the man opened his hand and stretched out his fingers. The point is that God's command was the *enablement* for this man to stretch out his hand.

The same goes for us. As believers, each one of us is ready, right now, to do all that God has commanded us to do, because again, His command is all the enablement we will ever need. So do not believe the lie that you are not able to do what God has commanded you to do, because the truth is, you have already been enabled to do that very thing.

It's important to point out that even though Jesus commanded this man to stretch out his hand, if this man did not have the faith to even try and stretch out his hand, he never would have been healed. Many times when God calls us to do something, we wait until we feel like we are ready to do it. Yet this is walking by sight, not by faith.

When God commanded Joshua to cross over into the Promised Land, the priests, who were carrying the ark of the covenant, had to first step into the Jordan River before the water receded. If the priests had waited for the water to recede, they never would have stepped foot into the Promised Land. So, believer, be encouraged. Whatever it is that God is commanding you to do today, step out in faith knowing that He has enabled you to do that very thing.

MARCH 26th

Jude 24: "Now to Him who is able to keep you from stumbling . . ."

Michelle and I love to go for long walks around our hometown of Redlands because the south side of the city has some amazing homes from the early 1900s. With that, though, the infrastructure is pretty old as well; the sidewalks are cracked, uprooted, uneven, and sometimes just stop—so you have to be very aware of your surroundings at all times.

One Saturday, as we were out walking, Michelle pointed out something for me to look at. As I looked to see what she was pointing at, the sidewalk dropped because of a tree root and I missed a step, causing me to tweak my back. About a block later, I pointed out something for her to look at, and she about broke her ankle as the sidewalk suddenly stopped. Then, as I was looking at my phone to see how far we had walked, I hit my head on a low-hanging tree branch. As we were laughing about our misfortune, and talking about the "dangers of walking in Redlands," I said to Michelle, "You can't take your eyes off of where you are going for two seconds without getting hurt."

For the Christian, the lesson here is an obvious one. Unlike my hometown sidewalk, I have always pictured the Christian walk as us walking on this perfectly smooth dirt path, up and down hills and valleys. But along this path, on both sides, is the world with all of its temptations and distractions. As we walk along this path, keeping our eyes straight ahead, we do not stumble or fall. But, if we take our eyes off where we are going and begin looking at the things of the world, we are slowly led off the path onto very uneven ground with lots of pitfalls and dangers. This is when we get hurt.

We have to remember, we have an enemy and a world and a flesh that purposefully tries to sabotage our walk with Jesus by getting us to focus on all of these other things. Jude reminds us that there is only One that can keep us from stumbling, and that is God. "Now to Him who is able to keep you from stumbling. . . ."

Notice that Jude says God is "able" to keep us from stumbling. The ability to not stumble is available to all of us, but we must work with God to receive it. This only happens through a habitual, *on-growing* relationship with Christ. So, believer, learn a lesson from walking around Redlands: Keep your eyes on where you are going, and not on what's around you.

MARCH 27th

> Genesis 3:6: "So when the woman saw that the tree was good for food, that it was pleasant to the eyes, and a tree desirable to make one wise, she took of its fruit and ate. She also gave to her husband with her, and he ate."

After Satan had deceived Eve into eating the forbidden fruit, Eve then took the fruit to her husband, Adam, so that she could share it with him. She did this because she thought the fruit was "good" and "pleasant." If Eve had truly believed and understood the consequences of eating the fruit, I doubt she would have taken it to Adam.

So many times we find something in the world that is, in our estimation, good and pleasant, and we bring it to others so that we might share it with them. The problem is, like with Eve, most of what we bring to other people is not good and pleasant in God's estimation. We call it sharing, God calls it gossip; we call it fiction, God calls it poison; we call it harmless, God calls it destructive. When we rely on our estimations, and not on God's, and bring these things to other people, we actually become a stumbling block for them.

It is also interesting to note that even though Eve was deceived about this fruit, Adam wasn't. David Guzik pointed out that Adam ate the fruit fully knowing and understanding the consequences that his actions would bring; yet "in open rebellion against God," he still chose to eat the fruit.[46] And notice that the consequences of their sin were not felt until after Adam ate the fruit. "Then the eyes of both of them were opened" (Genesis 3:7).

What would have happened if Adam had said no to Eve, and had not eaten the fruit that she brought him? Think about this for a second: Eve's eyes were not opened after she ate the fruit; they were only opened after Adam had eaten the fruit. The Bible confirms this in Romans 5:12, "Therefore, just as through one man sin entered the world, and death through sin, and thus death spread to all men [mankind], because all sinned." It makes me wonder, if Adam had said no to Eve, and had not eaten the fruit, would Eve's eyes still have been opened?

The point is that we have a responsibility not only in what we bring to others, but in what others bring to us. When someone brings us something that we know is not good and pleasant, we should not take part in it; instead, we should call it what it really is according to God's estimation and explain to them why it is not good and pleasant, so that their eyes might be opened to the truth of what they brought to us. So, believer, be on guard as to what you take and eat of in this world, because not everything is as good and pleasant as it seems.

MARCH 28th

> Genesis 3:24: "So He drove out the man; and He placed cherubim at the east of the garden of Eden, and a flaming sword which turned every way, to guard the way to the tree of life."

Michelle and I have been praying about having kids since we got married, and I admit, there is an aspect of fear involved because I know that you can never really be ready to have kids. You can prepare yourselves as much as possible spiritually, financially, mentally, and materially, but in the end, it is really a trial by fire with lots and lots of prayer. As we continued to discuss this, I was reminded of Adam and Eve and how ill-prepared they were for life as a whole.

After the fall in the Garden of Eden, God "drove out the man; and He placed cherubim at the east of the Garden of Eden, and a flaming sword which turned every way, to guard the way to the tree of life." How scary this must have been for Adam and Eve. All of the sudden the animals were not so friendly and docile; the weather was not so comfortable; the ground was not so soft; the food was not so easy to come by; but more importantly, no longer could they walk in the coolness of the garden with God as they once did. Everything they had ever known was now behind them, and they now faced a fallen world complete with danger and uncertainty.

It's crazy to think about, but at this time, they were the only two people on the earth. So who delivered the babies? Who started a fire for the first time? Who cooked the food? Who planted seeds for crops? What did they do when someone got hurt? Broke a leg? Cut themselves? You see where I am going with this. How did they know how to do any of these things? If there were ever two people who were not ready for marriage, children, and life as a whole, it was them, and yet somehow, here we all are today . . . amazing.

Understand that just because God had removed them from the Garden of Eden, it did not mean that He had removed His hand from them. In fact, we see God's great love for them in the Scripture above. Notice that the flaming sword specifically guarded the way to the tree of life. If Adam and Eve had been able to eat from that tree, they would have lived forever in a sinful world, separated from God. The Lord placed a guard at the tree because He loved them, not because He had abandoned them.

The truth is, if God had not kept His hand on Adam and Eve after they left the garden, they wouldn't have made it a day in the wilderness. But He did keep His hand upon them; He sustained them, and taught them, and provided for them in amazing and incredible ways. Will He not also keep His hand on us as well, sustaining us, teaching us, and providing for us? Of course He will, for He is the same God today that He was then, that He will be tomorrow.

MARCH 29th

> Romans 8:32: "He who did not spare His own Son, but delivered Him
> up for us all, how shall He not with Him freely give us all things?"

One of my favorite verses in the Bible is Isaiah 1:18, where God seemingly says to all of mankind, "Come now, and let us reason together." In other words, "Let's sit down and talk about My plan for salvation, the Bible, and My promises for you; let's think about all of this logically for a moment and consider what I am saying and see if it all doesn't make sense."

Well, Romans 8:32 is one of those verses where God says, "Come now, let us reason together." The thought here is quite simple: If God did not keep His own beloved Son from us, then what would He keep from us? Apparently nothing, as the Lord promises us that He will give us "all things." All things according to His will, that is—all things that will benefit us and not harm us.

Generally speaking, God's promises are never more sought after then when we find ourselves in a difficult situation. These are the times when we seemingly need hope and comfort the most. But we should remember that a promise is only as good as the one giving it. So our focus should not be on the promise itself per se, but rather on the One giving us that promise.

That's the logic we should take away from Romans 8:32: "He who did not spare His own Son, but delivered Him up for us all, how shall He not with Him freely give us all things?" Our focus in this verse should not be placed on being given "all things"; it should be placed on the One who did not spare His own Son, but rather delivered Him up for us all. This is the testimony of God's character and His faithfulness to keep His word to us no matter the cost. So, believer, we can find hope in all of His promises because of His unending faithfulness to us; and we can find comfort in every situation because of His eternal love for us.

MARCH 30th

Psalm 103:2: "Bless the LORD, O my soul, and forget not all His benefits."

The common theme found throughout the book of Psalms is that though life is difficult, God is good. Thankfully, we have been given the Bible which is an amazing source of truth and encouragement. It is full of historical events that reveal to us how faithful God has been to a wide variety of people in an assortment of different situations. In this we learn about God's nature, His character, His love for mankind, and how His promises have been fulfilled throughout history.

But a serious problem arises when we look only to the Bible for God's moving and not to our own lives. By doing this, we unknowingly develop a dysfunctional pattern of thinking that goes something like this: That is who God was then; that is what He did for them because they were more [spiritual, faithful, special . . . fill in the blank]. The result of this dysfunction is that we begin to doubt His faithfulness for us in the difficulties we face today.

It's important for us to remember that though we look to the Bible to learn about God, we look to our own lives today to experience God. This is why the Bible often challenges us to sing a new song to the Lord, because it forces us to think about all of the things that God is doing in our lives today.

I remember when Michelle started reading a book with her women's study about thankfulness. One of the assignments was to record all that she was thankful for. In just two days Michelle had filled up a quarter of a notebook with all of the things God was doing in her life. The end result in doing this for Michelle was a heart full of joy, peace, and excitement, because she realized just how special and significant she was to the Lord.

In the same way, the psalmist declares to us, "forget not all His benefits," because when we forget what the Lord has done in our lives, we then miss out on what He is presently doing, and we doubt what He is going to do. To combat this, the psalmist gave us an example of exactly what to do, as he listed just a few of the many benefits that we have already been given by God through Christ: "who forgives all your iniquities, who heals all your diseases, who redeems your life from destruction, who crowns you with lovingkindness and tender mercies, who satisfies your mouth with good things" (Psalm 103:3–5). On and on the list goes. So, believer, what is God doing in your life today?

MARCH 31st

> Psalm 10:1: "Why do You stand afar off, O Lord? Why do You hide in times of trouble?"

How many times have you asked this question when your world is falling apart? When the corruption in our government just seems never-ending? When evil seems to win and flourish without consequence? Or simply when the desires of your heart have gone unanswered? David was just as human as we are and when difficulty came into his life, he had the same questions that we have today. In Psalm 10 David asked God, "Where are You, Lord? Why do the wicked prosper? They steal and murder and oppress. They renounce You, Lord, and boast that there is no account for their actions. Aren't You going to do anything?"

When we find ourselves in this place of desperate confusion as David was here, we must remember that we are called to walk by faith, not by sight. David was clearly relying on what he saw, not on what he knew to be true. Because of that, he was frustrated, as all seemed hopeless. But once his focus shifted back to where it should have been, on who the Lord is, he said, "But You have seen, for You observe trouble and grief. . . . You are the helper of the fatherless. . . . The Lord is King forever" (Psalm 10:14, 16). David reminded himself that God is sovereign, and that He is fully in control of all things; nothing escapes His sight or His hearing.

We have to ask ourselves how we are going to live in this world. Are we going to be moved by every storm of life, as if our names are written in sand; or are we going to stand in faith, knowing that our names are forever chiseled into rock? In 1 Peter 5:10 we are told that after we have suffered a while, God will "perfect, establish, strengthen, and settle you." But notice that in order to be perfected, established, strengthened, and settled, we must first suffer for a time. We must first be tested and refined to make us free of those impurities of doubt and unbelief that weaken us and cause us to act like shifting sand. It's walking by faith during these difficult times that creates within us the deep-rooted faith that we so desperately need to endure this life.

Proverbs 10:25 reminds us, "When the whirlwind [think: tornado or hurricane] passes by, the wicked is no more, but the righteous has an everlasting foundation." Believer, remember, God's fire of testing does not burn us; it only refines us.

APRIL 1st

John 2:3: "They have no wine."

There was a wedding in Cana of Galilee that Jesus and His disciples were invited to. And at some point during the wedding celebration, they ran out of wine. Wisely, the servants went to Jesus and asked Him for help. Jesus then instructed them to fill six large stone pots with water. They did. He then told them to draw some water out and take it to the master of the feast. They did. Upon drinking the water, it turned into wine, and thus Jesus' first miracle was performed.

This was one of the passages that Brian and Cheryl Broderson spoke on at our married couples' retreat this past weekend. The point was a simple, yet very powerful one: At some point, we all run out. Whether it's in marriage or in life, we all run out of patience, joy, grace, strength . . . you name it, we run out of it.[47] Our first instinct when this happens is to try and refill ourselves by our own means. "I need a vacation; I need to go lie on the beach somewhere and do nothing; I need to get away from [my spouse, my children, my job, etc.]." Have you noticed that this never works? The reason is because you can't fix the flesh with the flesh. That is why Jesus never instructed us to work with the flesh; rather, He told us to destroy the flesh.

The problem we face is not with having deficits, mind you; rather, it is with how we try to fill those deficits. Just like the Law, deficits were never intended for us to fulfill them; rather, they are there to remind us of our desperate need for God. The servants in this story show us exactly what to do when we run out in life: We go to Jesus, and we do exactly what He says.

APRIL 2ⁿᵈ

> Joshua 1:7: "Only be strong and very courageous, that you may observe to do according to all the law which Moses My servant commanded you; do not turn from it to the right hand or to the left, that you may prosper wherever you go."

After the death of Moses, it was finally time for the children of Israel to make their way into the Promised Land and claim what was rightfully theirs. But before they crossed over the Jordan, God told Joshua, "Be strong and of good courage, for to this people you shall divide as an inheritance the land which I swore to their fathers to give them. Only be strong and very courageous, that you may observe to do according to all the law which Moses My servant commanded you; do not turn from it to the right hand or to the left, that you may prosper wherever you go" (Joshua 1:6–7).

Notice the difference between the two commands. God told Joshua to be strong and of good courage in dividing the land, but He specifically said for Joshua to be strong and *very courageous* when following the Law of Moses. As my good friend Darrell always says, "God will never allow us to escape our need for faith." We learn here that it will always take great courage and a certain measure of faith to step out and follow God—because chances are, when He calls us to do something, we will begin to experience fear and doubt about what He has told us to do. I think when this happens, our natural reaction is to wait for the fears and the doubts to leave us before we move forward and follow God. But having courage is not being obedient in the absence of fear; rather, it's being obedient in the midst of fear. God never said that we won't experience fear and doubt; rather, He said to be very courageous in the midst of fear and doubt and follow His commands.

So, believer, whatever it is that God has commanded you to do, whatever it is He is calling you to do today, be very courageous and do not fear, for "as I was with Moses, so I will be with you. I will never leave nor forsake you" (Joshua 1:5). Just be obedient and follow His commands.

APRIL 3rd

Psalm 139:7: "Where can I go from Your Spirit? Or where can I flee from Your presence?"

As we were closing in prayer the other night, a thought came on my heart: If God was physically with us, would we pray any differently? Would we hold anything back? Would there be anything we would not ask of Him? Would our prayers be more fervent, more passionate, more faith-filled? Would we leave His presence without an answer, or would we continue asking Him until He answered us?

I admit, there are many times when I pray that I struggle to grasp the fact that God is so intimately near me. I struggle to believe that I am truly in the midst of His Holy presence. When this happens, my prayers tend to lack faith and fervency and take on a sense of unbelief; I feel as though I am just praying to an empty room.

Part of the problem is the way we think about our relationship with God. I believe we naturally defer to the thinking that we are separated from God and so we have to do something *holy* in order to enter into His presence. But this could not be further from the truth. Once we surrender our lives to Jesus Christ, the veil is torn; nothing separates us from God as we are forever in His presence.

As David pondered, "Where can I go from Your Spirit? Or where can I flee from Your presence?" The reality is not that we have to enter into God's presence, but rather that we are always in His presence—for wherever we are, there He is.

APRIL 4th

Psalm 73:17: "I went into the sanctuary of God; then I understood."

In Psalm 73, Asaph, the psalmist, reflected on a time when he was struggling in his faith. "But as for me, my feet had almost stumbled; my steps had nearly slipped" (Psalm 73:2, ESV). The problem was that he stopped trusting in the Lord and he began trusting in his own understanding. "When *I* thought how to understand this, it was too painful for me" (Psalm 73:16, emphasis added).

It just didn't seem right to Asaph that the wicked were prospering while good people were struggling. The more he dwelled on these things, the more his depression overwhelmed him, and pretty soon self-pity had buried his faith. "Surely I have cleansed my heart in vain, and washed my hands in innocence. For all day long I have been plagued, and chastened every morning" (Psalm 73:13–14). But when

Asaph went to God about these things, everything changed. "I went into the sanctuary of God; *then* I understood" (Psalm 73:17, emphasis added). Notice that it was only when Asaph went to the Lord that his eyes were opened, and his perspective was changed from the carnal to the spiritual.

Believer, when we find ourselves in situations like Asaph did, we too need to go to God and praise Him for all that He is and all that He has promised us, because it is there, in those praises, that God is enthroned (see Psalm 22:3). Through thanks and praise, God takes His rightful place as Lord of our lives, and more importantly, as Lord of our situations. We are then refocused, and our trust is placed back where it should be—in Him, not in our own understanding.

APRIL 5ᵗʰ

> Romans 6:4: "Therefore we were buried with Him through baptism into death, that just as Christ was raised from the dead by the glory of the Father, even so we also should walk in newness of life."

One of the hardest things for us to do as believers is to let go of the past. Whether the past we struggle with is ten years ago or ten seconds ago, we regret our past mistakes to the point that we dwell on them for hours on end. As Michelle and I were praying on Sunday morning for the services that day, I was quickly reminded of this verse; more specifically, I was reminded of the fact that we are told to "walk in the newness of life."

Notice the word "walk" is written in the present tense, meaning that it is something that we are to do continually. It's a habitual lifestyle that we are to practice every minute of every day. So what are we to walk in? The "newness of life," Paul says. Well, what *is* the newness of life? It is exactly what it says it is: a new life. Ezekiel 36:26 reminds us that as believers, we have been given a new heart and a new spirit. Second Corinthians 5:17 tells us that "[we are] a new creation; old things have passed away; behold, all things have become new." Romans 6:4 seemingly affirms these truths as it refers to the regeneration of the believer; no longer are we defined by our sin (the old man); we are now defined by His righteousness (the new man).[48]

Walking in the newness of life is not only turning from sin and walking in the Spirit; it's not only following the leading of the Holy Spirit and going about our Father's business as He directs us—it's also understanding that every single minute that goes by is a fresh start for the believer . . . a clean slate, if you will. Regardless what we have done in our previous life, or what we did one minute ago, the past is gone. It's behind us, vaporized, and there is no remembrance of it in Christ Jesus as it has been completely removed. As Romans 8:1 declares, there is no condemnation in Christ.

We need to remind ourselves that we cannot change what we have done, but we can choose what we will do. We can go to Jesus and ask Him for forgiveness, because when we do, Jesus promises us that He will not only forgive us of our sin, but that He will also cleanse us from all unrighteousness (1 John 1:9).

APRIL 6th

Daniel 2:21: "And He changes the times and the seasons."

There are four seasons that break up our calendar year: fall, winter, spring, and summer. As a kid, I dreaded fall because it meant it was time to go back to school; winter wasn't too bad because it meant Christmas would soon be upon us; spring was always something to look forward to because we would get a spring break; but summer was my favorite because it meant complete freedom from school and homework. Year after year, though, no matter what I did, I could not stop fall from coming—and once it came, there was absolutely nothing I could do to make it end any sooner. I just had to wait and endure that season, knowing that one day it would end.

If you stop and think about it, the seasons in life are no different. We cannot stop them from coming, and we cannot make them end any sooner. They are completely in God's hands, for only "He changes the times and the seasons."

In Ecclesiastes 3:1, Solomon wrote, "To everything there is a season, a time for every purpose under heaven." He then lists out the times and seasons of life that we will all experience, such as: a time to be born and a time to die; a time to mourn and a time to dance, etc. But then he says something very profound in verse 11: "He [God] has made everything beautiful in its time." It's strange to think that death or mourning or affliction could ever be beautiful, but with God, they are all beautiful in that they are exactly what is needed at that time. Verse 11 essentially echoes Genesis 1:31: "and God saw . . . it was very good."

Michelle and I have been praying a lot about buying a house, having kids, etc. And as we were praying the other day, God led Michelle to these verses in the book of Daniel. "Blessed be the name of God forever and ever, for wisdom and might are His. And He changes the times and the seasons" (Daniel 2:20–21). Our prayer since that time has been for God to change our seasons in His time, not ours, because we know that in His time, all things are made beautiful.

It's important to realize that whatever season you are in right now, it is the best season for you at this point in your life. There is nothing you can do to stop it, and there is nothing you can do to make it go any faster. You definitely don't want to try to end it in your own strength (see Abraham and Sarah for an example; Genesis 21).

Our time of waiting and enduring is a time of learning and growing so that we will be ready for the next season. So, believer, don't waste this season by just closing your eyes and putting your head under the covers. Pray and ask the Lord what you need to learn and how you need to grow during this time, because only by doing this will the seasons change from fall to winter to spring to summer.

APRIL 7th

> Psalm 37:5: "Commit your way to the LORD, trust also in Him, and He will bring it to pass."

Michelle and I have been spending a lot of time around children lately, and I have to say, I have been amazed at how many lessons from the Bible I see come alive in and through their lives. One of the things that I love watching is how these one-to-three-year-olds interact with their parents. It always reminds me of how God is our Father and we are His children.

The other day as Michelle and I were visiting some friends, I noticed that their daughter would bring me a toy, hand it to me, and then just stand there and stare at me, anxiously awaiting to see what I would do with it. After a couple of seconds of inactivity, she would take it back, only to give it to me again. I was laughing because it reminded me of how we often *surrender* things to God, only to take them back a few seconds later.

The psalmist wrote in this psalm, "Commit your way to the Lord, trust also in Him, and He will bring it to pass." The word "commit" in this verse means to roll something over to the Lord. But notice that it is not enough to just surrender something to God; the psalmist says that we must "trust also in Him, and He will bring it to pass."

We are really, really good at surrendering things to God; the problem is that we don't *leave* them with God. If He's not moving fast enough for us, or moving how we think He should move, then we take those things right back and try to do them ourselves. But by doing this, we are essentially saying that we don't trust that God will bring it to pass.

Look carefully at this verse as it is broken down into three steps: First, "Commit your way to the Lord"; second, "trust also in Him"; and third, "He will bring it to pass." It's simple algebra: A + B = C. Notice the promise that we are given of God bringing that thing to pass only comes after we commit our way to the Lord *and* trust Him with it.

It's also important to remember that because our times and seasons are in His hands, things will come to pass in His time and in His way, not ours. So, believer, don't just surrender things to God; trust Him with them and don't take them back. Leave them in His care, knowing that He will bring them to pass in their perfect time and season.

APRIL 8th

> Psalm 34:1: "I will bless the LORD at all times; His praise shall continually be in my mouth."

David was a man who knew something about praising God because David was a man who knew what it was to be in a trial. As my good friend Darrell often says, "If you never had a problem, you would never know the One who can solve it for you." It was because of David's trials that he was able to write some of the sweetest psalms of praise you will ever encounter.

In Psalm 34, David opens by saying: "I will bless the LORD at all times; His praise shall continually be in my mouth." David knew that praise to the Father was not only fitting, but that it also enthroned God in whatever situation he found himself in. Listen and pay close attention to some of the justification that David gives as to why we should "exalt His name together" (Psalm 34:3):

> I sought the LORD, and He heard me, and delivered me from all my fears. . . . The angel of the LORD encamps all around those who fear Him, and delivers them. . . . There is no want to those who fear Him. . . . But those who seek the LORD shall not lack any good thing. . . . The eyes of the LORD are on the righteous, and His ears are open to their cry. . . . The LORD is near to those who have a broken heart, and saved such as have a contrite spirit. Many are the afflictions of the righteous, but the Lord delivers him out of them all. (Psalm 34:4, 7, 9–10, 15, 18–19)

Believer, God is faithful. God is good. God hears all of our cries of fear, worry, want, brokenheartedness, affliction, etc., and He comforts us in them and delivers us out of them all. He has never failed us, and He will never fail us. So when you find yourself doubting God's goodness, accept David's invitation to test these truths: "Oh, taste and see that the LORD is good; blessed is the man who trusts in Him" (Psalm 34:8).

APRIL 9th

> Acts 9:13: "Then Ananias answered, 'Lord, I have heard from many about this man, how much harm he has done to Your saints in Jerusalem.'"

Is there anyone in this world whom we should not pray for? I guess that depends on who you ask. Some people say, "Don't pray for them because of what they have done." Other people say, "Don't pray for them because they follow that religion." I once even heard a Christian say, "Don't pray for them because you don't know their heart."

Let me rephrase the question, then: Is there anyone in this world whom *God* does not want us to pray for? Or even better, is there anyone in this world whom Jesus does not pray for? Now the answer is much clearer: No, God's will is that we pray for all men. "Therefore I exhort first of all that supplications, prayers, intercessions, and giving of thanks be made for all men. . . . For this is good and acceptable in the sight of God our Savior" (1 Timothy 2:1, 3).

We see a great example of this with Ananias and Saul. One day the Lord spoke to Ananias and instructed him to go pray for Saul, to which Ananias replied, "Lord, I have heard from many about this man, how much harm he has done to Your saints in Jerusalem." I don't blame Ananias for not wanting to pray for Saul, because Saul was a persecutor and murderer of Christians. But the Lord responded to Ananias, "Go, for he is a chosen vessel of Mine" (Acts 9:15).

I was reminded of this the other day when I showed up to work and noticed that one of my coworkers had been crying. As I walked by her desk, I felt the Lord tell me to go and pray for her, but I was like, "I don't want to pray for her Lord. She does this, she is that," and I listed all of the reasons why I didn't want to go and minister to her. It was then that the Lord said to me, "Patrick, I died for her, too. She is My child and I love her. If that was someone who didn't bother you, you would pray for them without hesitation." That is when it became very clear to me that the problem was not with this woman or her personality quirks; the problem was with my heart.

Humbled, I went over to her and asked her if I could pray for her; she said yes. It was a very powerful few moments of prayer that, when finished, brought so much peace to my soul and joy to her heart. All of a sudden, those quirks that bothered me so much were gone and I saw this woman as God did. So, believer, remember, there is not one single person in this world whom God does not want us praying for, regardless of what they have done or who they are.

APRIL 10th

1 John 3:16: "By this we know love, because He laid down His life for us."

As I was preparing to teach on the crucifixion, I kept asking myself, "Do I go into detail about the crucifixion or not? Do I describe the suffering of our Lord to such a degree, that everyone leaves pondering His gruesome death rather than rejoicing in His magnificent love?" I think it is very telling that all four gospel writers are very reserved in describing Christ's crucifixion; they simply state, "and they crucified Him" (Mark 15:25).

This was done for two reasons: 1) everyone at that time knew exactly what the crucifixion entailed; and 2) as Alistair Begg pointed out, "the gospel writers were not focused on the physical aspect of the suffering, but rather were focused on what the suffering was actually achieving."[49] We must remember that the true intention of the Gospels—and really, the Bible as a whole—is to encourage our faith, not to evoke an emotional response within us. This is what I felt the Lord was compelling me to consider, "Do I want to evoke their feelings, or do I want to strengthen their faith? Do I want them to walk away contemplating how Jesus died on the cross, or do I want them remembering *why* Jesus died on the cross?"

I think it is important to understand that when Jesus took upon the cross, He did not do it to induce sympathy, empathy, or compassion in us; He did not do it so that we would be sorrowful and despondent, nor that we would memorialize His death by holding onto this image of Him beaten, bloodied, and broken. No, Christ took upon the cross so that we might be joyful at His remembrance, celebrating His victory in that He defeated sin and death, rose from the dead, ascended into heaven, and now sits at the right hand of the Father, glorified in all His splendor. Jesus took upon the cross so that we could be assured that it was His unending love for us that compelled Him to climb upon the cross, and it was that love for us that ultimately carried Him through His suffering.

Now, I fully agree that it is necessary for us to understand what lengths Jesus went to for us—how He suffered incredibly in our place, how He exchanged His righteousness for our sin, etc.—all with the condition, mind you, that the result of that understanding leads to a greater appreciation of His love for us, not an overwhelming sadness that clouds it. As Augustine well said, the cross is the pulpit from which God preached His love to the world.[50] First John 3:16 seems to echo this same sentiment, "By this we know love, because He laid down His life for us."

So we have a choice to make: We can either focus on the immense suffering that Jesus endured and find ourselves in the same state as those that left the cross on Calvary that day, or we can look upon the suffering He endured as confirmation of the abounding love that sent Him there in the first place. "For God so loved the world that He gave His only begotten Son, that whoever believes in Him should not perish but have everlasting life" (John 3:16).[51]

APRIL 11th

> Matthew 17:2: "He was transfigured before them. His face shone like
> the sun, and His clothes became as white as the light."

Over the last week or so, I have come across a lot of people who are struggling with the fear that they do not glorify God. And at every encounter, I immediately thought of the transfiguration. We often look at this amazing story and think to ourselves, "What a miracle—Jesus was transfigured into His eternal glory!" But is the greater miracle the fact that the glory of God was revealed, or that the glory of God can actually be hidden?[51]

In July of 2003, I was with a mission team on an overnight ferry, crossing the Adriatic Sea from Italy to Albania. It was my first mission trip and I was so overcome with fear and excitement that even though we had been traveling for thirty-six hours, I couldn't sleep at all. When the sun began to rise the next morning, I decided to go up to the top level of the ferry so that nothing would hinder my view of God's glorious creation. As I stood there watching the sunrise over the sea, I remember asking God to show me His glory. Nothing happened. Not to be deterred, I continued to pray this same prayer over and over again. Finally, I began begging God, "Please Lord, show me Your glory!" Still, nothing.

So I tried crafting His glory in the colors of the sky, the clouds, and the water, but it wasn't really His glory; it was just me creating things in my mind to appease my hunger of what I wanted to see. Discouraged, I finally gave up and turned around to see what the rest of the team was doing. It was then that I saw God's glory. I don't know how else to describe what I saw other than to say that it was a supernatural light and energy that was radiating from each member of the team. The amazing thing is that they weren't even doing anything *spiritual*; some were sleeping, some were talking, and some were just journaling. It was then, in that matrix moment of transfiguration, that I heard God say to me, "Patrick, My glory is in you."

So, believer, remember, "You are the light of the world" (Matthew 5:14). Just as a tree does not need to try and bear fruit, you do not need to try to be the light of the world; you *are* the light of the world. So, "Let your light so shine before men, that they may see your good works and glorify your Father in heaven" (Matthew 5:16).

APRIL 12th

> Genesis 2:24: "Therefore a man shall leave his father and mother and be joined to his wife, and they shall become one flesh."

We have been studying some couples from the Bible in our married couples' study, such as Adam and Eve, Abraham and Sarah, David and Bathsheba, and Joseph and Mary. Then we came across the couple known as Aquila and Priscilla, the ultimate team couple. The more I studied them, the more I realized that this couple was different than all of the other couples we had studied. There was a oneness about them that the other couples did not have.

I began thinking about what it is to be united as one flesh and what that means for husbands and wives, and so I went back to where it all started, Genesis 2:23–24. Here, God had caused Adam to fall into a deep sleep, took from his side, and made woman. Upon seeing her for the first time, Adam said, "This is now bone of my bones and flesh of my flesh; she shall be called Woman, because she was taken out of Man. Therefore a man shall leave his father and mother and be joined to his wife, and they shall become one flesh."

The thought of being one flesh has almost become a badge of honor that we wear around our neck, like we have accomplished this great thing because we went through premarital counseling, got married in the church by a pastor, go to church together, etc. But is there something more for us than just these things? Do we just become one flesh and then that's it? It's interesting that even unbelievers become one flesh when they get married. Even when a man and a woman engage in sex outside of marriage, they become one flesh (1 Corinthians 6:16). So there must be something more to marriage according to God's design than just becoming one flesh.

"But you shall receive power when the Holy Spirit has come upon you; and you shall be witnesses to Me in Jerusalem, and in all Judea and Samaria, and to the end of the earth" (Acts 1:8). And there it is, the something more: It is the anointing and filling of the Holy Spirit. Aquila and Priscilla differ from all of the other couples we studied in that they were born again; they were brand-new creations in Christ and had the Holy Spirit living within them, within their marriage, uniting them with the Lord as one spirit. "But he who is joined to the Lord is one spirit with Him" (1 Corinthians 6:17).

The point is, the mission for the believer has changed. No longer do we live under the Law, separated from God as those other couples did. No longer are we called to just occupy the land and make descendants. No longer are we called to drive people out of the land and look upon them as our enemies. Jesus Christ has fulfilled the Law. We are now called to make disciples of all nations. We are now called to love our enemies, pray for them, reach out to the lost, and win souls for the kingdom of God. The mission has changed. Our purpose has changed.

When I read about Aquila and Priscilla, I see power, I see purpose, I see fulfillment . . . quite simply, I see Jesus. Is that what people see when they see us, or are we still living under the Old Testament, barren of power, and just trying to survive, fill the earth, and drive out our enemies?

APRIL 13th

> Romans 4:20: "He did not waver at the promise of God through unbelief, but was strengthened in faith, giving glory to God."

We often talk about how hard it is to walk by faith because we are supposed to believe in something that is unseen. Even though God has never failed us, ever, we still somehow struggle to believe that He will deliver us in *this* circumstance. Yet have you noticed that we never seem to have a problem believing in the unseen when it comes to fear?

Fear allows our minds to paint vivid pictures and accurately depict detailed scenarios of exactly what is going to unfold when that fear is faced. We prepare ourselves a thousand different ways to handle this impossible situation, knowing for certain that if we don't lie, run away, or throw someone else under the bus, then we are doomed for the very worst. And as time drags us into that situation ever so slowly, we frantically try to find a way out of it, only to realize that the Goliath we were facing was only a tiny field mouse.

Last Thursday, Michelle and I were each battling with our own fear that we were going to have to face that day at our jobs. We prayed for one another, encouraged each other in the Scriptures, yet in the back of our minds we still believed that the worst was coming. As we each faced our own situation that day, the fear that we were so sure of never even came to pass.

While we were driving home after work, rejoicing in the Lord, I said to Michelle, "We really are like children, aren't we? We say to God, 'God, there's a monster under my bed!' So God turns the light on and says, 'See, there's nothing under your bed.' Then we say to Him, 'God, there's a monster in the closet!' So God opens the closet door and says, 'See, there's nothing in the closet.' Then we say to Him, 'God, there's a monster outside my window!' So God opens the blinds and says, 'See, there's nothing outside of your window.' Then we pause for a moment, look around, and say again, 'God, there's a monster under my bed!'" And on and on we go.

As Pastor Justin Alfred explained at our annual men's retreat, fear is simply "False Evidence that Appears Real."[52] It is all about deception and false truths that only appear to be real, whereas faith in the Lord is as real as real can ever get. God has proven His faithfulness to us over and over again, and yet we still lean toward believing in fear instead of faith. But let me ask you something: Which is harder to believe—a fear that never comes true, or a faith that is constantly proven over and over again? So, believer, what will you choose this day?

APRIL 14th

> Matthew 4:4: "Man shall not live by bread alone, but by every word that proceeds from the mouth of God."

About a month ago, I had this verse come up in my life three times in one day, from three different sources. I have learned in my walk with the Lord that when this happens, I need to stop whatever I am doing and focus on that verse, because God is trying to prepare me for something. And I am so thankful I did.

When we read this verse in context, we find that it was Jesus' response to Satan when Satan was tempting Him in the wilderness. "Now when the tempter came to Him, he said, 'If You are the Son of God, command that these stones become bread.' But He answered and said, 'It is written, "Man shall not live by bread alone, but by every word that proceeds from the mouth of God"'" (Matthew 4:3–4).

Jesus' point is that the Word of God is more vital to us than food itself. This is a very powerful statement as we all understand the desperate need we have for food. And notice that it's not just some of the Word, or most of the Word, but it is every word that proceeds from the mouth of God. Yes, that means even the books of Deuteronomy, Leviticus, and Numbers are essential to our walk with the Lord. It is the entire counsel of God.

Why is it so important for us to have the entire word of God? Because when the tempter comes—and he will come—this is how we defend ourselves. Notice that Jesus didn't use His divine power to defeat Satan; rather, He rebuked Satan as a man simply by using the Word of God.[53] In this, Jesus shows us how to defend ourselves against the attacks of the enemy, whether they are trials or temptations. But how can we stand as an individual, or as a family, if we don't know and practice the word of God? We can't—that is why we have been given the Bible. So, believer, do yourself and your loved ones a favor and stay in the Word. Learn it, trust in it, and apply it to your life so that you too might stand in the day of adversity.

APRIL 15th

1 Chronicles 21:11: "Choose for yourself."

Michelle works as a substitute teacher in the city of San Bernardino, and every now and then I will get a text from her saying that her school is on lockdown. When this happens, I immediately send out a text to some very faithful prayer warriors and we all pray. But then the horrible thoughts come to my mind of what could possibly be going on at her school. No one thinks it will ever happen to them, or their family, but when the reality hits that it could be happening to a loved one of yours, you come to realize just how helpless you really are. The limits of what you can control and what you cannot control are clearly defined.

So what do we have control over? Honestly, not much. As a society, we often think we have control over people, children, animals, nature, our health, travel plans, and sometimes even life as a whole . . . but the truth is, the only thing we have control over are the choices we make. This understanding is often manifested when a spouse cheats and wants a divorce, or a child rebels, or a loved one refuses to accept Christ. We try to do everything we can to remedy the situation, but ultimately every person has to choose for themselves because no matter what we do or how hard we try, we cannot make their choices for them.

Sure, they may make excuses, saying that we or something else caused them to make that choice—and unfortunately, we often believe them and put ourselves on the hook, feeling guilty that we didn't do or say the right things—but this is not true. God has given us all free will. Each one of us makes choices to our own benefit or to our own hurt; no one is forced to make any decision. The only thing we can do—which is actually the best thing to do—is to make the choice to pray for them, and then allow God to take control of that situation.

It's in these moments that we find out where our faith is truly placed. Is it in the unfailing, all-loving God, or is it in the illusion of control we thought we had? It's also in these moments that we find out how strong our faith really is, because when we realize that we have no control over a situation, our faith in God is all we have left.

APRIL 16th

> Mark 14:22: "And as they were eating, Jesus took bread, blessed and broke it, and gave it to them and said, 'Take, eat; this is My body.'"

When we find ourselves broken for others, we tend to look upon that time negatively because . . . well, quite simply, it hurts. Minutes seem to last for hours, our heart aches like our soul has been mortally wounded, and the concern and sadness for those loved ones consumes our every thought. It's pure torture. Yet when you really think about it, there is no other time in our lives that we are as Christlike as we are when we are broken for others—because it is there, in that state of brokenness, that our concern for others actually outweighs our concern for ourselves.

This is a rare experience for a people who are generally concerned with self. For us, self-preservation and self-promotion are what rule our thoughts day in and day out. It's no wonder why, though: Our entire society is focused on self and doing what is best for us as individuals, even if it means standing on the shoulders of others to get there. We have become a people who feast on the moldy bread and the sour wine of "me."

Yet when we are broken for others, we truly get to enjoy the sweet communion of Christ. Our prayers come to life. No longer are they weak and stale, but rather they become fresh and powerful as they are driven from the depths of our very soul, many times in the form of groaning and tears. This happens because our motives in these moments, what compels us to pray and intercede, are not the betterment of self but rather the healing and restoration of others. Oh, how we need this heart for all men.

Something the Lord reminded me about this is that the same way that our hearts break for the spouse who was cheated on, the wife who was beaten, the child who was abandoned, the people who were shot by the gunman. . . . God's heart also breaks for the spouse who cheated, the husband who abused his wife, the parents who abandoned that child, and the man who killed all of those people, because God died for them just as He died for us. He loves them just as He loves us. We are reminded that they are lost souls who need Jesus just as much as we do.

APRIL 17th

> Matthew 13:8: "But others [seeds of gospel] fell on good ground and yielded a crop: some a hundredfold, some sixty, some thirty."

Oftentimes when we think about salvation, we paint a picture of what that should look like based on how we were saved and the changes that took place in our lives. This never becomes clearer then when we compare our salvation to someone else's. I am not referring to how we are saved, but rather what happens after we are saved.

In Matthew 13, we read the parable of the sower. There, Jesus talks about the work of salvation in a person's life. "But others [seeds of gospel] fell on good ground and yielded a crop: some a hundredfold, some sixty, some thirty." I don't think Jesus was limiting the amount of fruit to these three choices; rather, I think He is making a point that some people will yield a lot of fruit with their lives, and some people will yield very little.

I know for myself, there are times when I look at someone else's salvation and I ask myself, "Are they really saved?" simply because I do not see the amount of fruit that I have assigned in my mind that is necessary for true salvation. This is especially true when it is someone I dearly care about like a family member or a close friend. In my heart, I want to see them on fire, diligently pursuing the Lord to the point where it is just obvious that they are saved. I do this because I want to have peace about their salvation and know that they will be in heaven with me.

Though well intentioned, this is actually pure selfishness because what I am really saying when I do this is that their salvation is not enough for me. They need more of this or that in order to be truly saved, yet this is not what the Bible teaches us: "if you confess with your mouth the Lord Jesus and believe in your heart that

God has raised Him from the dead, you will be saved. For with the heart one believes unto righteousness, and with the mouth confession is made unto salvation" (Romans 10:9–10).

So how much fruit does a person have to produce in order to be saved? One hundred . . . thirty . . . ten . . . how about one piece of fruit? Is that enough? How about none, like the thief on the cross? Or *did* he produce fruit? Don't you think that when he rebuked the other criminal on the cross and confessed that Jesus was Lord, he was producing fruit? Indeed he was. So, believer, let us not put our standards on salvation, but rather allow the Lord to be the Lord of salvation.

APRIL 18th

> Proverbs 4:5: "Get wisdom! Get understanding! Do not forget, nor turn away from the words of my mouth."

When Solomon was named king, the first thing he did was seek God and ask Him for wisdom; more specifically, he asked for the wisdom to govern God's people. God answered Solomon's prayer and gave him the wisdom and knowledge he needed to rightly govern and rule over Israel, as Solomon asked (2 Chronicles 1:11).

Unfortunately for Solomon, he did not govern himself very well. After God blessed Solomon with the wisdom to govern Israel, Solomon broke the three commands that God gave every king of Israel to follow, as listed in Deuteronomy 17:16–17. And because of that, Solomon's heart slowly began drifting away from the Lord.

"Get wisdom [for yourself]! Get understanding [for yourself]!" The point is that God's wisdom must be for us first and foremost. Too often we seek wisdom with the sole purpose to lead others, yet there is no application of it in our own lives. How many times have you listened to a sermon and thought to yourself, "You know who needs to hear this?" Meanwhile, you missed out on what God had for *you* that morning.

"Therefore we must give the more earnest heed to the things we have heard, lest we drift away" (Hebrews 2:1). God's Word must be real to us personally, individually. We must own it for ourselves, believe it for ourselves, trust in it for ourselves, or eventually we won't be able to help anybody because we will have drifted away from the Lord.

Sometimes when I am praying about a devotion that the Lord would have me write, I catch myself reading Scripture only for the sake of finding a devotion, not reading it for myself so that I can learn and be changed. And I think to myself, "Patrick, what about you? It does you no good if you don't learn it for yourself first." As James 1:22 says, "But be doers of the word, and not hearers only, deceiving yourselves."

Believer, it is really easy to find a sense of purpose in being the one who continually gives others wisdom in what to do and how to live life, but if your life is an empty wreck because you have drifted away from God, how far can you really lead them? Get wisdom and get understanding for yourself first; then you will be able to truly lead others.

APRIL 19th

Matthew 4:3: "Now when the tempter came . . ."

David Guzik said that "It is not a question of *if*" temptation will come, but rather *when* temptation will come.[54] So regardless of whether it is Satan, the world, or our flesh, we are going to be tempted. Unfortunately for us, our natural tendency is to try to figure out why we are being tempted, rather than just deal with the problem at hand. "What did I do? Why is this happening? What is causing this?" On and on we go trying to understand what we did that brought this upon us. But is that the best course of action when we are facing temptation? Should we focus on the why and how, or should we focus on standing firm in and through that temptation?

Think of it like this: Imagine that you are sitting in your house one night, and all of the sudden you realize that your house is on fire. Should you a) sit down in your favorite chair and try to figure out what started the fire; or b) get out of the house, call 9–1–1, and get the fire extinguished as soon as possible? Obviously the wise choice is b), yet oftentimes when we face temptation, we choose a). Just because temptation comes, it does not necessarily mean we did something wrong. After all, we are in a spiritual battle; we are going to face temptation no matter what we do. But remember, being tempted is not a sin, for even Jesus was tempted. It is what we do in that temptation that will determine if it is sin or not.

Temptation comes in many shapes and sizes; it is not just relegated to things of a sexual nature. We are often tempted to become anxious, fearful, worrisome, angry, etc. Yet throughout the Bible, God commands us to be anxious for nothing, to not fear, to not worry, to not give into anger, etc. We see in all of these things that we have a choice to make when facing these temptations. We either obey God's command to stand firm and not give into that temptation, or we choose to yield and allow that temptation have its way within us. It is very important to remember during these times that God's command is His enablement, meaning that we do not have to yield to that temptation because God has given us power over all temptation if we want it.

In Galatians 5:16 the apostle Paul wrote, "Walk in the Spirit, and you shall not fulfill the lust of the flesh." Notice that he did not say that you won't be tempted; he specifically said that you will not give into that temptation. So, believer, don't be discouraged when you are tempted; rather, walk in the Spirit and choose not to fulfill that lust.

APRIL 20th

> Psalm 78:34: "When He slew them, then they sought Him; and they returned and sought earnestly for God."

How many TV shows have used the line, "We can either do this the easy way, or we can do this the hard way"? More often than not, the person confronted with this choice chooses the hard way, only to eventually be caught or captured after some painful, drawn-out struggle. It is usually somewhat of a humorous scene, because I think deep down we know that is just how we are.

In Psalm 78, the psalmist reflects on all the miracles that God did for the children of Israel in the wilderness. "He divided the sea and caused them to pass through. . . . In the daytime He led them with the cloud, and all night with a light of fire. . . . He also brought streams out of the rock . . . rained down manna on them to eat . . . the bread of heaven . . . rained meat on them like the dust" (Psalm 78:13–14, 16, 24, 27). The psalmist also reflected on the miracles God did in Egypt: "Yet they tested and provoked the Most High God" (v. 56) with their unbelief, rebellion, idol worship and "did not believe in His wondrous works" (v. 32).

Yet, "When He slew them, then they sought Him; and they returned and sought earnestly for God." Why does it always have to be the hard way with us? Why can't it ever just be the easy way? For whatever reason, miracles, signs, and wonders do not work on us. We are a people who only respond when we are broken and in turmoil, because we have to see our need before we will ever turn and receive. Is it any wonder why we are referred to as sheep in the Bible?

God has proven to us over and over again how faithful He is toward us—how His ways always have our best interest in them. All we need to do is trust Him and follow His ways. Yet even the most faithful follower must be disciplined, because we just naturally drift away. This is why God reminds us so many times in the Bible that He disciplines us because He loves us. He allows difficulties to refine us, change us, and break us of those things that separate us from Him and lead us astray. If there were an easier way to get us to change, listen, obey, be saved . . . God would gladly do that. But unfortunately, we are a people who just love doing it the hard way.

APRIL 21st

Psalm 81:6: "I removed his shoulder from the burden;"

I love reading the Word of God slowly for two reasons: 1) It helps me pay attention to every word that is written; and 2) it helps me pay attention to the order in which the words are written. I do this because when I just breeze through the Bible, I often miss amazing truths like this one. Notice that God did not remove the burden from Israel, but rather He removed Israel from carrying the burden. The burden remained, but no longer was Israel struggling under it.

First Peter 5:7 (NIV) says: "Cast all your anxiety on him because he cares for you." Notice that it doesn't say that the situation will disappear; it says, give the situation to God and allow Him to carry it for you. Many parents come into the prayer room asking for prayer for a prodigal child; and as I am praying for them, I sense that they are carrying the weight of their child's choices—like they believe they did something wrong in raising their child, and because of that their child has drifted away. Or, someone comes in carrying the weight of a family member's salvation, like it is their responsibility to save that loved one and if they don't say or do the right thing, then that person won't be saved and it will be their fault.

Believer, as John 1:20 reminds us, "[We are] not the Christ." There is only One who can save, heal, restore, provide, and deliver . . . there is only One who can truly carry all of the burdens that this life casts onto us. We are unable to carry the burdens of this life because they were not meant for us to carry. Only Christ is strong enough, and has shoulders broad enough to carry the burdens of this world. Our job is to surrender them all to Him through prayer and supplication as we reflect on these truths. It's only when we do this that God can remove our shoulder from the burden and take our place under its weight.

APRIL 22nd

Proverbs 10:17: "But he who refuses correction goes astray."

The word "goes" that is used here literally means "leads." So he who refuses correction (instruction) not only goes astray himself, but more importantly leads others astray as well.

On April 22, 2000, the very day that I was saved, Jesus said to me very clearly, "Patrick, you are leading them to death. I want you to lead them to life." The "them" Jesus was referring to here were my friends and family. See, I was kind of the central hub in these relationships. I was the one who planned all of the events and who led others into doing the things we did. The sobering reality of what Jesus said to me on that day has always stayed with me, because I never realized I was leading others to death. It all seemed so harmless. But ultimately, if we are not leading people to Christ, then we are leading them to death. And that is the reality that we all must consider, because we are all leading somebody—family, friends, children. The question is, where are we leading them?

This is the seriousness that Solomon is portraying for us here in this verse. The choices we make do not just affect our own lives, because each one of us is leading someone; others will follow us wherever we lead them. So when we keep instruction, we do not just keep it for ourselves; we keep it for all of those who are following us as well.

Now, we know that each person will be held accountable for the choices that they make—meaning, I will never be held accountable for what choices someone else makes; but I believe I will be held accountable for where I lead people. I have heard many Christians talk about how they can do whatever they want, whenever they want, all because they are in Christ. The apostle Paul wrote about this in 1 Corinthians 10:23–24 (ESV): "'All things are lawful,' but not all things are helpful. 'All things are lawful,' but not all things build up. Let no one seek his own good, but the good of his neighbor."

So maybe you can drink alcohol and never have one too many drinks; maybe you can watch really dark or perverse movies and TV shows and never be stumbled by them; maybe you can walk right on the edge of the cliff and never slip and fall because you are so in control all of the time (can you hear the sarcasm?); but can you guarantee that those who are following you will never slip and fall? Can you guarantee that they won't be stumbled by what you are doing? No, you can't.

Understand, the Christian life is not about self; it is about others. We may not be held accountable for the choices others make, but we will be held accountable for where we lead them. Ours is to lead them to Jesus, not to the world and not to the things in the world.

APRIL 23rd

> Psalm 19:7–8: "The law of the LORD is perfect, converting the soul; the testimony of the LORD is sure, making wise the simple; the statutes of the LORD are right, rejoicing the heart; the commandment of the LORD is pure, enlightening the eyes."

W. Glyn Evans once wrote, "Lord, an emergency does not mean disaster to a disciple; it means a crossroads. The emergency means God's word is vitally at stake. The emergency gives rise to the question, 'Is your God . . . able . . . ?' as King Darius asked Daniel in the lion's den. . . . The den was not Daniel's death chamber but his pulpit. There, God's word was vindicated."[55]

There comes a point in every believer's life when we have to sit down and decide for ourselves if we really believe what the Bible says is true or not. There aren't *some* truths in the Bible; it isn't *mostly* true; it is either completely true or it's completely false—those are the only two options that we have to choose from; and whatever we choose will ultimately determine if we stand in the day of adversity or not.

I am not referring to the masks we put on at church that lead others to think that we fully believe that the Bible is true. I am talking about when no one else is around and all we have is our conscience; it's that moment when we look in the mirror and we know deep down that we either believe the Word of God because we have applied it to our lives and have rested in it, or, we have skipped around His Word and run from it because we don't trust in it.

Listen again and pay close attention to these verses: "The law of the LORD is perfect, converting the soul; the testimony of the LORD is sure, making wise the simple; the statutes of the LORD are right, rejoicing the heart; the commandment of the LORD is pure, enlightening the eyes." Notice that the Word of God is perfect, sure, right, and pure; it restores us to God, makes us wise, causes us to rejoice, and gives us clarity. The thing we must understand is that the only way we will ever overcome the unbelief and lack of trust that we have in God's Word is to actually place our full weight upon it by applying it to our lives and testing it out. Like Peter stepping out of the boat and walking on water, it is there, in that application, that His Word will be proven perfect and true. This is where our faith is grown; this is where our mind is renewed and we are transformed more into the image of Christ; and this is where our death chamber will become our pulpit to the world.

APRIL 24th

> Psalm 84:6: "As they pass through the Valley of Baca, they make it a spring."

The Valley of Baca can also be referred to as the Valley of Weeping. It was a very dry and parched valley that many people would pass through as they went up to Jerusalem.[56] This was an extremely difficult journey for many people to make, simply because of the heat and the lack of provision along the way, not to mention the time it took to travel in those days.

Yet listen to the psalmist: "Blessed is the man whose strength is in You, whose heart is set on pilgrimage. As they pass through the Valley of Baca, they make it a spring; the rain also covers it in pools. They go from strength to strength; each one appears before God in Zion" (Psalm 84:5–7). The psalmist is saying that when people were focused on the goal of getting to Jerusalem to praise and worship the Lord, the desert did not weary them. Rather, they were strengthened by the desire to be with God. And as they passed through the valley, the valley did not change them, they changed the valley. It became a spring, covered in pools of water. This all came from the knowledge that they would appear before God in Jerusalem.

The key to their perseverance was that they knew that they were just passing through. The Valley of Baca was not their destination; it was just something they had to travel through to get to their destination. Their eyes were not fixed on their immediate surroundings, but rather on the place where they would soon be.

Believer, we are pilgrims here on Earth. This is not our home; this is our Valley of Baca. It is a spiritually dry and barren land, and we must pass through it to reach our final destination. But when our hearts are set on the pilgrimage, knowing where our final resting place is, appearing before God, we too will be blessed as we are strengthened by that focus. And as we pass through the valley, and we have that focus, we too will make this dry and barren land a spring that will bring forth much refreshment and restoration for those in need.

APRIL 25ᵗʰ

Psalm 86:5: "For You, Lord, are good, and ready to forgive, and abundant in mercy to all those who call upon You."

If Michelle and I were ever to have children, this would be the first verse that I would write on their bedroom wall. It would be the first verse that I would teach them to memorize because in it we have the foundation of the gospel of Jesus Christ. We learn three vital things about our Heavenly Father that we desperately need to remember no matter where we go or what we do: 1) He is good; 2) He is ready to forgive; and 3) He has abundant mercy to all who call upon Him.

Oftentimes when we find ourselves in tough situations, we might remind ourselves that God is in complete control, but we forget to remind ourselves that He is also inherently good. He is not just good in some things; He is not just good in most things; rather, He is good in all things. It is who He is; He cannot *not* be good. "Oh, give thanks to the LORD, for He is good! For His mercy endures forever" (Psalm 136:1).

Oftentimes after we sin, we wallow in condemnation and self-loathing because we feel like we cannot go and ask God for forgiveness. We think to ourselves, "It's not right to go and ask for forgiveness again because I don't deserve it. I willingly chose to sin. Why would God forgive me?" Notice that God is ready to forgive, meaning that He is just waiting for us to ask for forgiveness and it will be done. First John 1:9 says as much: "If we confess our sins, He is faithful and just to forgive us our sins and cleanse us from all unrighteousness." But how many times? "O Israel, hope in the LORD; for with the LORD there is mercy, and with Him is abundant redemption" (Psalm 130:7). With the Lord, there is abundant redemption, more than we will ever need. In other words, it is impossible for us to ever exhaust His grace.

And lastly, notice that God has abundant mercy to all those who call upon Him. Not just some, not just most, and not just for the good ones; God has abundant mercy on *all* those who call upon Him. I have heard many unbelievers say that God would never forgive them for what they have done. I have heard many prodigals and backslidden believers say that God would never welcome them back. I have heard people offer reason after reason why they think God will not have mercy on them. To that I say, forget about what you think and what you feel and what you have heard . . . what does *God* say about it? What does He promise? The first step of faith is to take God at His word, regardless of what we may feel or think or hear.

So whoever you are, and whatever it is you are going through today, know this: God is good, He is ready to forgive, and He has abundant mercy to all who call upon Him.

APRIL 26th

> Romans 1:5: "Through Him we have received grace and apostleship for obedience to the faith among all nations for His name."

Condemnation is one of the biggest struggles we have as Christians; it drives us from God and tells us that we cannot go to Him for forgiveness because of what we have done. There is a lot of power behind this thinking, because we believe that we do not deserve to be forgiven—which, actually, is completely true. We don't deserve to be forgiven, so don't even try to argue with yourself about this logic. Fortunately for us, "Through [Jesus] we have received grace." Grace is unmerited favor, meaning that there is absolutely nothing we can do to earn it. It is given to us freely through Jesus Christ our Lord and Savior, and, as Paul was told in 2 Corinthians 12:9, God's grace toward us is sufficient for all of our needs.

Notice that we *have already* received this grace. It is not something that is yet to come; it is something that has already been given. When we gave our lives to Jesus Christ, we *received* all the grace we would ever need. Jesus died on the cross with all of our sin in full view. He knew every sin that every person had done, and would ever do, when He took our sin upon Himself. And yet He still says that we are forgiven, covered by His grace. This is how Paul could later write in Romans 8:1, "There is therefore now no condemnation to those who are in Christ Jesus." Notice the emphasis on the word "now." Right here, right now, in this moment, and for all the moments to come, there is *no* condemnation because we have received His grace.

So what do we have to do to receive His grace? The same thing we have to do when someone gives us a birthday present: We just have to receive it. The battle for us lies in believing it, not in receiving it; because if you really think about it, even if we don't fully believe or understand His grace, according to His Word, we have still already received it; we *are* forgiven. God's perfect measure of grace has afforded Him the ability to see us just as He sees Christ—righteous and without sin. And remember, when we sin, we sin only against the Lord; so if He can forgive us, why can't we? So, believer, stop fighting it, stop trying to understand it, and just accept it. Though we do not deserve His grace, we have already received it through Christ Jesus our Lord . . . be free!

APRIL 27th

Romans 1:19: "because what may be known of God is manifest in them, for God has shown it to them."

I have been thinking a lot lately about why we stumble during times of difficulty, and what I have concluded is that we often stumble because we confuse who God is with the way God does things. Let me explain.

We often quote Isaiah 55:8–9 when God does something that we just cannot understand: "'For My thoughts are not your thoughts, nor are your ways My ways,' says the LORD. 'For as the heavens are higher than the earth, so are My ways higher than your ways, and My thoughts than your thoughts.'" The premise here is that God's ways are, and always will be, a mystery to us. He does things that are so far beyond our understanding that it's impossible for us to ever see how it will all work out for our good. Yet it always does.

I think this is why Moses prayed in Psalm 90:16, "Let Your work appear to Your servants," because Moses wanted to see how God's ways in the present difficulties were working things out for a better future. But honestly, if God were ever to give us a perfect understanding of His ways, how would we ever have a need for faith?

All of this to say, God's ways may be a mystery to us, but God Himself is not. He is known by us, as Romans tells us, "what may be known of God is manifest in them, for God has shown it to them." There are certain things that we cannot know of God until we get to heaven, but for everything that we need to know about Him here on Earth, we know, as God has revealed to us who He is throughout the Bible. In it we see that He is love, incorruptible, eternal, immortal, omnipotent, omniscient, immutable, wise, glorious, perfect, just, true, upright, righteous, good, great, gracious, faithful, merciful, longsuffering, compassionate . . . on and on the list goes about who God is. And if we were to take a few moments, and just sit down and think about everything that God has done in our lives, we would see that all of these descriptions of Him are completely true. He has never failed us, and He has always done what is best for us. Though His ways of doing those things are often a mystery to us, God Himself is not a mystery. He is good, He is faithful, and He is in control of all things.

So believer, the next time you find yourself in a time of difficulty, do not confuse who God is with the way God does things.

APRIL 28th

Psalm 91:4: "His truth shall be your shield and buckler."

Where is our defense against the lies of the world, the enemy, and our flesh? How do we stand when difficulties, trials, and afflictions come into our lives? How do we move on when we have transgressed against our Lord and the condemnation we feel is crushing us? The Psalmist makes it very clear, "His truth shall be your shield and buckler."

He continues in Psalm 94:12–13, "Blessed is the man whom You instruct, O LORD, and teach out of Your law, that You may give him rest from the days of adversity." Notice the man whom the Lord instructs and teaches from His Word is blessed (beyond joyful); notice how he will receive rest from the days of adversity when he is taught and instructed by the Lord.

When we find ourselves in those hard times, only in the truth and promises of God's Word will we find rest from that which weighs us down. That's essentially the message of the Bible: "Come to Me, all you who labor and are heavy laden, and I will give you rest. Take My yoke (My teaching) upon you and learn from Me, for I am gentle and lowly in heart, and you will find rest for your souls. For My yoke is easy and My burden is light" (Matthew 11:28–30).

God not only promises us rest from trying to earn salvation through legalism, works, and rituals, but also from trying to stand physically while fighting a spiritual battle. His Word defeats all of those things that will ever come against us. No matter what it might be, there is a promise or an assurance that will cause us to rest from that very thing. But we have to know His Word; we have to trust in His truth; and we have to stand on His promises, or we will falter.

"In the multitude of my anxieties within me, Your comforts delight my soul" (Psalm 94:19). So, believer, do not run from God; rather, run to God. Open up His Word and receive that which you need today.

APRIL 29th

Psalm 94:22: "But the LORD has been my defense; and my God the rock of my refuge."

Recently, Michelle and I have been facing some pretty difficult circumstances—the kind where there is no easy choice to make because there are no black-or-white answers to them. No matter which direction we thought about going, it was a no-win situation for us.

Nothing seemed right; yet the time was coming when we had to do something. So instead of rashly making a decision, we prayed, asked for wisdom, and waited on the Lord until we absolutely had to say something. As the time got closer to making a decision, the anxiety level within us increased. We planned out in our minds how we would handle every possible scenario that came up, yet even this brought no peace at all. Eventually the time came when we were confronted with our no-win situation, and as the events unfolded before us, we never had to say or do anything . . . God completely worked it all out for us, and the situation was resolved.

The psalmist was completely correct when he stated, "But the LORD has been my defense." For every occasion, and every season of life, no matter how bad it looks or how hopeless it feels, the Lord is our defense in all things. Even when we see no possible way out, the Lord is still our defense. So believer, pray, seek wisdom, and wait on the Lord. Do not rush out into battle, for "The Lord will fight for you; you need only to be still" (Exodus 14:14, NIV).

APRIL 30th

Proverbs 10:17: "He who keeps instruction is in the way of life."

Have you tasted and seen that the Lord is good (Psalm 34:8)? I am not referring to salvation, mind you, but rather to the blessed application of God's perfect Word in your life. Christianity 101 tells us to apply His Word, and as new believers we fervently begin to do this by weeding out the big things in our lives such as drugs, alcohol, sexual immorality, etc. But God's Word is so much more than a list of do's and do not's. It is also wise instruction as to how to live rightly in the sight of both God and man.

In Proverbs 10:17 Solomon stated, "He who keeps instruction is in the way of life." I find it maddening when I am faced with a difficult situation and my imme-diate response comes from self rather than the instruction the Lord has provided us. Thankfully, the Lord continually reminds me of Proverbs 11:14: "in the multitude of counselors there is safety." What I find really unsettling about my initial response is that it seems so sensible and justified and righteous, and I am confident that the brethren will affirm it when I ask them. Yet when I am pointed to the Word and hear the instruction that the Lord has given for that situation, I am amazed at just how far off I really was. Solomon reminds us that when we keep the Lord's instruction, we will be in "the way of life" or literally, in the *path of living*. With that being said, we can rightly determine that when we do not apply His instruction, and we rely on the world or ourselves for our wisdom, we are in the way of death.

It's important to note that Solomon used the word "keep" rather than the words "receive" or "hear" in this verse. Ultimately, it's not enough to just receive or hear instruction; we must give heed to it or it is rendered useless in our lives. James reminds us of this very thing in James 1:22: "But be doers of the word, and not hearers only, deceiving yourselves." I think it's interesting that James specifically says for us to be doers of the word rather than just saying we need to be obedient to the word. The word "doers" is a description of who a person is, not just what a person does. James says this should be who we are at our very core—men and women who are continually keeping God's Word, for when we do, we shall be in the way of life.

MAY 1st

> Proverbs 24:27: "Prepare your outside work, make it fit for yourself in
> the field; and afterward build your house."

Waiting was never a strong suit for me until I became a believer. Like most people, I lived with the mentality of "Why wait? If you want something, go get it." But once I became a believer, the Lord taught me about the blessings that come with waiting. One of the more important aspects of waiting is to allow things to be done in the proper order and timing.

Solomon stated in Proverbs 24:27 that we should secure ourselves financially through hard work and wise planning, and then go build our houses. People in those days would live in tents while they planted the fields, and would not build their houses until after the harvest came in. The thought here is to establish a sound financial portfolio that will cover all of the necessities and possibilities that might come up before building your house.[57]

The Lord showed Michelle and I this verse when we were house-hunting last year, so we prayed about what He would have us do before we bought a house. The first thing He taught us was to budget our household so we would know exactly what we could afford. This has revolutionized our household structure and has built a financial base for us in that we are completely debt-free.

After praying more about the house, Michelle and I felt strongly that there was something the Lord still wanted to do before we went and bought a house.

So, we prayed and waited. Well, last Friday, Michelle and I found out that she is pregnant. What was so amazing about this is that, even though we had been trying to get pregnant since late August, we were not ready until last week. I think three months ago, even three weeks ago, we would not have been ready for this news; but last week, there was no fear, worry, or anxiety . . . just peace and excitement because we have trusted God to be the changer of our seasons. Believer, waiting on the Lord is not being idle; rather, it is faith in action, knowing that He is working out His perfect plans, in His perfect timing, for His perfect purposes.

MAY 2nd

> Psalm 105:1: "Oh, give thanks to the LORD! Call upon His name; make known His deeds among the peoples!"

The psalmist opens Psalm 105 with three things that we should always do as believers: 1) give thanks to the Lord; 2) call upon His name; and 3) make known His deeds among the people. The more I thought about this verse, the more I realized that these three things are what make up a believer's life in Christ.

First, we are to give thanks to God. Think about all that God has done, all that He is doing, and all that He has promised to do for us . . . that alone should cause us to fall on our knees and thank God without end. Not out of fear that He will stop being good to us, but simply because He is good and He deserves to be thanked. We must remember that thanksgiving brings peace to our souls, especially in difficult times, because it causes us to reflect on all that He has done for us, all that He has promised us, and all that He is right now in the situation we are currently facing. He is good, He is faithful, and He is in control of all things.

Second, we are to call upon His name. This should be an easy one for us, because in this life we need God every minute of every day. But we drift away at times, don't we? When life gets *easier* and things are going well for us, we just naturally drift from God because we don't *need* Him as much in those times. Well, don't believe the deception that good times might bring. We need God more in the good times than we do in difficult times, because in good times we tend to let our guard down; we tend not to pray as much, read as much, or be about His business as much. Our focus is skewed and we are much more vulnerable to making bad decisions, simply because our hands and minds are idle of the warfare that is going on in those moments.

And thirdly, we are to make known His deeds among the people. We often get all locked up when we are challenged to share with others, as we immediately start racking our brains as to what to say and how to say it; pretty soon, it's all about what we think we need to say and not about what God wants us to say. The psalmist reminds us to just keep it simple and share with others what God has done and is doing in our lives today. Just be honest with people about how you have experienced God, even if they don't believe in Him. This is witnessing at its finest, because all that you are doing is giving an eyewitness account of what God has done in your life.

So, believer, give thanks to the Lord, call upon His name, and share what He is doing in your life, that you may be blessed and that He may be glorified.

MAY 3rd

> Proverbs 10:18: "Whoever hides hatred has lying lips, and whoever spreads slander is a fool."

The commonality with hiding hatred and spreading slander that you see here is that both are done under the guise of secrecy. We conceal our hatred for someone by putting on a mask and deceiving them with flattery and kind words, all the while destroying them in our hearts; and of course, when we gossip about people, we do it behind their backs, not to their faces. The underlying theme here is that, although we might be able to hide things from man, we can't hide anything from God.

It is very easy to lose sight of this truth when we believe ourselves to be holy and righteous because we are able to live rightly in the sight of man. We slowly begin to lose our focus of reality when others give us acclaim about how wonderful we are, and we think, "Man, I am doing really good. Look at what everyone thinks of me. I *am* holy and righteous." Yet at the same time, we are cheating on our taxes, going to websites we shouldn't be going to, leaving work twenty minutes early without recording it on our timesheets, etc.

The reality in all of this is that ultimately, we do not live in the sight of man; we live in the sight of God. Nothing we think, do, or say ever escapes His sight or His awareness. That is why Solomon wrote in Proverbs 10:9, "He who walks with integrity walks securely." Back in the day, in the marketplace, when merchants would sell clay vessels, customers would walk up to them and ask them if a certain vessel had integrity—meaning, is there anything hidden that I should know about? See, because these items were made of clay, they would easily get cracked and broken, so merchants would use a crude form of wax to put the pieces back together, making it appear that the item was sound. But once the item was used for its intended purpose, it would quickly fall apart, because although it looked really good, it did not have integrity.

As believers, we need to be men and women who live rightly in the sight of God, because even though we can appear to have integrity before man, ultimately God is our judge.

MAY 4th

Psalm 18:35: "Your gentleness has made me great."

When Luke Skywalker first met Yoda in *The Empire Strikes Back*, he said to Yoda, "I'm looking for a great warrior." To which Yoda replied, "Wars [do] not make one great."[58] So what does? Society often determines whether someone is great or not by using worldly standards such as fame, power, wealth, influence, etc. The church often determines whether someone is great by how gifted they are . . . yet do any of these things actually make a person great?

"Your gentleness has made me great." David stated that it was God's gentleness that made him great—not the victories he had over his enemies, not the wealth he had accumulated, not the throne he sat upon, and not the gifts and talents he had been given. It was the gentleness that God showed him day in and day out that made David great, because once David learned this gentleness, he was then able to show that same gentleness to others.

W. Glyn Evans said that Jesus taught this same principle in His Sermon on the Mount, when Jesus stated that those who wanted to follow Him were to be gentle in word and in conduct. But Jesus did not just teach this principle; He lived it out for all of us to see when He faced His accusers at the cross. He did not defy His accusers or lash out at them; He simply surrendered the whole situation to God and allowed it to play out according to His Father's perfect will. We need to remember that when we choose the gentle way, as Jesus instructed us to do, we will be taken advantage of, cheated, and walked over by those who choose the worldly way.[59] Paul spoke of this in Romans 8:36–37, when he said: "'For Your sake we are killed all day long; we are accounted as sheep for the slaughter.' Yet in all these things, we are more than conquerors through Him who loved us."

When we choose the gentle way as Christ did—when we conduct ourselves in a manner that is worthy of Christ and not strike back at others through self-entitled justification—we are essentially laying down our situation before God, by faith, and placing the responsibility of the outcome completely in the Lord's hands. It is this type of radical faith that God desires for all of us to have because this is ultimately what makes us great in the sight of both God and man.

MAY 5th

Proverbs 10:20a: "The tongue of the righteous is choice silver."

When I meditated on this verse the other day, I immediately thought of expensive china and silver dinnerware that people only put out for very special occasions. Affirming my thoughts on this, John MacArthur pointed out that Solomon is reminding us that "good words are scarce," and because of that they are "precious and valuable."[60] It is important to understand that our words should be saved, planned, purposed, and thought-out for that perfect moment in time as ordained by the Holy Spirit, for as Proverbs 25:11 reminds us, "A word fitly spoken is like apples of gold in settings of silver."

Isaiah 50:4 is a fascinating section of prophecy that was written by the Holy Spirit through the prophet Isaiah. It is Jesus speaking, thousands of years before He was even born: "The Lord GOD has given Me [Jesus] the tongue of the learned, that I should know how to speak a word in season to him who is weary." MacArthur pointed out that this section of verses is about Jesus "being perfected through obedience and sufferings."[61] Guarding His tongue, knowing what to say in those precious moments, this was all part of the perfection process for our Lord.

But before Jesus could know what to say, He first had to learn to listen to the Father's voice. "He awakens Me morning by morning, He awakens My ear to hear as the learned" (Isaiah 50:4). As W. Glyn Evans well said, "I must also develop a sensitive ear . . . to keep tuned in to God's voice."[62] We must also learn to listen intently to what the Lord is saying so that we will know exactly what to say when situations present themselves. Think of it this way: If Jesus, the very Son of God, needed God the Father to empower Him to listen so that He would know how to speak at certain times, how much more do we need it? How much more should we spend time learning to listen to the Father's voice before we ever open our mouths to say anything?

Now maybe you are thinking to yourself, "That is not even practical." Why isn't it practical? Why do we feel the need to just open our mouths and fire away rather than listen first, pray, wait, think about it, and then speak? We have basically become a people who speak like we drive—always in a rush, cutting people off just so that we can be heard first.

This is where Galatians 5:16 comes in, "Walk in the Spirit, and you shall not fulfill the lust of the flesh." The apostle Paul reminds us that we need to have a daily, habitual lifestyle of sitting before God, listening and being still; then we are to apply what we learn, allowing the Holy Spirit to live His life through us by directing our words and our actions as we are obedient to His instructions. Because remember, "In the multitude of words sin is not lacking, but he who restrains his lips is wise" (Proverbs 10:19).

MAY 6th

Proverbs 10:20b: "the heart of the wicked is worth little."

Solomon is not saying that unbelievers are worthless, because that is simply not true. God created every single man, woman, and child, with the intent of having an intimate relationship with each one of us. We are all very valuable in the sight of the Lord, regardless if we are believers or unbelievers. Unfortunately, there are some Christians who go around saying that God hates unbelievers. Do not believe the lie; the Bible does not teach this, and this is definitely not God's heart. This is just man trying to play God.

The point that Solomon is making here is that people have nothing beneficial to offer anyone apart from God. Let me explain. In Proverbs 1:7, we are told that "The fear of the LORD is the beginning of knowledge." We are also told in Proverbs 9:10 that "The fear of the LORD is the beginning of wisdom." So if someone does not fear (respect, revere) God, then they do not have knowledge or wisdom, because that is where it all begins.

The beginning of knowledge and wisdom is when we recognize that we are sinners and that we need a Savior; it is when we accept God's free gift of salvation, surrender our lives to Him, and are filled with the Holy Spirit. If someone rejects God's free gift of salvation—if they reject His truth, and reject having a relationship with Him—then they do not have knowledge or wisdom. And if that is the case, how can they possibly help anyone, as they themselves are starving spiritually and lack that which is essential to help others? As John wrote in John 3:31, "he who is of the earth is earthly and speaks of the earth."

One of my desires ever since I was a kid was to help people. But I always thought that in order to do this I had to be a policeman, a firefighter, or a doctor.

Then I got saved, and God taught me about His Word and about the power of prayer. I realized that as a believer, I can help people in ways that I never even imagined—ways that go well beyond the physical.

Our pastor often tells the story of when he saved a man's life as a doctor at a local hospital. Afterward, as he was walking down the hall, God spoke to him and said something to the effect of, "You did not save his life; you merely extended it. It is a far better thing for you to save his soul." This is what Solomon is telling us here; helping people physically is good, but helping them spiritually is eternal.

Ultimately, Solomon says, "The lips of the righteous feed many, but fools die for lack of wisdom [heart]" (Proverbs 10:21). His point is that if your heart is of this world, it is worth little because you have nothing to offer anyone that is of eternal value. But if your heart is of God, then it is extremely valuable because you "are full of the word of God, which is the bread of life, and that sound doctrine wherewith souls are nourished up."[63]

MAY 7th

> Psalm 109:4: "In return for my love they are my accusers, but I give myself to prayer."

What should we do when people attack us . . . when we are wrongfully accused . . . when those we considered friends spread lies about us? David gives us some very practical wisdom in Psalm 109 as to how to handle these situations properly.

Apparently there were some people very close to David who launched a vicious assault of false accusations against him. David responded to their attack by saying, "In return for my love they are my accusers, but I give myself to prayer. Thus they have rewarded me evil for good, and hatred for my love" (Psalm 109:4–5). Notice David's amazing response to this situation: "but I give myself to prayer." He could have given himself over to hatred, anger, vengeance, anxiety, or fear . . . but he didn't. David knew that he had absolutely no control in this situation, and no matter what he said or did, nothing would change that. So he chose to give himself over to the one thing that would actually benefit him and the situation as a whole: prayer.

How many times a day do we have this choice before us? We could give ourselves over to any number of different things as situations unfold throughout our day, yet only one thing will benefit us, others, and the situation as a whole, and that is prayer. Prayer gives us God's heart and mind for that situation and for those involved. In essence, we take on God's divine perspective as we rise above the pettiness and adolescence of wanting to just strike back because someone has hurt us. Through prayer, our understanding of the situation changes; how we view the people involved changes; our motives change; and the words we are to say and things we are to do in that situation are revealed to us as wisdom and discernment become our compass, navigating us properly through that difficulty.

Most importantly, though, giving ourselves to prayer takes all of the control of the situation out of our hands and places it squarely in the hands of our Mighty Defender and Deliverer. It is only here, in this humble act of prayerful surrender, that we find freedom in the midst of that trial.

MAY 8th

Exodus 33:18: "And he said, 'Please, show me Your glory.'"

Moses had just led the nation of Israel in a time of worship and prayer when he made this request of God: "Please, show me Your glory." The thought here is that Moses wanted to draw closer to God and experience Him more. "Then [God] said, 'I will make all My goodness pass before you, and I will proclaim the name of the LORD before you'" (Exodus 33:19).

The thing about this incredible encounter with God is this: Moses only had to ask to see God's glory. He didn't need to do anything super-spiritual or perform some sort of sacrifice or penance; he simply needed to ask God, "Can I experience You more? Can I draw near to You, Father? Can I see You in a way that I have never known?" God's answer to this bold request was a resounding yes. But can it really be that simple? Can it really be as easy as, "Please, show me Your glory"? Yes, it can. Notice how ready and willing God was to say yes to this prayer. Truth be told, God had been eagerly awaiting Moses to ask so that He could draw Moses closer to Him.

Astounding I know, but think of it this way: Would God really ever say no to this prayer? "Sorry Moses, I don't want you to draw closer to Me. I don't want you to experience Me more. I don't want you to know Me more intimately." Of course not, because it is God's greatest desire that we all draw closer to Him and experience Him more. So, believer, let me ask you: What is keeping you from experiencing God more? What is keeping you from saying, "Lord, show me Your glory"?

MAY 9th

> Proverbs 26:20: "Where there is no wood, the fire goes out; and where there is no talebearer, strife ceases."

Anyone who has ever been around a campfire understands that when the wood runs out, so does the fire, because fire needs a source of fuel in order to burn; without that fuel, there can be no fire. Solomon takes this same train of thought and applies it to gossip and slander. He makes it very clear that these things create strife (contention); so, if you want to stop conflict in and around your life, workplace, ministry, etc., then stop the whispering.

Michelle and I have been dealing with some very difficult people for a while now, and in the past, I admit, it has caused some hardness in our hearts toward them. Recently, things had actually been going really well with them because, well honestly, we haven't had to deal with them one-on-one in a while. But of course, things picked back up with them and it's like nothing has changed.

But things weren't really that bad until Michelle and I started talking about them to one another; it was then, when we started *sharing* with one another about why we were so frustrated with them, that the strife in our hearts returned. That is when I remembered this verse and all the verses like it that remind us of the power of the tongue and how it directly affects us: "The words of a talebearer are like tasty trifles, and they go down into the inmost body" (Proverbs 18:8); "A man's stomach shall be satisfied from the fruit of his mouth; from the produce of his lips he shall be filled. Death and life are in the power of the tongue, and those who love it will eat its fruit" (Proverbs 18:20–21).

I understand the need and benefit to share with one another what we are feeling and how we are struggling, but we need to be honest and ask ourselves: Does that sharing lead to prayer, or does it lead to having more contention within our hearts? Please remember, conflict itself is not a bad thing, as it is an opportunity to make things better. For the believer, it is an opportunity to show Christ to others and to grow and mature as ambassadors of Christ. So again, conflict itself is not a bad thing; it is what we do in that conflict that can be bad.

A good barometer to know if we are slandering or sharing is to look at the state of our hearts after we begin talking. If bitterness, anger, or strife increases within our hearts, then a red flag should pop up in our minds, telling us that what we are doing is not a good thing. It's at this point that we need to stop talking and start praying because only prayer is going to change that situation, and more importantly, our hearts. So, believer, if there is strife in and around your life, stop listening to and partaking in gossip, slander, and the rumor mills of life, for this is how the fire of contention is ultimately quenched.

MAY 10th

Proverbs 11:3: "The integrity of the upright will guide them."

Ever since I was saved, I have learned the immense blessing of God's will coming to pass in my life. It is what Michelle and I long for in every single part of our lives. So how do we find God's will in a particular situation? There are a variety of ways to find it, such as searching the Scriptures, seeking wisdom from spiritually mature Christians, diligent prayer, etc. More often than not, Michelle and I are compelled to commit every situation to prayer by acknowledging the Lord in that situation, and then moving forward, allowing God to close the door if it is not His will for us (Proverbs 3:6). He has never failed us, nor has He ever led us astray.

But what does a closed door look like, and how does that happen? One of the ways that God closes doors is through our knowledge of what is right and what is wrong. For example, some friends of ours were seeking the Lord's will in where God would have them live. At this point they were in San Diego and were in the process of buying a house down there. It was then, in the final stages of buying a house, that the lender asked them to lie on some of their loan documents. It wasn't a big lie, and it probably never would have come back to them, but nevertheless, it was a lie. "Everyone does it," the lender told them; but our friends refused to compromise and they ended up losing the house.

Through that closed door, the Lord led them back to their hometown, gave them a much bigger house for a significantly lower price; gave them both wonderful jobs, and placed their children in great schools. This is exactly what Solomon was trying to get us to realize: "The integrity of the upright will guide them. . . . The righteousness of the blameless will direct his way aright. . . . The righteousness of the upright will deliver them" (Proverbs 11:3, 5–6). Notice that it is integrity and righteousness that guides, directs, and delivers us. Simply doing the right thing is one of the more common ways that the Lord directs us in His will and closes doors in our lives.

The key to all of this is to live rightly in the sight of the Lord, not in the sight of man. We can deceive and lie and cause people to think we are on the up and up, but ultimately, we are all accountable to God, not man. Living in His sight, not compromising in word or deed, walking in truth and integrity according to His righteousness, is really the essence of finding the Lord's will for our lives.

MAY 11th

> Psalm 51:6: "Behold, You desire truth in the inward parts, and in the hidden part You will make me to know wisdom."

I have been writing a lot lately about the need for us, as believers, to live rightly in the sight of God—mostly because this is the season Michelle and I are in right now. Ever since we found out that she was pregnant, we have been praying diligently that God would make us the parents that our child is going to need us to be. In answering those prayers, the Lord has been refining us by bringing the dross in our lives to the surface so that He can scrape it away. He has impressed on our hearts the desperate need for us to live rightly in His sight because ultimately our example of how we live behind closed doors is what will minister to our children the most.

One such lesson occurred when Michelle and I planned to vacation in Sedona over the week of New Year's Eve. The day before we were supposed to leave, the owner sent us an email with some last-minute details regarding the house we were renting. In the email, the owner quickly mentioned that the community where the house was located does not allow for short-term rentals, so if we were asked what we were doing there by the neighbors, we were to lie.

As I mulled this over in my mind, I could see God answering our prayers about teaching us how to live rightly in His sight. And I remember thinking to myself, "Even if no one else knows, God knows, and that is all that matters." And then I thought to myself, "What if your child was here right now, Patrick? Is this what you would want to teach them? That it's OK to lie and deceive?" Of course, this was all confirmed when I told Michelle what the owner had said and she immediately responded by saying, "I have no peace about this." So we politely explained to the owner why we had to cancel our trip, and asked for a full refund.

"Behold, You desire truth in the inward parts." Basically what we are talking about here is having character. Character has often been described as who you are when no one else is around. Yet even when no one else is around, God is around, and He knows and sees everything. God desires for all of us to be honest and sincere people who would honor the profession of faith we made to Him.

"And in the hidden part You will make me to know wisdom." Matthew Henry pointed out that God has worked within all of us the "truth and wisdom" we need to know right from wrong; and adhering to these things goes a long way in making "a man a good man," and a woman a good woman as they guide, direct, and deliver us in all things.[64] In other words, these are the things that keep us in the way of life.

MAY 12th

Proverbs 11:24: "There is one who scatters, yet increases more; and there is one who withholds more than is right, but it leads to poverty."

John MacArthur said that "the principle here" is an obvious one, and it's one that we come across a lot in the Bible: "generosity, by God's blessing, leads to increase, while stinginess leads to poverty."[65] I think the biggest reason why we do not often give, or why we do not give more, is because we do not believe this principle to be true. The math just doesn't add up for us. To us, the more we give, the less we have. Yet the Lord's math supersedes our math. He breaks the laws of physics and logic and does supernatural things in natural ways when we are obedient to Him. His math says that the more we give, the more we will receive; and as the old adage reminds us, "You cannot outgive God," because God will be a debtor to no man.

We learn here that giving as the Lord directs us to give is a matter of faith and perspective. It's faith in that we believe God will do as He promises and will provide for all of our needs; and it's perspective in that all that we have, He has given to us, so it's not ours that we are giving away, it's His. We see these principles clearly laid out for us in 2 Corinthians 9:6–15 (NLT):

> Remember this—a farmer who plants only a few seeds will get a small crop. But the one who plants generously will get a generous crop. You must each decide in your heart how much to give. And don't give reluctantly or in response to pressure. "For God loves a person who gives cheerfully." And God will generously provide all you need. Then you will always have everything you need and plenty left over to share with others. As the Scriptures say,
>
> "They share freely and give generously to the poor. Their good deeds will be remembered forever."
>
> For God is the one who provides seed for the farmer and then bread to eat. In the same way, he will provide and increase your resources and then produce a great harvest of generosity in you.
>
> Yes, you will be enriched in every way so that you can always be generous. And when we take your gifts to those who need them, they will thank God. So two good things will result from this ministry of giving—the

needs of the believers in Jerusalem will be met, and they will joyfully express their thanks to God.

As a result of your ministry, they will give glory to God. For your generosity to them and to all believers will prove that you are obedient to the Good News of Christ. And they will pray for you with deep affection because of the overflowing grace God has given to you. Thank God for this gift too wonderful for words!

Imagine if God did not give His Son to die for us; imagine if Jesus had decided not to give His life for us . . . where would we be then? Scary thought, isn't it? But because Jesus gave His life for us, two things happened (as described in 2 Corinthians 9): 1) Our need was met; and 2) God was glorified. And this is exactly what will happen when we give as well.

MAY 13th

Romans 6:22: "But now having been set free from sin, and having become slaves to God, you have your fruit to holiness, and the end, everlasting life."

At one point we were all slaves to sin; it was our lord and master and it ruled over our lives completely. And because of that, we were totally free from God's righteousness, meaning that we basically did whatever we wanted to do without adhering to the conviction of the Holy Spirit (Romans 6:20–21). But then we got saved and were given a new heart that was filled with the Holy Spirit. All of the sudden, those carnal things that we once did so peacefully were not so peaceful anymore as we began experiencing the gift of conviction.

This is what the apostle Paul was speaking of when he wrote, "But now having been set free from sin, and having become slaves to God, you have your fruit to holiness, and the end, everlasting life." The phrase "you have your fruit to holiness" is referring to the cooperative process of sanctification that takes place in a believer's life until the day we are taken home to be with the Lord. That is what Paul says ultimately happens for the believer, "and the end, everlasting life."

I am sure we all remember movies we watched before we were saved; at the time they seemed like really good movies, yet when we watch them now we are amazed that we could have ever liked them. Well, things have changed since then.

We have changed; we have been sanctified by the Holy Spirit, and our likes and dislikes have been aligned more with God's desires than with the world's perversions.

Please understand, the more we are sanctified, the more we become like Jesus in heart and in mind. So the list of things that need to be weeded out of our lives as we grow in the Lord is not going to get shorter, but rather will become longer. Now, this is not a bad thing because the more we are sanctified, and the more that list grows, the more we will realize just how much we need a Savior; the more we will depend on Him, the more we will appreciate His love and grace for us, and the more we will grow in humility.

But remember, this process does not end until we are taken home to be with the Lord. For example, the other day Michelle and I watched a movie that we each watched as believers about seven years ago. We originally loved the movie, and yet when we watched it again, we were both convicted by it. I remember thinking, "But I liked it as a believer; what happened?" Sanctification. We fool ourselves when we believe that we have already made it—that we are already there and we don't need to grow or change anymore. When we do this, we deceive ourselves and end up fighting the conviction of the Holy Spirit in our lives by saying, "I have always done this as a believer; all Christians are doing this, watching this, dressing like this . . . so why can't I?"

The thing we must remember is that we each have a personal, intimate relationship with Jesus Christ; and He grows us all at different speeds, different times, and at different levels. We should not concern ourselves with what others are, or are not, convicted by. We should only concern ourselves with the conviction that He brings in *our* lives, for He alone is our Lord and Master.

MAY 14th

Psalm 3:3: "But You, O Lord, are a shield for me, my glory and the One who lifts up my head."

Whenever I come across the word "shield" in the book of Psalms, I automatically think of the armor of God that we are exhorted to put on in Ephesians 6. There it tells us, "above all, taking the shield of faith with which you will be able to quench all of the fiery darts of the wicked one" (Ephesians 6:16).

It's important to remember that it is the armor of God that we are to put on, not the armor of man. "But You, O Lord, are a shield for me." *God* is our shield. Many times when we read Ephesians 6, we think it's our faith in God that is our shield, but in all reality it's God Himself who we are to rely on for our protection. It's His faithfulness to us that is our shield. If my shield of protection from the fiery darts of the wicked one was based on my faith, well, I would be in a world of trouble because my faith grows weary and it falters. I would lose every battle I would ever face, and I would crumble in every difficult situation.

David knew this to be true because of his own experiences. When David was going out to face Goliath, he first put on the armor of man, Saul's armor, and it hindered him because it was heavy and cumbersome. So he took off the armor of man, and put on the armor of God and walked out to face Goliath, knowing that his armor was in the fact that God was faithful. David knew that God would be his shield and that God would protect him from Goliath.

It's also important to note that the shield we have in God is not like the small shield that we see in movies such as the *Lord of the Rings*, where it only protects a small portion of our body. God's shield is more like a giant, protective bubble that completely surrounds us. That is what David wrote in this verse, "But You, O Lord, are a shield for me." The phrase literally means "to be placed around me." The Lord's shield of protection completely surrounds us physically, spiritually, mentally, and emotionally—which is comforting to know because many attacks come out of nowhere and we never even see them coming. Because God is our shield, and because God is faithful, we should lift up our heads in every situation because we know that He is fully in control. This is basically what Paul summarized in Romans 8:31: "What then shall we say to these things? If God is for us, who can be against us?"

MAY 15th

> Psalm 6:8: "Depart from me, all you workers of iniquity; for the Lord has heard the voice of my weeping."

David was going through a very difficult time of persecution when he wrote this psalm. "O Lord, do not rebuke me in Your anger, nor chasten me in Your hot displeasure. Have mercy on me, O Lord, for I am weak; O Lord, heal me, for my bones are troubled" (Psalm 6:1–2). David was pleading with God for mercy because he believed that he must have done something to anger God. Why else would he be in this situation? Oftentimes when we find ourselves in a season of difficulty, we believe that God is angry with us because of something we have done and we cry out, "Lord, what did I do? Why are You punishing me like this?"

We also begin to believe that we must have "finally done it"; we have finally crossed that line where grace stops and punishment begins, and the situation we now find ourselves in is because we have exhausted God's grace and He has finally left us. "Return, O Lord, deliver me! Oh, save me for Your mercies' sake! . . . I am weary with my groaning; all night I make my bed swim; I drench my couch with my tears. My eye wastes away because of grief; it grows old because of all my enemies" (Psalm 6:4, 6–7).

But none of these things are true because this is not who God is, nor is it how God works. David realized this in the midst of his despair and suffering as he finally gained an accurate perspective of who God really was. "Depart from me, all you workers of iniquity; for the Lord has heard the voice of my weeping. The Lord has heard my supplication; the Lord will receive my prayer" (vv. 8–9). Notice that David's situation had not changed, yet all of the sudden he boldly declares that God will deliver him. Why? How? Because David remembered who God is; he remembered God's abundant grace and His unwavering faithfulness. David realized that God had not left him, nor was God angry with him. Incredibly, David knew he would be delivered simply because God heard his prayers.

Believer, our greatest battle is never going to be the situation itself; our greatest battle is to remember and trust in who God is in the midst of that difficulty. This is where the battle will be won and lost for us because victory is not deliverance from a situation, but rather deliverance *in* a situation.

MAY 16th

Proverbs 2:9: "Then you will understand righteousness and justice, equity and every good path."

As Michelle and I were reading through the Bible the other day, we came across the parable of the sower in Matthew 13. The word that kept jumping out to me as we read Jesus' explanation of this parable was the word "receive." It hit me that each person in this parable received the gospel, just in different ways: some by the wayside, some in shallow soil, some among the thorns, and some in good soil. What I thought was really interesting when Michelle and I read this was that the focus was on the soil. The seed (the gospel) is unchanging; the sower is just someone who scatters the seed, but that which changes in this parable is how the person receives God's truth.[66]

The next day I was reading Proverbs 2, and there was that word again: "receive." As I kept reading, I realized that this is a picture of he who receives the Word of God in good soil:

> My son, if you receive my words, and treasure my commands within you, so that you incline your ear to wisdom, and apply your heart to understanding; yes, if you cry out for discernment, and lift up your voice for understanding, if you seek her as silver, and search for her as for hidden treasures; then you will understand the fear of the LORD, and find the knowledge of God. . . . Then you will understand righteousness and justice, equity and every good path. (Proverbs 2:1–5, 9)

Finding the knowledge of God, and understanding the fear of the Lord, righteousness, justice, equity and every good path is very appealing to me as I am sure it is to you as well. But it all comes back to how we receive the Word of God. Do we treasure it as truth above all truths? Do we meditate on it so we can properly understand it? Do we ask the Lord for insight and discernment in how to apply it to our lives? Do we search for it the way we do when we misplace twenty dollars?

In the parable of the sower, we can all see a part of ourselves when we read or hear the Word of God. Sometimes we read it but we make no time to actually understand it, and it just falls to the wayside. Sometimes we hear it and we get really excited about it, but then there is no application of it in our lives and it burns away like in shallow soil. Sometimes we receive His Word, and we know what we are supposed to do in a certain situation, but then we let the things of the world take priority over it and we choke out that truth. And then there are the times when we receive His Word and we treasure it; we seek to understand it and we apply it to our lives.[67] This is the good soil that brings forth much fruit. This is the good soil where we find the knowledge of God, and understand the fear of the Lord, righteousness, justice, equity, and every good path.

MAY 17th

> Romans 7:15: "For what I am doing, I do not understand. For what I will to do, that I do not practice; but what I hate, that I do."

We can all relate to this section of the Bible very easily. Why do we do what we don't want to do? That is the question that we are seemingly asking ourselves just about every time we sin. I remember a story that a friend once told me about her son when he was caught being disobedient. In response to the coming punishment he cried out, "I really wanna be good, Mommy!" I think we can fully relate to the exasperation of this little boy.

Paul definitely could as he wrote something very similar to what this little boy said, "For what I am doing, I do not understand. For what I will to do, that I do not practice; but what I hate, that I do." The word "understand" that Paul uses here means "to approve of." Paul makes it clear: I do not approve of what I do. Those things I want to do, I don't do; and those I don't want to do, I do. "For I know that in me (that is, in my flesh) nothing good dwells; for [to do good] is present with me, but how to perform what is good I do not find" (Romans 7:18). Paul says, "I have a problem. I really want to do good, but I don't know how."

David Guzik explained, "Paul's problem isn't desire—he wants to do what is right. His problem isn't knowledge—he knows what the right thing to do is. His problem is a lack of power. The law says, 'Here are the rules and you had better keep them.' But it gives us no power for keeping the law."[68] The point is that we cannot overcome sin following the Law; and we cannot overcome sin in our strength, in our desire, or in our knowledge of what is right and what is wrong. In order to overcome sin, we must have something that is greater, more powerful than sin itself.

This leads to Paul's conclusion: "O wretched man that I am! *Who* will deliver me from this body of death? I thank God—through Jesus Christ our Lord!" (Romans 7:24–25, emphasis added). Paul recognized that we all need a Savior to deliver us from sin; a Savior who is more powerful than sin itself. Enter Jesus Christ, the perfect Lamb of God, who is without sin and defeated all sin at the cross.

Understand, Romans 7 is not about how we can defeat sin; it is about *Who* will deliver us from sin. Only Jesus Christ living in us through the power of the Holy Spirit can empower us to overcome sin. We, as believers, now have the power to choose not to sin. How do we do that? "I say then: Walk in the Spirit, and you shall not fulfill the lust of the flesh" (Galatians 5:16). Zechariah wrote something very similar in Zechariah 4:6 when he said it's not by might (our strength), nor by power (the strength of many), but only by the Spirit of God that we can overcome.

MAY 18th

Psalm 11:4 (NLT): "But the Lord is in His holy Temple; the Lord still rules from heaven."

At some point during a very difficult situation, someone came up to David and painted him a hopeless picture of his circumstances: "Fly like a bird to the mountains for safety! The wicked are stringing their bows and fitting their arrows on the bowstrings. They shoot from the shadows at those whose hearts are right. The foundations of the law and order have collapsed. What can the righteous do?" (Psalm 11:1b-3, NLT). To this David responds, "But the LORD is in His holy Temple; the LORD still rules from heaven." David literally says to this person, "It doesn't matter what others may do . . . I take refuge in the Lord. He is my Protector and my Defender. He rules from heaven and is fully in control of all things."

It is so easy for us to feel helpless and have this hopeless outlook when we experience difficulties that are completely out of our control. Oftentimes it feels like the enemy is winning the battle, as our God is strangely quiet. Maybe the hopeless situation for you is the government, the economy, or the court system; maybe it's your job, or the lack thereof; maybe it's your prodigal child or a loved one's health; maybe it's a certain test that is coming up; maybe it's that you're not married, or that you can't have children; maybe it's that you have cancer or some other physical affliction; maybe you are even saying and believing these same things right now, "Run and hide! It's hopeless! There is nothing we can do!"

The answer to all of these things is exactly what David said, "But the LORD still rules from heaven." The easiest way to find a situation hopeless and helpless is to take God completely out of the picture and focus solely on what you see and feel and hear. This is exactly what happens when we face difficult situations and we believe that it's all on us to fix them. What we should be saying in these situations is, "But God. . . ." But God is my refuge; but God is my hope; but God is my deliverer, my provider, my healer, my defender, my banner, my advocate, my hope . . . and I trust in Him because He is good and He is faithful.

So, believer, do not lose hope by taking God out of your situation; rather, enthrone Him in that situation. Make Him the center of it, Lord of it, knowing that He alone is the Christ; that He alone is seated on the throne, and that He alone rules from heaven. Surrender that situation to Him in prayer and thanksgiving because He is for you, and He is in control of all things.

MAY 19th

Psalm 13:6: "I will sing to the LORD, because He has dealt bountifully with me."

How many times have you found yourself in a situation where it seemed like God was hiding from you? Where no matter how fervently you prayed or how desperately you cried out, God was seemingly nowhere to be found. It was as if all of your words fell right to the floor and never reached the heights of God's listening ear. This is where David was at when he penned Psalm 13.

"How long, O Lord? Will You forget me forever? How long will You hide Your face from me? How long shall I take counsel in my soul, having sorrow in my heart daily?" (Psalm 13:1–2). David was seeking the Lord; he was crying out for God to help him, yet the only voice he heard was from his own weakened and hopeless soul. But then something changed; David remembered how God had always dealt with him. "But I have trusted in Your mercy; my heart shall rejoice in Your salvation. I will sing to the Lord, because He has dealt bountifully with me" (Psalm 13:5–6).

Notice that David reflected on how faithful God had always been to him, "But I have trusted [past tense] in Your mercy. . . . He has dealt [past tense] bountifully with me." God had never failed nor forsaken David; and because of that, hope was restored. David's perspective had now changed from sorrow to joy. "My heart shall rejoice [present tense] in Your salvation. I will sing [present tense] to the Lord."

Nothing brings out our inner pessimist like having to wait on God in a difficult situation. When our world begins falling apart and our hope begins to fade, despair becomes our best friend. Yet if we were to reflect on God's faithfulness to us in every situation that we have ever faced, we would see that God has never failed us, nor has He ever forsaken us. In fact, we would see that He has always dealt bountifully with us. It's at these times that we should rejoice and sing to the Lord because we know that He is faithful, and we know that deliverance is coming for us. So, believer, do not place your trust in what you see or what you feel, but rather place your trust in the One Who always has been, and always will be faithful.

MAY 20th

Luke 6:11: "But they were filled with rage, and discussed with one another what they might do to Jesus."

What could have angered the scribes and Pharisees so much that they began plotting to kill Jesus? What could Jesus have done that caused these men to be so "filled with rage" that they were ready to break the very Law that they held so dearly and commit murder? Strangely enough, it was because Jesus healed a man on the Sabbath.

I have been thinking a lot about this story ever since Michelle and I read it the other night. I kept asking myself, "How could they be so blind and hardhearted to what Jesus was doing?" Answer: they were so caught up in their traditions, laws, and rituals that they could not see what, or Who, was right before them and the good that was coming from Him. Quite simply, these men became very comfortable in their religion.

I was very convicted by this thought as I started to reflect on all the times that I have responded in a similar manner. Generally speaking, when we are challenged to do things outside of the way that we normally do them, we become very uncomfortable. We even begin to criticize, label, and become so filled with rage that we miss all of the good that is coming from it.

So let me ask you, is there only one way to run a church service? Is there only one way to worship God? Is there only one way to preach or teach or share the gospel of Jesus Christ? No, there's not. God does not like to be put in a box, and He does not like to be limited to a particular method, because He is a diverse and wonderful God. We see this in the way that Jesus healed people. Sometimes He spoke words of healing, sometimes He touched them, and sometimes He used spit. Yet in each one of these situations, God was glorified.

And really, that should be our only concern . . . is God being glorified? If a person or a method is getting the glory, then something is very wrong. But if God is getting all of the glory and the Holy Spirit is moving and fruit is coming forth, then what is the problem? As Jesus told His disciples in Luke 9:50 when they were criticizing others, if they are not against us, then they are on our side. So, believer, are you getting too comfortable in your religion to let the Holy Spirit work in and around your life?

MAY 21st

Proverbs 13:2–3: "A man shall eat well by the fruit of his mouth, but the soul of the unfaithful feeds on violence. He who guards his mouth preserves his life, but he who opens wide his lips shall have destruction."

When carefully examining these verses, we find that verse 3 actually explains verse 2 for us. "A man shall eat well by the fruit of his mouth" because "He who guards his mouth preserves his life." And "the soul of the unfaithful feeds on violence" because "he who opens wide his lips shall have destruction." So the contrast here is between the person who speaks wise, or good things, and the person who speaks foolish, or evil things. The difference is that one brings life, and the other brings destruction.

Notice that Solomon uses eating and feeding as his metaphors in these verses. I thought this was very telling because when I eat something, it only affects me, not anyone else; only I receive the good or the bad from that food. Thus Solomon's focus is on what speech brings to the individual speaker. Notice also how he wrote these verses: "He who guards *his* mouth preserves *his* life, but he who opens wide *his* lips shall have destruction." So the focus is on the effects that our speech has on us. We reflect so much on how our words impact others that we often forget to consider how they impact us as well.

For example, have you ever been depressed and spoken depressing words about your situation and actually felt better? Have you ever been angry and spoken heated words and felt *less* angry? Have you ever felt hopeless and spoken words of hopelessness and despair and then felt joy just bubble up inside of you? No, of course not, because those words of depression, anger, and hopelessness just add on to what we are already feeling. They actually fuel our negativity and magnify our already destructive mental state. When we do this, we destroy our ability to think clearly and our attitude and perspective become corrupted in the state that we are already in. That is why the number-one rule in decision-making is to never make decisions while in an emotional or anxious state, because when we do, we generally make really bad decisions.

As Matthew Henry pointed out, ultimately, the warning that Solomon gives us here is for us not to be "ruined by an ungoverned tongue"; rather we are to guard our mouth, and preserve our life, because when we guard our mouth, we are guarding our very soul.[69]

MAY 22nd

> Proverbs 13:4: "The soul of a lazy man desires, and has nothing; but the soul of the diligent shall be made rich."

Solomon is pointing out the foolishness of the sluggard in this verse, and how ludicrous this kind of lifestyle and thinking really is. He says that the lazy man desires all of the increase that the diligent get, yet he doesn't want to put forth any effort to receive it. He covets what others have, but he will do absolutely nothing that needs to be done in order to obtain it. Therefore, he has nothing.

The irony here is that the greater pain for the sluggard is not the pain of working hard and putting forth effort; rather, it's the pain of not getting what he desires that really causes him to suffer. If he would just put forth the effort and work, not only would it be less painful for him, but he would also receive that which he longs for.[70]

We see this type of thinking a lot in marriage today. Everyone goes into marriage desiring to have a good marriage, yet many do nothing to make that happen. They just expect their marriage to be good without working at it. The truth is that it takes both the husband and the wife working together in a marriage to make it godly, strong, good, healthy, and successful. It's not going to just happen, and it's not going to just happen through one person's efforts.

This same truth is applied to our life as a whole, but more importantly, with our walk with God. Only those who put forth effort in a relationship to walk with, and know God more intimately, will find the pleasure, the purpose, and the profit in life.[71]

MAY 23rd

> Matthew 13:21c: "For when tribulation or persecution arises because
> of the word, immediately he stumbles."

Last Wednesday night, as a bunch of us were in the prayer room at church praying for the needs of those in the service, the Holy Spirit gave me insight into the parable of the soils that I had not seen before.

Now, we know that those who receive the Word of God in shallow soil are those who catch fire quickly, yet burn out when they face tribulation or persecution. So as we were praying, I was contemplating this and began asking myself, "Why would they stumble when facing tribulation or persecution?" The answer was simple; even though they know God's truth, they stumble because they do not believe God's truth.

That is when the Holy Spirit showed me that those who receive the Word in shallow soil are those who receive the Word in their minds, but not in their hearts. See, our hearts are the good soil that produces fruit; this is where we believe because this is where our faith comes from, not from our minds. Sure, we use our minds to weigh decisions and make choices, but it's what we believe in our hearts that ultimately fuels those decisions. I mean, you could know everything there is to know about packing a parachute and jumping out of a plane, but unless you actually believe that the parachute is going to open when you pull the cord, you are not going to jump.

So it's not enough to just hear God's Word; it's not enough to even know God's Word; we must believe it in our hearts, or else it is just head knowledge that will eventually be overpowered by what we really believe to be true. As it has often been said, many people will miss heaven by about eighteen inches, as this is roughly the distance between a person's heart and his or her brain. Do not be deceived, knowledge is not enough; we must believe.

So, believer, when was the last time you took true measure of your faith and honestly asked yourself, "What do I really believe to be true?" Here's a hint: You will know what you really believe by the choices you are making in those difficult situations. May we all be like the man who cried out to Jesus, "Lord, I believe; help my unbelief!" (Mark 9:24).

MAY 24th

> Acts 1:8: "But you shall receive power when the Holy Spirit has come upon you; and you shall be witnesses to Me in Jerusalem, and in all Judea and Samaria, and to the end of the earth."

When the Lord moves us to do something—like, say, share the gospel, pray, or speak a word of knowledge—why do we not do it? Why do we tell the Lord "no" in those situations? I would say the most common reasons are because: 1) We believe we are not able; 2) we believe we don't know how; or 3) we are afraid of how people will react.

This, I believe, is where Acts 1:8 comes in. "But you shall receive power when the Holy Spirit has come upon you; and you shall be witnesses to Me in Jerusalem, and in all Judea and Samaria, and to the end of the earth." The word "power" that is used in these verses is the Greek word *dunamis*; this is where we get our word "dynamite" from. But did you know that this word "power" is also translated as "ability"?[72]

Read Acts 1:8 again, only this time with the word "ability": "But you shall receive *ability* when the Holy Spirit has come upon you; and you shall be witnesses to Me in Jerusalem, and in all Judea and Samaria, and to the end of the earth." Interesting isn't it? You shall receive the ability to be witnesses for Me, Jesus says. I think we get ourselves into trouble when we take our focus off of the Holy Spirit's ability to do something, and place the focus solely on our own ability to do something. It is then that all of those excuses become very real truths for all of us. Rich Cathers explained it this way:

> If I was to take a glove and command it to play my keyboard, frankly I'm not going to hold my breath. It doesn't have the "ability" (*dunamis*) to accomplish it. But if my hand "fills" the glove, then whatever my hand does, the glove does too. Suddenly my glove has the ability to play the piano, just like my hand. When the Holy Spirit fills our lives, we are "enabled" to do whatever the Holy Spirit wants us to do.[73]

This is the picture that we have here in Acts 1:8. We now have the ability to do all that God instructs us to do through His Holy Spirit.

Having the ability is only half of it, though; the other half is knowing that God has gone before us and has readied that person's heart for what He is instructing us to do. For example, one morning I was standing outside of the prayer room in between services at church. As I was looking around the sanctuary, I noticed a young man sitting in the front row all by himself. It was then that I felt God say to me, "Go say 'Hi' to him." "What?" I replied. "Go say 'Hi' to him." The Lord repeated. "And then what, Lord?" "Just go," He said. My thoughts began racing. "This is dumb. Saying 'Hi' won't change anything . . . it's trivial."

But the Lord kept pressing on my heart to go, so reluctantly I walked over to this young man and said to him, "Hey bro, the Lord really impressed on my heart that I needed to come say 'Hi' to you, so . . . Hi." Immediately his eyes welled up with tears. He told me that he had been to our church seven times, and not one person had ever said "Hi" to him. He said, "I was just praying that God would please send someone over to say 'Hi' to me." After I shared with him what the Lord had told me to do, we both rejoiced and praised our amazing God.

So, believer, remember, the ability to do all that God wants you to do is there . . . but it only comes to fruition when we make ourselves available and do what He tells us to do.

MAY 25th

Ephesians 5:1: "Therefore be imitators of God as dear children."

Selfies are all the rage right now. They have consumed the social media landscape, and apparently have even made it to the Oscars. The funny thing is that people have been doing this for years; the only difference is that now it has a super-trendy name, so of course it's gone viral.

As I was thinking about selfies, I began thinking to myself, "If God were to take a selfie today, what would it look like?" The first answer I think people would defer to would be a picture of a sunset or a sunrise or some other amazing setting where God's artistic powers are revealed through nature's mighty splendor. But if we were to sit down and carefully consider this question for a while, I think we would all come to the same conclusion that God's selfie would not be a picture of nature, but rather a picture of one of His children loving another.

As glorious as nature can be visually, God's greatest glory is revealed through His children. This is why Paul encouraged the Ephesian church, "be imitators of God as dear children." There is no greater calling for us than to imitate our Lord Jesus Christ and the love that He showed others. This is where we will find our purpose in life as we are sanctified and refined more into the image of Christ. It is when we take on His heart and mind toward others that God's selfie is truly portrayed. This is what Peter wrote in 1 Peter 1:15 as well: "but as He who called you is holy, you also be holy in all your conduct."

The really convicting part about all of this is that every moment of every day, selfies are being taken by the choices we make and the words that we speak. The question we have to ask ourselves is, whom are those selfies reflecting? Are they selfies of the world, ourselves, Satan, or God? I wonder, if God had an Instagram account with all of the selfies of Him taken throughout time, would we be in any of them? Oh Lord, may it be so today!

MAY 26th

Acts 9:6: "Lord, what do You want me to do?"

It is so easy to get so caught up in what we want to do or what man thinks we ought to do, both in the world and in church, that we often forget to ask God, "Lord, what do *You* want me to do?" This is the challenge that Michelle and I have felt from the Lord a lot lately—to simply walk with Him, moment by moment, and just be obedient to how He leads us. No questions asked, no wondering why, no debating with the Lord—just take Him at His word and do what He says.

In doing this, the Lord has freed us from all of those distractions that make us ineffective tools for His kingdom, like: pleasing man; focusing on what others think we should be doing; trying to impress others with our spirituality; being concerned with what others are doing and how they are doing those things, etc. The focus on just living for God, and not man, has been completely liberating and refreshing for both of us.

I was reminded of this lesson last week when, for one night, I went to a men's retreat with a brother from church who was the guest speaker. See, for the last couple of weeks leading up to that evening, the Lord had really been moving in my life by giving me words of knowledge and wisdom to speak to others in all kinds of different settings; so I just assumed that when we were at the retreat, the Lord would continue to exercise those gifts in me and I would be able to share with and encourage the brethren.

The mistake I made in preparing for that night was not asking the Lord, "What do You want me to do?" Instead, because I expected the Lord to use me in a specific way, I became so consumed in trying to receive a word of knowledge or wisdom from the Holy Spirit that I was oblivious to what was going on around me, and I missed out on doing what the Lord really wanted me to do that night—which was to just pray for others.

I think the underlying theme of what the Lord showed me is that we are to serve Him, moment by moment, without expectation. When we expect the Lord to use us in a specific way that He has not revealed to us, we become ineffective to how the Lord really wants to use us in those moments and we end up feeling discouraged and frustrated. Please do not misunderstand me; we should absolutely be expectant that the Lord will use us. The question we need to remember to ask is, how does He want to use us in that situation?

I actually first learned of this lesson during the mission trips that the Lord would send me on. Sometimes I would teach, sometimes I would counsel, sometimes I would just clean the missionaries' house or do gardening for them; sometimes the Lord would give me a word of knowledge for a guy at a casual breakfast, and sometimes He sent me there to just pray for the missionaries' marriage. Regardless, every trip was different. The reminder for us is to serve the Lord, moment by moment, without expectation, so that whatever the Lord says to do, we will do, and His perfect purposes will be fulfilled, not ours.

MAY 27th

Proverbs 13:12a: "Hope deferred makes the heart sick."

When we have an expectation for something to come to pass—say, for example, like getting married or being healed from an affliction—and we diligently pray and wait for the Lord, and days, weeks, months, and maybe even years go by and that thing still hasn't come to pass as we desired, we begin to lose hope in that situation. The thing we have to remember to ask ourselves is this: Where is our hope placed? Is it placed in that thing coming to pass, or is it placed in the One who always does what is best for us, the ever-faithful God of all hope?

This is a very important question to answer because if our hope is placed in that thing, what happens if it doesn't come to pass? Where is our hope then? It's shattered and we are left devastated by our unfulfilled expectation. But when we place our hope in the Lord, even when an expectation is not met according to our desires, our hope is still intact because we are trusting in who He is and what His perfect will is for us.

We need to remember that when we come to God and pray, He is going to answer us in one of three ways: 1) yes; 2) no; or 3) wait. Though these three responses are completely different to us, if our hope is in God and not in that thing we are praying for, then they will all produce the same exact thing in us: faith. But again, where is that faith in prayer to be placed? Is it placed in that thing coming to pass, or is it placed in God's will for our lives? This is the faith that Jesus is looking for in us—the faith to trust in Him no matter how long we have to wait, and no matter what the answer might be, simply because we want His will for our lives and not ours.

Think of this verse like a warning and a barometer of our heart. First, it's a warning in that Solomon is telling us what is going to happen to us when hope is deferred. For example, we go to the doctor, we get a prescription, and on the prescription label it says, "May cause drowsiness." That warning is placed there so that if we get drowsy after taking the medication, we won't freak out and wonder what is happening to us. In a very similar way, this verse is a warning label for all of us in regard to waiting on the Lord. Solomon is basically saying to us here, "Hey, when you expect something to come to pass, and it is delayed, your heart is going to grow weary of waiting, so don't freak out when it does. Don't lose faith, don't lose hope, and don't take matters into your own hands; rather wait on the Lord."

It's at this point that the barometer portion of this verse kicks in. When we feel that weariness, and when we are tempted by hopelessness, a red flag should pop up telling us that something is very wrong. It's then that we need to ask ourselves, "Where is my hope placed?" Is it placed in that thing coming to pass, or is it placed in the ever-faithful God of all hope?

MAY 28th

Proverbs 13:12b: "but when the desire comes, it is a tree of life."

Yesterday, we talked about the first half of this verse, "Hope deferred makes the heart sick." And I asked the question, where is our hope placed when we pray for something? Is it placed in the thing we are praying for, or is it placed in the God of all hope? I remind you of this, because the answer to that question will determine if the second half of this verse comes to fruition or not: "but when the desire comes, it is a tree of life."

Notice that Solomon says when that expectation is fulfilled, it is "a" tree of life, not "the" tree of life. It is merely symbolic of the tree of life that we read about in Genesis and Revelation. John MacArthur said that the phrase "tree of life," as used here, refers to a time of "spiritual renewal and refreshment."[74] Now, with that thought rolling around in your head, let me ask you something: When that desire is met, whose desire is really being fulfilled?

We know from Scripture that the purpose of prayer is to bring about an awareness of what God's will is for our lives; as Jesus well said, God's will be done, not ours. And we know that if something is according to God's will, then it shall be answered yes; if it's not according to God's will, then it shall be answered no. So when that expectation comes to pass, it is not our desire that is ultimately being fulfilled; it is God's.

Here is the underlying theme in this verse that we cannot miss: When we place our hope in God *in* a situation, and pray and seek His will *for* that situation, we then take on God's heart and mind *about* that situation. And when this happens, our desires will align with His desires, thus ensuring that those expectations will always be met regardless if the answer is yes, no, or wait. This is how David was able to go and worship in the house of the Lord after his son died, because his hope was in God, not in his son being healed. And this is what brings about a spiritual renewal and refreshment in our lives.

Understand, answered prayer is not the fruit here; the fruit comes from the time of testing that we endure; it comes from the time of waiting in the crucible, because this is where we are refined more into the image of Christ. It is here that something is created within us that will bear fruit at a later date. "[W]e also glory in tribulations, knowing that tribulation produces perseverance; and perseverance, character; and character, hope. Now hope does not disappoint, because the love of God has been poured out in our hearts by the Holy Spirit who was given to us" (Romans 5:3–5).

How do you think Abram became known as Abraham, the father of faith, and listed in the "hall of faith" in Hebrews 11? It was learning from, and enduring, times of testing like these that enabled him to be the man of faith who took his son Isaac up to the altar to sacrifice him when the Lord commanded him to do so.

He would never have been able to do this if he had not had those times of testing in his life.

It's the process that bears fruit in our lives and becomes a tree of life, not the answered prayer. For example, when I got saved, the Lord taught me how to wait. It took years to learn, and was not fun, but when I eventually met Michelle, I was able to lead her in the time of waiting that God had for both of us, all because I had already been through that refining process. So, believer, do not place your hope in things coming to pass, rather place your hope in the One who will always do what is best for us, even if it hurts at times.

MAY 29th

Psalm 39:7: "And now, Lord, what do I wait for? My hope is in You."

Sometimes we can outthink ourselves in certain situations. For example, David found himself in a place where he was angry with God because of what was going on around him. The wicked were prospering and yet he was the one suffering with an affliction. Life wasn't fair, and he was angry. So instead of being honest with God and speaking to Him about it, David decided to be a good little Christian soldier and not say anything at all. "I was mute, I did not open my mouth, because it was You who did it" (Psalm 39:9).

The thinking here is that, "Though I am very angry with God in my heart, as long as I do not say anything to Him about it, all will be well and I will be good in His sight." There are a few problems that occur when we take on this approach of physically restraining ourselves from talking: 1) Even if we don't speak, everything is still in God's sight as He knows our hearts; 2) we not only lock ourselves out of saying what is bad, we also lock ourselves out of saying what is good; and 3) it just doesn't work. It simply makes us angrier until we finally blow a gasket.

This is what we see in David at this time. "I was mute with silence, I held my peace even from good; and my sorrow was stirred up. My heart was hot within me; while I was musing [meditating], the fire burned. Then I spoke with my tongue" (Psalm 39:2–3). David was so angry with God that he would not even speak the good things that needed to be spoken. Well, the pressure kept building until David finally had to speak to God about all of this. It was then, and only then, that he found peace. "And now, Lord, what do I wait for? My hope is in You." David realized after talking with God that his hope was in God, not in the wicked being punished, and not in him being healed.

Please understand, there is never a bad time to talk to God regardless what we are feeling. He compels throughout the Bible, "Come to Me; in whatever state you are in, just come." God already knows what we are thinking and feeling; He knows the thoughts and intents of our hearts, so why do we try to hide them from Him as if it makes a difference? God is big enough to handle our temper tantrums, frustrations, and impatience regarding this life. His desire is to have a relationship with us; not one of masks and topical performance, but one that is real and honest and true that comes from our hearts.

So, believer, do not try to keep things from God; rather, give Him all that you are, knowing that His love for you will never change. Be bold in the fact that you can be yourself with God and still be perfectly loved by Him. So what are you waiting for?

MAY 30th

> Psalm 40:3: "He has put a new song in my mouth—praise to our God; many will see it and fear, and will trust in the LORD."

I remember sitting at my desk one day at work and asking God, "Father, why have You not healed me of this physical affliction? What is the purpose behind it?" It was at that exact moment that an email came through from one of our devotional readers that said, "You have no idea how much I needed to hear this today." See, I had written a devotion that morning about my physical affliction, and as I read their response, it was then that God said to me, "That is why."

David reminds us of this very thing in Psalm 40 when he wrote in verses 1–2, "I waited patiently for the LORD; and He inclined to me, and heard my cry. He also brought me up out of a horrible pit, out of the miry clay, and set my feet upon a rock, and established my steps." David was going through a very rough time in his life, and so he prayed and waited "patiently" on the Lord. The thought here is that it took a while before David was delivered from this situation. Why, though? What was the point of it all? David answered that question for us in verse 3, "He has put a new song in my mouth—praise to our God; many will see it and fear, and will trust in the LORD."

Many things are allowed into our lives by the great Orchestrator that, not only teach us an important lesson, but also teach others an important lesson as well. And sometimes, those difficulties have nothing to do with us at all; they are simply allowed in our lives for the sake of others. This is what David meant when he said

"He has put a new song in my heart—praise to our God." In other words, I have experienced God's faithfulness in a way that I have not experienced before. Why? Because "many will see it and fear, and will trust in the LORD."

When we give our lives to Jesus Christ as our Lord and Savior, we essentially say to Him, "Lord, use me as *You* will." So when certain things are allowed into our lives, God is merely taking us up on our offer. He wants to use us for His great purposes so that, not only are we blessed and fulfilled and purposed, but also that others will know and trust in Him when they go through difficult times as well. So, believer, what new song has the Lord given you today? Look for those opportunities to share it with others, knowing that when we do, many will see it and believe and will trust in the Lord.

MAY 31st

> Psalm 44:6: "For I will not trust in my bow, nor shall my sword save me."

A couple of weeks ago, the electricity in our entire apartment complex went out. Normally when this happens the electricity is restored in just a couple of hours; this time, however, it was out for more than a day. Michelle and I learned a lot in that twenty-four-hour period—most of which was that we were not adequately prepared for a natural disaster that would leave us without electricity, water, food, and so on. And I admit, the thought of not being able to provide the necessities of life for my wife, and our soon to arrive baby girl, was a very scary one for me.

So I kicked my preparation into high gear and began researching all of the different ways that we needed to be prepared. But an interesting thing happened in all my planning and preparing: I noticed that I had slowly begun to place my trust in the preparation and supplies to save us, not in God. Now please do not misunderstand me, I think there is much wisdom in making sure that we are prepared in case a disaster hits, but there is a fine line between being prepared and being a prepper.

Listen to what David said when his enemies had surrounded him and he was in a battle for his life: "Through You we will push down our enemies; through Your name we will trample those who rise up against us. For I will not trust in my bow, nor shall my sword save me. But You have saved us from our enemies" (Psalm 44:5–7). David understood that even though he had to physically use a sword and a bow at times to defend himself, it was God who was ultimately his defense, and it was God who ultimately carried him though battle and gave him victory, not his bow and not his sword.

We need to remember, when disasters hit—whether they are natural, physical, economical, emotional, or spiritual, and we are shaken from every comfort zone that we have—God is still God. He is still in control, and He is just as faithful as our Protector, Provider, Healer, Defender, and Savior that He is when we are not facing a mountain of adversity. So, believer, where is your trust truly placed today? Is it in your retirement account, medicine, counseling, works, looks, titles, etc., or is it placed in the loving, ever-faithful God? Remember, there is nothing in this world that is reliable enough, or worthy enough, to have our hope and trust placed in it. Only One is ever faithful, and only One is our salvation from every disaster we face in life, and that is God.

JUNE 1st

Luke 22:13: "So they went and found it just as He had said to them, and they prepared the Passover."

As Passover was fast approaching, Jesus instructed Peter and John to go into the city and prepare the Passover meal for Him and the rest of the disciples. When they asked Jesus where He wanted to eat Passover, Jesus told them:

"Behold, when you have entered the city, a man will meet you carrying a pitcher of water; follow him into the house which he enters. Then you shall say to the master of the house, 'The Teacher says to you, 'Where is the guest room where I may eat the Passover with My disciples?' Then he will show you a large furnished room; there make ready." So they went and found it just as He had said to them, and they prepared the Passover. (Luke 22:10–13)

These instructions may not seem strange to us, but to Peter and John they may have seemed impossible. See, in those days, men did not carry pitchers of water as it was widely considered woman's work; so the odds of even finding a man carrying a pitcher of water were next to impossible.[75] Now add into that equation a man carrying a pitcher of water who will lead them to a house that has a fully furnished guest room, and it gets to that point where disbelief takes over. Yet, by faith, when

Peter and John followed Jesus' instructions, they found everything was just as Jesus had said it would be.

I was reminded of this very important lesson last Sunday morning as some of us were praying during first service in the prayer room. The Lord put the name "James" on my heart, along with a picture of a stone block wall and chains attached to it. I then prayed that the Lord would free James from the life of bondage that he was caught up in.

After service was over, an elderly gentleman came in and asked for prayer. As I began listening to him describe the situation with his son, the Holy Spirit emphatically told me that his son's name was James. I did not say anything at first because, I mean, what were the odds that this man's son was named James? Finally, I asked the man what his son's name was, and he said "James." I about jumped out of my chair. I then shared with this man what the Lord had placed on my heart during prayer and how we had prayed for his son. As it turns out, his son had just gotten out of jail and was basically on his last chance. It was just as the Lord had said it would be.

So, believer, what promise are you struggling to believe today? What impossible situation has you doubting the providence, deliverance, or healing ability of the Almighty God? Remember, as my good friend Darrell often says, "God will never allow us to escape our need for faith." So look to His Word and find the strength, hope, rest, and peace that is afforded to you today. Simply follow His instructions, and everything will come to pass just as He has said it will.

JUNE 2nd

Psalm 51:10: "Create in me a clean heart, O God, and renew a steadfast spirit within me."

What do we do when we are confronted with the wickedness of our sin? Some believe that penance is necessary so they might achieve right standing with God; for others, it is a matter of doing works so that they might earn their way back into God's good graces. Yet what did David do when God called him out on his adultery and murder? He confessed, "I have sinned against the LORD" (2 Samuel 12:13a). And then he prayed, "Create in me a clean heart, O God, and renew a steadfast spirit within me."

Why? Because "[God] desire[s] truth in the inward parts" (Psalm 51:6). It is always going to be about the heart with God because that is where our relationship

with God is, in our heart. It's not in works, or rituals, or even the law. Our relationship is one of the inward parts. "For You do not desire sacrifice, or else I would give
it; You do not delight in burnt offering. The sacrifices of God are a broken spirit, a
broken and contrite heart—these, O God, You will not despise" (Psalm 51:16–17).
God doesn't want our works or our penance; He wants a repentant heart.

So what was God's response to David when he confessed his sin? "The LORD
has put away your sin; you shall not die" (2 Samuel 12:13b). John reminds us of
this in 1 John 1:9, "If we confess our sins, He is faithful and just to forgive us our
sins and to cleanse us from all unrighteousness."

We must remember that God is always ready and willing to forgive us of our
sin. Our part is to confess our sin to God—to agree with Him that what He says
is sin *is* sin, and then simply receive His abundant grace of forgiveness. If we add
anything to this, or if we don't believe it, then we are saying that what Jesus did on
the cross was not enough for us and there must be more that needs to be done in
order for us to be forgiven.

I love what Jesus said to the woman who was caught in the very act of adultery,
"Neither do I condemn you, go and sin no more" (John 8:11). This is exactly what
God says to each one of us today when we come to Him with our sin.

JUNE 3rd

> James 5:16b: "The effective, fervent prayer of a righteous man avails
> much."

This verse is written to remind us just how powerful our prayers really are. To make
sure that we fully understand this, James gives us an example: "Elijah was a man
with a nature like ours, and he prayed earnestly that it would not rain; and it did
not rain on the land for three years and six months. And he prayed again, and the
heaven gave rain, and the earth produced its fruit" (James 5:17–18).

James says that Elijah was a normal person just like you and me, yet look at
how powerful his prayers were. So what was his secret? First, he knew God's Word
and He prayed according to God's promises; secondly, and probably more important, Elijah put forth effort in his prayers because he believed in the power of prayer.
This is ultimately what James tells us in this verse, "The effective, fervent prayer of
a righteous man avails much."

I think this is where most people get tripped up regarding this verse. The words
"effective" and "fervent" seemingly place specific conditions on prayers that avail

much; so if we do not pray "effectively" or have "fervency" when we pray, our prayers are powerless. I struggled to understand this verse for a long time because it is rare that I am fervent when I pray. Sometimes I would even try to drum up emotion or passion, just so my prayers would be effective. Well, this is not what the Lord wants, and this is not what this verse means.

The words "effective" and "fervent" actually combine to make up one word in the Greek, *energeo*. This is where we get our word "energy" from. The word *energeo* literally means "to be operative" or "to be at work." The thought here in context is to put forth power, or energy, into our prayers. To break it down even further, it means to put forth effort by praying; this, James says, is how prayer will avail much.

Let's go back to James' example regarding Elijah. When he prayed for it to rain, we are told that he knelt down on the ground, put his head between his knees, and prayed. Elijah did this seven times as his servant ran to the top of the mountain each time to see if any rain clouds were coming. Finally, on the seventh time, his servant saw a cloud the size of a man's fist, and Elijah knew it was going to rain. Notice how Elijah had to put forth effort in his prayers. The Bible doesn't describe him as being fervent; it describes him as being humble, diligent, and faithful to continue praying until he received an answer from God. This is the prayer that avails much.

But when it really comes down to it, it is all about belief, because if Elijah did not truly believe in the power of prayer, he never would have put forth the effort needed to pray. So, Christian, what do you believe?

JUNE 4th

Psalm 57:1: "Be merciful to me, O God, be merciful to me! For my soul trusts in You; and in the shadow of Your wings I will make my refuge, until these calamities have passed by."

It's reassuring to know that we have a place to run to when calamities hit. Whether it is sickness, death, persecution, sorrow, or heartache, we always have a place to go in our time of need, as God is our refuge from the storms of life. But what does that look like in a practical sense? What does it mean to make our refuge in Him?

About seven weeks ago, our doctor told us that there appeared to be a cyst on our daughter's brain. As Michelle and I faced the reality of "what could be," we called upon our brethren to pray with us during this very difficult time. After a short cry of about fifteen seconds, Michelle was overcome with peace that Kate would be just fine. I carried it a little bit longer, but the next day the peace of the Lord overwhelmed me, as I also knew that she would be OK. For us, we made our refuge in the Lord with our brethren through prayer. When we got the report last Thursday that Kate was fine and there was no cyst on her brain, we rejoiced and praised our amazing God.

So much of making a refuge in the shadow of God's wings means not going through difficulties alone, but rather having brothers and sisters who will walk down that road with you in prayer, support, encouragement, etc. It's having people constantly point you to the God of all hope during temptations of hopelessness. Lately, Michelle and I have had to stop numerous times and just thank the Lord for all of the amazing people He has placed in our lives. We recognize the embarrassment of riches that we have in these people, and are so thankful that we are not alone on this journey.

So what do people do when they do not have God to run to because there is no relationship with Him? Where do they make their refuge? I remember being prepped for shoulder surgery a couple of years ago, and while I was there, I overheard a nurse saying that the guy in the bed next to me was getting prepped for some kind of heart surgery. As I watched the multitudes of this man's family come and go, the last thing each person said to him before they left was, "Good luck." My heart broke for this man because all that he had to trust in was, "Good luck." That is where his refuge was, and there is absolutely no hope in that. So let me ask you, where have you made your refuge?

JUNE 5th

> 1 John 3:24: "Now he who keeps His commandments abides in Him, and He in him. And by this we know that He abides in us, by the Spirit whom He has given us."

For the last week or so, I have been really struggling spiritually. Normally when I struggle in this manner, it feels as though I am really far away from God—but this time it's different. This time it feels as though God is still near me; there is just nothing coming through from Him—kind of like if you had your TV turned on, but all you saw was a black screen because there was no feed coming in from your cable box or satellite dish. It feels like that.

So yesterday I decided to ramp up my time in the Word, figuring that I was going through a spiritual growth spurt and needed more time studying; but as I was going out to my car to read during my break, the Lord said to me, "Patrick, you need to come to Me, not My Word." He then asked me a question, "When do you feel closest to Me?" That was when I realized that I am closest to God when I am making decisions to deny myself for the sake of others, and I had not been doing that.

Things had been going so well in and around my life, and I was being so blessed by God, that I had become very complacent in my walk with Him. Sure, I was still in the Word and serving in ministry and praying for others, things like that, but my heart was drifting far from God because of a lack of compassion and love for those around me. On paper everything looked great, but truth be told, my heart began to grow cold and hard and rebellious; I had stopped keeping God's commandments to love Him with all my heart, soul, and mind, and to love my neighbor as I love myself. Jesus said in Matthew 22 that these are two greatest commandments, and this is essentially what John is talking about in 1 John 3:24.

In Luke 9:23 Jesus said, "If anyone desires to come after Me, let him deny himself, take up his cross daily, and follow Me." Notice that before we can take up our cross and follow Jesus, we must first deny ourselves. Without that, there is no following Jesus. Without that, there is no abiding in Him and Him in us. If we are choosing to not follow His commandments, and we serve self rather than others, then we cannot remain in Him or Him in us. This does not mean that we are not saved anymore; it just means that we have turned off the cable box or satellite dish. John says we will know that He is abiding in us and us in Him by the power of the Holy Spirit. I had no power. There was no feed from God coming through because I had quenched the Holy Spirit in my life—not by one choice, mind you, but by constantly choosing to put myself in front of others.

It's really easy to believe that denying ourselves and putting others first is a huge burden for us to carry. Yet John wrote in 1 John 5:3 that "[God's] commandments are not burdensome." Denying ourselves actually frees us from the burden of our flesh and fills our lives with purpose and blessing. Understand that we are never more like Jesus then when we deny ourselves for the sake of others, because in this, God is manifested. "No one has seen God at any time. If we love one another, God abides in us, and His love has been perfected in us" (1 John 4:12). May it be so this day for all of us.

JUNE 6th

Proverbs 14:4: "Where no oxen are, the trough is clean; but much increase comes by the strength of an ox."

In ancient Israel, the ox was probably the most valuable possession a man could own. Oxen were used to plow the ground for crops and to power grain mills; basically, they did all of the heavy work that was needed to be done back then. So the thought here is a simple one: If I don't have any oxen, then I don't have to clean up after them, care for them, etc.—but I don't have any increase, either.

The Lord impressed this verse on my heart this morning as I was getting ready for work, and He reminded me of the decisions that this pattern of thinking can lead to. More specifically, the Lord told me that there are people reading this right now who are afraid to get married because of the effort that it takes to make a marriage work. I totally understand this thinking. When I was single, I had my cool apartment, my sports car, my big TV, my video games . . . I could do anything I wanted to do, whenever I wanted to do it. Life was *easy*.

But I was also alone all the time. I had no helper, no best friend, no one to share my heart with, experience life with, grow together with. Life may have been *easier* for me in the sense of being selfish and lazy, but it was also much emptier because there was no true sacrifice in my life; and without sacrifice, how could I ever truly know the Lord? The Lord told me when I was single that I would never be the man that He wanted me to be if I did not marry Michelle, and I am so thankful that I did because life has never been better.

We all face these types of decisions in life. Maybe for you it's that you don't want to have children, you don't want to get involved serving in a ministry, or you don't want to reach out and befriend other people. We become so comfortable in our lives and our schedules that we don't want to do anything that would upset that perfect balance that we have established. We just want an easy, stress-free life. Yet there is no increase in our lives when we live like this—no growth, no purpose, no fulfillment, no challenge. The problem with this thinking is that our circle of "imagined control" keeps shrinking to the point where pretty soon we are not even living anymore; we just exist in a prison of fear, afraid to do anything different because it might involve effort and take us out of our comfort zones.

Ultimately, though, this type of thinking leads us to disobey the leading of the Holy Spirit in our lives. Walking with the Lord is not an easy thing to do, especially in the world we live in today. God will call us to do many things that will take us out of our comfort zones, things that will cause us to be vulnerable and that will require us to put forth effort and sacrifice. God wants us to invest our hearts into the lives of others—because it is there, and only there, that we will find true increase in our lives.

JUNE 7th

John 3:16: "For God so loved the world that He gave His only begotten Son, that whoever believes in Him should not perish but have everlasting life."

I was studying for a teaching this last week, and I found myself so focused on all of the original Hebrew text, punctuation, grammar, etc., that I had nothing to put down on paper. It was as if my mind had completely seized up and I couldn't see or think about anything other than that one verse. This is what happens to me when I zoom in too far on one verse and I forget the bigger picture. It's at these times that I have to take a step back and just ask myself, "Why did God write this? Why did God want this verse in the Bible? What is His heart for this verse?" And it is there that I gain God's perspective on His Word, and things begin to clear up for me a little bit.

I often tell people that we need to read and teach God's Word in context—and rightly so, because it keeps things in their proper perspective. Well, the fundamental context for reading and teaching all of God's Word, even books like Leviticus and Numbers, is this: God desires that all men be saved (1 Timothy 2:4). That is the really the context for the entire Bible.

This is where those who say that God has created certain people for destruction get it wrong; this is where those who say God hates unbelievers get it wrong, because they are taking God's Word out of context. They are looking at God's Word without considering God's overriding purpose behind all that He has done ever since the very beginning. John 3:16–17 basically sums up God's *mission statement* for us: "For God so loved the world that He gave His only begotten Son, that whoever believes in Him should not perish but have everlasting life. For God did not send His Son into the world to condemn the world, but that the world through Him might be saved."

Believer, God is love. All that He does is out of love. His most fundamental desire is that all of mankind would be saved. This is the context in which the whole Bible was written, and this is the context that we should read and teach the Bible in.

JUNE 8th

Matthew 5:44: "But I say to you, love your enemies, bless those who curse you, do good to those who hate you, and pray for those who spitefully use you and persecute you."

There have been many times that I have come across a verse in the book of Psalms that seemingly contradicts this verse, and I think to myself, "This is not the heart of God. The heart of God desires all men to be saved, so why are these verses in the Bible?" The Lord showed me recently that the verses I have read in the book of Psalms just need to be examined more carefully; upon further review, they actually line up with God's heart and reveal to us how we should be praying for those who come against us.

Psalm 58:6 declares, "Break their teeth in their mouth O God! Break out the fangs of the young lions, O LORD!" When we first look at this verse, it seems to be a very violent, destructive prayer that is fueled by hate; yet, upon further review, we see it actually aligns with God's heart perfectly. David's prayer is not for God to physically harm his enemies; rather, it is for God to disarm them. David prays that God would take away from his enemies their means of doing evil so that they could not do those things anymore. Think of it like that of a police officer arresting a suspect. The first thing the officer does is disarm that person so that they can no longer harm anyone. This is what David is praying here.

David continues, "When he bends his bow, let his arrows be as if cut in pieces" (Psalm 58:7). Next, David prays that the intentions of wicked would be rendered ineffective, leaving them once again, disarmed. This time, David is not addressing the weapons they have; rather, he asks God to change the intentions of their heart. We see this same type of prayer in Psalm 70:2–3 as well: "Let them be ashamed and confounded who seek my life; let them be turned back and confused who desire my hurt. Let them be turned back because of their shame." Again, David is praying that God would convict, not condemn, the hearts of these people so that they might recognize what it is they are doing, realize that it is wrong, and repent from those wicked ways.

So why should we pray for our enemies and not against them, you ask? First, it changes us; and second, it changes them. "[Pray for your enemies so] that you may be sons of your Father in Heaven; for He makes His sun rise on the evil and on the good, and sends rain on the just and the unjust" (Matthew 5:45). Remember, God does not hate anyone. He loves all mankind, even His enemies; that is what this verse means: "He makes His sun rise on the evil and on the good, and sends rain on the just and the unjust."

So, believer, do not pray against those who buffet you. Rather, pray for them. Pray that God would disarm them and would change their hearts so that they too might be sons and daughters of God, and walk in the newness of life.

JUNE 9th

> Romans 12:2a: "And do not be conformed to this world, but be transformed by the renewing of your mind."

I have been thinking a lot lately about the battles that we face every day with sin, fear, doubt, unbelief, etc., and I am continually reminded that it all begins with the mind. This is why directly after Paul wrote in Philippians 4:6, "Be anxious for nothing," he wrote, "Finally, brethren, whatever things are true, whatever things are noble, whatever things are just, whatever things are pure, whatever things are lovely, whatever things are of good report, if there is any virtue and if there is anything praiseworthy—meditate on these things" (Philippians 4:8). This is essentially what Paul is saying in Romans 12:2. There has to be a change in our conscious, purposed thought life. We have to stop thinking as the world does; stop dwelling on what the world says, and purpose our minds to a new pattern of reason and deduction.

The apostle Paul exhorts us here to not model who we are and what we do after the world anymore, but rather to purposefully change ourselves into a form that is more like Christ by allowing Him to renovate our understanding, our reason, and our recognition of what is good and what is evil, because only when we do this will we be able to "know what God's will is for [us], which is good and pleasing and perfect" (Romans 12:2b, NLT).

To do this, we need to stop asking ourselves how we feel and what we think we need to do, and start asking ourselves what God's Word says about this and what is true.[76] It is here, in applying God's Word to our lives, that we will be transformed by the renewing of our minds, because our faculty of making decisions, believing, trusting, perceiving, etc., will change from the world to the Word. It is essentially what Paul spoke about in Philippians 2 when he told us to take on the mind of Christ and put away the foolish things of the world. So, believer, do not align yourself with the world; rather, align yourself with the Word and be transformed by the renewing of your mind.

JUNE 10th

> Isaiah 40:31: "But those who wait on the LORD shall renew their strength."

The beginning of this verse implies that there are those who do not wait on the Lord, but rather move out in their own strength, in their own wisdom, creating their own path in what they perceive to be the best time and the best way for a particular situation to unfold. Solomon addresses the results of this type of thinking in Proverbs 19:2b–3a: "[H]e sins who hastens with his feet. The foolishness of a man twists his way." But "those who wait on the Lord shall renew their strength; they shall mount up with wings like eagles, they shall run and not be weary, they shall walk and not faint."

The truth as to why we do not wait on the Lord is not hard to figure out: We simply do not trust that God is going to move in that situation because we lack faith in His ways and in His timing. To this Isaiah says, "Have you not known? Have you not heard? The everlasting God, the LORD, the Creator of the ends of the earth, neither faints nor is weary. . . . He gives power to the weak, and to those who have no might, He increases strength" (Isaiah 40:28–29).

Understand that waiting on God does not mean being idle in a situation; rather, it is expecting that God is going to move in a mighty and perfect way. The mistake we often make is thinking that waiting is a time of inactiveness rather than a time of growing our faith in God. Isaiah exhorts us here to wait on the Lord because as we do, He passes on His strength to us so that we will be able to run and not be weary, to walk and not faint. When we do this, we essentially exchange our weakness for His strength, and our weak faith for the persevering faith that we can only find in God.[77] Only when this exchange takes place, Isaiah says, can we run and not grow weary, can we walk and not faint. So, believer, wait on the Lord and trust in Him, for He will move in the perfect way and in the perfect timing.

JUNE 11th

> Ecclesiastes 4:12: "Though one may be overpowered by another, two can withstand him. And a threefold cord is not quickly broken."

Our desperate need for fellowship and accountability is radically understated in the church today. Too often we have seen spiritual giants fall into sin simply because they did not want to have a transparent circle of accountability in their lives. I believe that if they had someone with whom they were open and honest about what was going on in their lives, and the thoughts they were having toward that other woman, they would not have chosen to follow the paths that they did.

This is what Solomon is reminding us of here in this verse, the need for accountability. "Though one may be overpowered by another, two can withstand him. And a threefold cord is not quickly broken." Most times when I hear this verse quoted, people are focusing on the threefold cord of marriage . . . a man, a woman, and God. Though it is true that God is needed in every marriage, that is not what this section of verses is talking about. If you were to read verses 9–12, you would see that Solomon is directly referring to the value of a friend, not about God's necessity in marriage.

I was reminded of this when I was reading the book of Joshua the other day, and I came across the story of Achan. Here is a perfect example of what happens when we do not have accountability in our lives. After the fall of Jericho, God spoke to the children of Israel and specifically told them not to take part in any of the gold, silver, bronze, or iron that they came across, because those things were consecrated to the Lord. Yet Achan became tempted. He desired these things. In his own estimation, he did not see the harm in taking some of the treasure for himself because, I mean, who would it hurt? Eventually, when his sin finally came into the light, Achan and his entire family were killed.

If Achan had a brother in his life that he was honest with, and shared with this man what he was thinking about doing, how he was being tempted, etc., I guarantee you that this brother would have spoken wisdom into Achan's life about what a horribly bad idea it was. But he didn't have any accountability, and he fell into temptation.

Having this type of accountability is not a suggestion for us; it is a mandatory guideline for every single believer. Proverbs 18:1 reminds us of the danger we face without accountability: "A man who isolates himself seeks his own desire." The qualification for an accountability partner should not just be that the person is a friend of ours we like talking to; no, they should be a man (for men) or a woman (for women) who is mature in the Lord and will call us out when we are going down a slippery slope. Just having a friend there, who is not mature in the Lord, is just adding to the problem. So, believer, remember, "Two are better than one, because they have a good reward for their labor. For if they fall, one will lift up his companion. But woe to him who is alone when he falls, for he has no one to help him up" (Ecclesiastes 4:9–10).

JUNE 12th

Philippians 4:8: "[M]editate on these things."

I love reading the book of Psalms because I gain so much insight into the human condition. In Psalm 77, the psalmist found himself in a time of deep despair. "In the day of my trouble I sought the Lord; my hand was stretched out in the night without ceasing; my soul refused to be comforted. I remembered God, and was troubled; I complained, and my spirit was overwhelmed. . . . You hold my eyelids open; I am so troubled that I cannot speak" (Psalm 77:2–4).

So what was the psalmist going through, and what was causing his suffering? Like many psalms, the situation itself is not revealed to us because the situation is not the real problem. We often think that the affliction, or the persecution, or the relationship is the reason why we are in turmoil, but is that really the reason why we struggle in times like this? Or is it something completely different? Notice that the psalmist wrote, "I remembered God, and was troubled." The psalmist began reflecting on who God is and it troubled him greatly because he knew of God's faithfulness; yet here he was suffering, without any help from his mighty Savior. And it's here that we find the real reason for his suffering.

"Will the Lord cast off forever? And will he be favorable no more? Has His mercy ceased forever? Has His promise failed forevermore? Has God forgotten to be gracious? Has He in anger shut up His tender mercies? . . . And I said, 'This is my anguish'" (Psalm 77:7–10a). The problem was not the situation the psalmist was in; the problem was that he began to doubt God. He began to question if God would save him, heal him, provide for him, deliver him, etc.

"'But I will remember the years of the right hand of the Most High' . . . the works of the LORD . . . Your wonders of old" (Psalm 77:10b–11). The psalmist made a choice in his time of suffering to reflect on the promise of God's faithfulness, even though it seemingly was not present with him. He began to remember all that God had done for him and his people, and it is there that he found peace.

This is what the apostle Paul instructed us to do in our times of difficulty: "Finally, brethren, whatever things are true, whatever things are noble, whatever things are just, whatever things are pure, whatever things are lovely, whatever things are of good report, if there is any virtue and if there is anything praiseworthy—meditate on these things" (Philippians 4:8). This is not positive thinking; this is choosing to meditate on that which we know is true. It is choosing to continually fill our minds with truths about God that are far greater than our circumstances. And if you were to look at the list that Paul compiles for us here, you would see that Paul addresses every type of struggle that we will ever face in this life.

Believer, the situation you are facing right now is not the problem; the problem is that there is a battle going on in your mind between fear, doubt, and anxiety vs. having faith in God. So stop dwelling on the things that you see and feel, and choose to fill your mind with the things that you know to be true of God. For "Who is so great a God as our God?" (Psalm 77:13).

JUNE 13th

Joshua 9:14: "[B]ut they did not ask counsel of the LORD."

As we grow and mature in the Lord, certain things should become more natural for us to do than others. I am not speaking about doing things out of legalism or obligation, but simply doing them because we recognize the wisdom and blessing that comes from applying them to our lives. One of those things is to seek the Lord in all the decisions we make.

In the case of Joshua and the Gibeonites, Joshua did not seek the Lord to find out if these people were telling the truth or not. Instead, he and the other leaders of Israel sampled the provisions that the Gibeonites brought with them and determined that they were a people from a faraway land just because the bread was moldy, the wineskins were old and cracked, and their clothes were tattered and worn. As David Guzik pointed out, Joshua and the leaders of Israel were walking by sight, not by faith. They relied on what seemed right to them by trusting in their senses (sight, touch, taste, smell), rather than just seeking the Lord and asking Him for wisdom and discernment in the matter.[78] This process of decision-making can only end in one way: badly. Proverbs 14:12 reminds us of this: "There is a way that seems right to a man, but its end is the way of death."

Too often I have seen believers (including myself) get into bad situations and make bad decisions simply because we "did not ask counsel of the LORD." We make these decisions based on what seems right to us, and then we complain to God and ask Him why He allowed the consequences from that decision to come about. Yet if we just considered the promise that we have in Proverbs 3:6, we would see that God wants to direct all of our paths for us: "In all your ways acknowledge Him, and He shall direct your paths."

God's heart is for all of us to make wise decisions and be in the center of His perfect will, so if we go astray, or if we make foolish decisions, whose fault is it really? Isaiah 30:1 speaks to this, "'Woe to the rebellious children,' says the LORD, 'who take counsel, but not of Me, and who devise plans, but not of My Spirit, that they may add sin to sin.'" So, believer, seek the Lord in every decision; wait, and allow God to direct your paths. You will be glad you did.

JUNE 14th

Psalm 80:3: "Restore us, O God; cause Your face to shine, and we shall be saved!"

Psalm 80 was written in a time of despair, as Israel was being overrun by its enemies. So the psalmist cried out to the Lord, "Restore us, O God; cause Your face to shine, and we shall be saved!" The phrase "cause Your face to shine" was a direct reference to when a king would have favor on his people, meaning that whatever request was made of the king was going to be fulfilled.[79] So the dilemma that the psalmist was struggling with was not "if God *could* save them," but rather, "if God *would* save them." We see this summed up in verse 14: "Return, we beseech You, O God of hosts." In their thinking, God had left them. But, truth to be told, they had left God.

I have come across many people in the prayer room lately who have told me that they are trying to get right with God. My response to them is, "How long does it take to get right with God?" The point is that God never leaves us. If there is any type of barrier between us and God, it is because we have placed it there through disobedience, sin, rebellion, unbelief, etc. Yet all it takes to remove that barrier is for us to ask, because God is always ready to forgive (Psalm 86:5). Since the very beginning, God has stretched out His hands to all of mankind imploring us to come to Him so that He might save us. Nothing has changed. God is still stretching out His hands to us today, inviting all of us to come to Him and find shelter in the shadow of His wings. So the thought of "Will God save me?" is not of God; it is of the world. God responded to the psalmist:

> You called in trouble, and I delivered you . . . "Hear, O My people, and I will admonish you! O Israel, if you will listen to Me! . . . But My people would not heed My voice, and Israel would have none of Me. So I gave them over to their own stubborn heart, to walk in their counsels. Oh, that My people would listen to Me, that Israel would walk in My ways! I would soon subdue their enemies, and turn My hand against their adversaries." (Psalm 81:7–8, 11–14)

It's times like these that we need to own up to the old adage that has been used in so many relationships, "It's not You, it's me." So, believer, how long does it take to get right with God? I don't know . . . how long does it take to ask God for forgiveness?

JUNE 15th

Proverbs 14:31 (NIV): "Whoever oppresses the poor shows contempt for their Maker, but whoever is kind to the needy honors God."

One of the pitfalls that we as Christians can easily fall into is when we begin to think too highly of ourselves. It's the attitude, "Man, the church is lucky to have me." This usually happens because we know we are saved, we know that God has promised us amazing things, and we know how much He loves us. Though all of these things are true, and we should rest in them, we need to remember that it's not because of who we are that we have these assurances; rather, it's because of who God is that we have them.

I was reminded of this truth when we were going over Proverbs 14:31 in the married couples' study last week. Notice the words "whoever" that Solomon uses in these verses. He is not just talking about believers or unbelievers here; he is referring to all of mankind. "Whoever [even believers] oppresses the poor shows contempt for their Maker, but whoever [even unbelievers] is kind to the needy honors God." Is it possible for unbelievers to honor God through their actions? Absolutely.

We often think that because we go to church, attend Bible study, read our Bibles, pray, and tithe, that we honor God. Yet we are not instructed to do these things to honor God; we are instructed to do these things so that we will stay grounded and focused on how we should live our lives. In other words, all of these things are for our benefit, not God's. Honoring God, on the other hand, comes when we take on the mind and heart of Christ toward other people. We honor God when we serve others just as Jesus did. That is what Solomon says here: "Whoever is kind to the needy honors God."

Jesus once told a parable about a man who was lying on the side of the road, half-dead. A certain priest walked by and did nothing, as did a Levite (both were fellow Jews of the man who was half-dead). But along came a Samaritan (a people despised by the Jews), who had compassion on the man and took care of him. Jesus then asked the man He was talking to, "'So which of these three do you think was neighbor to him who [was half-dead]?' The man replied, 'He who showed mercy on him.' Then Jesus said, 'Go and do likewise'" (Luke 10:36–37). So, believer, do not get too comfortable in your religion, for without love, it is all just clanging cymbals (1 Corinthians 13:1–3).

JUNE 16th

Proverbs 24:10: "If you faint in the day of adversity, your strength is small."

There is no beating around the bush with this verse as Solomon gives us both barrels in regard to running away when facing adversity. Essentially what he is saying here is, "If you fall to pieces in a crisis, there wasn't much to you in the first place" (Proverbs 24:10, MSG). Please understand—this verse, like every other verse in the Bible, is written in full view of all of the promises of God, and that is how we should look at it.

The rebuke that Solomon gives us here, by calling us weak-faithed individuals when we faint in times of adversity, is not a pleasant one, but it is an accurate one. There is no reason for us to ever yield to fear during adversity or life in general. The Lord has not only instructed us to not fear, but He has also given us unlimited power through His Holy Spirit. When we faint in times of adversity, it is because we have chosen to rely on our strength rather than relying on the mighty power that God has afforded us. Zechariah 4:6 reminds us of this: "'Not by might [our strength] nor by power [the strength of many], but by My Spirit,' says the LORD."

Last week I faced a lot of adversity as I was taken out of just about every comfort zone I have; the temptation, when we face these situations, is to just run away from them because it is so uncomfortable for us to walk in faith. Yet the Bible says, "without faith it is impossible to please [God]" (Hebrews 11:6). And as my good friend Darrell often reminds me, "God will never allow us to escape our need for faith." So walking in faith is a vital part of our lives if we are to grow and mature in the Lord.

It was then that the Lord said something very profound to me, He said, "Patrick, before you take control of the situation in your strength and understanding and run away from it, will you give Me the opportunity to be faithful to you? Will you give Me the chance to show you that I am the ever-faithful God that you read about in the Bible?" I was blown away by this amazing insight, as I was quickly reminded how often I never give God a chance to be faithful to me. I choose to faint in the days of adversity, instead of just walking through them with God as my strength and shield.

Maybe you are reading this right now, and you are struggling to believe that God is faithful, or will be faithful in your time of adversity. To that I ask you, have you ever given God the opportunity to be faithful to you? Have you ever marched into a hopeless situation that the Lord has allowed into your life, and basically said, "Let it be unto me as You desire, Lord"? Has the Lord ever failed you?

Believer, do not choose to faint in the day of adversity by relying on your perception of the situation, or the limited strength you have to endure it. Rather, tap into the power of God through His Holy Spirit and walk in faith, knowing that in Him there is always victory.

JUNE 17ᵗʰ

Psalm 138:8: "The LORD will perfect that which concerns me."

The Lord will complete and bring to an end that which you are in the midst of. That is what this verse essentially promises us. I know this doesn't seem true when we are in the midst of a difficult situation, but we have seen this promise come to pass all throughout the Bible, as the Lord has continually stayed true to His Word by delivering all of those who called upon His name.

The important thing for us to remember is that this promise is not only for those we read about in the Bible; it is also for us today. And it's not just for certain situations either; no, this promise is for every single situation that we will ever face, big or small. So whatever it is that concerns you, wherever it is that you find yourself, God promises that He will bring it to an end in His timing and in His way.

I find it amazing that God, the Creator of the universe, loves us so much that He cares about every concern that we have, regardless what it might be. Even if everyone else in the world thinks that it's ridiculous—if it concerns us, it concerns God. But it's not just that God will bring our situation to an end; more importantly, He will perfectly complete it in our lives, meaning that we will be changed through it all. We will become stronger as our faith and trust in Him and His Word grows; and we will gain the endurance, character, and hope that we need to make it through this life.

But here is the condition of this promise that we cannot miss: Only the Lord can bring this situation to an end and perfectly complete it in our lives. It won't come to an end by our hand, our wisdom, our works, our pastor, our spouse, our friends, drugs, alcohol, sex, anger, lying, etc . . . only "The LORD will perfect that which concerns [you]."

So, believer, what are you concerned with today? What are you in the midst of right now that has you anxious and fearful? Wherever you are, whatever it is you are going through, God knows—and more importantly, God cares. So look to God for deliverance, and rest in the fact that He will bring it to an end when the work is perfectly complete, for He is "full of compassion, and gracious, longsuffering and abundant in mercy and truth" (Psalm 86:15).

JUNE 18th

1 Corinthians 13:8: "Love never fails."

This week, our married couples' study started reading *The Five Love Languages* by Gary Chapman for our summer study. As we were going through the introduction to the book, the Lord impressed a question on my heart that He wanted me to share with the men when we separated into groups of men and women: "Do we even care what our wives' love language *is*?" The point came across very clearly to the men in my group because if we really do not care to grow and apply the things we hear and learn, then going through the book would just be just a waste of time as we would be just going through the motions. For without love, it profits us nothing (1 Corinthians 13:3).

I remember when the movie *Fireproof* came out, and everyone started buying the *Love Dare* books thinking that the book would save their marriages. Yet if you remember the movie, the dare itself did not work until the husband got saved and received the love of Christ. It was then, and only then, that the dare began working to restore their marriage, because the husband began loving his wife *through* these acts, and not just loving her *by* the acts . . . big difference.

This is essentially what Paul was speaking of in 1 Corinthians 13. Many in the church at Corinth were focusing solely on the gifts of the Holy Spirit while ignoring the importance of love (1 Corinthians 13:1–3). So Paul says to them, "Love never fails. But whether there are prophecies, they will fail; whether there are tongues, they will cease; whether there is knowledge, it will vanish away" (v. 8). Only love will remain. When considering this, David Guzik said that the gifts of the Holy Spirit are the tools for God's work, but love is actually "the work itself." Without love, these gifts are merely empty vessels.[80]

Love never fails. I think this is a great reminder for all of us because there will be times when we don't know what to do or what to say to someone; and yet, if we just love on them, that is what will minister to them the most. At the end of the day, love alone is what will remain. It is what will change and heal and restore because when we truly love someone as God loves us, God is clearly manifested to that person and that is what they will remember, that they were loved by God.

JUNE 19th

1 Samuel 3:1: "And the word of the LORD was rare in those days; there was no widespread revelation."

There is a saying that my good friend Darrell often says, "Some things are taught, and other things are caught." Well, this morning, as I was reading through 1 Samuel, I caught this verse: "And the word of the LORD was rare in those days; there was no widespread revelation." This verse literally says that there was no breakthrough of divine revelation during that time. The obvious question is, why?

If we were to look at where Israel was at this point, we find out exactly why. This was written during the time of the judges—a time when Israel continued to live in rebellion against the Lord. The question that came to me as I was studying this was, "Was God's divine revelation rare in those days because God held it back, or was it rare because the people were not seeking the Lord?"

I was very challenged by this as it made me consider my own walk with the Lord. Lately, there seemingly has been no "divine revelation" in my life, and I have been very frustrated by that. But whose fault is it that I have not heard from the Lord—mine, or the Lord's? It's my fault, because the Bible clearly says that if we seek the Lord, we shall find Him.

We need to remember that God *wants* to reveal His divine revelations to us. He wants us to learn, grow, mature, and be used for His mighty purposes. The truth is, He is speaking today, right now, and mightily I might add. The question is, are we listening? Do we even desire to hear what the Lord has to say to us through His Holy Spirit? Our role in the relationship with our Father is to break through the static and noise from this world, set ourselves apart, and be still so that we might hear His voice. He has given us instructions for this, such as fasting and prayer, for example. When was the last time that we fasted and prayed just because we wanted to hear from Him?

The truth is that we want God's divine revelations, but we often don't want to work for it. We just want God to be our drive-thru God and get our order right so that we can get on with the rest of our day. But there is no relationship in that. All of this is to say, there can be great revelation in all of our lives today if we want it.

JUNE 20ᵗʰ

> 1 Samuel 14:6: "Come, let us go over to the garrison of these uncircumcised; it may be that the LORD will work for us. For nothing restrains the LORD from saving by many or few."

The Philistines had encamped against Israel and the Bible tells us that their force was so large that it caused the people of Israel to fear and tremble (1 Samuel 13:6). When King Saul *saw* this, he took matters into his own hands and disobeyed what the Lord had instructed him to do; for Saul was a man who based his decisions on what he *saw*, rather than on who the Lord was and what the Lord had said.

On the other hand, Saul's son Jonathan was a man who walked by faith and not by sight. When he saw this multitude gathering against Israel, he decided to go and face them with only his armor-bearer, saying, "Come, let us go over to the garrison of these uncircumcised; it may be that the LORD will work for us. For nothing restrains the LORD from saving by many or few." Rather than let the situation determine his actions for him, as his father did, Jonathan stepped out in faith, knowing that the Lord could do the impossible.

But how did Jonathan come to this decision? The Lord had not instructed him to do this, and the Holy Spirit had not moved his heart to do it . . . so what was the basis for Jonathan's faith? First, he knew who God was, meaning that he had a relationship with Him. And second, he knew God's promises for that situation as detailed in Joshua 1:9: "Be strong and of good courage; do not be afraid, nor be dismayed, for the LORD your God is with you wherever you go." This is how Jonathan could look at the situation and do as the occasion demanded, because he knew that God was with him (1 Samuel 10:7). Jonathan was a man who knew how to walk in faith, because Jonathan was a man who knew God's mind and heart toward His people.

Oftentimes we will look at a situation and determine the outcome of that situation based on what we see and think; we then end up making our decisions based upon those factors alone. But where is God in this decision-making process? Do we give Him an opportunity to be faithful, as Jonathan did here? As believers, we should allow God to open and close doors for us as we consider who He is and what He has said about that situation, for "it may be that the LORD will work for us. For nothing restrains the LORD from saving by many or few." So, believer, as Ron Daniel well said, "It doesn't matter how small, how few, how weak, how unimpressive you are," if God is for us, who can possibly be against us (Romans 8:31)?[81]

JUNE 21st

Philippians 2:8: "And being found in appearance as a man, He humbled Himself and became obedient to the point of death, even the death of the cross."

Jesus simply amazes me. The more I learn about Him, the more I am simply in awe of all He has done and is doing for us today. Look at this verse, for example. Jesus—God—willingly came down from heaven and was "found in appearance as a man" for our sake. Other verses affirm this as well: "And the Word [Jesus] became flesh and dwelt among us" (John 1:14); "For God did not send His Son into the world to condemn the word, but that the world through Him might be saved" (John 3:17).

I cannot state in words how this must have been for Jesus. I can only liken it to us becoming a cockroach to save cockroaches. Imagine what that would be like—knowing everything you know right now about living, eating, and cleanliness, and then becoming a cockroach and living in the slime and filth of their world, all the while knowing you would die an excruciating death for them. Would you do that? Yeah, neither would I.

We also see that Jesus "humbled Himself and became obedient to the point of death, even the death of the cross." This is what really hit me, the obedience that Jesus had to the will of the Father. In Isaiah 53:1–12, the prophet Isaiah foretells of Jesus' sufferings for us. So much of what Isaiah wrote revealed how awesome Jesus really is, but something specific jumped out to me: "He was oppressed and He was afflicted, yet He opened not His mouth. He was led as a lamb to the slaughter, and as a sheep before its shearers is silent, so He opened not His mouth" (Isaiah 53:7).

This is pure unadulterated obedience. Jesus was an innocent man. He did nothing wrong, never once sinned, and yet here He was being crucified by the very people that He was saving—and yet, we are told that He did not say a word. He was silent. He didn't spite them, He didn't rebuke them, and He didn't try to defend Himself. Jesus was obedient unto death, even the death of the cross. The most painful, excruciating, humiliating death you can possibly imagine, Jesus endured, and He never even said a word. That is simply incredible to me. We are all very aware of how hard it is to not defend ourselves when we are wrongly accused for anything, but unto death . . . even death on the cross?

And after it was all over, and Jesus endured the cross for our sake through His own willing obedience, Isaiah wrote, "He [God] shall see the labor of His [Jesus] soul, and be satisfied" (Isaiah 53:11). Here is the promise that makes it all worthwhile. Willing obedience to the Father's will always leads to a satisfaction that goes beyond this world and beyond our understanding. And this is what has encouraged me to try and be obedient to all that Jesus has called me to be obedient to, because I want to look back and see the labor of my soul and know that God was satisfied.

JUNE 22ⁿᵈ

2 Samuel 22:20: "He delivered me because He delighted in me."

It is very easy for us to have a relationship with God that is based on us trying to earn His favor. Why wouldn't we naturally defer to this type of relationship, when that is basically what we have experienced from the time we were brought into this world? When we do something good, people like us more; when we do something bad, they like us less. And so we do the same with God. When adversity comes into our lives, we feel that we must have done something wrong to cause this to happen; we begin to believe that if we do enough good things for God, then He will rescue us from that situation. And on and on it goes.

In 2 Samuel 22, David recounts a time "When the waves of death surrounded me, the floods of ungodliness made me afraid. The sorrows of Sheol surrounded me; the snares of death confronted me" (2 Samuel 22:5–6). So what did David do when he found himself face to face with death? "In my distress I called upon the LORD, and cried out to my God; He heard my voice from His temple, and my cry entered His ears" (2 Samuel 22:7). It was then that the Lord "delivered me from my strong enemy, from those who hated me; for they were too strong for me. They confronted me in the day of my calamity, but the LORD was my support" (2 Samuel 22:18–19).

Notice that all David did was call upon the Lord for help in his time of need, and the Lord delivered him. Why, though? Was it because David was such a good man? Was it because he followed the Law, or because he did so many good deeds? No, "He delivered me because He delighted in me." Isn't it awesome to know that God delights in you, not because of what you do or don't do, but simply because that it is just who God is? We love to put conditions on why God delights in us, but the simple truth is that God delights in us because He is God, and that is just His nature.

So let us be like David today and sing this song of praise to the Lord: "The LORD is my rock and my fortress and my deliverer; the God of my strength, in whom I will trust; my shield and the horn of my salvation, my stronghold and my refuge; my Savior, You save me from violence. I will call upon the LORD, who is worthy to be praised; so shall I be saved from my enemies" (2 Samuel 22:1–4).

JUNE 23rd

> 2 Samuel 22:25: "Therefore the LORD has recompensed me according to my righteousness, according to my cleanness in His eyes."

We often make the mistake of defining ourselves by how we see and what we think of ourselves. Being that we know ourselves best, we can justify the conclusion that we come to about who we are based on what we have done. Yet here is David, singing a song of praise to God as he declares his innocence and righteousness. How can this be, though? This is the man who willingly committed adultery and murder, who made numerous bad decisions by not seeking the Lord and was a sinner just like you and me. Yet he says here, "The LORD has recompensed me according to my righteousness." What righteousness did David have? By himself, none; but by God, he had abundant righteousness through God's amazing grace.

In 2 Samuel 12:13, Nathan the prophet told David that "the LORD also has put away your sin." David fully believed in what the Lord had said to him through Nathan; because of that, David could confidently say that his hands were clean "according to my cleanness in His eyes." Notice whose viewpoint David was looking from when he defined himself. It wasn't according to what David saw, or what others saw; rather, it was according to what God saw. He was clean in God's eyes. Herein lies the victory from the burden of condemnation that sin brings into our lives: We are completely clean from sin in God's sight, according to how He sees us. And really, that is all that matters.

So how does God see believers? "For He made Him who knew no sin to be sin for us, that we might become the righteousness of God in Him" (2 Corinthians 5:21). When God looks at us, He does not see our sin; He only sees His Son Jesus Christ. This is not to say that we should take our sin lightly, or take for granted the amazing grace that He has afforded us through what Jesus did on the cross; but it is to say that we can live free of the condemnation of sin. We can be free of what we think of ourselves and rest in the truth of how God sees us. So, believer, stop defining yourself by how you or others see you, and start defining yourself by how God sees you.

JUNE 24th

Luke 10:33: "And when he saw him, he had compassion."

While I was at work yesterday, Michelle called me from home and told me that the police had blocked off the only street into our apartment complex. She said there were a lot of police cars, a couple fire engines, and an ambulance in the gym parking lot right across the street. She found out a little bit later that there was an armed gunman sitting in his car, threatening to kill himself. So what was my first prayer upon hearing this? "Lord, please clear all of this up so that I can get home." Really, Patrick? It was then that Michelle awakened me to the reality of the situation, and we prayed for this man and for his salvation.

This whole thing reminded me of the story that Jesus told of the good Samaritan. A Jewish man once went down to Jerusalem and fell among thieves. They stole his belongings, beat him to the point where he was almost dead, and then just left him lying on the side of the road to die. A priest walked up, saw him lying there, and then went to the other side of the road and kept on walking. So did a Levite. "But a certain Samaritan, as he journeyed, came where he was. And when he saw him, he had compassion." So he bandaged the man up, brought him into town and took care of him. The most important part of this story that you need to know is that Samaritans were despised by the Jews; yet this Samaritan had compassion on the man that, by the culture in that day, despised him.

So why did the priest and the Levite pass on by and not help one of their own? I believe it was because they bought into the same exact lie that we buy into today when we choose to not have compassion on someone: They were on a tight schedule that did not allow room to get involved and help this man. I will admit it, when I heard of our street being closed because of this man in the gym parking lot, my first reaction was that my daily schedule had been interrupted; he became an inconvenience to me rather than a human being who was struggling with life. He became a burden rather than a lost soul who needed to be prayed for.

We have become so comfortable in our daily routines that if there is one deviation from our normal routine, we get thrown into a tailspin. We become very angry because we are taken out of our comfort zone. The truth is that our daily routines have become a form of bondage for us as they keep us from following the leading of the Holy Spirit. Having deviations from our daily routine actually frees us from living the life of the zombie, where we just mindlessly go about our day.

These divine interruptions are what keep us alive, if you will; they keep our hearts from growing cold and callous. Our daily routines, and the comfort we find in them, are focused all on self; and when we are focused only on self, it is very hard to choose compassion when others are in need. So, believer, break free from your daily routine today by purposefully praying for opportunities that would help you deviate from it. You will be glad you did, as "whoever is kind to the needy honors God" (Proverbs 14:31, NIV).

JUNE 25th

> 1 Kings 12:8: "But he rejected the advice which the elders had given him, and consulted the young men who had grown up with him, who stood before him."

One day, my eight-year-old nephew Sean walked into my room and asked me how to get through a certain level in a video game that he was playing. Now, if you are not a gamer, you need to understand that there are multiple ways to try and get through each level in a video game, but only one way gets you through it properly. Sean knew that I had already been through that level, and so he came and asked me to show him how to get through it the right way.

I was reminded of this as I was reading 1 Kings 12. King Rehoboam, Solomon's son, was faced with a situation where he needed wisdom and guidance. So he went and consulted with the elders who had advised Solomon during his reign and they gave Rehoboam very wise counsel. "But he rejected the advice which the elders had given him, and consulted the young men who had grown up with him, who stood before him."

There are a couple of problems here as I see it. First, Rehoboam relied on his friends rather than on those who were more spiritually mature than him. When I got saved, the first place that God led me to was a men's Bible study where I was surrounded by older, more mature men. This is where I learned and grew the most as a believer, because I listened and gleaned wisdom from these men. They were the ones I would go to when I needed counsel, not my friends.

Too often today, I see believers avoid certain Bible studies simply because the people in those studies are older than they are; they would rather be around people their own age, or on their same level. But if we do this, how will we ever grow? How will we ever know how to get through all of the different levels of life, if everyone we seek wisdom and counsel from is on the same level we are? Please understand, I am writing this under the assumption that we all go to the Lord first and foremost in all things; but also note that the Bible says in Proverbs 11:14 that in the multitude of counselors there is victory. The Lord wants us to seek out mature believers for wisdom and counsel; and when we receive that wisdom, we are to hold it up to the Bible and ask the Lord to confirm it, allowing Him to direct our paths.

Second, Rehoboam was seeking those who would give him the advice that he wanted to hear. Too many times, we bounce around seeking wisdom from others until we finally find someone who will tell us exactly what we want to hear. This is why we often go to our friends rather than the elders of the church, because we want to hear what we want to do and not be corrected. This is not wisdom. I purposefully have men in my life who I know without a doubt will correct me when I am wrong and will give me sound wisdom even if it is not what I want to hear. This is the wisdom the Lord wants us to exercise when we seek counsel from others.

So, believer, who do you go to when you need counsel, and why do you go to them? Is it because they are your friends, or because they are more mature in the Lord? Are you seeking them so you can hear what you want to hear, or are you seeking them because you know that they will tell you the right thing to do?

JUNE 26th

> 1 Kings 13:9: "For so it was commanded me by the word of the Lord, saying, 'You shall not eat bread, nor drink water, nor return by the way you came.'"

There will be many times in our walk with the Lord when we will be instructed to do or say something that will be very difficult for us to follow through with. And as hard as that thing might be to do, the real challenge will come after we have been obedient to the Lord, because it is there that we will be confronted with the temptation to compromise where we just stood firm.

For example, one day "a man of God" went to King Jeroboam and gave him a word from the Lord that basically foretold of Jeroboam's destruction. When Jeroboam ordered this man to be arrested, Jeroboam's hand became withered and lame, thus leading Jeroboam to beg the man of God to pray for him that God might heal his hand. The man of God graciously prayed for Jeroboam and his hand was restored.

As a reward for his service, Jeroboam invited the man of God to come back with him and "refresh" himself with food and drink, to which the man of God said, "For so it was commanded me by the word of the Lord, saying, 'You shall not eat bread, nor drink water, nor return by the way you came.'" So the man of God left Bethel, following what the Lord had instructed him to do.

But then, as the man of God was resting under an oak tree—tired, hungry, and thirsty from his journey—"an old prophet" came from Bethel and invited the man of God to go back to town for food and drink. The man of God stood firm once again and repeated to the old prophet what the Lord had told him. The old prophet replied to the man of God, saying that he too was a prophet and that an angel spoke to him by the word of the Lord saying, "Bring him back with you to your house, that he may eat bread and drink water" (1 Kings 13:18). And so the man of God went with the old prophet, back the way he came, and ate food and drank water in Bethel—doing exactly what the Lord had specifically told him not to do. Ultimately, that act of disobedience would cost the man of God his life.

The temptation to compromise after we have stood firm in obedience will always seem less significant than that in which we were instructed to stand firm. Because of that, the temptation to give in usually wins out because it seems so harmless. I remember when Michelle and I cancelled our vacation the day before we were supposed to leave because the property owner asked us to lie to their neighbors about renting the place out. We were very firm in the fact that deception is wrong, and we were not comfortable taking part in that. Later that night, as we went to the movies, we brought in water and snacks even though the movie theatre specifically says that those things are not permitted. As we talked about it after the movie, we were both convicted by our act of deception, even though it seemed so insignificant to us at the time.

So, believer, be on guard against the temptation to compromise after you have had a victory in obedience; and never, ever, take man's word over God's, even if it comes from another believer.

JUNE 27th

1 Corinthians 2:10: "But God has revealed them to us through His Spirit."

When Michelle and I brought home our baby daughter from the hospital, there were many decisions we had to make regarding feeding, sleeping, wake times, etc. We had read books and sought counsel from other parents about these things, but nothing seemed to work for Kate. Ultimately, we came to realize that no one knows Kate the way that God does, and so we began diligently seeking the Lord as to what

His schedule for her was. That has been our prayer ever since, "Lord, give us Your heart and mind to know how to raise Kate this day."

The apostle Paul was trying to get a similar point across to the church in Corinth when he wrote 1 Corinthians 2. He wanted the believers there to understand what true wisdom was and where true wisdom came from. "Eye has not seen, nor ear heard, nor have entered into the heart of man the things which God has prepared for those who love Him" (1 Corinthians 2:9). The first thing that Paul says to them is that wisdom cannot be attained through human efforts, meaning that we cannot attain wisdom by using our strengths or our senses. Paul was essentially quoting Zechariah 4:6, which says, "'Not by might nor by power, but by My Spirit,' declares the Lord." That is why Paul made it clear, "But God has revealed them to us through His Spirit. For the Spirit searches all things, yes, the deep things of God" (1 Corinthians 2:10).

Throughout the Bible we learn that God is the only source of wisdom. Everything else apart from God is not wisdom, but rather a feeble attempt at wisdom by using human means. The only way to truly attain wisdom is through God's Holy Spirit, "Even so no one knows the things of God except the Spirit of God" (1 Corinthians 2:11). And this wisdom is only available to believers, "But the natural man [unbeliever] does not receive the things of the Spirit of God [wisdom, truth, etc.], for they are foolishness to him; nor can he know them, because they are spiritually discerned" (1 Corinthians 2:14).

What Paul is getting across to us here is that, if God is wisdom—which He is—and if wisdom is revealed through His Holy Spirit—which it is—then how can anyone who does not have the Holy Spirit dwelling within them through a personal relationship with Jesus Christ have wisdom? They can't—which is a very uneasy notion to ponder when you consider how many people are in positions of power throughout the world today and are not saved. This is ultimately why Paul reminds us to pray for all men, especially those in authority, so that we might live quiet and peaceable lives (1 Timothy 2:1).

JUNE 28th

> 1 Corinthians 2:12: "Now we have received, not the spirit of the world, but the Spirit who is from God, that we might know the things that have been freely given to us by God."

So how do we receive the Lord's wisdom that He has "freely" given to us? Well, logic has it that if something has been freely given to us, then we don't have to try to work for it; rather, we just need to ask for it. "If any of you lacks wisdom, let him ask of God, who gives to all liberally and without reproach, and it will be given to him" (James 1:5).

The problem that we get ourselves into, when asking for wisdom, is that we often expect some huge, divine outpouring of wisdom the very moment we ask for it—and when that doesn't happen, we begin to believe that our prayer did not "take." God either did not hear us, or He just decided not to answer us. This is when we begin to get anxious and rashly take on the belief that either James 1:5 is not true, God is not faithful, or that we must have to do more to get the Lord's wisdom.

Listen to James 1:6: "But let him ask in faith, with no doubting, for he who doubts is like a wave of the sea driven and tossed by the wind." Have you ever seen a balloon being tossed around by the wind? That is what we go through mentally when we ask God for wisdom and do not believe that He has given it to us. James makes it clear that when we ask for wisdom, we are to know, by faith in God, that He has given it to us, even if we do not "feel" like we have received it.

As Michelle and I have been asking God for wisdom as to what feeding/sleeping schedule our daughter Kate should be on, we never once felt a surge of wisdom or clarity at any moment after praying. And at times we became very frustrated, because we did exactly what the Lord instructed us to do and asked Him for wisdom. We know He is good, we know He hears us, so what is the problem? The challenge for us in these times is to know that God is faithful, and that He will give us the wisdom when it is needed because He knows exactly what we need and exactly when we need it. When it is time for us to make that decision, we will have His perfect wisdom.

One thing that Michelle and I had to remember about Kate is that babies are a moving target, as they are always changing. Ultimately God knows the seasons that Kate will be going through day by day, and as we ask for His wisdom, He continually gives us divine insight in how to raise her that day. He has done this mostly through conversations with other parents at just the right moment. One day Mandy will give us a word of knowledge; the next day it will be Coral, or Julie, or Holly, or Korine, or a host of others whom God has used to help us. Regardless, each day He meets our need for wisdom.

So, believer, when you ask God for wisdom, even though you may not feel that He has given it to you, know that you will have it exactly when you need it. Think about it like this: If we ask God for His wisdom so that we could make wise decisions, do you really think God would say no to that prayer? Of course He wouldn't, because He desires for us to walk in His wisdom.

JUNE 29th

> Isaiah 41:10: "Fear not, for I am with you; be not dismayed, for I am
> your God. I will strengthen you, yes, I will help you, I will uphold you
> with My righteous right hand."

As I was reading the Bible this morning, I realized something: No matter how hard I may try, I cannot give you the hope, faith, and belief in the Lord that you need for today. All I can do is point you to where these things are in the Bible, and pray that you take them to heart as truth above all other things.

The weird thing about unbelief is that when we do not believe what someone says, it is not a reflection on us, but rather is a reflection on the one we do not believe. For example, if your child comes to you and tells you something and you do not believe them, the reflection of unbelief is not on you, but it is on them. When we do this, we are essentially saying to them, "I don't believe you because you are not trustworthy in this situation." So when difficult situations arise in our lives, and we allow them to move us into fear and despair instead of standing firm on what God's Word promises us, we are basically telling God that we do not believe Him because He is not trustworthy in that situation.

Well, truth be told, God is trustworthy in every situation, and that's what makes this verse so incredibly powerful to me. "Fear not, for I am with you; be not dismayed, for I am your God. I will strengthen you, yes, I will help you, I will uphold you with My righteous right hand." The first thing we see is that God commands us to "Fear not." This command is for every situation in life that we will ever face. And He tells us why we are to never fear: "for I am with you." We are never alone, misplaced, or forgotten. God is always with us, no matter where we are or what we are going through.

Then God gives us another command: "be not dismayed." This means that we should never look to any other person or go to any other place for help, "for I am your God." God says, come to Me for help because I am your God and I will help you. The phrase "I am" cannot be overlooked. It's not that He might be all that we need—no, the Lord Almighty says, "I am," present tense, all that you will ever need. You won't need anything else because "I will strengthen you, yes, I will help you, I will uphold you with My righteous right hand." Notice that all of the promises God makes here state, "I will." He does not say that He will have someone else do it, or that He will leave it for you to do, or that He might do it. No, God specifically and emphatically says, I will do it all myself, because I am your God and I love you.

Did you also notice how God personalized this verse for each and every person who reads it? He says "you" or "your" five times in this one verse. In doing this, He makes it clear that all of these promises are for you. Yes, even you. I think God is trying to tell you and me something very important. He knows exactly where we are, and He knows exactly what is going on in our lives. Nothing about us is ever lost on Him, no matter how small or insignificant it might seem to be. He knows, and He cares. So, believer, find your hope, faith, and belief in His Word, for He is faithful, true, and trustworthy in every situation.

JUNE 30th

Luke 4:10: "For it is written . . ."

A good friend of mine was going through a very difficult time earlier this week, and as I listened to him share about what was going on, how he was feeling, and what he believed to be true, I began to wonder where the truths that he was sharing with me came from. I heard nothing but hopelessness, discouragement, and a powerless, watered-down god. It hit me that what my friend believed to be true in the midst of this difficulty was a gospel of deception, and not the gospel of truth we find in the Bible.

This false gospel stems from a lifelong exposure to wrongful truths, misgivings, misconceptions, Scripture taken out of context, partial truths, etc.—all received from someone, who at some time said to us, "For it is written. . . ." And oftentimes when we are in a trial, believer or not, we often revert and cling to the things that we have heard other people say to us as truth. I don't even think we realize what we believe until another brother or sister comes along and points out to us what the truth really is for us and for our situation, according to the Bible.

I have heard it said that the devil has no new tricks, just new victims. After talking with my friend, and meditating on Scripture, I couldn't agree more. Understand that Satan's most powerful weapon against us is deception. "He [the devil] was a murderer from the beginning, and does not stand in the truth, because there is no truth in him. When he speaks a lie, he speaks from his own resources, for he is a liar and the father of it" (John 8:44). When Satan attacks us, deception will always be involved in his attack. So how do we combat this deception? With the truth. "Sanctify them by Your truth. Your word is truth" (John 17:17).

One of the ways that the devil will often try to deceive us is with the Word of God. For example, in Luke 4, when the devil was tempting Jesus in the wilderness, he said to Jesus, "For it is written . . ." and then quoted most of Psalm 91:11–12. The deception here was taking those verses out of context—and of course, leaving a few key words out of those verses as well. Jesus, knowing the whole counsel of God, in context, rebuked Satan and overcame his deception. And I guarantee you, if Satan tried to pull this on Jesus, the very Son of God who is the Word that became flesh, he will absolutely try to use this tactic against us as well.

So, believer, study, memorize, and know the Word of God, for "Whoever gives thought to the Word will discover good" (Proverbs 16:20, ESV).

JULY 1st

2 Kings 19:6: "Do not be afraid of the words which you have heard."

One day, King Hezekiah received a troubling letter from the king of Assyria, stating that Assyria was going to attack and destroy Jerusalem just as it had done to all of the other kingdoms in the land. "Do not let your God in whom you trust deceive you saying, 'Jerusalem shall not be given into the hand of Assyria.' Look! You have heard what the kings of Assyria have done to all lands by utterly destroying them" (2 Kings 19:10–11). It was true; no other kingdom had been able to withstand Assyria's onslaught. But notice the real attack was neither on Hezekiah nor on Jerusalem; rather, it was on God.

The king of Assyria essentially told Hezekiah, "You cannot trust your God to deliver you, because no other god has been able to stop us. Your God will fail you, just as all of those other gods failed them." This was a spiritual attack on Hezekiah's faith in God. So Hezekiah went to the house of the Lord and "spread [Assyria's letter] out before the LORD" (2 Kings 19:14). The Lord answered Hezekiah by saying, "Do not be afraid of the words which you have heard. . . . I will cause him to fall by the sword in his own land" (2 Kings 19:6–7). And the Lord delivered Hezekiah and the people of Judah just as He said He would.

There are going to be many times in our lives when we are going to receive a bad report about something that is going on with us, our loved ones, or the world. And when the shock of this news reverberates through our hearts and minds, the temptation for us will be to fear and panic and lose all hope in that situation. That's also about the time we will hear the same thing that the king of Assyria said to Hezekiah, "Do not let your God in whom you trust deceive you saying" that everything will be OK, I will deliver you, I will defend you, I will provide for you, etc. It's in these moments that our faith in God is truly tested.

Rather than give in to the temptation to fear and panic and lose hope, and allow that situation to dictate to us what the outcome is going to be, we need to follow Hezekiah's example and take it to the Lord; we need to spread it out before God and see what He has to say about it. I guarantee you that the first thing the Lord will say to us will be the same exact thing that He said to Hezekiah: "Do not be afraid of the words which you have heard," for I am God, I am faithful, I am good, and I am in control. Trust Me, acknowledge Me, and I will direct your paths. So, believer, stand firm, and do not allow the words which you have heard remove your faith from the One who is ever faithful in all things.

JULY 2nd

> Philippians 3:8: "Yet indeed I also count all things loss for the excellence of the knowledge of Christ."

The apostle Paul's greatest aspiration in life was to have a more profound knowledge of who God is. In fact, his desire was so demanding that he essentially counted all things that would hinder this pursuit of God as a loss to him. Please understand, Paul was not satisfied with being saved or with having a topical knowledge of who God is; that is why he basically gave up everything that he had, and everything that he was, just so that he could be free to pursue God without entanglement.

We see a similar example of this fervent desire in the Old Testament when King Josiah went through and purged Jerusalem from every idol, high place, and act of perversion that had taken place in and around the temple; this was all done just so he could draw closer to God through unblemished devotion.

This fervor seems to be missing in the church today. Christians often fall into a measured relationship with God where we go to church, pray, and read our Bibles just so that we can check off the boxes on our list of what being a Christian is; then, once we have done our good Christian duty for the day, our conscience is clear to pursue all the other things that we truly desire to fill our lives with.

When Moses pleaded with God to show him His glory, Moses already knew God, he was already called a friend to God, yet the unrelenting zeal he had to go deeper with God is what ultimately led him to cry out, "Show me Your glory! I want to know You more, Lord!" And if we do not have this same kind of hunger to know God more, we will never be compelled to cry out, "show me Your glory!" (Exodus 33:18, NASB).

Believer, a true relationship with God cannot be sustained by a checklist and it will never be one that is stagnant or tempered, as the hunger to know Him more should never be satisfied. A true relationship with God is an eternal pursuit that requires less of us and more of Him, for "this is eternal life, that they may know You, the only true God, and Jesus Christ whom You have sent" (John 17:3).

JULY 3ʳᵈ

Luke 18:23: "But when he heard this, he became very sorrowful, for he was very rich."

Have you ever thought about what God could do through you if you fully sold out to Him and walked in the power of the Holy Spirit by faith and obedience every day? Notice I did not say "be perfect." I have often heard that if someone were to fully give themselves to the Lord, the Lord could use that person to change the world. Imagine being a modern-day Elijah in the world we live in today. It's a very intriguing thought to have, yet that is all it is—a thought. It never seems to make it past that point because there are things in our lives that we just do not want to give up for the Lord.

And that is the true madness about this thinking, because if we were to fully surrender all things to the Lord, and enthrone Him in our hearts above everything else, all of those "things" would fade away. The desire for them would soon leave us and we would be fulfilled in ways that we cannot even imagine. But even knowing this truth—that completely selling out would actually make us richer and more fulfilled—we still do not do it because we are afraid to give certain things up. We just cannot picture our lives without the things that we have even though deep down we know that God would fulfill us more than having those things ever could.

The rich young ruler in Luke 18 is a classic example of this very thing. This young man was seeking eternal life; he desired it. But when Jesus told him to sell all that he had and give it to the poor, "he became very sorrowful, for he was very rich." His sorrow was not because eternal life was out of his grasp; no, it was because he did not want to give up his riches for God. Now, even though we are saved in Jesus Christ, and our eternity is secure in Him, we often fall way short of who we could be in the Lord because we just don't want to give up our things for Him. We want the things of this world more than we want God, and that is why there are no modern-day Elijahs today. But there can be . . . if we so choose.

Believer, we were made for something much more than the levels of unsatisfaction that this life affords us. We were made to change the world. I pray that we allow God to change the world through us today, one soul at a time.

JULY 4th

> Matthew 27:51: "Then behold, the veil of the temple was torn in two from top to bottom."

I once heard someone say that if you teach a message from your head, you will only reach a person's mind; but if you teach a message from your heart, then you will reach that person's soul. This is the struggle that I found myself facing this morning, finding a devotion to write from my own experiences with God so that your soul, and my soul, might be uplifted and enlightened this day.

Well, as I sat there and thought about the huge, thick, burdensome veil that was seemingly covering my heart this morning, I began to ask myself, "Why do you think there is nothing stirring in your heart, Patrick?" The answer was as easy as it was convicting . . . because at times I can become so familiar with the things of God that I often forget to actually spend time experiencing God.

We often say that prayer is just talking to God, but how many times do we actually talk to God as if He were a person sitting right next to us? How many times do we actually take the time to sit and listen to what God has to say to us? We can get so caught up in theological arguments and doctrines in doing things for God, and doing things of God, that we begin to make those things our relationship *with* God. In turn, that is what we preach to others . . . a heady, cold, distant theology that encourages people to just be content with the things of God, rather than seeking to experience God in the way Moses did when he cried out, "Lord, show me Your glory!" (Exodus 33:18, NASB).

The greatest knowledge of God is not an intellectual knowledge of God, but rather a heart knowledge of God through experience. A friend once told me that it was the prophets who were the greater instruments of change, not the scribes. The scribes shared what they read, but the prophets shared what they experienced.

Believer, remember, when Jesus took our sin and shame on the cross, the veil was torn so that we could go into God's presence and experience Him personally. We are not to follow Him from a distance as Peter once did, finding fellowship outside the temple in the courtyard. No, we are meant to boldly go into the very presence of God and experience Him so that our hearts might be changed; so that we can share those experiences with others so that they might change. God longs to have intimate fellowship with us; His arms are open wide; all we need to do is just "Come" (Matthew 11:28).

JULY 5th

Ezra 8:21a: "Then I proclaimed a fast there at the river of Ahava."

As I was reading through the book of Ezra, I came across this very interesting passage of Scripture. Ezra was in charge of leading a large group of Jews from Babylon back to Jerusalem. Before leaving Babylon, Ezra had everyone spend three days resting, organizing, and rendering vows in preparation to go to Jerusalem; it was then that Ezra realized that something even more important was needed before they could leave the land. "Then I proclaimed a fast there at the river of Ahava, that we might humble ourselves before our God, to seek from Him the right way for us and our little ones and all our possessions" (Ezra 8:21). Ezra knew that even though they were prepared physically, mentally, and materially for this journey, they were not prepared spiritually; and so he had everyone fast and pray so that the Lord would direct their paths and protect them on their journey.

As a new parent, the portion of this verse that really jumped out to me was when Ezra said, "to seek from Him the right way for us and our little ones." Notice that Ezra had the people seek the Lord so that they would know how to lead and protect their children. I was extremely convicted when I read this, because even though Michelle and I have been praying diligently for wisdom and guidance with our baby girl, Kate, we have yet to fast and pray for her; we have yet to humble ourselves before our God, and really seek the right way for her. With all of the decisions that we have to make for our children, just throwing up a prayer every now and then is not going to get it done. We need to deny self for the sake of our children, and fast and pray and seek the Lord so that He might lead us in the right way for them.

This also reminded me that being a parent is so much more than just providing the necessities of life such as food, water, shelter, clothing, hugs, kisses, toys, etc., for our children. We have to battle for them in prayer because our enemy is their enemy, and he "walks about like a roaring lion, seeking whom he may devour" (1 Peter 5:8). It's no coincidence that the day after we dedicated Kate to the Lord, she began waking up in the middle of the night crying. That was when I realized I had been praying so much for the Lord to protect her physically from disease and such that I had neglected to pray for the Lord to protect her spiritually as well. I will never make that mistake again. As Nancie Carmichael wrote regarding the desperate need for parents to pray for their children, "The courses of our children's lives are changed and their history is altered because of prayer."[82] May it be so today!

JULY 6th

> 1 Peter 4:8: "And above all things have fervent love for one another, for 'love will cover a multitude of sins.'"

A brother from church sent me this verse Thursday morning. As I read it, the Lord showed me something that I had never seen before. I have always believed that this verse was instructing us to love others in such a way that when they sin against us, we could show them the same grace that has been shown us through our Lord and Savior Jesus Christ. And rightly so, we should love others in this way so that they would come to know Christ. But this morning I realized that we are to love others not so much for their sake, but for our sake, so that when they sin against us, that love will keep us from harboring anger and bitterness toward them. In other words, having this love will cover the multitude of *our* sins, not theirs.

In this section of verses, Peter begins by writing, "But the end of all things is at hand; therefore be serious and watchful in your prayers" (1 Peter 4:7). John MacArthur explained that the realization of Christ's return is being fulfilled as we speak; because of that, we need to keep the "proper eternal perspective" about who we are in Christ and where our home truly is.[83] First John 3:3 reminds us that when we keep this perspective, we will be purified just as He is pure, meaning that we will be able to live above this world and not let it change us or influence our decisions.

"And above all things have fervent love for one another, for 'love will cover a multitude of sins.'" Loving others the way that God instructs us to should always be a choice that we make first and foremost. We shouldn't think about it, pray about it, or consider it; we should do it right away, without hesitation, before the sin of anger can so easily ensnare us. Loving others will also stretch us to our very limits, especially when people purposefully go out of their way to trouble us. And lastly, we need to remind ourselves in these situations that the choice to love others, even when we do not feel like it, will not only hide what they have done to us, but more importantly, it will keep us from committing a multitude of sins against our Lord. For when we hate them, we hate Him.

JULY 7th

Nehemiah 4:20: "Wherever you hear the sound of the trumpet, rally to us there. Our God will fight for us."

Last Wednesday night, Michelle and I got a text from some very close friends of ours. The text was asking for people to meet at their house that night to pray against a false Child Protective Services claim that was going to be submitted by a divisive and troubled family member. Now, even though the claim against them was blatantly false, the threat was still very real; and prayer was definitely needed. So Michelle and I, and some of our beloved brethren, went over to their house and had a great night of fellowship and prayer.

One of the things that I shared with the group that night was this verse from Nehemiah: "Wherever you hear the sound of the trumpet, rally to us there. Our God will fight for us." Nehemiah had been called by God to return to Jerusalem and rebuild the wall around the city. When he got there and began this great undertaking with his brethren, they immediately faced opposition by many of the locals. First, the locals began a whisper campaign to try to frustrate those that were working on the wall, saying that it was a foolish endeavor because it was an impossible task and would never be completed.

When that did not work, the locals began making physical threats against the Jews, saying that they were going to attack Jerusalem and kill all of those who were working on the wall. Understandably, those working on the wall began to fear for their lives and the lives of their families. "The strength of the laborers is failing" (Nehemiah 4:10).

"Then I said to the nobles, the rulers, and the rest of the people, 'The work is great and extensive, and we are separated far from one another on the wall. Wherever you hear the sound of the trumpet, rally to us there. Our God will fight for us'" (Nehemiah 4:19–20). Nehemiah understood the need for all of the workers to stand together in unison against a common enemy. By sending out that text on Wednesday night and having people come over to pray for them, our friends exercised great wisdom and did exactly what Nehemiah said to do here—they sounded the trumpet, the brethren rallied together, and God fought for them.

Believer, sounding the trumpet and rallying together should be the rule for us, not the exception. So whatever it is that you are facing today, tomorrow, or the next day, do not face it alone. Rather, sound the trumpet, rally together, and watch as our God fights for you.

JULY 8ᵗʰ

Psalm 139:7: "Where can I go from Your Spirit? Or where can I flee from Your presence?"

God is here. Wherever we are, there God is. There is no place we can go on this earth where God is not. There are approximately 7.6 billion people scattered throughout the earth right now, and each one of us can rightly say, "God is here with me." God is not nearer to some and farther from others. He is the same exact distance from each person on this earth, whether that person is a spiritual giant or the most carnal of men. God is here. He is with you, and He is with me. Did you know that? More importantly, do you believe that? Have you grasped the fact that God is with you . . . that He is all around you? There is absolutely no place you can go where God will not be.

David knew this for a fact. It was what inspired him to write Psalm 139 and intimately detail for us how personally God has been, and is right now, involved in our lives. On the day I was saved, God very clearly said to me that He had always been right by my side; He assured me that He never left me, not even when I was His enemy and continually rebuked Him time after time. If He was with me then, how much more can I find peace that He is with me now that I am His?

Jacob ran away from his home and believed he had also run away from God's presence; yet after he slept that night in the wilderness, and had that divine encounter with God, he awoke and said, "Surely the LORD is in this place; and I knew it not" (Genesis 28:16). Oftentimes we deceive ourselves by thinking that we can go to those "certain places" and escape God's presence, but we can't. He is in all of those places—whether they are physical locations like Las Vegas, or mental places like where we take a vacation and leave our Christianity behind us. He is also in those private places in our homes when we believe we are all alone. Yes, God is there, too.

I share all of this because the reality that God is with us should help us experience Him more and rejoice in our Lord daily. Think about all of those people in the Bible who had powerful, amazing, divine encounters with God—and then remember that God has no favorites. All that He did for them, He will do for us if we so desire it. Understand that God wants us to discover Him. He longs to manifest Himself to us in new and amazing ways every day. Does that surprise you? Have you always thought that you had to beg and plead for God's presence, or maybe that you had to do enough good things to warrant His attention? The only distance between God and us is not measured by feet or miles, but rather by experience. Those who truly desire to know God more will be "closer" than those who do not, because being "close" to God is a matter of the heart, not distance.

So, believer, know this: God earnestly awaits us to ask Him to manifest Himself that we might know Him and experience Him more. We all have the ability to do this; all we have to do is ask.

JULY 9th

> Proverbs 3:1–2: "My son, do not forget my law, but let your heart keep my commands; for length of days and long life and peace they will add to you."

A couple of years ago, as Michelle and I were talking about all of the different temptations that we face in this life, a question suddenly popped up in my mind: "Are we ever tempted to do good?" And it quickly hit me, yes, we are. Just as we are tempted to do evil things by our flesh, we are also tempted to do good things by the Holy Spirit.

I find it very convicting that when temptation comes to us from our flesh, the world, or Satan, we have to fight with all that we are just to keep from giving in to those evil desires. Yet when we are tempted to do something good by the Holy Spirit, we are able to say no to that temptation without much fight at all.

I was reminded of this last Saturday as I walked out of Costco. A woman approached me and asked me if I had any spare change that I could give her. Before I even considered what the Lord would have me do or say in this situation, I was already doing the "check your pockets" routine while saying, "Sorry, I don't have any cash on me." As she walked away and I got in my car to leave, I had a conversation with myself about my life that went something like this: "Patrick, what good is it to say you are a Christian, go to church, write devotions, teach Bible studies, serve in the prayer room, etc., if you never live it outside of your church bubble? What's the point if it's not real and you do not have the mind and heart of Christ?"

I came to realize that all of the "stuff" I do in and around church is useless if I do not live it out in the lives of others—because by doing just these things, I am no different than the Pharisees of old who looked great on the outside but were rotten bones on the inside. It makes me wonder how narrow the gate that Jesus spoke about in Matthew 7 really is.

Proverbs 3 implores us, "let your heart keep my commands." In other words, get out of the way of the Holy Spirit and allow Him to live His life through you—for as believers, it is no longer you who live but Christ who lives in you (Galatians 2:20). Being obedient to Christ's leading and allowing Him to use us for His purposes is not so much for others as it is for ourselves. In all reality, we are the ones who benefit from obeying Christ because "length of days and long life and peace they will add to you." It's not just eternal life that we receive in Christ; it's quality of life here on Earth as well.

So, believer, when the temptation to do good comes upon your heart and you feel that fear, or that tightening of your daily schedule that quenches out the love of Christ, get out of the way and allow your heart to follow Christ's leading. You will be so glad that you did.

JULY 10th

Nehemiah 2:2: "Why is your face sad, since you are not sick?"

There was nothing physically wrong with Nehemiah, yet the king could see that Nehemiah was struggling mightily on this day. So the king asked Nehemiah, "Why is your face sad, since you are not sick?" Nehemiah responded to the king, "Why should my face not be sad, when the city, the place of my fathers' tombs, lies waste, and its gates are burned with fire?" (Nehemiah 2:3). The city of Jerusalem was completely in ruins. The walls were torn down, the gates were burned, and weeds had overrun the dilapidated structures. Jerusalem was now a shell of its former self—where, at one time, it was the place where God Himself dwelled and where His Shekinah glory shined ever so brightly. Yet now, because of Israel's sin and rebellion against the Lord, it lied in ruins, overrun by those who despised God.

The imagery here could not be more obvious to those of us that have ever felt the ruin that comes from sin and rebellion against God. Whether it was living a life apart from God since birth, or walking with the Lord for a time and then allowing the thorns of this world to choke out His glory, we know all too well why Nehemiah's countenance was so dim. We understand the despair and heartache he was experiencing as he went about his daily duties. We understand the hopelessness he felt because restoration seemed so impossible.

Yet our God is the God of the impossible. He specializes in restoring those things that have been ruined—those things that the world says are damaged beyond repair. God will never "crush the weakest reed or put out a flickering candle" (Isaiah

42:3, NLT). Rather, He gives "beauty for ashes" (Isaiah 61:3) and makes "all things new" (Revelation 21:5). Where we see ruin, God sees opportunity. Our Lord fervently desires to rebuild that which has been ruined and devastated by sin and rebellion. He longs to restore those places where the things of this world have overrun that which was once so precious and pure. Our Savior came and died for this very reason, that He would restore all things unto Himself.

Whatever you have done, wherever you find yourself today, no matter how "ruined" you might be from the things of this world, know that you have a loving Heavenly Father who passionately longs to restore that ruin into something beautiful—because in His eyes, you are of immeasurable value. So return to your loving Stronghold, you prisoners of hope, for the Lord declares that He will set you free from the waterless pit and "restore double to you" (Zechariah 9:11–12).

JULY 11th

> Job 1:1: "There was a man in the land of Uz, whose name was Job."

It seems like whenever Job's name is brought up in a teaching or a casual conversation, trials and suffering are the subject matter. Yet there is so much more that we can learn from this man other than how to endure trials.

The first thing we are told about Job is that he "was blameless and upright, one who feared God and shunned evil" (Job 1:1). The word "blameless" used here actually refers to Job being a complete man. The idea is that he did not follow the ways of the world; rather, he followed the ways of God. In other words, what God instructed him to do he did, and what God instructed him not to do he didn't do. As Ray Stedman explained, Job was blameless because he feared the Lord, and he was upright because he "shunned evil."[84]

This is not to say that Job was perfect, because he wasn't. Normally when we see someone described as "blameless" in the Bible, we automatically think that they are being described as sinless or perfect. Yet we know this is not the case, because all men sin (Romans 3:23). What Job shows us here is that even though we may sin and fall short of God's glorious standard, we can still be considered blameless in the eyes of the Lord if we know how to deal with our sin properly. Job dealt with his sin the way that God had instructed him to, and because of that, he was considered blameless in the eyes of the Lord.[85]

I find it very comforting to know that even though I sin and fall short of God's glorious standard every day, I am still considered blameless in the eyes of the Lord, because the blood of Jesus Christ has removed my sin as far as the east is from the west (Psalm 103:12). The Bible says that when we confess our sin to Jesus, He is faithful and just to forgive us of our sin and cleanse us from all unrighteousness (1 John 1:9). As I tell my three-month-old daughter every day, there is only one name under heaven by which we are saved, and that is Jesus Christ (Acts 4:12). There is no other way to deal with sin and still be considered blameless in the eyes of the Lord.

JULY 12th

Psalm 118:8: "It is better to trust in the LORD than to put confidence in man."

Confidence is a very tricky thing. Not only can it be gained or lost in a matter of seconds; more importantly, it only helps us if it is placed in that which can never fail us. This is what the psalmist was referring to when he wrote, "It is better to trust in the LORD than to put confidence in man."

When our daughter Kate was born three months ago, I quickly gained confidence that I could take care of her when Michelle was out of the house. And for the past two months and three weeks it was, dare I say, easy. Well, this last week was not so easy, and my confidence went right out the window. After I shared this with Michelle, she asked me a question: "Is your confidence in yourself, or is it in God?" She then confessed to me that she has no idea what she is doing day to day with Kate. "That is why I pray so much," she said. Quite simply, Michelle places her confidence in the Lord, not in herself.

This reminded me of something one of our pastors said after he had spent many years successfully planting churches in Europe as a missionary: "Every day, I had no idea what I was doing. I had never planted churches or negotiated deals on large buildings before. That is why we prayed so much, because we had no idea what we were doing." Do you see the pattern here?

Believer, if we place our confidence in anything but the Lord, we will surely fail. This is what Isaiah said in Isaiah 31:1 (NIV), "Woe to those who go down to Egypt for help, who rely on horses, who trust in the multitude of their chariots and in the great strength of their horsemen, but do not look to the Holy One of Israel, or seek help from the LORD." And it's not just trusting God in those certain areas of life that we "feel" inadequate in, but rather in every area of life—especially those that we feel confident in because ultimately those are the areas that we need the most help in. So, believer, place your confidence in the Lord, for the help of man is useless (Psalm 108:12).

JULY 13th

John 15:15: "I have called you friends."

When we first call on the name of Jesus to be our Lord and Savior, we enter into a life we never knew existed; a life where we can find peace, joy, truth, and hope; a life where we can finally find rest for our souls. And much like a newborn baby, we spend all of our time experiencing the newness of life that comes with being adopted into the heavenly kingdom. For many believers, this is where their growth ends; they are content to just be accepted into the kingdom of God and are satisfied with being in the courtyard of the temple.[86]

For others, though, just sitting in the courtyard soaking up their newfound life is not enough for them anymore; they desire purpose and want to be used by Jesus and so they follow Him and do what He tells them to do. Yet even here, serving in the temple just steps away from the Holy of Holies, is where the growth ends for many more believers as they become content with following Jesus and serving Him in ministry.[87]

But there are a rare few who hunger for more of God. Sitting in the courtyard warming themselves by the fire and following Jesus in a master-servant relationship is just not enough for them anymore; they desire to enter into the Holy of Holies, the very presence of God, so that they may walk with Him in the coolness of the garden. These are the ones that Jesus spoke of when He said, "No longer do I call you servants, for a servant does not know what his master is doing; but I have called you friends, for all things that I heard from My Father I have made known to you" (John 15:15).

Those who are called "friends" of God are those who take on the mind and heart of Christ as their own; they are those who forsake their own desires and take on Christ's in their place. Amos 3:3 says, "Can two walk together, unless they are agreed?" To be a friend of God, we must have the same purpose for our life that Christ has for us.

Isaiah wrote in Isaiah 41:8, "But you, Israel, are My servant, Jacob whom I have chosen, the descendants of Abraham My friend." The differences in the three relationships that are described above do not have to do with salvation, but rather intimacy. One is a servant, one is chosen, but only one is called friend and is invited into the secret counsels of God.[88] Believer, do not be satisfied with anything less than this.

JULY 14th

Psalm 118:5 (NIV1984): "In my anguish I cried to the LORD, and he answered me by setting me free."

The psalmist found himself in a very desperate situation: "All the nations surrounded me. . . . They surrounded me on every side. . . . They swarmed around me like bees" (Psalm 118:10–12, NIV1984). In the psalmist's eyes, death was certain; there was nowhere for him to go. So he did what all of us would do in a situation like this: "In my anguish I cried to the LORD, and He answered me by setting me free." God heard this man's prayer and set him free, though the freedom this man received is not what you think.

Let's finish verses 10–12 (NIV1984): "All the nations surrounded me, but in the name of the LORD I cut them off. They surrounded me on every side, but in the name of the LORD I cut them off. They swarmed around me like bees, but they died out as quickly as burning thorns; in the name of the LORD I cut them off." Truly God gave this man victory over all of his enemies, but notice that he still had to face the battles. God did not remove him from his situation; rather, He strengthened him *in* it. "In the name of the LORD I cut them off."

So what was the psalmist referring to when he said that God had set him free? Well, look at what the psalmist wrote directly after he prayed to God for deliverance: "The LORD is with me; I will not be afraid. What can man do to me? The LORD is with me; he is my helper. I will look in triumph on my enemies" (Psalm 118:6–7, NIV1984). I want you to notice that this man's situation hadn't changed; he was still surrounded by enemies on every side. Yet his perspective was completely different now. Why? Because he remembered that God was with him and that God was for him; he knew that nothing could come against him with the Lord by his side, and so his perspective went from defeat to "triumph."

Even though God did not set this man free *from* his circumstances, God set him free *in* his circumstances. No longer did he look at God through his situation; he now looked at his situation through God—big difference. Believer, God will always set us free when we call on Him; just remember, it may not be freedom *from* our circumstances, but rather freedom *in* our circumstances.

JULY 15th

Psalm 1:3 (NLT): "They are like trees planted along the riverbank, bearing fruit each season without fail."

There are certain fruit trees that bear fruit almost every calendar month of the year, and yet sometimes these same trees do not bear fruit every year. There are some fruit trees that bear fruit every year, but yet do not bear fruit every month of the calendar year. To put it simply, none of these trees bear fruit in every season of their lives. Yet the psalmist seemingly states in Psalm 1:3 that there is a specific kind of fruit tree that can bear fruit in every season "without fail." This would be a tree that is "planted along the riverbank."

Of course, the psalmist is not talking about an actual tree here; rather, he is talking about a specific kind of person: "Oh, the joys of those who do not follow the advice of the wicked, or stand around with sinners, or join in with scoffers. But they delight in doing everything the Lord wants; day and night they think about His law. They are like trees planted along the riverbank, bearing fruit each season without fail. Their leaves never wither, and in all they do, they prosper" (Psalm 1:1–3, NLT1996).

Ecclesiastes 3:1 (NIV1984) tells us, "There is a time for everything, a season for every activity under heaven." Solomon then lists all of the different seasons of life, including death, mourning, crying, losing, war, etc. If we were to think about every season of life we go through, who could honestly stand up and say, "Yes, I bear good fruit in every season of life without fail, no matter what season it may be"? I couldn't. Maybe we are like the fruit tree that can bear fruit every month, but not every year. Maybe we are like the fruit tree that can bear fruit every year, but not every month. But who can bear fruit in every season of life without fail? The psalmist makes it clear that only one person can do this: It is the person who does not go to the world for wisdom or fellowship or fulfillment, but rather delights in walking with the Lord, trusting in His commands, constantly filling themselves with Him.

As believers, we should never be content to just endure and survive the seasons of life when the Lord has already told us that we are more than conquerors in Him. We should be purposed to bear fruit in every season of life, regardless what it might be because we know He is good, we know He is in control, and we know He is faithful. We are not being told to be perfect here; we are told to keep our eyes, heart, and mind on Him, because when we do, we will bear fruit in every season. I pray it would be so today for all of us.

JULY 16th

John 1:42: "You are Simon the son of Jonah. You shall be called Cephas."

When Andrew brought his brother Simon to Jesus, Andrew told Simon, "We have found the Messiah (which is translated, the Christ)" (John 1:41). It was then, when Jesus looked at Simon, that He said to him, "You are Simon the son of Jonah. You shall be called Cephas." It is very easy to overlook what Jesus said here because it seems insignificant. Yet upon further review, we learn that it is very significant.

Back in the day, most parents would give names to their children that would describe something very specific about them. Esau, meaning "hairy," was named because he had a lot of hair; Jacob, meaning "heel-catcher," was named because he was holding onto Esau's heel when Esau came out of the womb. The difference is that when God names someone, or changes someone's name, it is always based on who they will become spiritually, not who they are physically. That is why what Jesus said here is so significant.

The name Simon means "little rocks," or "shifting sand." That is who Simon was at that time, as Jesus well said, "You are Simon son of Jonah." In other words, "You are shifting sand. You have no foundation." By saying this, Jesus was describing who Simon was spiritually, not who he was physically. That's what makes the next part of this verse so significant: "You shall be called Cephas," meaning "the rock." "You are Simon, but you shall be Peter. You are shifting sand, but you shall be a rock," Jesus says. Jesus was prophesying about who Simon would become after he gave his life to Jesus Christ and grew in Him spiritually. And notice that this wasn't something that was going to happen overnight; no, this was going to be a process that would take some time.

Peter would also have a new ancestral heritage that would define him. No longer would he be identified by blood or earthly relations or what he did or didn't do on this earth; he would now be identified by who he was in Christ. The same goes for us. When we met Jesus for the first time and gave our lives to Him, He gave us a new name that identifies who we are in Him, not who we were in this world. So, believer, let go of the past; break free from who you once were in this world; remove those things that restrict your growth, and walk in the newness of life.

212 Renovating Your Mind

JULY 17th

1 Corinthians 2:5: "[Y]our faith should not be in the wisdom of men but in the power of God."

I once heard that if you can talk someone into the kingdom of God, then they can be talked right out of it as well. In other words, we all have to come to salvation by the power of God, not by the power of man's words. In order to truly repent of our sin, we need to understand that we are sinners in need of a Savior. Thus, the apostle Paul only preached "Christ crucified" (1 Corinthians 2:2)—not some prosperity gospel, and not the Law, but the simple yet profound truth of Christ crucified.

To the Jews and the Greeks, this didn't make any sense. A Messiah who was crucified? By their mere definitions, these two words completely contradict one another. This is why Paul said it was a stumbling block to the Jews and foolishness to the Greeks (1 Corinthians 1:23). But in this, Paul teaches us a very valuable lesson in how to share the gospel with others. He says that we should not come with "excellence of speech [as a gifted or talented speaker] or of wisdom [as a logical thinker]" nor with "persuasive words [think of a used car salesman]," but rather "in demonstration of the Spirit and of power that your faith should not be in the wisdom of men but in the power of God" (1 Corinthians 2:1, 4). For it's only the gospel of Jesus Christ that "is the power of God to salvation" (Romans 1:16).

Quite simply, Paul says that we are to speak the truth of the gospel and nothing further. We should not strive or stress ourselves to try and think of creative ways and wise arguments to win people for the kingdom, but rather we should speak the truth of the gospel as we are led by the Holy Spirit. When we do, there will be a demonstration of the power of God through the working of the Holy Spirit in that person's life. It is here that our faith will grow in the power of God, not in the wise words we use or the way that a person came to salvation. So, believer, keep it simple. Preach the gospel and allow the power of the Holy Spirit to do the rest.

JULY 18th

Leviticus 13:3: "deeper than the skin . . ."

I once heard a story about a pickpocket. Apparently, this man was the best; yet even he was not perfect and was eventually caught by the police. The first time he was caught, he was given a warning. The second time he was caught, he was thrown in jail. The third time he was caught, his right hand was cut off; and the fourth time he was caught, his left hand was cut off. Yet even after losing both of his hands, this man still tried to pick people's pockets by using his teeth.

Oftentimes when we hear a story like this, we say to ourselves, "When is enough, enough?" Yet deep down, there is a part of us that can somewhat relate to this man's "plight" as we are all "repeat offenders" with our sin. Maybe the consequences were not as severe as with this man, but nevertheless, we understand all too well the temptation to continue doing that same sin over and over again, even though we know the severe consequences that come from it.

The Bible teaches us that the answer to sin is never going to be rehabilitation, but rather rebirth.[89] And contrary to what some people may say today, we do not have a gun-control problem, or a race problem; we have a sin problem. In other words, there has to be a changing of our heart, spiritually, not a changing of our flesh—because our flesh will never change. We gain some great insight into our sin problem in Leviticus 13:3 when the Lord gave Moses and Aaron instructions on the characteristics of leprosy, which in the Bible represents sin: "The priest shall examine the sore on the skin of the body; and if the hair on the sore has turned white, and the sore appears to be deeper than the skin of his body, it is a leprous sore."

Notice we are told that leprosy is "deeper than the skin." It doesn't matter if you cut off a person's hands, gouge out their eyes, confiscate all the guns, or have more race-sensitivity training. Unless there has been a changing of the heart, there is going to be a sin problem because sin goes deeper than the skin; it goes all the way to the heart.

Thankfully there is an answer to our sin problem; it is found in the promise we have in Jesus Christ. The Bible tells us that Jesus will give us a new heart and a new Spirit to live within us when we surrender our lives to Him (Ezekiel 36:26). At this point, we are no longer slaves to sin. We now have the power to choose not to sin even though we may be tempted to sin. We do this by walking in the Spirit because when we continually pursue God, we shut out the world, including our flesh (Galatians 5:16). So, believer, do not battle the flesh with the flesh, but rather overcome the flesh through the power of the Holy Spirit.

JULY 19th

Judges 5:23: "'Curse Meroz,' said the angel of the LORD, 'Curse its inhabitants bitterly, because they did not come to the help of the LORD, to the help of the LORD against the mighty.'"

A bunch of guys from the couples' study gathered together for a men's Bible study last month, and one of the questions we were asked as part of our homework was, "If you could use one word to describe your walk with God to this point in your life, what would it be?" As I carefully considered this question, the answer that I thought best described my walk with the Lord to this point was "potential." Let me explain.

The Lord has gifted me with incredible spiritual gifts; I have the Spirit of the risen Christ living within me, leading me, and empowering me in all things, for all things. I have access to the Creator of the universe, God Most High, for everything that I will ever need. So the potential for me to be the instrument that God uses to change this world is there, but if I discard my gifts, deny His power, and do not access His throne, then that's all it is—just potential. And that's the thing with potential; you can have all the potential in the world, but if you never fulfill that potential, then it means absolutely nothing.

This is what is said of the people of Meroz in the book of Judges. Apparently they had an opportunity to help the Lord against His enemies, but as W. Glyn Evans pointed out, rather than use their talents for His service, they discarded them and chose to not get involved. "Discarded talent is responsibility shunned, power unexpressed, authority unused."[90] So instead of being deemed worthy in the eyes of the Lord, they were cursed. But it wasn't just the city of Meroz that did this; many others in the Bible have done this as well. Remember when the children of Israel chose not to drive out the inhabitants of the Promised Land, or when John Mark refused to go with Paul and Barnabas on their mission to Asia Minor?[91] On and on the stories go of unfulfilled potential—of believers discarding those things which would bring change and victory and light to those who need them.

Believer, God has gifted every one of us in amazing and incredible ways. We have the Spirit of the risen Christ living within us, empowering us for great and mighty works. We have access to the God Most High for everything that we will ever need. So, the potential for us to be the instruments that God will use to change this world is there . . . but, will that potential be fulfilled, or will it be wasted? The choice is ours to make.

JULY 20th

Romans 8:24: "For we were saved in this hope."

It is said that if you only considered the external circumstances of a believer and an unbeliever, there would be no difference between the two.[92] This is because believers and unbelievers alike will go through hard times physically, emotionally, mentally, economically, etc. So what separates the believer from the unbeliever? Hope.

In society today, we use the word "hope" as something that may or may not come about, such as, "I hope my team wins on Sunday." But in the Bible, the word "hope" means to know something for certain—to expect it to happen. This is the difference between a believer and an unbeliever. As believers, we should be different from unbelievers in that we should never be given to hopelessness or despair in our situations, because we know that all things work together for the good of those who love God (Romans 8:28). Yes, we will all have trouble in this life, but we know that God will use that trouble for His glory and for our betterment. The unbeliever has no such hope.

We see a great example of this in Hosea 2:14–15 as the Lord says that He will often bring His people into the wilderness, into the Valley of Achor (which means Valley of Trouble), and will speak comfort to their hearts and provide for their every need so that the Valley of Achor will not be a valley of despair, but rather "a door of hope." This mirrors what Romans 5:3–5a says, "And not only that, but we also glory in tribulations, knowing that tribulation produces perseverance; and perseverance, character; and character, hope. Now hope does not disappoint." We will never have the hope we need to endure the trials of this life if we never go into the Valley of Achor, because it is there that sin—and impurities like unbelief, despair, and the world—are purged out of our lives so that we may be free of them.[93]

It's interesting to note that the Valley of Achor is named after the stoning of Achan and his family. If you recall, Achan took some treasures that he was not supposed to take and hid them under his tent, thus bringing sin into Israel's camp. That sin had to be purged out of Israel if they were going to continue conquering the Promised Land. So it is with us. We all have things hidden deep down within us that need to be purged. Some things are known to be there and some things aren't. Regardless, they need to be removed so that our hope will be strengthened and purified. So, believer, though we might be in the Valley of Achor right now, with Jesus, it is always a door of hope.

JULY 21st

Isaiah 59:2: "But your iniquities have separated you from your God."

The day after Kate was born was really the first time that I was able to spend some quality time with her; and I must say, it was life-changing. All we did was hold hands and stare at one another for more than an hour. It was then that I began to experience a love that I had never known before. It was as if something within me woke up that was previously dormant and unused. It was the love of a father for his child.

When I went back to work two weeks later, I began experiencing something else that I had never experienced before . . . the separation between a father and his child. My heart ached that day like it never had before. It was not because my daughter was in danger or because she was in pain; it was simply because I was separated from her. All I could think about was getting back home so I could be with her again.

On a much larger and deeper scale, this is how God feels about each one of us. We learn throughout the Bible that the love a parent has for their child is a symbolic picture of the love that God has for us. I say symbolic because God's love for us is not only perfect, but it is also far greater than any love we could ever have for our children, and that is saying a lot. "But your iniquities have separated you from your God."

So imagine how God must feel when He is separated from us because of our sin and rebellion. It is one thing to be separated from your child because of your job; it is quite another to be separated from your child because of sin. It must crush God to see His children willingly choose death over life. I honestly don't know what I would do if Kate treated me the way that I often treat God. I don't know how I could handle watching her destroy herself, suffering through pain and anguish, all the while rebuking my desperate pleas to love and help her. This is what God experiences on a daily basis and on a much larger scale.

I think when we begin to fully understand the Father-child love affair that God has with us, we will begin to make different choices for our lives, as we often sin believing that it hurts no one. Yet this is not true. Sin separates us from our Father, and it hurts Him greatly when we do this. So, believer, the next time you look at your child with those loving eyes, always wanting the best for them, always wanting to protect them and keep them from danger, remember, this is exactly how God looks at you.

JULY 22nd

Zechariah 7:14c: "This is how they made the pleasant land desolate."

There was a time when Jerusalem was filled with children laughing and playing in its streets; when the elderly could sit around and feel safe and secure behind its great walls (Zechariah 8:4–5). There was a time when Jerusalem prospered greatly, had the most magnificent temple ever seen, and thoroughly defeated all of its enemies that rose up against them. Yet here in Zechariah, we read about how Jerusalem's streets were now vacant, its walls were torn down, the temple destroyed, and their enemies victorious over them. What changed?

> They refused to pay attention [to God]; stubbornly they turned their backs and stopped up their ears. They made their hearts as hard as flint and would not listen to the law or to the words that the LORD Almighty had sent by His Spirit through the earlier prophets. So the Lord was very angry. "When I called, they did not listen; so when they called, I would not listen," says the LORD Almighty. "I scattered them with a whirlwind among all the nations, where they were strangers. The land was left so desolate behind them that no one could come or go. This is how they made the land desolate." (Zechariah 7:11–14, NIV1984)

It is very easy for people to blame God and say that He brought all of this on the nation of Israel, but Zechariah makes it very clear who is at fault here. "This is how *they* made the pleasant land desolate." God did not bring this on His people; they brought it on themselves. Understand that this was not just a onetime thing that all of the sudden happened one day. No, this took years of compromise, slowly drifting away from God until they were so far gone that they refused to even listen to God anymore. "Then they despised the pleasant land; they did not believe His word" (Psalm 106:24). They despised God and all He had done for them. They basically got to the point where they said, "God, we don't need You, nor do we want You. We don't need to follow Your instructions, nor listen to Your commands. We know what is best. Thanks, but we are good." So God let them have what they wanted: a life without Him.

I see the same thing happening in America today. God has blessed this country tremendously because it was built on Him and His Word; in the beginning, our Founding Fathers listened to His instructions and followed His commands. But slowly, over time, we have drifted away from Him and are now saying the same exact thing that the people of Israel said, "We don't need You, God." If we continue down this path, it will be said of us as well, "This is how they made the pleasant land desolate."

But the term "pleasant land" does not only refer to our country; it also refers to our personal lives as well. The pleasant land is also your business, your family, your marriage, and your life. Have these things become desolate and run-down, a shell of what they once were? God wants to bless and enrich and cultivate these things so that they will prosper and bear much fruit. But that can only happen if we make Him our Lord and Savior every day, listening to His instructions and following His commands.

So what will be said about your pleasant land: "This is how they made the pleasant land desolate," or "This is how they made the pleasant land fruitful"?

JULY 23rd

Philippians 2:12: "[W]ork out your own salvation."

In seventh grade, my math teacher gave us the complete freedom to do our math problems as fast or as slow as we needed to. The only requirement she had was for us to show all of our work in how we came up with our answers. My teacher knew that if we didn't have to show our work, we would just go to the back of the book and get all of the answers. In the long run, if we did not know how to work out mathematical problems, we would not know how to solve them later in life.

When the apostle Paul wrote to the believers in Philippi, he told them something very similar, "Therefore, my beloved, as you have always obeyed, not as in my presence only, but now much more in my absence, work out your own salvation with fear and trembling; for it is God who works in you both to will and to do for His good pleasure" (Philippians 2:12–13). Paul is not saying that salvation comes through works because that would be incorrect; salvation comes by grace, through faith in Jesus Christ (Ephesians 2:8–9). Rather, Paul is saying that we have a responsibility to actively take part in the process of being set apart for God's great purposes.[94]

Part of the sanctification process we go through comes about when facing difficult situations. This is where we are refined and our faith is strengthened. The Bible tells us over and over again that we will face hard times in this life, and if we do not know how to mentally work out our faith during those trials, we will fail to allow that perfect work to be completed within us. But it's not just hard times that are used for our sanctification; it's also those times when God calls us to do something. If we do not know how to mentally work out our faith in those callings, we are going to basically be like the children of Israel in that we will just walk around the desert for forty years.

Now, when I say "work out our faith," I am referring to an actual mathematical process that takes place in our mind. Here is the formula: A + B = C. A = God's

Word, B = His character, and C = the answer in our situation. The answer, most often, is not *to* our situation, but rather is *in* our situation—more specifically, to strengthen us in it and through it. But in order to get this answer, we need to know how to show our work, meaning that we need to know what God's Word says, and we need to know who God is. Remember, the only expectation we should have of God is that He will do what He has said He will do, and that He is who He says He is. It is only by having these two things will we be able to work out our faith properly and effectively in every situation. So, believer, what is God calling *you* to do today? How does He want *you* to work out *your* salvation today?

JULY 24th

John 6:68: "Lord, to whom shall we go?"

There have been more times than I would like to admit where I have made the decision to stop walking with the Lord. Frustration, unbelief, and misunderstanding of what the Lord was or was not doing in and around my life fueled my self-righteous indignation against Him. And it was at that point, in that one millisecond when actually I decided to leave the Lord, that I was struck with the same reality that Peter was struck with when the Lord asked him, "Do you also want to go away?" (John 6:67). The reality we both faced was this: Where else can we possibly go? What else *is* there other than the Lord? He alone is life and truth and grace and love. I lived without Him for twenty-nine years, and I found nothing in this world but death. The truth that Peter and I both understood so clearly in these very trying moments is that there is nowhere else *to* go, because there is absolutely nothing in this world better than Jesus.

There will be many times in our lives that we will be given a very "hard saying" from the Lord that we will not understand (John 6:60). It might be a situation that just seems incredibly unfair to us; it might be a lack of the Lord moving when we believe He should be doing something . . . anything! Or, it might be an answer to prayer that we just do not want to hear. Regardless, these are the times when we are most tempted to quit and walk away from the Lord because we just do not understand why it has to be like this. And so, in our carnal and adolescent logic, we believe that leaving Him will force Him to do what we want Him to do.

The truth of the matter is that "many of His disciples went back and walked with Him no more" because of these types of situations, so we are not alone in our thinking (John 6:66). In fact, it was after one of these hard sayings that Jesus looked at the twelve and said to them, "Do you also want to go away?" Yet when faced with the reality of leaving Jesus, Peter rightly said, "Lord, to whom shall we go? You have the words of eternal life. Also we have come to believe and know that You are the Christ, the Son of the Living God" (John 6:68–69).

Peter and the other eleven did not understand what Jesus was saying; they were confused and troubled by the truth of what Jesus had proclaimed. Yet they did not walk away from Jesus. Even though they did not understand, even though it didn't make sense to them, they knew that Jesus was the Christ, the Son of God, the only name under heaven by which all men are saved . . . where else could they possibly go?[95]

This is the same truth that we must gird our minds with, because there will be many times in our walk when we will not understand or even fathom why God is doing what He is doing. It is there, in those moments of temptation to just quit and walk away, that we must stand firm in our faith in Jesus Christ and trust in who He is and in what His Word says. We must grasp onto the reality of what we know to be true—because, honestly, where else are we going to go? Jesus alone has the words of eternal life and He alone is the Christ, the Son of the Living God. So, believer, when faced with these times of difficulty, remember the promise Jesus gave to His disciples: "What I am doing you do not understand now, but you will know after this" (John 13:7).

JULY 25th

> Mark 8:36: "For what will it profit a man if he gains the whole world, and loses his own soul?"

I was speaking with a brother from church the other day about some of the struggles he has been having and why he has been failing in them so often. Below is our conversation:

> Me: "What would happen if you stopped working out and stopped your martial arts training?"
>
> Him: "I guess I would be unfit."
>
> Me: "Would you then be in more danger at work (as a police officer)?"
>
> Him: "Well, yeah, definitely. That's the main reason why I do those things. So that way when a challenge arises, I can overcome it with ease."
>
> Me: "Interesting. If you could picture yourself spiritually, how would your spiritual body look right now?"

Him: "Definitely unfit."

Me: "If your physical body is in better shape than your spiritual body, then there is a problem with your priorities. You said it yourself . . . you train physically so that you can overcome challenges as they arise. Now apply that same truth spiritually. What does it profit a man if he gains the perfect body, but loses his soul?"

The point here is not about whether we should work out or not; it is about having our priorities in the correct order. Last Saturday, myself and a bunch of men from our church gathered together for our monthly Bible study. The challenge that the Lord gave me at the end of Saturday's study was this: "What are you striving to finish strong as?"

For myself, the Lord instructs me to fulfill my role as the spiritual leader of my home as husband to my wife and father to my children, and thus I need to finish strong in those areas. That is the ministry that I am to fulfill first and foremost, after my relationship with the Lord. So my priority should be to involve myself in the things that help me fulfill that ministry, not take away from it.

See, the married couples' study, the men's study, the accountability groups, and all the things like them are not my ministries; they are merely tools to help me fulfill my ministry, which is my wife and children. For what would it profit me if I was the most successful (fill in the blank), but I neglected my wife and children? Absolutely nothing. The same goes for all of us in life as a whole. What would it profit us to have/or be (fill in the blank) if we lost our soul in the process? Absolutely nothing.

So, believer, take an honest assessment of yourself and picture your spiritual body right now. Are you in shape and ready to endure the battle that awaits you? Or are you so spiritually unfit that you cannot even engage in the battle for your soul and for the souls of your loved ones?

JULY 26th

1 Corinthians 4:2: "Moreover it is required in stewards that one be found faithful."

What is the difference between a pastor who faithfully leads his congregation of 20,000 people, has annual crusades where thousands come to salvation, hosts a radio show, writes books to encourage others, goes on mission trips to spread the gospel . . . and a stay-at-home mom who faithfully manages the house, cares for her children, teaches them about Christ, serves her husband, and prays for her family?

In man's eyes, there is no comparison. The pastor is more special; what he is doing is much more important and significant. Yet in God's eyes, He only sees one thing; He only asks one question: "Is that person faithful to what I have called them to do?" God does not look at production as man does; He looks for faithfulness, because ultimately man does not give the increase in any work, God does. God looks for faithfulness because "it is required in stewards that one be found faithful."

My good friend Darrell has a saying, "Comparison is the thief of joy." And he is right. When we compare ourselves to others, sooner or later we will come across someone who is *better* or *more successful* or *more gifted* than we are. And it is there, in that place of comparison, that we lose our joy in the work that God has called us to. We become depressed and discouraged as we begin believing that what God has called us to do is "not as important" as what that other person is doing; and because of that, we stop being faithful to the ministry God has called us to.

In God's eyes, there is no big or small ministry. All God cares about, all that He asks of us, is to be faithful to do what He has called us to do, and to go where He has called us to go . . . that's it. That is all that we can do. Our job is to love the Lord with all of our heart, mind, and strength, and do whatever He says. Yes, it really is that simple. So, believer, be faithful to what God calls you to do, knowing that faithfulness is all that is required of you.

JULY 27th

> Jeremiah 31:34: "For I will forgive their iniquity, and their sin I will remember no more."

One of the worst feelings for a believer is to go to God and ask for forgiveness for something that you just "repented of" yesterday; or to go to God and confess yet another sin, different from the one you just confessed earlier that morning. It begins to feel like a burden to even ask God to forgive us, like we are wearing on Him. Yet in Psalm 86:5, the psalmist reminds us that the Lord "is ready to forgive." Not only does God want to forgive us, but He is also ready and willing to forgive us of our sin.

That is why the Lord said in Jeremiah 31:34, "For I will forgive their iniquity, and their sin I will remember no more." It is extremely difficult to believe this verse when the weight of condemnation is placed squarely on our hearts, yet these are the

Lord's words that He spoke; they are not anyone else's words. This is not a transliteration or an opinion, and it's not debatable or open for interpretation. The Lord said that He will not remember our sin, period.

To reinforce this very important truth, the Bible is littered with this same sentiment over and over again. Psalm 103:12, "As far as the east is from the west, so far has He removed our transgressions from us." Notice that the psalmist did not say "north from the south." If you were to travel north, eventually you would reach the North Pole. Once there, you begin traveling south; whereas, if you were to travel east, and continue on traveling east, you would never meet the west. The Lord says our sin is as far from us as the east is from the west. In other words, it is gone forever.

Think of it like this: On the Day of Atonement, when the high priest would go into the Holy of Holies once a year and confess all of Israel's sin, the blood of the animals would "cover" their sin. Yet, when Jesus Christ shed His blood for our sin and died on the cross, our sin was not covered—it was removed for all time. As Jon Courson well said, "We never need to go to God and say, 'I sinned again Lord' because God doesn't remember the first time we sinned."[96]

"[Insert your name here], I will remember your sin no more." –God

JULY 28th

> Psalm 9:10: "And those who know Your name will put their trust in You."

Matthew Henry said, "The better God is known, the more He is trusted."[97] That is what this verse is literally saying to us right here. It sounds so simple and yet it is so difficult to do . . . or is it? The psalmist reminds us here that when we know who God is, His character, His attributes, then we will trust Him in all of life's issues. But notice the emphasis that is placed in this verse, "will." We *will* trust God, the psalmist says—not we *might* trust God, but we *will* trust God. This is a bold statement to make as trusting God is a choice that we each to have to make every day in every situation. Yet there seems to be a law of trust that is being identified here by the psalmist, and that law says that if we know God, we will trust Him.

The psalmist could make this proclamation without reservation because he knew God; and he was confident that if anyone truly knew God, as he did, there would be no way that person could ever *not* trust God. The key is in the word "know." This does not speak of a knowledge *of* someone, but rather refers to a knowledge that is gained by experience through a personal relationship. Job exemplified this for us in Job 13:15 as he did not understand why everything was taken from him, or why his children were killed, or why he was severely afflicted. Yet because he knew God so intimately, he could rightly say, "Though He slay me, yet I will trust Him."

Job knew full well that God had allowed all of these things to come about in his life and yet even when presented with such a perplexing truth, he still proclaimed, "yet I will trust Him." This kind of trust supersedes understanding and circumstances because it does not take into account either one of these things when making the decision to trust God or not; it only looks at God and makes the decision to trust based on who God is, not at what the situation says.

The challenge the psalmist presents to us here is one that is very revealing and yet very convicting: "those who know Your name *will* put their trust in You."

JULY 29th

1 Corinthians 6:11: "And such were some of you."

The day after I got saved was Easter Sunday, and it marked the first time I went to church as a brand-new creation. But as I walked up to the church, something strange happened: I began to tremble with fear; so much so that the only thing I could do to keep moving forward and not turn back was to look at the ground and avoid making eye contact. Throughout the entire service my eyes never left the floor, because I was absolutely sure that everyone there knew I did not belong. I was completely convinced that they saw all the filth, muck, and sin that I had basked in for twenty-nine years. It wasn't until about a year-and-a-half later that the Lord showed me I wasn't that person anymore.

In his first letter to the church in Corinth, Paul was addressing a myriad of issues, most of which had to do with the church allowing the ways of the world to creep in. So Paul reminded them, "Do not be deceived. Neither fornicators, nor idolators, nor adulterers, nor homosexuals, nor sodomites, nor thieves, nor covetous, nor drunkards, nor revilers, nor extortioners will inherit the kingdom of God" (1 Corinthians 6:9–10). It is a pretty comprehensive list, one in which none of us can escape. But then Paul puts it all in perspective for them, "And such were some of you." Notice that Paul wrote this in the past tense. "You were those things," Paul stated. "But you were washed, but you were sanctified, but you were justified in the name of the Lord Jesus and by the Spirit of our God" (1 Corinthians 6:11).

Again, notice that Paul was writing in the past tense, meaning that these things had already taken place. "You were fornicators and idolaters and covetous and all of these other worldly things, but you were washed clean from all of your sin, you were set apart for a significant purpose, and you were made righteous in God's sight. You were freed from shame and death by the blood of our Lord Jesus Christ and you were made brand new through the power of the Holy Spirit. You are no longer that person, so stop thinking that you are. Stop living life as though you are still that person of old." David Guzik pointed out that these worldly ways should not "mark the life" of a believer because we have been made new; we have been given a new heart, a new mind, and a new set of values and desires.[98] Put away the old things, Paul says, and walk in the newness of life.

Believer, it doesn't matter who you once were; it doesn't matter what you once did. All that matters is who you are now and what you do now. So put away those worldly ways and begin living life as who you are in Christ Jesus—because you have been washed, set apart, and made right with God.

JULY 30th

> Genesis 29:35: "And she conceived again and bore a son and said, 'Now I will praise the LORD.'"

Thanksgiving and praise naturally follow the acknowledgment of benefits received. For example, when the Lord saw that Leah was unloved, He opened her womb and gave her many children. After she had her last child, Judah, Leah said, "Now I will praise the LORD." Notice that she only praised the Lord after her *last* child was born.

This is a common occurrence among believers today as well. When God answers a prayer, or when He blesses us in some amazing way, we praise Him and thank Him for His favor. And rightly so: We should always thank and praise the Lord, confessing that it was only because of Him that we have that favor. Yet at the same time, we are told in the Bible to walk by faith and not by sight. So if we are in the habit of only praising the Lord after benefits have been received, are we walking by faith or by sight?

Praise is essentially the natural reaction to trust. Before Jesus raised Lazarus from the dead, He praised God. Before He fed the five thousand, He praised God. Jesus fully trusted in God the Father that is why He could praise Him before, during, and after any situation. If we truly believe that God is who He says He is, and if we truly believe that God will do what He says He will do, then we should praise God just as Jesus did.

When we face difficulties and hard times, we need to believe that Romans 8:28 is in fact true, that "all things work together for good to those who love God." We need to believe that God will take that which is meant for evil against us and use it for our good (Genesis 50:20). We need to trust that just as God always has been, He always will be.

David is a great example of this very thing. When David faced lions and bears as a shepherd, he was being prepared to face Goliath. This is the reason David gave to Saul as to why he wanted to face Goliath: "The LORD, who delivered me from the paw of the lion and from the paw of the bear, He will deliver me from the hand of this Philistine" (1 Samuel 17:37). The truth is that difficulties prepare us for victory. Knowing this, believing it, trusting in it, will move us to praise God before, during, and after every situation.

JULY 31st

Philippians 4:6: "Be anxious for nothing."

As Michelle and I celebrated our daughter's first birthday, we took some time to look back over the last year and we were amazed to see how much Kate has taught us about being Christians. I would say the biggest example she has set for us is the outlook that she has in everyday life.

I find it very convicting that though our daughter is completely helpless, defenseless, and fully reliant on Michelle and I to provide for her, she never worries about where her next meal will come from; she is never anxious about what tomorrow might bring. She just lives life without concern because she fully trusts that we will take care of her. I seriously doubt that the thought even enters her mind that she will not be taken care of. Well, if we, being evil, know how to take care of and provide for our daughter, how much more will God take care of us, being that we are His children? If Kate can trust Michelle and I to the extent that she has absolutely no concern or worry in her life, how much more should we be able trust God in that same regard?

I believe that worry and anxiety come into our lives because we quit relying on God and begin relying on ourselves. It's when we believe that the final outcome in a situation is fully reliant on us, or what we do, that worry and anxiety comes rushing in. The reason why Kate can be at peace is because she is completely helpless, defenseless, and fully reliant on us. If we would get back to that reality—that we are fully reliant on God and we can do nothing apart from Him—we too would be at peace because it would force us to trust in God and not in ourselves.

I remember when a missionary friend came back from Africa and told me all about the amazing faith and joy that the children over there have. The reason for their incredible faith, she said, was because they had absolutely nothing . . . no food, no shelter, no money . . . nothing. And because they had nothing, they had to fully rely on God, every day, to provide for them, and He always did. These children have amazing faith and joy because they could not rely on themselves for anything, but rather had to rely on God for everything. So believer, "Be anxious for nothing, but in everything by prayer and supplication, with thanksgiving, let your requests be made known to God; and the peace of God, which surpasses all understanding, will guard your hearts and minds through Christ Jesus" (Philippians 4:6–7).

AUGUST 1st

> Genesis 17:1: "When Abram was ninety-nine years old, the LORD appeared to Abram and said to him, 'I am Almighty God; walk before Me and be blameless.'"

A couple of weeks ago, I was talking to a brother from church about his addiction to alcohol and drugs. He said to me, "If I only had God's power, I could stop falling back into my addiction." I quickly reminded him that God has made His Holy Spirit readily available to all of us to overcome every form of bondage and addiction—but at some point, we have to receive that power and walk in it by making wise decisions that are based on God's Word, not on feelings, and not on what *we* want to do.

This is what the Lord was speaking to Abram about in Genesis 17:1. See, a while back, God had promised Abram that he would have a son. When that didn't happen soon enough for Abram and Sarai's liking, Abram took on his wife's maidservant as his wife and had a son with her. Thirteen years of turmoil, bitterness, unhappiness, and unrest later, God appeared to Abram again and said, "I am Almighty God; walk before Me and be blameless."

The name "Almighty God" in Hebrew is *El Shaddai*, which means the God who is sufficient. Basically what the Lord was saying to Abram here is, "My sufficiency of power will be revealed in your life as you live out your life wholly before Me." God was not telling Abram that he had to live a perfect life, but rather that he was to live a life that was fully committed to God. As David Guzik explained it, "God wanted all of Abram," not just part of him.[99]

Abram was now at a place where his divided mind could no longer exist. He could no longer live for God and live for himself; it had to be one or the other. The same goes for us today. We have a standing in Christ that says we are forgiven of our sin through no efforts of our own. Yet we also find that there is a responsibility for us to walk before God and be blameless as His servant.[100] "But the blameless in their ways are His delight" (Proverbs 11:20). This is also what David was talking about when he wrote in Psalm 24:3–4: "[W]ho may stand in His Holy place? He who has clean hands and a pure heart, who has not lifted up his soul to an idol, nor sworn deceitfully." David is specifically speaking about having pure intentions and making personal decisions on how we live out our lives before God.

I see so many believers today with the attitude of, "How much can I get away with and still be called a believer?" Basically, they live careless lives with no accountability, and then justify their actions by stating, "Back off, man; I am forgiven." God will not tolerate this kind of life. He will eventually just give them exactly what they want: a life based on self, as He did with Abram. How'd that work out for him? Believer, we should absolutely rest in the finished work of Christ as we are forgiven; but we should also remember that we will be held accountable for how we lived out our lives before Him.[101] "I am Almighty God; walk before Me and be blameless."

AUGUST 2nd

John 17:17: "Sanctify them by Your truth. Your word is truth."

Over the last couple of weeks, Michelle has been repeating the same truth over and over again, "It's not an event; it's a process." She does this to remind herself that teaching and training up a child is not a onetime event, but rather is a lengthy process that takes place within a child over time. The same exact thing can be said about the sanctification process that takes place in the life of a believer; it is not a onetime event, but is rather a lengthy process that takes place within a believer over time.

So what is sanctification? To be sanctified is to be set apart for a specific purpose. For example, after Michelle and I got engaged, she went out and bought a beautiful white wedding dress. This dress was not for everyday use. In fact, it had only one purpose assigned to it—it was set apart for the day we got married. The same goes for us as believers. We have been set apart specifically for God's great purpose. So what does sanctification do? It separates us from the evil and perverse ways of this world and transforms us more and more into the image of Jesus Christ.

We first enter into the process of sanctification when we place our faith in Jesus Christ as our Lord and Savior (Acts 26:18). But this is only where the sanctification process begins, from that point on it must be pursued earnestly by each and every believer in order to possess it. It is not something that is imputed or transferred to us; rather, it is something that must be learned from God as He teaches us His Word through the power of His Holy Spirit.

Even though I gave my life to Jesus Christ on April 22, 2000, I still continued on in my perverse lifestyle for about another year. But throughout that year, as I read the Word of God, I slowly began changing. My desires began to go from darkness to light and my friends had no idea what to make of me. I was being sanctified by God's Word through the power of the Holy Spirit even though I did not understand what I was reading half the time. Little by little, through God's Word, I was becoming more like Jesus.

This is what Jesus meant in John 17:17 when He prayed to God the Father, "Sanctify them by Your truth. Your word is truth." Notice that Jesus spoke in the present continual tense when He asked the Father to "sanctify" us. By doing this, Jesus made it clear to us that sanctification is not a onetime event, but rather is an ongoing process that will continue on until the day we are taken home.

AUGUST 3rd

John 14:27: "Peace I leave with you, My peace I give to you; not as the world gives do I give to you. Let not your heart be troubled, neither let it be afraid."

After Kate was born, things changed for Michelle and me—not just in our lives and in our home, but in our thinking as well. All of a sudden we had someone else that we had to consider and take care of. So we decided that it would be wise for us to have a living trust put into place just in case something happened to us and we were taken home to be with the Lord. We did this because we wanted to leave Kate in good standing spiritually, emotionally, physically, and financially.

In John 14, Jesus did something very similar for His disciples as He knew that in about two days' time He would be arrested, crucified, and buried in a tomb. He also knew that His disciples would be confused, broken, and full of anxiety because of everything that was going to happen to Him. So Jesus, in a sense, set up a living trust for His disciples because He wanted to leave them in good standing as well.

But what would Jesus leave them? He had no money or possessions, so what could He leave them that would ensure they would be taken care of? "Peace I leave with you, My peace I give to you; not as the world gives do I give to you." Jesus basically said, "I do not leave you something that can be lost or stolen; something that is temporary and can be altered by this world. No, I leave you that which can never be taken from you and will always be available to you no matter where you are or what you do—My peace I leave with you." He was, of course, referring to the coming of the Holy Spirit and the life-altering work that He would perform in our lives (John 14:26).

But I thought it was interesting that Jesus made it a point to say that He does not give as the world gives. See, the world gives things that have to do with the physical world, whereas Jesus' gifts are both spiritual and eternal. And, unlike Jesus, the world gives peace only through temporary means, such as: If we are stressed or anxious, we are told to take pills; if our lives are chaotic, we are told that we need to escape it by taking a vacation. But what happens when the drugs wear off and we come back from our vacation? Our problems are still there. Nothing has changed.[102]

But the peace that Jesus gives is a "peace . . . which surpasses all understanding" (Philippians 4:7). Circumstances do not affect it, as it is an internal peace that overcomes stress, anxiety, and hopelessness. His peace will never be found through drugs, or vacations, or by having no problems in this life.[103] No, the peace that Jesus leaves to us is found in the midst of the storms of this life, not apart from them. The thing that we must remember about His peace is that it is a possession of ours as believers in Christ. Through the power of the Holy Spirit, we already have it available to us whenever we need it.

So, believer, "Let not your heart be troubled, neither let it be afraid." In other words, be at peace, because the One who dwells within you is more than able to handle whatever it is you are facing right now. He knows and He is in control.

AUGUST 4th

Proverbs 19:11: "The discretion of a man makes him slow to anger, and his glory is to overlook a transgression."

Grace has been a hot topic around our house lately. Our discussions have ranged from how to show grace to a child when disciplining them to how to show grace to believers when they sin. And of course, there is no shortage of books or opinions on how these things should be done, either. So Michelle and I prayed and asked the Lord to give us wisdom so that we might gain a better understanding of how to show grace to others. That is when the Lord led me to this verse, "The discretion of a man makes him slow to anger, and his glory is to overlook a transgression." Essentially, Solomon is saying that a wise man defers anger until he can properly weigh the entire situation, and then he responds accordingly. So if we want to be more like God in those situations, we need to pass over the penalty for those sins.[104]

The Bible defines for us what it is to be a person of understanding in Proverbs 9:10: "knowledge of the Holy One is understanding." This knowledge of God does not come to us naturally; rather it must be sought after and learned. And the more we seek after God, desiring to know Him more intimately, the more we will become like Him. Thus, when a situation arises where someone has sinned against us, we defer our anger toward that person and that event until we have thoroughly considered all of the details as to what may have provoked such an action.

That brings us to the second half of this verse: "and his glory is to overlook a transgression." Solomon said that if we really want to be like God, if we really want to shine brightly before man, then we need to take on God's attitude toward sin and pass over the penalty for that sin.[105] This is essentially what Jesus did on the cross; He took the penalty of our sin upon Himself so that we might be free from the snares of eternal death.

With that being said, it is important to note that we are not told to pass over the sin itself, because sin is evil and God hates evil (see Proverbs 8:13). We are to hate sin just as God hates sin. Nowhere in the Bible does God ever say to someone, "It's OK that you committed that sin. Keep on keepin' on." No, God always exposed sin for what it was, and yet He did so without condemnation.

When Jesus told the woman in John 8:11 who was caught in adultery, "go and sin no more," He was not saying, "It is OK that you committed adultery." No, it was very clear that what she did was wrong and that she needed to turn from that sin; but what Jesus did say to her was, "I will pass over the penalty for your sin," which was death by stoning.

God says to us that we are to have this same attitude toward others. We are to pass over the penalty for their sin because that is what God's amazing grace does. "And be kind to one another, tenderhearted, forgiving one another, even as God in Christ forgave you" (Ephesians 4:32).

AUGUST 5th

2 Corinthians 1:3: "Blessed be the God and Father of our Lord Jesus Christ, the Father of mercies and God of all comfort."

We often confuse the biblical term "comfort" with the worldly term "comfortable." Comfortable has a soft, weak connotation attached to it, like when we go on vacation and sleep in a bed that is not as comfortable as the one we have back home; we often long for our bed so that we will be comfortable again.[106] That is not what this verse is talking about. In fact, I do not believe that God ever wants us to be spiritually comfortable in this sense, because with this kind of comfort comes spiritual laziness and complacency.

The word comfort that is used in 2 Corinthians 1 speaks of intensive strengthening, "Blessed be the God and Father of our Lord Jesus Christ, the Father of mercies and God of all comfort, who comforts us in all our tribulation." Paul praises God for the strengthening that God gave him while he was suffering through his tribulation—not for taking away his suffering, and not for making him comfortable during his suffering, but rather for strengthening him through it.

So why does Paul praise God for this strength? "[T]hat we may be able to comfort those who are in any trouble, with the comfort with which we ourselves are comforted by God" (2 Corinthians 1:4). Paul thanks and praises God for strengthening him, so that he can strengthen the brethren with the same strength that God gave him. It's important for us to recall the law of giving here: Before we can ever give something out, we first have to receive it for ourselves. So if we do not go through trials, and if God does not strengthen us in them, we will never be of use to anyone else who is struggling.

It's interesting that God often gives this strengthening to us through other believers. That means that before we can share that strength with others, we must first make ourselves vulnerable so that others can share it with us. This is why many never receive the strengthening that God wants to give them, because they are too prideful to open up and share their needs with others.[107] In turn, it makes them less effective tools for the kingdom's work.

Another reason why we may not reveal our problems to others is because we believe that if they have not gone through the same exact situation that we are in, or if they have not had the same exact struggle that we struggle with, then they cannot possibly help us. Wrong. As Gene Pensiero pointed out, "God comforts us in *all* tribulation" so that we can comfort others in "*any*" situation.[108] Remember, we are sharing the strengthening that God gave us, not the situation we may or may not have experienced. The focus, Paul says, is on the strengthening that God gives us, not on the situation we went through.

AUGUST 6th

Proverbs 28:12: "When the righteous rejoice, there is great glory."

A couple of weeks ago, a number of us from our home church gathered together for a night of worship and prayer at a friend's house. There was no agenda specified for that night; we just wanted to come together and praise God for all that He is, all that He has been, and all that He is going to be. Well, I will let you in on a little secret about God in case you didn't know: When God's children gather together to seek Him, He will manifest Himself in glorious ways.

From the very beginning of the night, it was ridiculously obvious to all of us that God was orchestrating each and every aspect of this evening. It got so obvious, in fact, that at one point I actually started laughing during worship (and I was one of the worship leaders). I would love to describe in detail everything that happened that night, but alas, I will just say that our faith was strengthened, our chains were broken, our lives were changed, and God was completely glorified.

The next morning, as I was reading through Proverbs 28, I came across this verse: "When the righteous rejoice, there is great glory." I smiled as I stared at this verse, because it was a perfect description of what had happened the night before. I believe God shared this verse with me because He wanted me to understand what happened that night and how it can happen every night . . . for when the righteous rejoice, there is great glory. The encouragement I took from this verse was that nights of prayer and worship should not be the exception for the believer, but rather should be the rule because God's glory is readily and abundantly available to all of us if we want to experience it.

The more I thought about this verse, the more I realized that it is not just when we gather together and rejoice that His glory is revealed, but it is any time that we rejoice. So whether we are at church, at work, or at home . . . whether the sun is shining down upon us that day, or whether we find ourselves in a fiery trial, when we rejoice, there is great glory because God is being glorified, not man. We do not rejoice because of our circumstances and we do not rejoice because of the things in this world . . . no, we rejoice because of the promises and assurances that God has given us through His Word that are sealed in our hearts by His Holy Spirit. I remember sharing my testimony with a good friend of mine shortly after I got saved, and as I was rejoicing in the new life that I had been given through Jesus Christ, my friend said to me, "You are absolutely glowing!"

Our pastor said a couple of weeks ago that there are about 3,573 promises in the Bible for us, ranging from life here on Earth to eternal life in heaven. We rejoice because Jesus is our Lord and Savior, and He is the Yes and the Amen to all of God's promises (2 Corinthians 1:20). So believer, make it a point today to rejoice in Him and experience His great glory.

AUGUST 7th

> Romans 12:1: "I beseech you therefore, brethren, by the mercies of God, that you present your bodies a living sacrifice, holy, acceptable to God, which is your reasonable service."

As I was getting ready for work last Tuesday morning, Michelle hurt her back in such a way that she could not even walk without me helping her. So I took off work and stayed home to take care of both her and our eight-month-old daughter Kate.

The first day I was like a machine, as my whole focus was on serving my wife and my daughter. The second day I was a little slower, but I was still moving pretty good as I kept the needs of Michelle and Kate my top priority. The third day I began dragging a little bit because I stayed up late the night before so I could have some "me" time. The fourth day I was exhausted because I stayed up even later the third night so I could have even more "me" time. By the fifth day, even though I continued serving my wife and daughter as much as I could, there was more "me" than there was Michelle and Kate in my heart.

As I reflected on all of this, I was reminded of something that a friend of mine once told me: "The problem with a living sacrifice is that it keeps crawling off of the altar." How very true that is. Crawling up on the altar is never the problem—the problem is staying there and enduring the altar.

When we think about sacrifice, we often think of it in terms of a onetime event. For example, one night at a men's study we were all asked if we would take a bullet for our loved ones. Every man in the study gave a resounding "Yes!" without hesitation. Yet when asked if we would deny ourselves every day and serve our families by putting their needs before ours—spiritually, physically, mentally, and emotionally—there was a resounding pause before anyone said anything. Ask a man to die for his family and he would do it without hesitation—but ask him to live for his family and there is pause, because being a living sacrifice takes endurance and requires the continual denying of self.

We often forget that God did not create us so that He could serve us; no, He created us so that we can serve Him by serving others. Paul said it very clearly; being a living sacrifice "is your reasonable service." In other words, this is the very least we can do considering all of "the mercies" God has given us. David Guzik pointed out that those mercies include the gift of His Holy Spirit, justification, adoption into His kingdom, "identification with Christ," being freed from the Law and covered by grace, help in times of need, a love that is unfailing, and of course the guarantee "of coming glory." "In light of all of these mercies—past, present, and future—Paul begs us to 'present [our] bodies a living sacrifice,'" because this kind of sacrifice is "holy (and) acceptable to God."[109]

Consider this thought: When we are on the altar, denying ourselves, that is when we are most Christlike. The simple truth in all of this is that there is no better place for us to be than on the altar of sacrifice.

AUGUST 8th

James 4:8: "Draw near to God and He will draw near to you."

Last Sunday morning, one of the brothers in the prayer room asked if the gift of repentance was available to everyone today. The answer was a resounding yes, as God has done everything needed to make repentance available to all men. As I was meditating on this thought, the Lord reminded me of a great truth that we often forget about Him: He is readily available.

We see a symbolic picture of this in Proverbs 9:1–4: "Wisdom has built her house, she has hewn out her seven pillars; she has slaughtered her meat, she has mixed her wine, she has also furnished her table. She has sent out her maidens, she cries from the highest places of the city, 'Whoever is simple, let him turn in here!'" In this passage of Scripture, Solomon makes it clear to us that everything has been done that needs to be done in order for us to receive God's wisdom; all we have to do is to come and receive it. In fact, in James 1:5, we are told that we just need to ask for His wisdom and it will be given to us.

Likewise, and in a much broader sense, God has done everything needed to make Himself readily available for all of our needs today. Yet many do not receive that which they need from God simply because they do not accept His invitation to come and receive. James reminds us in James 4:7–8 that there is an order of events that takes place in a believer's life. "Therefore submit to God. Resist the devil and he will flee from you. Draw near to God and He will draw near to you." David Guzik said about this verse, "The call to draw near to God is both an invitation and a promise. It is no good to submit to God's authority and to resist the devil's attack and then fail to draw near to God."[110]

So why don't we draw near to God? The main reason is unbelief. We believe that either He won't help us, or that He's unable to help us. Either way, our unbelief keeps us from drawing near to God. This last weekend I spoke with a friend who, for the last thirty years or so, has been living out the book of Judges. She wrecks her life with drugs and alcohol, calls on God for help, He delivers her, then she walks away and wrecks her life again. So I invited her to church Sunday morning, only to see her make an excuse as to why she couldn't come. She states that she has submitted to God's authority as Lord of her life, yet she refuses to draw near to Him and receive that which she truly needs. Change, freedom, salvation, hope, strength . . . these things, and all that God promises, do not start tomorrow; they start today, right now, if we want them. Believer, God has done everything needed to make Himself readily available for us. So draw near to Him, and He *will* draw near to you.

AUGUST 9th

Proverbs 23:5a: "Will you set your eyes on that which is not?"

I once heard a story about a man who was learning how to fly a plane. Every time he landed the plane he would hit this huge pothole that was in the middle of the runway. Finally, the instructor asked him, "What are you looking at when you're landing the plane?" The man replied, "The pothole." So the instructor said back to the man, "The reason why you keep hitting the pothole is because that is what your eyes are fixed on. Stop looking at the pothole and you won't hit it anymore."

In Proverbs 23, Solomon gives us a warning about those things that we set our eyes upon, "Do not overwork to be rich; because of your own understanding, cease! Will you set your eyes on that which is not?" (Proverbs 23:4–5). Solomon is not saying that we should not work to support our families; rather, he is speaking to those who overwork and weary themselves for the sake of attaining more. Many men today are working extra shifts because they believe that providing their families with bigger, nicer, or more material possessions is what their family needs most. Yet what their wives and children really need more than anything else is for their spiritual leader to be at home, loving on them, spending time with them, teaching them, leading them, and washing them with the Word of God. I have never heard of anyone on their deathbed say, "I wish I would have worked more." Riches, possessions, titles, they're all temporary and eternally meaningless. Only that which is in Christ is eternal.

"But the more money I have, the more people I can help!" This is probably the most popular reason people give God as to why they think God should let them win the lottery. Yes, money has its purpose in life, but it is never the answer in helping people. I remember when a missionary from one of the poorest countries in Africa came back on sabbatical and told me that the children there do not need schools, shoes, or more money . . . they need Jesus. I think about when Jesus helped others, He always gave them that which they needed most, that which was eternal. Even the spiritual gifts that are given to us through the Holy Spirit are given for the edification of the body (minus the gift of tongues, which is given for personal spiritual edification). These gifts are not to benefit the one who receives the gift, but rather are used to benefit others so that they may be built up in the Lord.

It is not just riches, though. There are many things in this world that we set our eyes upon which do not have eternal value or significance yet can still consume our lives. So how do we know what our eyes are really set upon? Well, ask yourself, what do I always sacrifice and make time for? What do I talk about most in conversations with others? What do I share on Facebook or Instagram? That which occupies our mind the most will come out through these different avenues. More importantly though, that which we set our eyes upon is all we will have to offer other people when they are in need. So, believer, "Will you set your eyes on that which is not," or will you set your eyes on that which is Christ?

AUGUST 10th

Philippians 4:14: "Nevertheless you have done well that you shared in my distress."

Last Sunday morning, Michelle threw out her back for the second time this month. The first time this happened it took a week before she was recovered enough for me to go back to work. Needless to say, we were both very discouraged as we began thinking about the days ahead.

The biggest concern for us was having me miss work. Because I missed so much work the first time she hurt her back, we were unsure how all of this was going to work out this time around. So we prayed for the Lord to do a mighty work. We called for the elders to come over and anoint Michelle with oil and pray over her (James 5:14), and we asked for prayer through Facebook and text messages. In our hearts, we were looking for a miracle from God in the form of a miraculous healing, but what we found was so much sweeter. As word got out about what had happened to Michelle, and people began praying for us, we began receiving phone calls and text messages from our brethren, offering to come over and take care of Michelle and our nine-month-old daughter, Kate, so that I could go to work. As the schedule for the week unfolded before us, it became very clear that I would hardly miss any time at all.

In Philippians 4:10–19, Paul thanked the believers in Philippi for their continued support of him, even though he had learned to be content in whatever state he found himself in because he knew that the Lord would always strengthen him through whatever he faced. "Nevertheless, you have done well that you shared in my distress." Even though he knew the Lord would carry him through it, Paul was still very thankful that there were those who would willingly share in his distress.

Michelle and I have often talked about the riches that we have in Christ. We have always considered ourselves to be extremely wealthy simply because of the people the Lord has placed in our lives. This is why I often feel very sad for believers who do not have the rich fellowship we have, simply because of the choices they make to not have it. If I were to count the glimpses of heaven I have experienced since I got saved, and the life-altering events that have shaped my life, I would say ninety-nine percent of those times were because I was in fellowship with other believers. For us, the riches in Christ we treasure the most are those people we fellowship with . . . those who willingly share in our distress no matter what road we are walking down. To them we say thank you and we love you.

AUGUST 11th

John 16:4: "But these things I have told you, that when the time comes, you may remember that I told you of them."

I once heard a pastor say, "I really hate teaching through the book of Job because I always have to live out what I am teaching." I have heard many other pastors/teachers say something very similar to what this man said, but what if they are wrong? What if they have it all backward? Is it that we have to live it out because we are teaching on it, or is it that we get to teach on it because we are going to have to live it out?

When I began teaching Bible studies in 2002, I also thought as these men did. But then the Lord spoke to me, and told me something very similar to what He told His disciples in John 16:4, "But these things I have told you, that when the time comes, you may remember that I told you of them." Jesus prepared His disciples for the coming persecution by telling them what was going to happen. He warned them about these things so that they wouldn't "abandon their faith" (John 16:1, NLT) when those things came to pass. His disciples were not going to go through persecution because He told them; no, He told them because they were going to go through persecution.

In 2007, after Jesus had spoken to me about this very thing, I had a verse come across my path three times in one day from three different sources. Whenever that happens to me, I know the Lord is trying to tell me something, so I meditated on this verse and prayed that the Lord would reveal to me what it was He wanted to teach me. By the next day, I realized that the Lord was not trying to teach me something; rather, He was trying to warn me of something that was going to happen in the near future and He wanted me to be prepared for it so that I would respond properly in that situation. Sure enough, a few days later that very thing came to pass and I was able to endure it and not lose heart because the Lord had prepared me for it. So that situation did not come because of the verse I read; rather, I was led to that verse because that situation was coming.

It's not just the big things that the Lord prepares us for, either; it is also the seemingly insignificant things that He prepares us for simply because He cares for us. For example, a couple of years ago my wife and I decided to cancel our cable TV. Now, I am a huge NFL draft guy, and cancelling cable meant that the only way I would be able watch the draft was if I went to someone else's house to watch it. Well, earlier this month, I got a free month's subscription to a streaming service, which gave me unlimited access to the very channels the draft is televised on. I realized this morning that because my wife hurt her back and is currently unable to take care of our baby girl without me, I would have not been able to watch the draft this year. God knew what was coming and He provided for me so that I could stay home and take care of my family and still be able to watch the draft. This is how good our God is. This is how much the Lord loves us and wants to bless us. If He provides for us even in the most insignificant things in life like the NFL draft, how much more will He prepare us for the significant things in life when they are coming? So much more!

AUGUST 12th

1 John 3:1: "Behold what manner of love the Father has bestowed on us, that we should be called children of God!"

Whenever I look at my daughter Kate, I just have to smile. Regardless if I am looking at a picture of her on my desktop at work, a video on the iPad at home, or just sitting down and watching her play with her toys, I smile. I don't have to choose to smile; it's just a natural occurrence when I see her because I love her so much.

With this love, though, comes an innate instinct to defend and protect her at all costs. The mere thought of her suffering, even for a minute, in any way is more than I can seemingly bear. This is why I do not understand how certain believers can say that God has created some people for heaven and some people for hell. How can that be? If I, being evil, and having an imperfect love for my daughter, cannot even fathom her suffering for a minute, how can God, who is inherently good, and has a perfect love for all mankind, stand the thought of anyone suffering for an eternity in hell? How can our loving God willingly create His own children, made in His image, for eternal damnation?

If you look at the Bible as a whole, it paints this beautiful picture of a Father's love for His children. From beginning to end, God says to each one of us "I love you," and He proved this love by sending His only begotten Son, Jesus Christ, to die for all of mankind so that whosoever chooses to believe in Him shall be saved. To say that Jesus only died for the "elect" cheapens His great sacrifice and changes the entire Bible, as it places conditions on His unconditional love for all of mankind.

Imagine a pastor delivering a sermon to thousands of people, and at the end of the sermon he gives an altar call with this condition, "Now, regardless what you want to do here today, some of you have been elected to go to heaven, and some of you have been chosen for hell. So, good luck with all that. Maybe it will only seem like an eternity!" There is absolutely no hope in this message, and we know that the God of the Bible is the God of all hope.

It all comes down to knowing who God is. You can know the Bible inside and out, and have all sorts of degrees in theology, but if you do not know the Author personally, intimately, relationally, you will develop a distorted view of who God is and what His Word says. So believer, what view of God do you have?

AUGUST 13th

> Psalm 37:3: "Trust in the LORD, and do good; dwell in the land, and feed on His faithfulness."

Our natural instinct when facing a difficult situation is either fight or flight. We either want to strike back in that situation, or we want to just run away from it altogether. David understood this all too well, as there were many times when he fought back in a situation only to experience the internal corruption that comes from such a response. And there were many times when he fled from a situation only to see that he could not outrun it; sooner or later, he would have to return and face that situation whether he wanted to or not. This is why David could write, "Trust in the LORD, and do good; dwell in the land, and feed on His faithfulness."

Oftentimes when difficulties come, the first thing we do is complain about it to a friend, a family member, or a coworker. We call it "sharing," but really we are fighting back and trying to recruit other people to our side so that our complaining or slander is justified. This is where the corruption begins as it quickly leads to some sort of physical response rooted in bitterness or fear. David reminds us that when the temptation comes to fight back, we are to "Trust in the LORD, and do good." Trusting God and doing good is easy when everything is going well and the sun is shining down on us; the true test for a believer is to do good when we face difficulties because it is there that we find out if we really trust God or not. If we say we trust God, yet we do not do good, do we really trust God? Our circumstances should never determine whether or not we do good; we do good because we trust that God is who He says He is, regardless of the circumstances.

Maybe you are not a fighter; maybe you are more of a runner when it comes to difficulties. It seems like I have been running my entire life. I have learned, as David did, that you cannot run forever. Sooner or later you are going to have to face that situation head-on. The problem is that the longer you run, the harder it is to go back and face that situation, as fear poisons your mind and distorts your perspective. David reminds us when the temptation comes to run, "Dwell in the land, and feed on His faithfulness." Stay where you are, David says, and dwell where the Lord has you, for His faithfulness will sustain you.

So, believer, do not give in to fear, rather, "Rest in the Lord and wait patiently for Him. . . . I have been young, and now am old; yet I have not seen the righteous forsaken" (Psalm 37:7, 25).

AUGUST 14th

Matthew 5:45: "[F]or He makes His sun rise on the evil and on the good, and sends rain on the just and unjust."

As a believer in the death and resurrection of our Lord and Savior Jesus Christ, it is very easy for me to think that God favors me over, say, someone who does not believe. It is very easy for me to justify why I am more special to God than someone who flat-out rejects God and wants absolutely nothing to do with Him. It is very easy for me to esteem myself as God's favorite over a terrorist, a murderer, a thief, an adulterer, an atheist, a denominationalist, a cultist, etc.—and yet when I do this, when I take on this thinking, I begin looking down on people; I begin thinking that I am somehow better than they are and that things should fall my way and not theirs because God loves me more. This is the thinking that compelled David to ask God why the wicked had everything and seemingly always got away with their wickedness; he believed that God should have more favor on the righteous than on the unrighteous.

Yet nowhere in the Bible do we ever read that God favors believers over unbelievers. In fact, in Matthew 5:45, Jesus said, "for He [God] makes His sun rise on the evil and on the good, and sends rain on the just and unjust." Romans 2:11 echoes this same sentiment, "For there is no partiality with God." God has no favorites. He has absolutely no partiality toward anyone regardless of their standing in Him or their standing in this world. Believer, unbeliever, man, woman, black, white, Jew, Gentile, rich, poor, Republican, Democrat . . . God loves us all *exactly* the same. Does that offend you? Understand that God blesses and pours out favor because that is who He is; it has nothing to do with being a believer or not. He makes His sun rise on all men, and He brings forth rain on all men. Yes, God loves us immeasurably, but He also loves those we hate with the same measure.

The point Jesus was making in Matthew 5:45 is that we are all going to receive blessings in this life and we are all going to go through trials and tribulations in this life, regardless if we are believers or not. The difference lies in how we go through these seasons. A believer will recognize that their blessings are from God and will give Him thanks and praise; an unbeliever will give glory to luck, self, or others. A believer will have the absolute assurance of God with them during the storms of life; the certainty of coming glory; and the intimate knowledge of a personal, faithful, loving Father who comforts, delivers, and sustains. An unbeliever only has luck, self, and others to place their hope in. So in this regard, we are much more blessed than unbelievers—but it's only because we have God, not because He has us.

AUGUST 15th

2 Timothy 3:16: "All Scripture is given by inspiration of God, and is profitable for doctrine, for reproof, for correction, for instruction of righteousness."

There are many verses that are taken out of context by the church today, but probably none more than Matthew 18:20: "For where two or three are gathered in My name, I am there in the midst of them." I hear people quote this verse all of the time when gathering together, and though it is true that Jesus is in the midst of two or three believers who gather in His name, this is not the correct application of this verse. If it is, what does that say about the person who is alone? Is Jesus not in their midst?

It has been said that there are three rules for understanding and applying God's Word properly: 1) context; 2) context; and 3) context.[111] When we quote a verse out of context, even though our application might be true in a general sense, we are missing the proper application of God's Word in our lives. To gain the proper context of Matthew 18:20, you need to go back to verse 15, where Jesus began instructing us on how to keep unity within the church when disputes arise. Verse 20 is not a standalone verse; rather, it sums up and affirms to us that when we follow the entire disciplining process that Jesus laid out for us in verses 15–19, the power and authority of His presence will be there to direct and guide us in that outcome.

Why is this so important, you ask? Because "All Scripture is given by inspiration of God, and is profitable for doctrine, for reproof, for correction, for instruction of righteousness." First, the Bible is given by God, or literally is "God-breathed." Understand that God laid out the Bible with a specific purpose in mind, so "that the man of God may be complete, thoroughly equipped for every good work" (2 Timothy 3:17). Second, it is by His Word that we are taught, convicted, set straight, and trained. When we take His Word out of context, we miss out on these key essentials that make us capable and fully prepared for His good work.

In the example of Matthew 18, the instructions we see in verses 15–19 can be very daunting for any believer to want to follow. Yet when we understand the context that verse 20 is written in, and we receive the promise that Jesus will bless that situation and establish it by His presence, power, and authority, all of the sudden those instructions become much easier to want to follow and obey. Believer, know this: understanding God's Word correctly will lead to correct living; this is not only true for us, but for those we are leading, teaching, and sharing it with as well.[112]

AUGUST 16th

Psalm 50:14: "Offer to God thanksgiving."

The children of Israel were following God's instructions to the letter. They offered sacrifices just as God told them to, in the way He told them to do it, and at the exact time when He said they should occur. Yet in Psalm 50 the Lord said to them "Hear, O My people, and I will speak, O Israel, and I will testify against you" (Psalm 50:7). The Lord had something against His people.

"I will not rebuke you for your sacrifices, or your burnt offerings, which are continually before Me" (Psalm 50:8). The Lord had no problem with their sacrifices as, again, they did exactly what He had told them to do. The problem God had with His children was their attitude in sacrificing. For them, the sacrifices they offered to God had become a ritual, a work, a list of items that had to be checked off so they would be made "right" with God. Their sacrifices became more habit then a heartfelt offering, as they forgot why they were sacrificing in the first place.

So the Lord spoke and said to them, "I don't need your bulls and goats because everything is already Mine. If I were hungry, would I really need to tell you? Do you think I need flesh to eat and blood to drink?" (see Psalm 50:9–13). The Lord reminded them that the sacrifices were not for Him, but rather were for the children of Israel. They served as a reminder of the serious nature of sin, and were a symbolic picture of the coming Messiah who would eventually save them out of their sin. Offering sacrifices to God meant absolutely nothing to Him if their hearts were not right in the offering.

Rather than sacrifice, "Offer to God thanksgiving" (Psalm 50:14), the psalmist wrote. God does not want ritual, He wants relationship; He wants a thankful heart. David penned Psalm 51 after he had committed adultery with Bathsheba and murdered her husband Uriah, and in this psalm he wrote, "For You [God] do not desire sacrifice, or else I would give it; You do not delight in burnt offering. The sacrifices of God are a broken spirit, a broken and contrite heart – these, O God, You will not despise" (Psalm 51:16–17). David got it; he understood that sacrifice without true repentance (without the heart) was meaningless to God. God desires truth in the inward parts (Psalm 51:6), not outward signs of religion.

We can easily fall into this works-based relationship as well by reading the Bible, worshipping, praying, giving, serving, etc., and yet not once actually talking with God. We do great at talking about God, or talking at God, but when was the last time we really sat down and talked *with* God? It is crazy to think about, but we can actually develop a relationship with the acts of the things we do, rather than with God in the things we do.

So, believer, remember, everything God instructs us to do is for us and for our benefit, not His. Our obedience to Him should be the natural result of having a thankful heart for all He has done, all He is doing, and all He is going to do.

AUGUST 17th

> 2 Corinthians 6:17: "'Come out from among them and be separate,' says the Lord."

As my wife and I do our best to train up our daughter in the Lord, one of the tougher issues we have discussed is how to protect our daughter from the world, and yet not shelter her so much that she cannot be a light to the world. Where is the line drawn between being *in* the world and being *of* the world? Ask ten different believers and you will probably get ten different answers. David Guzik explained it like this: "A ship should be in the water, but water shouldn't be in the ship!"[113] It is a difficult topic to say the least, but it is not alone as there are many topics such as this one that are not clearly defined in the Bible for us. So what do we do in these situations?

The apostle Paul, when instructing believers about being equally yoked in binding relationships, referenced Isaiah 52:11 when he said, "'Come out from among them and be separate,' says the Lord" (2 Corinthians 6:17). Paul was specifically telling believers to distance themselves from the ways and influence of the world, for "what communion has light with darkness?" (2 Corinthians 6:14, KJV). Many have taken this verse and drawn all kinds of reckless conclusions from it, specifically focusing on how we need to radically isolate ourselves from the world completely. Though I agree that Paul was saying there must be a separation from the world for the Christian, I also believe Paul was more emphatically saying that we need to separate ourselves *unto the Lord*.

The way that we successfully navigate the undefined situations life throws at us is not through isolation, but rather through transformation. We are to come out from among the world and separate ourselves to the Lord, fully opening ourselves up to Him, allowing His Holy Spirit to come in and transform us by the renewing of our minds through His perfect Word. It's only when we take on the mind of Christ that we will know where the lines are drawn between being in the world and being of the world. We will know what dressing modestly means; we will know how to lovingly and truthfully respond to those who come against us. When we take on the mind of Christ, we will know, and have conviction, in all of the grey areas that life has. Ultimately, the more we open ourselves up to the Lord, the more we will not be of the world. So, believer, where is your focus? Is it on isolation, or transformation?

AUGUST 18th

> Deuteronomy 31:8: "And the LORD, He is the One who goes before you. He will be with you. He will not leave you nor forsake you; do not fear nor be dismayed."

I found it interesting that Moses was giving Joshua encouragement upon entering the Promised Land. This was Joshua, after all—the battle-tested general who, upon spying out the Promised Land some forty years earlier, encouraged the children of Israel to go and take possession of the land despite the strong people and the fortified cities that existed there (Numbers 13). Yet here was Moses, encouraging Joshua to "not fear nor be dismayed."

In this encouragement, we learn a lot about what causes us to become fearful. First, we become fearful when we go before God. Oftentimes fear comes because we, in our minds, go before God and create the magnitude of the situation that is coming, how it will play out, and what the outcome will be. One of the many problems with this is that God is nowhere to be found in our estimation of these future events, as they are all based on self-salvation. This is why the first thing Moses said to Joshua was, "And the LORD, He is the One who goes before you." Moses reminded Joshua that the Lord goes before him to prepare the way and to make the crooked places straight, not the other way around (Isaiah 45). We will always invite fear into our lives when we go before the Lord.

Second, we become fearful when we believe we are alone. Oftentimes fear comes because we believe that we have to overcome a situation in our strength, with our knowledge, and by our abilities. There is no hope for us in this thinking. Thus Moses said to Joshua, "He will be with you. He will not leave you nor forsake you." God is always with us. He will never leave us, nor will He ever forsake us. Yet we often believe God has left us because of mistakes we have made, or even because we have not read our Bibles this morning. Do not believe the lie; God has not moved. He has not left us, and nothing can separate us from His love (Romans 8).

Lastly, notice that it is God Himself who goes before us and never leaves us. "He is the One who goes before you. He will be with you. He will not leave you nor forsake you." God does not just set things in motion and then leave us to some mechanical fate, nor does He send some appointed representative to accompany us. No, it is the Lord Almighty, the Creator of heaven and Earth, the all-powerful, all-knowing, and ever-present God Himself who goes before us and walks with us.

So, believer, do not fear nor be discouraged, for the Lord, He is the One who goes before you. He will always be with you, and He will never, ever leave you or forsake you.

AUGUST 19th

> John 1:4–5: "In Him was life, and the life was the light of men. And the light shines in the darkness, and the darkness did not comprehend it."

Regardless what many say or choose to believe, the truth of the Bible is not subjective but absolute. People can alter it, add to it, subtract from it, or ignore it all together, but in no way does that change what is actually true. There are some today who want to change the Bible because they do not agree with what it says; some call portions of the Bible hate speech; others want to start calling God "She"; and then there are certain religious groups who say that Jesus was a created being, was not the Son of God, and that He is dead and buried in some unknown tomb. The fact is, people can scream, hate, argue, protest, persecute, and deny until they are blue in the face—they can even get a whole nation to agree with their point of view and make laws that instruct others as to what they must believe—but in no way does any of this ever change what is actually true.

"In the beginning was the Word [Jesus Christ], and the Word was with God, and the Word was God. He was in the beginning with God. All things were made through Him, and without Him nothing was made that was made. In Him was life, and the life was the light of men. And the light shines in the darkness, and the darkness did not comprehend it" (John 1:1–5). Jesus was, is, and will always be God. He was in the beginning before time began, He is the Creator of all things, and in Him is life, and this life is the "light of men."

The phrase "light of men" is very interesting, in that it gives us the concept of bringing forth revelation. Jesus brought revelation to the darkness of this world, but "men loved darkness rather than light, because their deeds were evil" (John 3:19). It is very important to understand that men love the darkness because they can do whatever they want to do without conviction, not because they do not believe that the light exists. They hate the light because with it comes the revelation of truth. So even though men may choose the darkness over the light, they still cannot deny the truth of that light, which is: 1) Jesus is God; and 2) man is sinful. This is the light that Jesus brought forth; this is the light that continually "shines" in the darkness that men cannot overcome; this is the life that Jesus brought into our world that cannot be extinguished no matter how many may oppose it. This, my friend, is absolute truth.

"Then Jesus spoke to them again saying, 'I am the light of the world. He who follows Me shall not walk in darkness, but have the light of life'" (John 8:12).

AUGUST 20th

> John 2:9: "When the master of the feast had tasted the water that was made wine, and did not know where it came from (but the servants who had drawn the water knew), the master of the feast called the bridegroom."

"Why are there no miracles in our day?" I have asked this question a few times in my walk with the Lord, as I am sure many others have as well. The truth is that miracles are being performed around us every single day. We just do not see them, because we are not involved in the process of those miracles coming to pass.

Take the miracle that Jesus performed at the wedding in Cana, for example. At some point during the wedding they ran out of wine, so Jesus instructed the servants to take six large stone pots (about twenty to thirty gallons each), fill them with water, and then draw some water out and take it to the master of the feast. "When the master of the feast had tasted the water that was made wine, and did not know where it came from (but the servants who had drawn the water knew), the master of the feast called the bridegroom."

Notice that the master of the feast did not know where the wine came from. All that he knew was that he was drinking really good wine, and so he called on the bridegroom to thank him for providing it. This was the extent of his blessing: really good wine. The servants, on the other hand, received a much richer blessing because they knew where the wine came from; more specifically, they knew that Jesus had miraculously turned the water into wine. The servants were able to share in the joy of this miracle because they were directly involved in the process by being obedient to do what Jesus had instructed them to do. It was here that their faith in Jesus grew, "and His disciples believed in Him" (John 2:11).

Believer, you are never going to see miracles just sitting on the sidelines, and your faith is never going to grow if you are just going through the motions. Make yourself available to God and get involved in His work. Put feet to your faith by being obedient to do what He tells you to do—and I guarantee you, you will see miracles.

AUGUST 21ˢᵗ

> John 4:10: "If you knew the gift of God, and who it is who says to you, 'Give Me a drink,' you would have asked Him, and He would have given you living water."

In the book of James, we are told that we do not have because we do not ask (James 4:2). This truth is supported in Luke 11:9–10: "So I say to you, ask, and it will be given to you; seek, and you will find; knock, and it will be opened to you. For everyone who asks receives, and he who seeks finds, and to him who knocks it will be opened." The obvious question then is, why don't we ask? It's simple, really: because we don't believe. Well then, why don't we believe? Because we don't really know the One we are praying to.

When Jesus encountered the woman at the well, He said to her, "If you knew the gift of God, and who it is who says to you, 'Give Me a drink,' you would have asked Him, and He would have given you living water." Jesus was essentially telling the woman at the well, "If you knew Me, that I was the Son of God and that I take away the sins of the world, then you would have asked Me for forgiveness and I would have gladly given you everlasting life." This woman hadn't received everlasting life because she had not asked for it. She hadn't asked for it because she did not know who Jesus was.

"If you knew [Me] . . . you would have asked . . . and [I] would have given. . . ." There is an underlying truth here that goes well beyond salvation. It says that the extent of our asking will always be determined by how well we know the One we are asking those things from. For example, if we do not know Jesus as the great provider, we will not ask Him for provision when we are in need; if we do not know Him as the source of all wisdom, we will not ask Him for wisdom when making decisions; if we do not know Him as the great healer, we will not ask Him for healing when we are sick, etc. More importantly, though, if we do not believe that Jesus is willing and able to help us, we will never ask Him for anything.

Ultimately, how well we know and trust Jesus will always be reflected in our prayer life. So, believer, how is your prayer life doing today? "If you knew [Me] . . . you would have asked . . . and [I] would have given. . . ."

AUGUST 22nd

2 Corinthians 10:3: "For though we walk in the flesh, we do not war according to the flesh."

Some of the recent decisions by the Supreme Court have sent shockwaves throughout the Christian community. I saw a myriad of reactions on social media, most of which consisted of frustration, anger, and even a hate for those who were celebrating these decisions. It is at times like these we need to remember that "though we walk in the flesh, we do not war according to the flesh."

The apostle Paul made it clear that "the weapons of our warfare are not carnal, but mighty in God for pulling down strongholds" (2 Corinthians 10:4). As David Guzik explained, Paul was not referring to "swords and spears" and things of that nature. No, he was referring to the way his opponents battled, using tactics such as hate, deceit, manipulation, intimidation, etc. Paul made it clear that as believers, we are not to war in such ways.[114]

In Ephesians 6:12, we are told why these carnal weapons will not work in the battles we face: "For we do not wrestle against flesh and blood, but against principalities, against powers, against the rulers of the darkness of this age, against spiritual hosts of wickedness in the heavenly places." Our battle is not with the Supreme Court or with those who support their recent decisions, for we do not battle with flesh and blood. Yelling at them, cursing them, criticizing them, complaining about them . . . none of these things are going to bring good to these situations, nor will they bring about the necessary changes that we so desire. Ours is a spiritual battle against the rulers of the darkness of this age, not against man.

Only the weapons God has given us are mighty "for pulling down strongholds, casting down arguments and every high thing that exalts itself against the knowledge of God" (2 Corinthians 10:4–5). The arguments that contradict the very nature of God are the strongholds that Paul is referring to here. And even though our weapons may seem foolish and powerless to the carnal man—and maybe even to some believers—the truth is that no principality or power can stand against us when wield them as Christ has instructed us to.

So believer, put aside the flesh. Put aside the anger, the hate, the despondency, and take on the mind and heart of Christ and wage war the way we have been gifted to war—with diligent prayer, the truth of God's Word, righteousness, faith, and the message of salvation. This is where all of our battles will be won.

AUGUST 23rd

1 Corinthians 13:6: "[Love] does not rejoice in iniquity, but rejoices in the truth."

There has been a common response I have noticed from some believers whenever the subject of witnessing to unbelievers is brought up, and it goes something like this: "We just need to love them." Though I fully agree that we should love all of mankind just as we are loved by our Father in heaven—unconditionally, for Jesus died for all of mankind (John 3:16)—I also believe that just loving others is not the answer. For what is love without truth?

First Corinthians 13, also known as the love chapter, says in verse 6, "[Love] does not rejoice in iniquity, but rejoices in the truth." In other words, love does not rejoice in unrighteousness, nor does it ever support it; rather, love rejoices when the truth is spoken. Likewise, "Now the purpose of the commandment is love from a pure heart, from a good conscience, and from sincere faith" (1 Timothy 1:5). Notice that the whole purpose of truth (the commandment) is to love others. If we are to truly glorify God to others as Jesus did, we must realize that there cannot be love without truth, and there cannot be truth without love. They are inseparable.

For example, one night in December, Michelle and I were out witnessing at the Mission Inn with another couple from our church. As we were sharing the gospel with this man, Ahman, he said to us, "I believe God will forgive me because He loves me." Yes, God does love Ahman, just as He loves all of us, but we are not saved by God's love; we are only saved by the blood of Jesus Christ. "For without the shedding of blood, there is no forgiveness" (Hebrews 9:22, NLT). So if I just loved this man and never told him the truth—that he must repent of his sin and ask for forgiveness—am I really loving him? If I just loved him and supported whatever decisions he wanted to make, but never told him the truth of where those choices will lead him, am I really loving him? No, because love without truth is not really love.

"[B]ut, speaking the truth in love, [we] may grow up in all things into Him who is the Head—Christ" (Ephesians 4:15). Notice that when we speak the truth in a loving way, with patience and gentleness, yet being firm and bold about what is truth, we grow to be more like Christ. Likewise, "For this is the love of God, that we keep His commandments. And His commandments are not burdensome" (1 John 5:3). We will know we are loving others by whether or not we are keeping the commandments of God toward them. In all of this, we see that love cannot be separated from God's truth because love rejoices in truth.

Ultimately, the goal of all truth is love, and the goal of all love is truth. So "Let us hold fast the confession of our hope without wavering" (Hebrews 10:23); "not that [they] should be grieved, but that [they] might know the love which (we) have so abundantly for [them]" (2 Corinthians 2:4).

AUGUST 24th

> John 5:44: "How can you believe, who receive honor from one another, and do not seek the honor that comes from the only God?"

In John 5, Jesus was having a conversation with the Pharisees regarding His deity. This all began when the Pharisees got upset because Jesus healed a man on the Sabbath; "For this reason the Jews persecuted Jesus and sought to kill Him, because He had done these things on the Sabbath" (John 5:16). So Jesus gave them undeniable proof that He was the Son of God.

In John 5:31–35, Jesus reminded the Pharisees that John the Baptist gave testimony to His deity. In John 5:36, Jesus showed them that the works He was performing were the very works that the Father had sent Him to do, and these works, Jesus said, "bear witness of Me, that the Father has sent Me." In John 5:37–39, Jesus pointed out that the Father had given testimony to Jesus through the Scriptures, for "these [Scriptures] are they which testify of Me." These men knew the Scriptures inside and out, yet they were "not willing to come" (v. 40) to Jesus because they did "not seek the honor that comes from the only God," but rather only sought to "receive honor from one another" (v. 44).

The gospel of Jesus Christ essentially says to each one of us that Jesus must increase and we must decrease. It is a message of humility. It is also a message that will offend. The Pharisees hated this message because they loved the honor and respect that their position brought them. They did not want to receive Jesus as Messiah because His message did not fit their greatest desire, which was to receive glory from man—not the coming glory that the Father would give them through the Son. To this Jesus asks them, "How then can you possibly believe Me or what I say, since you seek glory from man and not from God?"

It's a great question that we each must ask ourselves as well. Whose honor are we seeking, man's or God's? Today, many conservatives in the GOP are changing their platforms to fit that which is politically correct and popular; many pastors are altering their stance on certain cultural issues, and some are even refusing to teach on these issues because of the persecution and unpopularity it might bring them. Believer, in the days we are living in, the question of whose honor we are seeking is going to become more and more prevalent in our lives, as we are challenged to give answers to certain topics that the majority does not want to hear. And in those moments, we are going to have to decide whose honor we are really seeking: man's honor, which is temporary, or God's honor, which is eternal.

AUGUST 25th

John 6:6: "But this He said to test him, for He Himself knew what He would do."

As Jesus and His disciples were sitting on a hillside one day, Jesus looked up and noticed a multitude coming to Him. So He leaned over to Philip and asked him, "Where shall we buy bread that these may eat?" (John 6:5). Philip looked at the amount of people coming, considered how much money they had, and then gave his answer, "Two hundred denarii worth of bread is not sufficient for them, that every one of them may have a little" (John 6:7).

Essentially, Philip said to Jesus: We can't feed them because we do not have the resources to do it. "But this [Jesus] said to test him." Jesus was testing Philip, as He already knew that there was no town nearby and that they were low on cash. As Ray Stedman explained, the question was asked so that Philip would see that there was "no human solution" to the problem, "for [Jesus] Himself knew what He would do."[115]

Oftentimes we find ourselves in similar situations, where there is seemingly no solution to our problems. We look at every angle, we consider every possibility, and when we have determined that there is no answer to the situation we are facing, we cry out in utter despair, "It's hopeless!" Well, suppose Jesus asked an unbeliever the same exact question He asked Philip; suppose an unbeliever was facing the same situation we are facing right now where there is no human solution. How would they respond? The same exact way we often respond; they would cry out in utter despair, "It's hopeless!" [116]

It should grieve our hearts greatly when we have the same response that an unbeliever has in these situations, because it means that we are both consumed by the same thing: unbelief. Their unbelief is based on the fact that they do not know God; ours is simply because we doubt God. Which is worse? Our response as believers should be much different because we know God. We know His Word, His character, His faithfulness, His goodness, His promises, etc. We should handle these situations differently, simply because His Holy Spirit lives within us and we have complete access to the Father through His Son, Jesus Christ. So, believer, though we may not know how God will resolve the situation, we should respond in faith because we know that He will resolve the situation.

AUGUST 26th

Hebrews 11:6: "But without faith it is impossible to please Him."

There will never be a moment in our walk with God where we will not need faith. In fact, as my good friend Darrell often reminds us, God will never allow us to escape our need for faith—because without faith, it is impossible to please God (Hebrews 11:6).

So, how much faith do we need to "please God"? The Bible says that if we have the faith of a mustard seed, we can move mountains (Matthew 17:20). When you consider the size of a mustard seed (one or two millimeters in diameter), that's not saying a lot.

For the last couple of weeks, our eleven-month-old daughter Kate has been taking her very first steps. Granted, she may only walk a couple of feet before she stumbles and dives into our arms; but regardless, she is still walking, and Michelle and I are completely overjoyed no matter how far she walks. I think it's interesting that we often do not consider a child to be *officially walking* until they reach a certain distance that, in our minds, is enough to be considered successful. Yet even if Kate only takes two steps and then falls down, isn't she still walking?

I am reminded of the time when Peter walked on water. So many people focus on Peter's failure as he saw the wind and waves and began to sink; yet they overlook the fact that there were twelve men in the boat that night and only one had the faith to step out of the boat and walk on water. Did you catch that? He *walked on water*! Do you think God was upset that Peter only took two steps? Do you think

Jesus chided Peter for being afraid and losing focus on Him? No, I think Jesus was overjoyed with Peter as Peter stumbled and dove into Jesus' arms crying, "Lord, save me!" (Matthew 14:30).

So how much faith does it take to please God? Is one step enough, or do we have to walk a mile before God is pleased? Believer, as long as we continue to walk in faith, as long as we continue to step out of the boat and walk as far as our faith will carry us in that situation, God will be pleased.

AUGUST 27th

John 8:11: "Neither do I condemn you; go and sin no more."

A few years ago, a coworker of mine told me something very interesting about her experience while serving on a jury. She said that throughout the trial, the defense attorney barely said anything in defense of his client. He had a brief opening statement, didn't call a single witness for the defense, barely cross-examined anyone, and had almost no closing argument. After the verdict was handed down, the jury was given an opportunity to ask questions of the judge and the attorneys in a private room. One of the questions posed to the defense attorney was, "Why didn't you defend your client?" He said to them, "I had no defense for him."

I was reminded of this when I was reading through John 8 and came across the story of when the Pharisees and scribes brought a woman to Jesus who was caught in the very act of adultery (John 8:4). That morning, Jesus was teaching at the temple in Jerusalem, and it was very crowded as "all the people came to Him" (John 8:2). It was then that these men brought this woman and put her in the midst of everyone that was there that morning. She was naked, humiliated, and had no defense.

As these men asked Jesus what He thought should be done with her—since the law instructed such to be stoned to death—Jesus said to them, "He who is without sin among you, let him throw a stone at her first" (John 8:7). Notice that Jesus did not condone this woman's sin, nor did He say she was not guilty of adultery. In fact, if you carefully examine Jesus' response to them, you will see that Jesus agreed with these men in that, according to the law, this woman should be stoned to death for her sin. Yet when Jesus put the onus back on these men by saying, "Let the person who is sinless among you go ahead and stone her to death for her sin," the men were "convicted by their conscience" and left one by one (John 8:9).

The law states that there had to be multiple accusers in order for the law to be enacted in such a case, so without anyone left to accuse her, Jesus looked at the woman and asked her, "Woman, where are those accusers of yours? Has no one condemned you?" (John 8:10). To which the woman responded, "No one, Lord" (John 8:11). Notice that she did not say, "No one, Rabbi" or "No one, Jesus," but clearly stated, "No one, Lord." At some point during this whole ordeal, this woman came to recognize Jesus as Lord and believed on Him as Messiah. Jesus then responded to her, "Neither do I condemn you; go and sin no more."

It is said that when Satan speaks to us about God, he lies; yet when he speaks to God about us, he tells the truth. The story of this woman is very symbolic of how we often feel after we have sinned. There we are, standing before God . . . naked, humiliated, and completely defenseless, as Satan rattles off all that we have done. And yet, just like with this woman, if Jesus is our Lord and Savior, we shall not "die in [our] sin" (John 8:21), because we have no accusers who can condemn us; not even Satan himself can do that. Only One has the right to judge, because only One is sinless and can exact a perfect, righteous judgment, and that is Christ Jesus. And He says to all who call on Him as Lord and Savior, "Neither do I condemn you, go and sin no more."

AUGUST 28th

John 8:37: "My word has no place in you."

About seven years ago I received a phone call from an old friend of mine from high school. She told me that she saw some of my posts about God and wanted to ask me some questions about my faith. After hours of conversation scattered over a couple different nights, I began to realize that my friend was not seeking Jesus; rather, she was seeking a religion that would suit her interests and lifestyle. The problem for my friend, and for so many others today, is that she would not make a place in her heart for the Word of God (John 8:37). Rather than seek what is true, she was seeking that which was pleasing to her ears.

This is the problem that Jesus encountered with the religious leaders in His day. His message of salvation and freedom did not make progress in the lives of these men because they would not make room for it in their hearts. They refused to receive Jesus' teaching as truth because it did not suit their lifestyles and was not what they wanted to hear. So, rather than receive what is true and find complete freedom in Jesus, they rejected Him and His message of grace and filled themselves with hate, anger, and murder.

I think it speaks volumes that the litmus test for every religion used to be whether it was true or not. Today, most people couldn't care less about what is true; they just want something that scratches their itching ears—something that feels good and doesn't offend anyone else. What was once a search for absolute truth has now been transformed into a carnal yearning to be entertained.

As odd as it may sound, people reject the gospel of Jesus Christ simply because it *is* true. "But because I [Jesus] tell you the truth, you do not believe Me" (John 8:45). The truth of the gospel offends man to the core of his being because it sheds light on our sinful nature and it calls evil what is evil, and sin what is sin. The gospel calls for recognition and repentance of sin, not blind acceptance to every perverse thing that man feels the need to do. The Bible says that it's not an affair, it's adultery; it's not abortion, it's murder; it's not love, it's sexual immorality. These are not easy things to hear or speak about in this day and age, but again, are they true?

The danger for us as believers comes when we stop making room for God's Word in our lives because it doesn't suit what we want to believe as truth. We would rather fill ourselves with something that is more pleasurable, something not so challenging or difficult to follow, something not so offensive to others. We close up our hearts to His truths so that His teaching can no longer make progress in our lives. It is there that we begin to replace God's truth with the lie . . . with false truths that are pleasing to the world and its itching ears that we think are more suitable for the times and the culture of today.

Jesus made it very clear, "If you abide in My word, you are My disciples indeed. And you shall know the truth and the truth shall set you free" (John 8:31–32).

AUGUST 29th

John 15:11: "These things I have spoken to you, that My joy may remain in you, and that your joy may be full."

In John 15, Jesus spoke about the relationship we are to have with Him by using the analogy of a vine and its branches. "I am the vine, you are the branches. He who abides in Me, and I in him, bears much fruit" (John 15:5). The interesting thing about being a branch is that though we produce fruit, we never take part in it. Our fulfillment, as branches, comes simply from abiding in the vine. The fruit

258 Renovating Your Mind

we produce is not for us, but rather is for others; thus "every branch that bears fruit He prunes [cleans], that it may bear more fruit" (John 15:2).

John continually emphasized what Jesus often spoke about: the need for believers to abide in (remain in, continue in) the Word of God, because it is by His word that God cleanses us from the world and from ourselves. But, as my good friend Darrell often reminds us, "You may be in the Word, but is the Word in you?" The cleansing that we receive from God's Word only comes through the obedience and the application of His Word. It is an essential characteristic of the Christian walk as this is what compels us to bear fruit for others.[117]

"If you abide in Me, and My words abide in you, you will ask what you desire and it shall be done for you" (John 15:7). Notice that Jesus is not referring to desires for our own gain here, but rather our desires to bear fruit for the sake of others. These desires, Jesus says, only come from us abiding in Him, and His Word abiding in us. Ultimately, He says, this is how God is glorified. "By this My Father is glorified, that you bear much fruit; so you will be My disciples" (John 15:8). Jesus expounded on what it is to be His disciple in John 13:35, "By this all will know that you are My disciples, if you have love for one another."

The fruit that Jesus is referring to here is love. "As the Father loved Me, I also have loved you; abide in My love" (John 15:9). The apostle Paul wrote about this fruit as well in Galatians 5:22, "But the fruit of the Spirit is love." God's greatest desire for us, as believers, is to love, because this is where our joy is ultimately sustained and fulfilled: "These things [in John 15:1–10] I have spoken to you, that My joy may remain in you, and that your joy may be full."

Jesus knew a little something about this enduring joy and how it only comes when bearing fruit for others, "who for the joy that was set before Him, endured the cross" (Hebrews 12:2). Joy that endures only comes when we produce fruit for others, not fruit for ourselves. And if you really think about it, a branch does not need fruit if it already has the vine that is the source of that fruit. In other words, Jesus is all we need.

AUGUST 30th

John 11:6: "So, when He heard that he was sick, He stayed two more days."

Lazarus was dying, and like any loved one would do, Mary and Martha pleaded with Jesus to come and save their brother. "Now Jesus loved Martha and her sister and Lazarus. So, when He heard that he was sick, He stayed two more days" (John 11:5–6). Doesn't that sound odd? Jesus loved Martha, Mary, and Lazarus—so, because He loved them, He stayed two more days and allowed Lazarus to die. This is so contrary to our thinking and understanding of how things should be done. In our estimation, if Jesus really loved them, then He would have gone and saved Lazarus, not waited around for two more days allowing him to die.

The truth is that by the time the message from Mary and Martha reached Jesus (it took about two days), Lazarus had already died. The reason why Jesus waited two more days before He began His two-day journey back to Bethany was so that there could be no doubt that Lazarus had in fact died; this way, he would have been dead for four days by the time Jesus brought him back to life.

We learn here that there was a greater purpose in this sickness—one that superseded the temporary comfort that Martha, Mary, and Lazarus so desired. "This sickness is not unto death, but for the glory of God, that the Son of God may be glorified through it" (John 11:4). God, the Father, gave Jesus, the Son, certain works to perform while He was here on Earth. These works would testify of Jesus' deity as the Son of God so that people might believe on Him as Messiah. Lazarus was allowed to die so that Jesus would be glorified.

I think we often forget that when we gave our lives to Jesus Christ, we signed over all of our rights to Him. At one time or another, we have all said something to the effect of, "God, take my life and use me as *You* will." God does not look upon these words lightly; He will take us at our word and use us in ways that we often do not understand or even like. I think it is very important for us to remember during these times that the trials we go through are not only for us, but are for the sake of others as well. In this case, Martha, Mary, and Lazarus were allowed to go through this very difficult time for the sake of the disciples. "Lazarus is dead. And I am glad for your sakes that I was not there, that you may believe" (John 11:14).

Believer, though God's ways and purposes are far above ours, and though we may never understand why He does what He does, God's character is clearly revealed in and through the Bible; He is good, He is faithful, He is in control of all things, and most important, He is love. So when in doubt, do not rely on what you see, but rather rely on what you know to be true.

AUGUST 31st

1 John 2:1: "And if anyone sins, we have an Advocate with the Father, Jesus Christ the righteous."

I think it's interesting that in a court of law, a defense attorney tries to prove that his client is innocent, yet Jesus Christ, our "Advocate with the Father," does no such thing. He never tries to hide the fact that we are guilty; in fact, as David Guzik pointed out, Jesus fully "admits our guilt."[118] As believers, we should never fear or worry about the Father's judgment for our sin because "[Jesus] Himself is the propitiation for our sins" (1 John 2:2). Jesus presented Himself as the sacrifice for all of our sins so that, though we are guilty, we are still counted righteous by the Father.

So we know that Jesus is our Advocate with the Father, our defender from Satan, and our deliverer from this world . . . yet our worst enemy we often overlook. Sure, we love to throw Satan, the world, and others under the bus and blame them whenever we are attacked; but honestly, there is nothing in this world that can torment us, cause us to doubt, or create depression in our lives like our own selves. After all, we know our thoughts, our intentions, our desires, our perversities, etc., and we constantly condemn ourselves for embracing them. Yet even here, in the depths of our soul, we must realize that Jesus is our Advocate—because unlike our other enemies, we have absolutely no defense against our own conscience.

The reason why we forget to rely on Jesus as our Advocate is because we are too busy trying to prove our innocence to ourselves;[119] we are too busy trying to make ourselves feel better by justifying why we committed that sin. The truth is that, as believers, we should never *feel better* about our sin, because it completely goes against our new nature. We should be greatly disturbed when we are confronted with our rebellion. Yet we put forth so much time and effort trying to free ourselves from the truth of our guilt that we actually open ourselves up to the lie that what we did was really not that bad.

How can we ever rejoice in Jesus' great sacrifice if we continually fail to recognize why we need that great sacrifice? We struggle to believe in Jesus' love, grace, and forgiveness for us because we refuse to accept the truth of our sinful nature. There is no growth in this, no maturity, no great victory. We are sinners. We are guilty. We are completely bankrupt and hopeless without Him. The sooner we can admit this to ourselves, and call what we do what it really is, the sooner we can move on and rejoice in the glorious truth of our Advocate's amazing grace. Because if we are not guilty, why do we need Jesus? If we are not guilty, how great is His grace, really? As Ray Stedman well said, "The blood of Jesus Christ cannot cleanse excuses. It only cleanses sins."[120] It is only when we look in the mirror and admit how sinful we are that we truly begin to appreciate what we have been given. It is here that we start to believe. It is here that we refuse to take His grace for granted. And it is here that we are forgiven.

So, believer, remember, Jesus made the greatest exchange in the history of the world for us. He died as though He lived our life, and we live freely as though we lived His. Stop trying to prove your innocence; just admit your guilt, stand on His promises as your Advocate, and receive His amazing grace.

SEPTEMBER 1st

Acts 1:8: "[Y]ou shall be witnesses to Me."

After Jesus raised Lazarus from the dead, people came from all over to see him. This made the Sadducees very angry because "on account of [Lazarus] many of the Jews went away and believed in Jesus" (John 12:11). The Sadducees were angry because Lazarus was living proof that their beliefs were wrong, as they did not believe in the resurrection—but even more so, because people were withdrawing from the influence of the religious leaders and believing in Jesus as Messiah.

In Acts 1:8, Jesus told His disciples that when the Holy Spirit came upon them, they would "be witnesses to [Him]." In other words, they would be witnesses for Jesus based solely on what He did in their lives, not because of anything they would have done or would later have to do. The same held true for Lazarus. Here was a man that did nothing but die; and yet because of the work of Jesus in his life, many came to believe in Jesus as Messiah.

I am reminded of the man in Mark 5 who had a legion of demons within him. After Jesus cast out the demons into a herd of swine, this man pleaded with Jesus to allow him to stay with Jesus. Yet Jesus told him, "Go home to your friends, and tell them what great things the Lord has done for you, and how He has had compassion on you" (Mark 5:19). When Jesus later returned to this area, the masses came rushing to Jesus, simply because of the testimony of this one man.

Neither Lazarus nor the demon-possessed man had to try to be witnesses; they were witnesses simply because they were living proof of the power of God. All they had to do was just share with others what God had done in their lives. Because of their testimonies, many believed in Jesus as the Christ.

Believer, the same holds true for us. We were once dead but are now alive in Christ. We are witnesses because we are living proof of the power of God, and when we share what God has done in our lives, many will come to call on Him as Messiah as well. As the old saying goes, "You are not a human *doing*; you are a human *being*."

SEPTEMBER 2ⁿᵈ

Leviticus 20:26: "You shall be holy to Me, for I the LORD am holy, and have separated you from the people, that you should be Mine."

The theme of the book of Leviticus is found in Leviticus 20:26: "You shall be holy to Me, for I the LORD am holy, and have separated you from the people, that you should be Mine." The word "holy" generally means to be set apart or sanctified; but interestingly enough, it also comes from the same root word that our English word "wholeness" comes from.[121] I believe that if you were to theologically paint a picture or create a diagram of what it is to be holy, you would eventually end up with an image that perfectly portrays wholeness.

Ray Stedman explained that wholeness means to have everything that we were intended to have, functioning as we were "intended to function." This is how it was when the Lord first created Adam. Adam had everything that he was intended to have and he functioned just as he was intended to function. But then came the fall, and everything changed. Adam was still in the image of God, but he was no longer in the likeness of God. Something was now missing. Thankfully, God saw our brokenness and had great mercy on us. He knew our ways of wickedness and our flawed nature, and yet He still graciously chose to reach down so that we could be whole again.[122] We find this great purpose in Isaiah 61:1–3:

> The Spirit of the Lord GOD is upon Me [Jesus], because the Lord has anointed Me to preach good tidings to the poor; He has sent Me to heal the brokenhearted, to proclaim liberty to the captives, and the opening of the prison to those who are bound; to proclaim the acceptable year of the LORD, and the day of vengeance of our God; to comfort all who mourn, to console those who mourn in Zion, to give them beauty for ashes, the oil of joy for mourning, the garment of praise for the spirit of heaviness; that they may be called trees of righteousness, the planting of the LORD, that He may be glorified.

Jesus Christ came and fulfilled God's great purpose. He was empowered by the Holy Spirit to preach good tidings to the poor; to heal the brokenhearted; to proclaim freedom to all those in bondage and free all of those that are imprisoned; to comfort and console those who mourn; to give beauty for ashes, the oil of joy for mourning, and to replace the spirit of heaviness with the garment of praise. Regardless how sin would break us in this life, Jesus was empowered to restore that brokenness and make us whole again.

SEPTEMBER 3ʳᵈ

John 13:1: "He loved them to the end."

Your unbelief in something cannot take away my freedom to choose, just like my unbelief in something cannot take away yours. This is the law that God has put into place regarding freedom of choice. Unfortunately, we see people attempting to do this all too frequently in our country today. And though we are quick to criticize this kind of dysfunctional thinking because we recognize the foolishness in it, we often do this very thing with God.

For example, we are a people who incessantly examine ourselves and meticulously record our motives, thoughts, and choices throughout the day; then, at the end of the day, by our own estimation of who we are and what we have done, we judiciously determine that there is no way God can love us. Yet God has repeatedly said to each one of us throughout the Bible, "I love you, unconditionally." Even if we choose not to believe that God loves us, even if we can prove without a shadow of doubt that we are not worthy of such amazing love, it still doesn't mean that it's not true. God has freely made the choice to love us, and our unbelief cannot take away His choice.

In John 13, as John was reflecting on the hours before Jesus gave up His life for us on the cross, he wrote, "when Jesus knew that His hour had come and that He should depart from this world to the Father, having loved His own who were in the world, He loved them to the end" (John 13:1). As David Guzik pointed out, this means that Jesus loved His disciples "to the fullest extent" possible.[123] What is important to note about this statement is that Jesus knew these men would betray Him, deny Him, and desert Him in His hour of need, and yet Jesus still loved them to the very end because that was the choice that Jesus made.[124] Nothing His disciples could say or do could rob Jesus of His choice to love them.

This same truth can be applied to just about every area of our lives in regard to our relationship with God. Even when we are not faithful to Him, He is still faithful to us; even when we do not listen to Him, He still listens to us; even when we run away from Him, He still chases after us; and even when we do not love Him, He still loves us. Believer, our unbelief cannot take away God's freedom to choose. He has spoken very clearly to each and every one of us through His Son Jesus Christ that He always has, He presently is, and He forever will love us. So stop equating God's choices by how you see yourself, and just accept what God has said as truth.

SEPTEMBER 4th

> John 13:7: "Jesus answered and said to him, 'What I am doing you do
> not understand now, but you will know after this.'"

While Jesus was washing His disciples' feet, Peter questioned Jesus as to why He
was doing this. "Jesus answered and said to him, 'What I am doing you do not
understand now, but you will know after this.'" Peter then rebuked Jesus, saying,
"You shall never wash my feet!" To which Jesus responded, "If I do not wash you,
you have no part with Me" (John 13:8).

It's interesting to me that Peter objected to having his feet washed simply
because he did not understand why Jesus was doing it. It wasn't that Peter didn't
need his feet washed or didn't like having his feet washed. No, Peter protested Jesus
washing his feet because he needed an answer to satisfy his innate compulsion to
understand. But notice that even though Peter did not understand, Jesus still did
not give Peter an explanation of His actions, but rather made Peter a promise:
Though you do not understand what I am doing right now, you will understand
afterward. Jesus was telling Peter to trust Him.

The world we live in is a "reason-focused" world that demands an explanation as to why things happen. The problem for us is that we carry over this same
reason-focused thinking into our walk with God. So when the Lord allows certain
things into our lives that we do not understand, we rebuke that which He wants
to do, simply because we do not understand why He is doing it. We, like Peter,
cry out and demand an explanation from God for His actions, or lack thereof—
but the Lord's reply to us is the same that it was to Peter: Though you do not
understand what I am doing right now, you will understand afterward. In other
words: Trust Me.

The reason why we incessantly demand an answer from God is because we
think an explanation of "why" will actually make the situation better. Yet in my
experience, peace is never found in searching for, or even finding, the why—but
rather, in knowing the Who. These are the times that our faith in the Lord is grown
the most. I understand that it is just part of our natural self to want to understand,
but that doesn't mean it's who we have to be in those situations. When speaking
about being content in every season of life, the apostle Paul wrote that he had to
learn to be content because it was not part of his nature to be so (Philippians 4:11).
As believers, we have to learn not to rely on our natural self, living by reason and
explanations, but rather live by faith in the God who is always faithful to us. So,

believer, "You don't understand now what I am doing, but someday you will" (John 13:7, NLT).

SEPTEMBER 5th

John 13:15: "[Y]ou should do as I have done to you."

Jesus said in John 13:34, "A new commandment I give to you, that you love one another." This seemed a little odd to me at first, because I remember reading in Leviticus 19:18 when the Lord said to Moses, "love your neighbor as yourself." So how is this a new commandment? The answer is found in the second half of John 13:34: "as I have loved you, that you also love one another." Jesus was not referring to the *commandment* to love one another as being new, but rather the *standard* by which we are to love others.

Moments after Jesus washed His disciples' feet, He said to them, "For I have given you an example that you should do as I have done to you" (John 13:15). Washing the disciples' feet was one example of how to love one another, but it was not *the* example. The more significant portion of this verse is when Jesus said, "you should do as I have done to you." Not just in serving, not just in loving, not just in forgiving—but in all things, Jesus says, you should do to others as I have done to you.

Some of the greatest challenges we face as Christians is to choose to love and forgive those whom we deem unlovable and unforgivable. Yet even in these situations, I believe we all still make the choice to love and forgive as God has instructed. The problem is that we love and forgive one another according to what we determine love and forgiveness to be. These determinations are usually based on our own experiences of being loved and forgiven, or by what we believe that person might deserve according to what they may or may not have done, rather than loving and forgiving just as Jesus loves and forgives us.

"Most assuredly, I say to you, a servant is not greater than his master" (John 13:16). Jesus' point is very simple: If He, our Lord and Savior, chooses to love and forgive us, then we, being His servants, must do the same—not according to our standards of love and forgiveness, but according to His. We are to love just as He loves us, and we are to forgive just as He forgives us. "If you know these things, blessed are you if you do them" (John 13:17). The amazing thing about all of this is that when we obey Jesus' instructions, and we do to others just as He has done to us, we are the ones who are truly blessed—because it is there, in that obedience, that Jesus manifests Himself to us (John 14:21).

266 Renovating Your Mind

SEPTEMBER 6th

> John 13:37: "Peter said to Him, 'Lord, why can I not follow You now?
> I will lay down my life for Your sake.'"

After Jesus told His disciples that He would be leaving them and would go to a place where they could not come, Peter said to Him, "Lord, why can I not follow You now?" After all that they had been through together, after all the places they had followed Jesus to, why now were they not allowed to follow Jesus? This is what Peter was asking: Why can I not follow You now, Lord? Is it because it is dangerous? "I will lay down my life for Your sake."

I have no doubt that Peter meant what he said. I believe that he would have absolutely given up his life for Jesus had the occasion arose. We saw proof of this in the garden of Gethsemane, when Peter drew his sword and attacked one of the servants of the high priest as they came to take away Jesus. Yet Jesus never asked for Peter to die for Him; rather, He asked Peter "to live for Him."[125] Courage in the battlefield is one thing, but courage in everyday life . . . that is an entirely different thing, and it was one that Peter was not prepared for.

Peter was ready to take a life, but he was not ready to save one. He was ready to die as he wanted, but was not ready to live as Christ wanted. Just hours earlier Jesus had girded Himself and washed the disciples' feet. Yet when Jesus was setting aside His garments and girding Himself to wash their feet, none of the disciples stood up and said, "No Lord! Please, let me do that. Let me wash my brother's feet." Their hearts were not right.

Like Peter, we often boast about what we are willing to do for Christ or for others, but rarely, if ever, do we boast about what Christ asks us to do. It is easy to pick and choose our battles and be strong in situations we are comfortable with being strong in, but living for Christ, doing what He wants us to do, that is an entirely different way of dying. What He asks us to do always requires a measure of faith, not a measure of self.

Sure, we will blast the guy who cuts us off on the freeway, but will we show him grace? We will defend ourselves fervently when someone speaks harshly about us, but will we hold our tongue? We will strike back at the person who hurts us, but will we forgive? We will gladly put ourselves in harm's way and die for our loved ones, but will we put down the remote control and actually lead them spiritually?

SEPTEMBER 7th

> 2 Corinthians 5:17 (ESV): "Therefore, if anyone is in Christ, he is a new creation. The old has passed away; behold, the new has come."

When we surrender our lives to Jesus Christ and make Him Lord and Master of all that we are, we have to change the way that we think about ourselves, others, and even Jesus Christ Himself. "From now on, therefore [because we have given our lives to Christ], we regard no one according to the flesh [not even ourselves]. Even though we once regarded Christ according to the flesh, we regard Him thus no longer" (2 Corinthians 5:16, ESV).

No longer are we to think as we once did, according to our flesh; rather we are to think according to what the Bible says is true. Our wisdom, the things we trust in, the truths that we are to live by, are no longer according to the world or our feelings. We are now to walk in the newness of life physically, mentally, and spiritually. Unfortunately, this change in thinking is not something that will just happen automatically, nor is it something that will come naturally to us; a transformation must take place within us as we renew our minds by reading, believing, and applying the Word of God to our everyday lives and circumstances (Romans 12:2).

One of the biggest changes that must take place in our thinking is how we view ourselves. Second Corinthians 5:17 (ESV) tells us, "Therefore, if anyone is in Christ, he is a new creation. The old has passed away; behold, the new has come." In my experience, one of the hardest things to do as a born-again believer is to accept this truth when we begin living out our new lives in Christ and then *we* stumble and fall by sinning. Our first reaction is that we really haven't changed at all, that we are still the same old people doing the same old things—and it can be very discouraging.

When I got saved, I boldly proclaimed to all of my friends how much I had changed and how I was not that same old person anymore. One year later, I made the foolish decision to go to Vegas with my friends and I repeated the same foolish behavior that I had sworn I had left behind. It was then that one of my best friends said to me, "I knew you didn't really change." I was devastated. My heart was broken because I knew I had just ruined my witness. I remember thinking to myself, "I thought I had changed. . . ."

"Therefore, if anyone is in Christ, he is a new creation. The old has passed away; behold, the new has come." I want you to notice the emphasis on who we are in Christ: "he is a new creation." I am a new creation in Christ, as are you. Notice that this verse is not written in the past tense in that it is a onetime deal, or even the future tense where it has not yet taken place. No, it is written in the present tense as a continual state of living. We are new creations, every second of every day.

Though I had made a very foolish decision by going to Vegas and taking part in those old behaviors, it still did not change who I was in Christ. I was not the same person I used to be, as "the old has passed away; behold, the new has come." I had to renovate my mind through the Word of God by reading, believing, and applying it in that situation, no matter how badly I felt about what I did. And as 1 John 1:9 promises us, "If we confess our sins, He is faithful and just to forgive us our sins and cleanse us from all unrighteousness." The real difference between the old and the new is that the old self would just keep on sinning without hesitation; the new self repents and seeks forgiveness.

SEPTEMBER 8ᵗʰ

> Isaiah 1:11 (ESV): "'What to me is the multitude of your sacrifices?' says the LORD."

It is really easy in our walk with God to go from devotion to religion. It can happen so subtly that we don't even realize that we are just going through the motions and that our hearts have become cold and hard. If this is not dealt with quickly, it can become such a way of life that the motions become our religion, or our "salvation," and we begin to live a life far apart from God.

This is what happened to Israel back in the days of Isaiah. God had given His people certain rites to engage in that were designed to help them walk in their faith. Blood sacrifices were vivid reminders of the seriousness of sin in that sin brings forth death. The Sabbath was to remind them of the need for rest and worship; burning incense was a reminder of how sweet prayer is to God. Yet God told Israel through the prophet Isaiah, "I hate all your festivals and sacrifices. I cannot stand the sight of them!" (Isaiah 1:14, NLT1996). Why, you ask? Because these rites had become their religion, not their devotion. Though they were meticulously performing these rites as God had instructed, their hearts were far from God. Like a painting of a fire putting off no heat, there was no devotion in these acts of worship.

Today we have many rites as well—communion, baptism, worship, praying before meals, tithing, going to church, etc. Very quickly, these things can become religion rather than devotion. Very easily we can look at these things as our "salvation" as we meticulously perform them; but, simply taking part and performing these rites is sickening to God if our hearts are not in them: "I am sick of your sacrifices" (Isaiah 1:11, NLT1996). Understand that God wants the devotion of our hearts, not our acts of religion, because He knows that when He has our hearts, He will have all of us.

So how do we combat falling from devotion to religion? By spending intimate time with God every day; focusing on Him, talking to Him, listening to Him through prayer and the reading of His Word. I once heard a pastor say that our experience at church on Sunday is a direct result of what we do with God Monday through Saturday. His point was that our works and deeds will be acts of devotion, and not religion, if we are daily at the feet of our Father.

Performing rites devoid of the reality of Who those rites are to, and why we are performing those rites in the first place, brings much displeasure to the Lord. We need to be real with God and truly consider why we take part in these things. We need to turn those acts of religion into heartfelt acts of devotion, so that they will be a sweet incense to our Father in Heaven and in turn, produce much fruit in our lives.

SEPTEMBER 9th

> Psalm 40:1 (NIV): "I waited patiently for the LORD; He turned to me and heard my cry."

In Psalm 40, David shares with us a time in his life when he prayed and waited on the Lord: "I waited patiently for the LORD; he turned to me and heard my cry. He lifted me up out of the slimy pit, out of the mud and mire; he set my feet on a rock and gave me a firm place to stand. He put a new song in my mouth, a hymn of praise to our God. Many will see and fear the LORD and put their trust in him" (Psalm 40:1–3, NIV).

When we read passages like this, we quickly capture and hold tightly to the promises for our own circumstances. We say to ourselves, "God will turn and answer me, and deliver me from this slimy pit! Thank You, Lord!" And He absolutely will. But there is one little section in these verses that we seemingly skip right over and disregard: "I waited patiently." We love to claim the final outcome, but rarely do we ever want to acknowledge and embrace the process.

Let's just admit it: We hate waiting. The light turns green and the car in front of us doesn't move for one, maybe two seconds, and yet we are compelled to lay on our horn and scream at the person because, for us, sitting at a green light for one or two seconds is a painful time to endure. "I have places to be, things to do, and you are obstructing where I want to go!" And that's really it, isn't it? When we pray for things to come to pass and God tells us to wait, in our minds God is obstructing where we want to be and what we want to do. He is keeping us from where we want to go. In our minds, there is absolutely no point to just sitting there, waiting.

Well, contrary to popular belief, waiting is not inactivity. G. Campbell Morgan said it best: "Waiting for God is not laziness. Waiting for God is not going to sleep. Waiting for God is not the abandonment of effort. Waiting for God means, first, activity under command; second, readiness for any new command that may come; third, the ability to do nothing until the command is given."[126] Waiting is exercising an active faith in God.

David knew a lot about waiting as he was anointed king very early on in his life and yet he had to wait many years before it came to pass. That is why he could write, "Wait for the LORD; be strong and take heart and wait for the LORD" (Psalm 27:14). And also, "Blessed is the man who makes the LORD his trust" (Psalm 40:4, ESV). It is important to understand that waiting is a valuable part of the Christian life; it is a time of growing our faith and learning to trust in God.

So believer, remember, though difficult and trying, waiting is often the most important method of carrying out God's will in your life, because waiting for an answer from God is often part of the answer to your prayer.

SEPTEMBER 10th

> Matthew 9:4 (NIV): "Why do you entertain evil thoughts in your hearts?"

I think the word "entertain" that the NIV uses in this verse is very interesting, because it not only refers to turning over something in your mind again and again, but also refers to welcoming in, showing hospitality to, and making something comfortable. If you think about when you entertain people at your house, generally speaking, you welcome them in, make them comfortable, and engage in fellowship with them. This is what Jesus is asking the Pharisees in regard to evil thoughts: "Why do you entertain evil thoughts in your hearts?" "Why do you welcome evil thoughts into your hearts, make them comfortable, empower them by giving them a foothold in your life, and engage them with an open mind?"

The problem for us is that we often do not recognize these evil thoughts for what they truly are, kind of like wolves in sheep's clothing. They may not be as obvious to us as thoughts about murder, stealing, adultery, and the occult, but nevertheless, they are just as toxic. Maybe for you, the evil thought is that you are not pretty enough; or that you are not smart enough; or that God will never deliver you from this trial or answer your prayer or meet that need. Maybe it's that shopping, a relationship, food, or work will fulfill the emptiness you feel in your life. Maybe it's that you are now damaged goods from that past relationship and no one would ever want to be with you; maybe it's that you are not adequate for God's calling in that ministry. Regardless what the lie may be, it can quickly be camouflaged into something that it isn't, and before we know it, we are entertaining it in our hearts.

This is why it is so important to be in the Word of God, because His truths dispel all the lies and expose those things that hide in the darkness. His Word transforms our minds so that we will recognize these lies from the very beginning and rebuke them rather than entertain them. This is what the apostle Paul meant when he wrote, "We demolish arguments and every pretension that sets itself up against the knowledge of God, and we take captive every thought to make it obedient to Christ" (2 Corinthians 10:5, NIV). So, believer, before you entertain any thought, take it to Christ and hold it up to His truths—see if it is worthy to be entertained in your heart and mind.

SEPTEMBER 11th

Hebrews 13:3: "Remember the prisoners as if chained with them— those who are mistreated— since you yourselves are in the body also."

One morning as I was driving to work, I heard the DJ on the radio say, "News update: Terror in the east." I immediately felt my heart grow hard toward whatever was going to be said next because in my mind, the people in the Middle East were always fighting and killing each other—and, to be perfectly honest with you, I couldn't have cared less about what was going on over there because it didn't affect me. But that was all about to change. As the DJ continued, she said that two commercial airliners had crashed into the Twin Towers. She was not talking about the Middle East—she was talking about back east, in New York City. All of a sudden fear, sadness, and shock came over me. All of a sudden, it mattered.

The author of Hebrews understood this part of the human condition very well, and so in chapter 13, as he is writing about brotherly love, he gives us some practical ways to "Let brotherly love continue" (Hebrews 13:1). He says, "Remember the prisoners as if chained with them—those who are mistreated—since you yourselves are in the body also." Notice that he doesn't just say, "Remember the prisoners . . . those who are mistreated." No, he specifically says "Remember the prisoners *as if chained with them*—those who are mistreated—*since you yourselves are in the body also.*"

We can be such self-serving people in that if something doesn't directly affect us, we generally don't care about it. To help us remember to support others through prayer and provision, the author of Hebrews says, "Pray and provide for them as though you are in their situation with them." When we take on this perspective, all of a sudden their situations matter to us. If we were in that situation with them, we would be on our knees praying fervently and without ceasing; we would be pleading for people to come and provide for us.

The amazing thing I have learned through all of this is that since I have been praying for others as though I am in that situation with them, and thinking about how I would want to be provided for if I were in that situation, my perspective on life has been radically changed. All of the sudden those little, meaningless problems that I have been so fixated on lately have disappeared. I am no longer concerned with what I do not have, but rather have become so extremely grateful for all that the Lord has blessed me with. When we realize what others are going through, and pray and provide for them as though we are in that situation with them, it changes us and teaches us to truly appreciate what we have. And it is here, the author of Hebrews says, that brotherly love continues in us and through us.

SEPTEMBER 12th

John 16:27: "[F]or the Father Himself loves you."

Do blessings only come from the prayers we lift up to God, or does God bless us because He is good and because He loves us? I have been thinking a lot about this lately as I found myself in this place where I subconsciously believed that goodness only came if and when I prayed. So if I did not pray, then God would not move and nothing good would happen. By having this type of belief, I completely removed the very nature of God from the whole process. I was living as if His action to bless was fully dependent on my prayers. Essentially, I removed God's willingness to be good.

When Jesus was speaking to His disciples in John 16 about His death, resurrection, and ascension into heaven, He said to them, "In that day you will ask in My name, and I do not say to you that I shall pray the Father for you; for the Father

Himself loves you, because you have loved Me, and have believed that I came forth from God" (John 16:26–27). The word "for" at the beginning of verse 27 indicates that what is said next will explain what was previously said. Jesus' point was that once He ascended into heaven, the disciples would have direct access to God the Father, "for the Father Himself loves you." Everything Jesus was pointing to here was based on the fact that God loved them, not on whether they prayed or not.

We need to remember that the purpose of prayer is not to move God to do our will, but rather to reveal the Father's will to us that we might be of His mind and purpose. Ultimately, when we focus too much on prayer and not enough on who God is, we lose sight of the fact that He is good, He has good plans for us, and He wants to bless us; we begin believing that His goodness is based solely on our prayers and we have to convince Him to have mercy and grace on us; we have to convince Him to do good things in and around our lives or else nothing good will ever happen. When we have this type of mindset, our prayer life gets all the glory and we quickly forget who our God really is.

So, believer, when God moves mightily—when He blesses, when He heals and saves and delivers—it is not just because we prayed; it is because He is good, He loves us, and that is what He had planned.

SEPTEMBER 13th

Philippians 1:1: "Paul and Timothy, bondservants of Jesus Christ . . ."

The term "bondservant" that Paul uses here describes a slave who willingly commits himself to serve a master that he loves and respects. As Ron Daniel explained, the origin for this word was established in Exodus 21 where we are told that if a Jewish person was forced into slavery because they "committed a crime or got into debt," they were forced into slavery; but after six years of service, according to God's law, all slaves were allowed to go free as they would have paid their debt for that particular circumstance. Yet, even after their required service was over, many slaves did not want to leave their masters. They quickly realized that there was no better place for them to be as they loved their masters and more importantly, they knew their masters loved them; and so they chose to serve that master for the rest of their lives.[127] These slaves became known as bondservants.

This is what Paul was alluding to when he described himself and Timothy as bondservants of Jesus Christ. He was saying: We have made the choice to willingly give ourselves over to Jesus Christ because there is no better place for us to be. There is no better Master to serve, no better life to live, no better joy to be had, than that of a bondservant, because for me, Paul says, to live is Christ.

In this we find one of the keys to having a joyful life. Paul says there must be a change in our thinking from being a bondservant to self to being a bondservant to Christ. David echoed this same sentiment as he stated that there was no situation or circumstance that could move or shake him because he had fully submitted his life to God: "I have set the Lord always before me; [and] because [of that] He is at my right hand [and] I shall not be moved. Therefore [because I have submitted my life to God] my heart is glad and my glory rejoices. . . . [For] in [the Lord's] presence is fullness of joy" (Psalm 16:8–9, 11). Like David, Paul stated that he could be joyful in any situation, because he placed God first in his life through acts of submissive obedience to the Father's will.

For many, the idea of being a bondservant to anyone is ludicrous. Yet the truth is that every person in the world is a bondservant to someone; some are bondservants to Christ, and some are bondservants to self. Romans 6:16 confirms this very thought: "Do you not know that to whom you present yourselves slaves to obey, you are that one's slaves whom you obey, whether of sin leading to death, or of obedience leading to righteousness?" So we see that there are only two masters available for us to choose from: self, which leads to bondage and death; or Christ, who leads to freedom and life. Who will you choose?

SEPTEMBER 14th

> Psalm 23:6 (NLT): "Surely your goodness and unfailing love will pursue me all the days of my life."

Chasing around our fourteen-month-old daughter Kate obviously has its challenges physically, but I never really stopped and considered the emotional challenges that come with being in a constant state of pursuing your child. Wednesday night, as Michelle and I were praying, Michelle reminded me how incredibly special it is when Kate stops running around and actually makes a choice to come and interact with us. And Michelle was right; it brings us so much joy when Kate acknowledges us in some way, shape, or form. It doesn't matter if she is showing us her baby, asking for help, or giving us a hug; any interaction with her is powerfully precious to us because we love her and we just want to spend time with her.

I imagine it is very similar with God. Ever since the fall in the garden, God has been in a constant state of pursuing us; desiring any semblance of the intimate fellowship that He once had with Adam and Eve. When His children stop running around and actually make a choice to interact with Him, not because they have to but because they actually want to, I imagine it is incredibly special to Him. It doesn't matter if we are crying out for help, or just wanting to talk to Him about life . . . those moments are powerfully precious to our Abba Father as He longs for that special time with each one of us. So, believer, make it a point today to stop running around and spend some quality time with your Heavenly Father. He will be glad you did, and so will you.

SEPTEMBER 15th

2 Corinthians 1:10: "who delivered us from so great a death, and does deliver us; in whom we trust that He will still deliver us . . ."

One of the first rules of communication is to make eye contact with the person you are talking to. Doing this accomplishes two things: 1) It helps the listener focus on what is being said; and 2) it confirms to the speaker that what they said has been heard. I know at home there have been times when Michelle will ask me a question or share something with me when I am occupied doing something else. If I do not respond to her with an answer or acknowledge that I was listening by making eye contact with her, she is sure to get my attention and repeat what she said because she wants to be certain that I heard her.

This is where we often struggle when praying to God. Obviously we cannot make eye contact with God to ensure He has heard us, and we are not going to hear Him audibly answer us, so when we are praying about something and we do not get any type of response or acknowledgment from God, we often believe the lie that God is not working in that situation.

With God, we should never confuse silence with inactivity. Just because there is no acknowledgment or response from God does not mean that He has not heard us, and it does not mean that He is not working in that situation—quite the opposite, actually. The psalmist reminds us in Psalm 46:1 that God is a very present help in times of trouble. Jesus said in John 5:17 that God is always working. Paul assures us in 2 Corinthians 1:10 that God, "who delivered us . . . and does deliver us . . . will still deliver us." In other words, God was faithful, God is faithful, and God will always be faithful.

There comes a point for all of us when we have to begin to walk with God by the knowledge of His Word and not by our feelings. We have to choose to believe

His promises by faith, and trust in who He says He is and what He says He will do. It is here that we will find peace in the midst of silence.

SEPTEMBER 16th

> John 18:4: "Jesus therefore, knowing all things that would come upon Him, went forward and said to them, 'Whom are you seeking?'"

When Judas brought about two hundred men armed with weapons to arrest Jesus in the garden of Gethsemane that night, Jesus did not try to escape or fight His way out of the situation even though He knew "all things that would come upon Him." Jesus had the power to overcome these men, He had the choice to run away from this situation, but He didn't. Rather, He humbly yet firmly submitted Himself to the will of God. "Jesus therefore, knowing all things that would come upon Him, went forward and said to them, 'Whom are you seeking?'"

There will be many times when God will ordain something for us that will not be pleasant, comfortable, or fun—yet we must consider the fact that if the Father has ordained it for us, perfectly suited it for us in timing and method, should we really try to escape or fight it? Should we not, like Jesus, humbly yet firmly submit ourselves to the will of the Father because we trust His will for our lives?

There is such a difference in spiritual and personal growth by how we endure these times of testing. I have fought these situations all the way through to the very end, stubbornly refusing to accept them; I have reluctantly submitted to them simply because I was exhausted from fighting; and I have tried to escape them by running as fast and as far as I could. And though I eventually came through these situations, I hadn't really changed at all. My faith in God had not changed. I was still a fair-weather Christian whose faith only shined like gold in the sunlight.

But when I willingly embraced the situation and humbly submitted to the Father's will for my life, by faith . . . that is when I grew the most, changed the most, and received the most blessing. Believer, these are the situations that we train for. These are the moments in time when we really get to test out our faith and experience, firsthand, if what the Bible says is true. Is God who He says He is? Will God do what He says He will do? These are the moments in life when we get to look in the mirror and say to ourselves, I trust in God, and genuinely know that we mean it because we are actually living it out just like Jesus did. It is an exciting time for us as believers, because these are the times we get to experience life outside of ourselves.

SEPTEMBER 17th

Acts 2:1: "When the Day of Pentecost had fully come, they were all with one accord in one place."

There are numerous times in the New Testament where we read that the disciples "were all with one accord." In fact, the phrase "with one accord" is found eleven times in the book of Acts alone,[128] so there is something very significant about coming together as brothers and sisters and being in one accord. Speaking on this, Matthew Henry said, "For where brethren dwell together in unity, there it is that the Lord commands His blessing."[129]

The *NKJV Study Bible* says that the phrase "with one accord" is made up of two different words that mean "having the same mind." Specifically, it refers to people who share the same thinking for a specific purpose. It does not mean that everyone thinks and feels "the same way about everything," and it does not mean that everyone agrees with one another on every topic. Rather it refers to a group of people "who set aside [their] personal feelings," biases, and varying points of view, "and commit themselves" to one specific purpose for a greater good.[130] This is the mindset that the disciples took on after Christ ascended into heaven, and the results were nothing less than miraculous as the early church grew exponentially every day.

Today, rather than be unified in one accord, we often magnify our differences and use them as platforms to promote self while tearing others down. This is not what Christ would have us do, as this is the way the world functions. Can you imagine how effective the body of Christ would be today if no one cared who got the credit; if we stopped fighting amongst ourselves over all of those foolish little things; if everyone denied self and embraced Jesus' determined purpose, which was to win souls for the kingdom of God?

It's a very sobering thought to consider, because it causes us to face the reality that the only thing stopping another revival from taking place in our lives, in our family, in our community, in our country, in this world . . . is us. We need to stop arguing and bickering amongst ourselves about who the greatest in the kingdom is, and come together with the same heart and same mind, uniting with the same purpose. As the apostle Paul well said, "Now may the God of patience and comfort grant you to be like-minded toward one another, according to Christ Jesus, that you may with one mind and one mouth glorify the God and Father of our Lord Jesus Christ" (Romans 15:5–6). May it be so this day.

SEPTEMBER 18th

> Isaiah 1:2: "I have nourished and brought up children, and they have rebelled against Me."

I used to think there was only one kind of rebellion toward God: the complete rejection of Jesus Christ and all that He stands for. So as long as I was not standing in rejection to His gospel, I was not rebelling. But after meditating on this verse for a while, I have realized that there are multiple levels of rebellion that we can have toward our Heavenly Father who has "nourished and brought" us up. As the *NKJV Study Bible* tells us, the word "rebelled means 'to refuse to submit to someone's authority and rule.'"[131] So the only way we *cannot* be in rebellion toward God, in any way, is to fully submit to God's authority and rule in every area of our lives. Jesus, of course, is our perfect example of this.

I was watching our fifteen-month-old daughter Kate refuse to eat her dinner last night. It wasn't that she was full; it was that she just did not want to eat the food we gave her, even though it would nourish her, fulfill her, and sustain her. She refused to submit and trust that what we were asking her to do was going to benefit her. Later that night, she placed her hand on something that I specifically asked her not to touch. When I removed her hand from it, she looked me straight in the eye and brashly placed her foot on it. Hilarious, I know, but rebellion in its purest form nonetheless.

We are no different. How often does God step in and try to keep us from doing something we should not be doing only to see us find another way to do it? How often do we reject the promptings of the Holy Spirit, the instructions of the Bible, and the endless opportunities to sit and spend time with our loving Father when we know these things will bless us and benefit us? We know they will nourish, fulfill, and sustain us throughout this life and prepare us for all of the adversity we will face; yet we often refuse to submit, simply because we just don't want to.

The mistake here is for us to take this thought and believe we have to be perfect. No, the goal for us is not to be perfect, but to have the intent to submit to God in our hearts. The key to submitting to God's authority and rule is less about choice and more about trust. When we truly trust the God who has "nourished and brought" us up, we will willingly submit to His authority and rule in our heart, mind, and body.

SEPTEMBER 19th

John 1:17: "For the law was given through Moses, but grace and truth came through Jesus Christ."

One of the things that I have noticed with believers today is that we are confusing grace with truth. We think that showing grace toward someone means that we do not tell them that what they are doing is wrong. Because of that, accountability among the brethren is almost nonexistent and we find ourselves with a lukewarm church that is compromising more and more every single day.

When God spoke through Isaiah to the children of Israel, God was very clear that what Israel was doing was wrong. He didn't show them grace by not telling them the truth because that is not what grace is. He told them the truth by pointing out their sin and rebellion, and then He showed them grace through the promise of His Son. "Though your sins are like scarlet, they shall be as white as snow" (Isaiah 1:18). The truth is that Israel willingly turned their back on God; the grace is that instead of striking Israel, God struck His Servant. "All we like sheep have gone astray; we have turned, every one to his own way; and the LORD has laid on Him [Jesus Christ] the iniquity of us all" (Isaiah 53:6).

God has called us to share this same truth with others about sin and our sinful nature, and then show them the grace of God by pointing them to Jesus Christ. The Bible makes it clear that there can be no grace or truth without Jesus because "grace and truth came through Jesus Christ." The message Jesus brought was one of hope—that though we are sinners, we can be forgiven by His grace. But if we do not believe we are sinners, why would we ever need grace? If we do not believe we are sinners, why would we ever need Jesus? So believer, remember, grace does not supplant truth; rather, it is received because of the truth that we are all sinners and we all need a Savior.

SEPTEMBER 20th

Isaiah 2:2: "Now it shall come to pass in the latter days that the mountain of the LORD's house shall be established on the top of mountains, and shall be exalted above the hills."

Oftentimes when we look forward to something in this world, it can very subtly become the focus of our hope, especially if we view it as an escape from the realities of this life. In fact, we can focus on this thing so much that we actually begin believing that it will make our lives better and that we will be happier because of it. But after it has come and gone, we quickly realize that it didn't fulfill or change us as we thought it would, and now we must go back to our lives just as they were before—only now, we are discouraged and depressed because nothing has changed.

Well, as believers, we have many things to look forward to that will fulfill and change us for the better. Remember that this life, and all that it entails, is as bad as it will ever get for us. Once we are in the Lord's presence, either by death or by rapture, it only gets better—so much better, in fact, that the Bible tells us we cannot even think or imagine how much better it will be. So not only will our joy be full and remain forever, but our eternal life will far exceed any and all expectations we can ever have.

The prophet Isaiah wrote of one such thing we should look forward to, "Now it shall come to pass in the latter days that the mountain of the LORD's house shall be established on the top of mountains, and shall be exalted above the hills." Notice the guarantee, the assurance of the Lord's coming millennial reign: "it shall come to pass . . . the LORD's house shall be established . . . and shall be exalted." The time is quickly coming when our Lord and Savior will return and establish His rule and reign on this earth. It will be a time of peace and righteousness, where all will go up to Jerusalem to worship God.

The apostle John reminds us in 1 John 3:3 that when our hope is firmly placed in Jesus Christ and in His imminent return, we will be purified just as He is pure. In other words, the world will fade away and we will have the proper perspective on what is, and what is not really important. In this, our thinking will change, our desires will change, and we will fulfill the purpose that God has set us apart for. So, believer, there is nothing wrong with looking forward to things in this world—just be sure that your hope is firmly placed in the Lord Jesus and not in those things.

SEPTEMBER 21ˢᵗ

Isaiah 3:10: "For they shall eat the fruit of their doings."

In the book of Isaiah, we see a symbolic picture of our nation today. Judah and Jerusalem had forsaken the Lord as they were "a people laden with iniquity, a brood of evildoers, children who are corrupters!" (Isaiah 1:4). The Lord spoke through the prophet Isaiah and told His people that He would turn the hand that once diligently protected them, against them, in order to "rid [Himself] of [His] adversaries, and thoroughly purge away [their] dross" (Isaiah 1:24–25).

The Lord made it very clear who had led His people astray: "O My people! Those who lead you cause you to err, and destroy the way of your paths." Thus, "The Lord will enter into judgment with the elders of His people and His princes" (Isaiah 3:12, 14). This purging process had to be done so that "Afterward you shall be called the city of righteousness, the faithful city" (Isaiah 1:26).

It can be a very wearisome and troubling thing to find yourself under the leadership of those who forsake the Lord. Thankfully, the Lord has also made it very clear that each person will be held accountable for the decisions that they make in spite of what their leaders do. "If you are willing and obedient, you shall eat the good of the land; but if you refuse and rebel, you shall be devoured by the sword. . . . Say to the righteous that it shall be well with them, for they shall eat the fruit of their doings. Woe to the wicked! It shall be ill with him, for the reward of his hands shall be given to him" (Isaiah 1:19–20, 3:10–11).

I find it very comforting that even though the leaders of our nation are making decisions that go against the very heart of God, I shall only eat the fruit of my doing. If I am willing and obedient to follow the Lord and all of His ways, I shall eat the good of the land. A huge part in bringing this about is when we follow the Lord's instruction to pray for our leaders: "Therefore I exhort first of all that supplications, prayers, intercessions, and giving thanks be made for all men, for kings and all who are in authority, that we may lead a quiet and peaceable life in all godliness and reverence" (1 Timothy 2:1–2). Notice that when we pray for our leaders, we are blessed with a quiet and peaceable life in all godliness and reverence. So, believer, choose for yourself whom you will serve and what you will do because you will eat the fruit of your doings; as for me and my house, we will serve the Lord.

SEPTEMBER 22nd

Psalm 106:15: "And He gave them their request, but sent leanness into their soul."

One of the more important lessons I have learned as a believer is that when we strive to get what we want for ourselves, and not what the Lord wants for us, we are always left with a leanness in our soul. This whole process begins when we manipulate with the specific purpose to make room for what it is we desire to have or to do.

When this happens, our lives take on a shallowness, a lack of meaning, and we find ourselves in a place of spiritual barrenness because our selfish desire for the things of the world was the driving force, not a selfless desire for the things of God.

It is here that we begin drifting away from the Lord as our priorities quickly change. We soon forsake our time with God and stop serving others because they are in the way of that which we want most; we begin sacrificing them for that which we so foolishly desire. Our thinking strays from seeking the things of the divine to seeking the things of the world, and soon, after we have received that which we desired so much, we ask ourselves, "Isn't there more than this?"

This is what happened to the nation of Israel when they sacrificed God for the idols they desired. "For they shall be ashamed of the terebinth trees which you have desired; and you shall be embarrassed because of the gardens which you have chosen. For you shall be as a terebinth whose leaf fades, and as a garden that has no water" (Isaiah 1:29–30). Notice the underlying theme here—"you shall be" what you worship. For the nation of Israel, the Lord said they shall be as a tree whose leaf fades and as a garden that has no water, for that is the natural consequence of what they truly desired. This same truth applies to us as well.

Thankfully, when we stray, we have a loving Father in heaven who sends leanness to come into our souls so that we will be drawn back to Him, and back to the things that truly bring richness to our lives.

SEPTEMBER 23rd

Romans 1:17: "The just shall live by faith."

The rallying cry for the believer who gazes upon the full weight of the cross is simply this: "I am justified!" It is a glorious moment indeed when we come face to face with the life-altering truth that, through the shed blood of Jesus Christ, we are completely forgiven of all our sin. As many Bible scholars have well said before me, it is literally just as if we never sinned. But what happens then? Does our life of justification end with the forgiveness of our sin, or is there more for us?

"For in [the gospel of Jesus Christ] the righteousness of God is revealed from faith to faith; as it is written, 'The just shall live by faith'" (Romans 1:17). The righteousness of God is not just revealed the moment we surrender our lives to Jesus Christ and are forgiven of our sin. No, the righteousness of God is revealed "from faith to faith," meaning from the moment of surrender to the moment of coming glory when we are in His very presence. For as it is written, "The just shall live by faith." Notice that the word "live" is written in the present continual tense, meaning that it is an ongoing, recurring action, not just a onetime event.

Too often we justify our salvation by faith, but we do not justify our way of life by faith. I find it interesting that we can trust God with something as big as forgiving our sin and the eternal weight attached to it, yet we do not trust Him with the temporary things and decisions of everyday life. If we live our lives in this manner, why would an unbeliever ever listen to us and place their trust in God to forgive them of their sin, if we cannot simply trust in God to pay our bills? But when we live a life of faith by applying God's Word, standing on His truth, and trusting in His promises, the righteousness of God is revealed and He is justified, not only as our Lord, but also as our Savior.

SEPTEMBER 24th

2 Chronicles 26:15: "So his fame spread far and wide, for he was marvelously helped till he became strong."

As a young believer in 2003, I was given the opportunity to street-preach for the very first time while serving on a mission trip in Albania. Scared and trembling at the prospect of sharing the gospel to a sizable crowd, I sought prayer from just about every member on our team because I knew that I couldn't do this without God. The Lord was faithful to answer those prayers as He empowered me to share His message of salvation. Afterward, I was so overjoyed by the fruit of that experience that I could not wait for the next opportunity to speak. The very next day I was asked to speak again. This time though, I felt much stronger; I was more confident in myself and my abilities, so I didn't ask anyone for prayer because "I've got this." Let's just say it did not go so well and leave it at that.

King Uzziah was a great king, general, and inventor, and "his fame spread far and wide, for he was marvelously helped" by the Lord. Uzziah was blessed in all that he did because he "did what was right in the sight of the Lord" (2 Chronicles 26:4)—until, that is, Uzziah "became strong." In other words, until King Uzziah began reading his own press clippings and soon believed that he no longer needed to rely on the Lord. He became strong in his own mind, relying on his own strength and wisdom, and allowed his pride to take over. "But when he was strong his heart was lifted up, to his destruction, for he transgressed against the Lord his God" (2 Chronicles 26:16). Notice that it was only when Uzziah became strong, relying on self, that he lifted up his heart against the Lord and transgressed.

Oh, how we need to understand the danger of self, pride, and arrogance. They come so subtly, so deceptively, so innocently, but when we allow these things to come in and take over, we stop doing what is right in the sight of the Lord and begin doing what is right in the sight of self because we think we know best. And just like with King Uzziah, and so many others before and after him, it will only lead us away from the Lord.

I think it's important to realize that though we are made in the image of God, we are nothing like Him. In fact, we are His complete opposite. He is good, He is wise, He is strong, and He is able—and we are none of these things. The prophet Isaiah realized this all too well when he saw the Lord sitting on His throne; when faced with such righteousness and glory, all Isaiah could muster was, "Woe is me, for I am undone!" (Isaiah 6:5). Oh, how we need to have this same mindset every day because our strength, our pride, and our self-reliance is God's weakness in our lives; whereas our weakness, our humility, and our meekness is His strength.

SEPTEMBER 25th

> Isaiah 6:6: "Then one of the seraphim flew to me, having in his hand a
> live coal which he had taken with the tongs from the altar."

We all know that everything in this life is temporary, because we have experienced it in every area of our lives since the moment we were born. So when we consider the promise that we are forgiven by grace through faith in Jesus Christ, we stumble ourselves by naturally attaching a temporary characteristic to it in that it was done when we gave our lives to Jesus Christ, but it is not being done currently. So now when we sin, we are not forgiven as we once were and something more is needed to atone for those *new* sins.

I often catch myself feeling this way. That is why this passage in Isaiah really spoke to me when I was meditating on it. "Then one of the seraphim flew to me, having in his hand a live coal which he had taken with the tongs from the altar. And he touched my mouth with it, and said: 'Behold, this has touched your lips; your iniquity is taken away, and your sin purged'" (Isaiah 6:6–7).

Notice that the seraphim brought Isaiah a "live coal" from the altar. This was a coal that was alive and active, continually burning, constantly purging, and by it, Isaiah was forgiven of his sin, past, present, and future. We are reminded here that forgiveness is not something that was given once and then faded out after it lost its power. No, the Lord's forgiveness is a continual, living, breathing thing that endures forever.

Yes, we were forgiven the moment we gave our lives to Jesus Christ for all that we had done up to that point, but the Lord's forgiveness does not stop there; rather, it continues on for the rest of our lives and throughout eternity, because it is alive and active just as He is alive and active. Remember, this coal came from the Lord's altar, a heavenly altar, not an earthly altar built by man where things fade and die. No, this was the Lord's altar where things are perfect and complete and continue on for all eternity. It is important to realize that God's forgiveness is a direct reflection of who He is in character and in nature. So just as the Lord always was and always will be, so is His forgiveness toward you and me.

SEPTEMBER 26th

Isaiah 7:9: "If you will not believe, surely you shall not be established."

When Ahaz was king of Judah, word came to him that Syria and Israel were gathering together to attack Jerusalem. Upon hearing this, he and the people of Judah became very afraid; so the Lord sent word to Ahaz through Isaiah, promising that the plans to overtake Jerusalem by Syria and Israel "shall not stand, nor shall it come to pass" (Isaiah 7:7).

Ahaz now had a choice to make: He could either choose to believe the Lord's promises and place his trust in Him, or he could choose to reject the Lord's promises and place his trust in other things. One choice would establish him; the other choice would lead him to destruction. As David Guzik pointed out, regardless what Ahaz chose, his choice would "not affect the outcome of the attack against Jerusalem," for God had already promised that it would not come to pass; rather, the decision would affect "Ahaz's life and [his] reign as king."[132]

The Lord, in His amazing mercy and grace, even gave Ahaz the opportunity to ask for any sign he wished from heaven or Earth to prove that God was going to keep His word, yet Ahaz still foolishly chose to not place his trust in God. Instead, Ahaz chose to place his trust in the king of Assyria, Tiglath-Pileser, in which Ahaz gave him silver and gold from the house of the Lord to protect Jerusalem (2 Kings 16:7–9). It was through this "good-intentioned" alliance that Ahaz was eventually corrupted and destroyed.

There is a great lesson here for all of us. We can choose to place our trust in the Lord and His promises, or we can choose to reject the Lord and place our trust in other things. One choice will establish us; the other choice will lead us to destruction. Regardless what we choose, though, the Lord's promises and truths will stand, and they will come to pass just as He has said they will. It doesn't matter if we think they are fair, it doesn't matter if we disagree with them, and it doesn't matter if we choose to believe them or not—they will come to pass just as God has promised, and we will each face the consequences to the choices we have made.

This truth extends well beyond salvation. It also has to do with the everyday life decisions we make as well. As stated in the *NKJV Study Bible*, as believers, we need to know God's Word, accept the fact that it is true, and then place our trust in Him to keep it, for it is by believing in the Lord and placing our trust in Him that we are ultimately established.[133] Or, as Ray Stedman explained it, "If there is no belief, you will find no relief."[134]

SEPTEMBER 27th

Psalm 3:3: "But You, O LORD, are a shield for me, my glory and the One who lifts up my head."

There will be certain times in our lives when situations and people convince us that we are finally getting exactly what we deserve—that our past has finally caught up with us, God has finally had enough of our rebellion and sinful nature, and we are now left to fend for ourselves against the cold and the wolves. This is what David was experiencing when he wrote Psalm 3.

It all began when David was forced to abandon his throne and all of his possessions because his own son, Absalom, rose up against him in rebellion. To make matters worse, many of David's most trusted friends joined Absalom's assault on the throne; and those who did stick by David's side told David that God was not going to help him. "There is no help for him in God" (Psalm 3:2). Notice how personal their attack was against David. It wasn't that God *couldn't* help David; it was that God *wouldn't* help David—there was no help "for him" in God, they said. Many were convinced that David's sins had finally caught up with him, and because of that, God had forsaken him.

To all of this David replied with the two most important words we can ever speak in such situations, "But God. . . ." David acknowledged the situation—how it looked, how it felt, and what it was pointing to—but rather than allow any of those things to move him, David said, "But what does God say about all of this? I get the situation and how it looks and what my friends are all saying, but what does God say about it?"

In the face of personal bankruptcy, emotional distress, physical fear, and spiritual hopelessness, David purposed to set his mind above all of those things and place it on that which he knew to be certain about the Lord. "But You, O LORD, are a shield for me, my glory and the One who lifts up my head." David confessed that even though Absalom was hunting him down and trying to kill him, the Lord was a shield around him; even though he had abandoned his throne and had nothing to his name, the Lord was his glory; and even though man was giving his opinion of everything that was going on, discouraging David, the Lord was the lifter of his head.

Because David knew God so intimately, he did not go to man for help, but rather cried out to the Lord in his distress, "and He heard me from His holy hill" (Psalm 3:4). That is why, even though "ten thousands of people . . . have set themselves against" him (Psalm 3:6), David was still able to lie down and sleep at night. He knew it was the Lord who sustained him, not the situation, not his throne, and not his friends.

SEPTEMBER 28th

Proverbs 6:27: "Can a man take fire to his bosom, and his clothes not be burned?"

There is a great lie that we tell ourselves when we want to justify our sin, and it goes something like this: "No one will get hurt." Yet Proverbs tells us otherwise: "Can a man take fire to his bosom, and his clothes not be burned?" Solomon's warning to us is very clear: The likelihood of sinning without anyone getting hurt is as likely as setting your clothes on fire and not getting burned. Yet we still believe the lie that sin doesn't hurt anyone, don't we? Why? Mostly because we can't see the damage that is being done until it is too late.

Before I was saved, I lived in sexually immoral relationships for thirteen years; I never saw the damage that was being done inside of me until it was too late. It wasn't until after the damage was already done that I noticed the severe consequences of that sin in my life. This is why Solomon warns us throughout the book of Proverbs of the damage that sin, and especially sexual immorality, causes in our lives.

It is important to understand that God has placed something very precious inside of each one of us; it is something that is meant to be shared only between a man and a woman in marriage. When we take for granted that which He has given us and chase after the false treasures of this world and give ourselves over to sexual immorality, we are giving that precious gift away—and pretty soon, we will have nothing left to give anyone. That is why Solomon tells us in Proverbs 6:32 concerning those that practice sexual immorality, "He who does so destroys his own soul." I can attest to this being true because after years of living in sexual immorality, it literally felt as if my soul had been destroyed. I had foolishly given away all of the preciousness that God had given me and there was just nothing left for me to give.

Thankfully, we have hope in Jesus Christ, as He is the restorer of our souls (Psalm 23:3). He faithfully restores that which the locusts have eaten (Joel 2:25), for in Christ, old things have passed away, and all things have become new. But the warning still stands for all of us: Just as fire burns, sin destroys.

SEPTEMBER 29ᵗʰ

> Isaiah 10:20: "That the remnant of Israel . . . will never again depend on him who defeated them, but will depend on the LORD, the Holy One of Israel, in truth."

Contrary to what you may have been taught, or what others might say, God is not out to get you. In fact, the Bible promises that God is for you (Romans 8:31). His greatest desire is to bless you—to see you overcome this world and receive the crown of eternal life (James 1:12). Yet many paint a picture that God is some grumpy old man just waiting to strike us with His cane when we break one of His rules, and so rather than see discipline as an act of love (Hebrews 12:6), we see it as a punishment for our bad behavior.

Discipline from the Lord has nothing to do with breaking rules or God angrily lashing out at us when we do so. In fact, if we were to sit down and carefully examine the discipline process, we would see that, more often than not, discipline from the Lord is Him merely respecting our freedom to choose and allowing us to have what it is we really want. We see a perfect example of this with the people of Judah.

The Lord had promised the king of Judah that He would protect Jerusalem from its enemies, but rather than trust in what God had promised, the king of

Judah chose to bribe the Assyrians to come in and defend his city. When Jerusalem was eventually saved just as the Lord had promised, the people of Judah rejoiced and praised the Assyrians for their deliverance. So rather than strike His people, as some would have you believe God would do, the Lord simply stepped aside and allowed Judah to have the Assyrians as their chosen savior. The Assyrians then turned on Judah and forced them into bondage.

Eventually, the discipline and refining process of allowing Israel to have what they wanted served its perfect purpose, "And it shall come to pass in that day that the remnant of Israel, and such as have escaped of the house of Jacob, will never again depend on him who defeated them, but will depend on the LORD, the Holy One of Israel, in truth" (Isaiah 10:20). Through this very long and painful process, the people of Israel finally realized their foolishness and came back to the Lord, faithfully trusting in Him as their Lord and Savior. So discipline is not God raising His hand against us when we mess up; it is God lifting His hand from us and allowing us to have what it is we have chosen.

Ultimately, we will all learn to faithfully trust in God. The only question is, how do we want to learn this lesson—through discipline, or through faith? I pray we choose faith this day, and trust in all that the Lord says.

SEPTEMBER 30th

Isaiah 11:9: "For the earth shall be full of the knowledge of the LORD as the waters cover the sea."

I think it is obvious to just about every single person in this world that change is needed if there is ever going to be peace. The problem is that just about every single person has their own idea of what that change looks like. Some believe peace should be imposed through acts of violence and aggression; others believe that peace is the direct result of tolerance and acceptance. Yet none of these changes will ever bring peace to this world because none of these changes will ever fix the fatal flaw that is within man. In order for there to be peace in this world, man's nature must be changed.

The Bible tells us that a time is coming very soon when peace will reign throughout the earth. It will be a time when the wolf will lie down with the lamb and the leopard will lie down with the young goat; a time when the cow and the bear will graze together in a field and the lion will eat straw; it will be a time when children can safely play with cobras and vipers and have no threat of being harmed

(Isaiah 11:6–8). It will be a time when "the earth shall be full of the knowledge of the LORD as the waters cover the sea." Do not miss this: Peace only comes through the knowledge of the Lord.

This is not merely an intellectual knowledge of God, mind you; rather, it's a personal, intimate, relational knowledge with God. This is where man's very nature is changed, because it is through this relationship that we are transformed more into God's image (2 Corinthians 3:18). Saul knew more about God than just about anyone else in his day, yet it wasn't until after he had a relationship with Jesus Christ that his nature actually changed and he stopped murdering Christians. It was only then that the wolf could lie down with the lamb in peace.

OCTOBER 1st

> Psalm 139:23–24: "Search me, O God, and know my heart; try me, and know my anxieties; and see if there is any wicked way in me, and lead me in the way everlasting."

October is Breast Cancer Awareness Month, and with that come many slogans to remind women of the danger that this particular cancer brings. One slogan I saw on a t-shirt was "Screening Saves Lives." It is a reminder for women to have regular checkups to see if there is any cancer forming, so that it might be dealt with before it spreads. But as good as that is for women to do, doctors say that the best preventative against this cancer spreading is for women to perform self-examinations on a regular basis and not rely solely on the annual screenings.

There is much wisdom here that we can apply directly to our spiritual lives. We should be performing spiritual self-examinations on a regular basis to see if there is any cancer forming within us as well. Too often we rely on annual screenings at a conference or a retreat to reveal possible cancers growing within us; all the while the cancer has metastasized to other parts of our lives, making it much more difficult for us to deal with.

The idea behind this spiritual self-examination is not to create a list of sins so that we might condemn ourselves; rather, it is for us to be aware of what is going on in our spiritual lives so that we might take that sin to the Lord and have it dealt with immediately. Jesus has promised us that if we confess our sin to Him, He is faithful and just to forgive us of our sin and cleanse us from all unrighteousness (1 John 1:9). That is why He came and saved us, after all.

Throughout the Bible we are encouraged and instructed to perform self-examinations in every aspect of life and Christianity for this very reason:

Let us examine and probe our ways. (Lamentations 3:40, NASB)

Consider your ways! (Haggai 1:5)

But a man must examine himself. (1 Corinthians 11:28, NASB)

Test yourselves. (2 Corinthians 13:5)

All of these admonishments are spoken with the sole purpose of us returning to the Lord and walking in a worthy manner. The danger, of course, in neglecting this practice is seen in Psalm 32:3 (NASB): "When I kept silent about my sin, my body wasted away." Sin destroys, both physically and spiritually.

The important thing to remember about self-examinations is that we do not examine ourselves based on our standard or by what we think is right or wrong; rather, we hold ourselves to God's standard, as stated in His Word. Whereas we can justify just about anything we do as being OK, the Lord is very clear about what is and what is not sin. We need to remember that it does us no good to perform self-examinations if we are just going to call our cancer a harmless mass, because ultimately we are just hurting ourselves. As Ezekiel 18:28 reminds us, "Because he considers and turns away from all the transgressions which he committed, he shall surely live; he shall not die."

May we earnestly pray as the psalmist prayed and cut that sin out of our lives, no matter what it might be: "Search me, O God, and know my heart; try me, and know my anxieties; and see if there is any wicked way in me, and lead me in the way everlasting."

OCTOBER 2nd

Isaiah 12:1: "Though You were angry with me, Your anger is turned away, and You comfort me."

Throughout our lives we have seen and experienced the world's relational cause-and-effect system that goes something like this: When we do good things, we make people happy and we are loved; when we do bad things, we make people angry and we are not loved. So naturally, when we come into a relationship with God through

Jesus Christ, we bring into the relationship this same type of dysfunctional mindset. When we do good things, we make God happy and He loves us; when we do bad things, God becomes angry and His love for us wanes.

Yet Isaiah 12:1 reminds us that "Though You were angry with me, Your anger is turned away, and You comfort me." Notice that God was (past tense) angry with us because of our sin; but also notice that is no longer the case as all of God's anger was poured out on Jesus Christ at the cross. In other words, it has been "turned away" from us forever. Jesus stated as much when He said *Tetelestai*, or "It is finished," while on the cross (John 19:30). Not only was sin defeated, but God's anger had been completely exhausted. Now, God only has comfort for us through His grace. Though it might feel like God is angry when He disciplines us, we must remember that God's discipline always comes out of love, not anger. The apostle Paul reminded us of this when he vehemently stated in Romans 8 that nothing could ever separate us from the love of God.

And even though Jesus Christ proved His perfect love for us by dying on the cross, we still fall victim to the thought that what we do determines His love for us. But as Ephesians 1:4 reminds us, before the world ever was, before you and I were ever created, before we could ever do anything to earn His love, God loved us. He made the choice to love us with every single thing we would ever do in full view, and He did so by His own volition. Nothing we do will ever change that.

OCTOBER 3rd

Isaiah 12:2: "Behold, God is my salvation, I will trust and not be afraid. For Yah, the Lord, is my strength and song."

It is one thing to trust God for our salvation; it is quite another to trust Him *with* our salvation. As believers, we have come to trust that God has provided the way of salvation through His Son Jesus Christ, yet we often struggle to trust God to preserve our salvation. We recognize our sinful nature and we begin to fear that our salvation will default due to our iniquity, so we try to preserve our salvation by offsetting the bad behavior with the good. At that point our security in the cross and all that Jesus did becomes so fragile that instead of God being our salvation, we become our salvation.[135] What we must remember is that Jesus Christ is not only our Savior by whom we are saved, but He is also our salvation itself, in whom we are saved. "Behold, God is my salvation."

The key to trusting God with our salvation is to trust in God Himself, "I will trust and not be afraid." Fear comes in when we believe that God will fail us; when we believe that our sin is greater than our God and we must do something to mitigate for His shortcomings. Whereas faith in the sovereign God of the Bible, in all that He says about who He is and what He will do, dispels all of those fears and brings peace to our souls, allowing us to confidently proclaim, "For YAH, the LORD, is my strength and song" (Isaiah 12:2).

Yah, the eternal and unchanging God, is the strength of our minds and the song of our hearts. He is not just an aid to find strength when we are in need; He Himself is our strength. He is not just an aid to find joy when we are troubled; He Himself is our joy.[136] And He is not just an aid to the way to salvation; He *is* our salvation.

OCTOBER 4th

Isaiah 19:22: "He will strike and heal."

A few years back, a good friend of mine was a guest speaker at a church function, and being that he was my friend, I was asked to introduce him. I gave the audience the usual information such as his name, his occupation (police officer), how long I had known him, etc. But I really wanted them to know his heart for others so I gave them this analogy: "If you were to point a gun at someone, or at (my friend), he would put you down without hesitation. But he would then walk over to you, bandage you up, and explain to you why he put you down so that you might learn from it. This is the heart of God."

The Lord's greatest desire is that all men be saved by grace, through faith, in His Son Jesus Christ (1 Timothy 2:4; Ephesians 2:8–9); but that is not man's greatest desire. By nature, we are a rebellious and sinful people, and oftentimes the Lord must strike us physically in order to heal us spiritually. We see this type of "tough love" throughout the book of Isaiah, as the Lord not only struck Israel for their rejection of Him, but also Moab, Assyria, Ethiopia, Egypt, etc. All were held to the same standard, and all were struck with the sole purpose of saving them from their sin.

In my own experience, I knew that when I prayed for God to do whatever it took to save my family that it was probably going to hurt. But, "the LORD binds up the bruise of His people and heals the stroke of their wound" (Isaiah 30:26). The spiritual fruit that I have seen in their lives, because the Lord struck them, far outweighs the temporary physical discomfort they went through, or are still going through today.

This does not mean, however, that once we are saved, the Lord will never strike us again. We are continually being sanctified, and sometimes our sanctification can only come through being struck by the Lord. But even though the Lord may need to strike us physically in order to purge the evil from our hearts, we can rest assured knowing that He is healing us spiritually. "Now no chastening seems to be joyful for the present, but painful; nevertheless, afterward it yields the peaceable fruit of righteousness to those who have been trained by it" (Hebrews 12:11). The victory in the midst of this chastening is not to focus on what is happening to us, but rather on what is happening within us, because the result of the Lord's discipline is always the peaceable fruit of righteousness.

OCTOBER 5th

> Ephesians 4:11–12: "And He Himself gave some to be apostles, some prophets, some evangelists, and some pastors teachers, for the equipping of the saints for the work of the ministry, for the edifying of the body of Christ."

I was talking with a brother from church the other day and he was explaining to me why he was leaving our church and going to another one. He said that the pastors at our church were not out evangelizing enough, and he wanted to find a church where the pastors were more given to this area of ministry. I quickly explained to him that it is not the role of the pastors to go out and evangelize; that is our job.

Like this brother, there are many Christians today who believe it's the sole responsibility of the church leadership to visit the sick, witness to the lost, minister to the poor, pray for those in need, serve in ministry, etc. Because of this outlook, when the Holy Spirit stirs our hearts to move in a certain capacity, we take on this attitude that it's not our job to do that, it's theirs. The excuses that we often defer to in these situations are that we are not gifted in that particular area, or we just do not have the time to serve in that capacity, so "someone else can do it." Having this outlook is why there is such a huge need in just about every ministry in the church today.

Yet this is not what Scripture teaches us regarding the roles of believers. First Corinthians 12–14 teaches us that all believers are given spiritual gifts—not just some, or most, but all believers are gifted. First Timothy 4 reminds us that we are not to neglect the gifts that have been given to us, but rather we are to use them as the Holy Spirit leads us—because the gifts are not given for our benefit but for the benefit of others so that we might stir up, build up, and cheer up. We must continually remind ourselves that our role is to serve and bless others, not the other way around.

We are also taught that the primary purpose of church leadership is "for the equipping of the saints for the work of the ministry, for the edifying of the body of Christ." Notice that the primary role of pastors is to equip the saints (all believers)—meaning, they are to outfit us. For example, if we were going on an expedition to the South Pole, we would have to be outfitted with certain equipment so that we would be ready for the harsh environment that we were going into.[137] This same idea applies to the pastor's role in our lives today. They are to equip us spiritually through the preaching and teaching of God's Word for the work of the ministry, so that *we* might be equipped to visit the sick, witness to the lost, minister to the poor, pray for those in need, and serve in ministry. For it is when we do this that the church is built up and "we come to such unity in our faith and knowledge of God's Son that we will be mature and full grown in the Lord, measuring up to the full stature of Christ" (Ephesians 4:13, NLT1996).

OCTOBER 6th

Isaiah 26:3: "You will keep him in perfect peace, whose mind is stayed on you, because he trusts in You."

Many times we struggle in life simply because we believe that our minds are supposed to be remote-controlled by God. We go to church, worship, pray, read our Bibles, and then we just hit cruise control and assume that our work is done—it's now God's turn to work, His responsibility to cleanse our minds and fill them with the things of the kingdom. Yet the Bible teaches us something different.

According to Isaiah 26:3, God will keep the person "in perfect peace, whose mind is stayed" on Him. Notice that having perfect peace is contingent on our minds staying on God. The Hebrew word "stayed" used here means "to lean on" or "to take hold of." It is not something that is just going to miraculously happen; it is something that we must purpose ourselves to do. Colossians 3:2 confirms this: "Set your mind on things above, not on the things of the earth." The apostle Paul also reminds us in Philippians 4 that we must purposefully meditate on those things which are true, noble, just, pure, lovely . . . things that are of good report, things with virtue and anything that is praise worthy. It's by doing these things that we will have the "mind of Christ" (1 Corinthians 2:16).

The trap for the believer is when we forget that the Christian life is a thinking life. Somewhere along the line we separated faith and reason and placed them into two different categories as if they were complete opposites from one another. Well, contrary to what the world might say about faith, it is not some mindless leap we take when there is nowhere else to go. It is a thought-out, deliberate decision we make, based on what we know to be true because we have placed our trust in God. Proverbs 3:5 mirrors this truth: "Trust in the LORD with all your heart, and lean not [stay] on your own understanding." The battles we face in who or what to trust always begins in the mind; when we trust in the Lord, our mind will stay on Him, and He will keep us in perfect peace.[138]

OCTOBER 7th

Genesis 22:1: "God tested Abraham."

What determines if what we do is a success or not? For us, it's all about the results, as we live in a results-driven world. If the results of what we do are not to the standard we have predetermined for the outcome of that situation, we conclude that we have failed. But what if success has nothing to do with results or the outcome of a situation? What if success was solely reliant on an individual's submission to follow instructions?

When "God tested Abraham" and told him to sacrifice his son Isaac, was Abraham deemed successful because his son was sacrificed, or because he obeyed the Lord's instructions? If we define success as the achievement of something planned or attempted, as the world does, how does that translate into the kingdom of God when we do not know the plans of the Lord? "'For My thoughts are not your thoughts, nor are My ways your ways,' says the LORD" (Isaiah 55:8). For Abraham, the plan was never to sacrifice his son; rather, it was to test Abraham's faith and obedience to God, "for now I know that you fear God, since you have not withheld your son, your only son from Me" (Genesis 22:12).

It is easy for us to believe that we have failed the Lord when we share the gospel with someone and they do not come to salvation. Yet, are we the Christ? Can we convert a heart of stone to a heart of flesh? Do we have the power to bring the dead to life? No, only God has the power to save the lost. What we must remember is that the gospel will "accomplish what [the Lord] please[s], and it shall prosper in the thing which [He] sent it" (Isaiah 55:11).

I remember a young gal being asked to share her testimony to a group of missionaries on our mission trip in 2004. Her objection to doing so made sense: Why share her testimony to a bunch of people who are already saved? What she did not realize was that our unsaved bus driver was sitting right behind her, and he heard every word she said. Like ripples in a pond ever expanding outward, we cannot fathom the purpose or plan for the things the Lord calls us to do—and honestly, it's not for us to know. We are simply to be obedient to do what God has called us to do and leave the results in His hands.

OCTOBER 8th

1 Corinthians 1:18: "the message of the cross . . ."

A few years ago, Michelle and I were asked to lead worship at a couples' conference. In the days leading up to the conference, I began to feel a lot of pressure about the responsibility we had been given to usher others into the throne room of grace. It was then that the Lord spoke to me about the cross. He reminded me that I contributed absolutely nothing to the victory at Calvary. All I brought was my brokenness, my sin, my shame, and my weakness; victory was all His, as He did it all. So why would the conference be any different?

I was reminded of this as I have been considering the cross a lot lately. I think it is important for us to remember that when Jesus took the cross upon Himself, a deal was brokered between God and man. The terms of the agreement were basically these: We offer to bring our brokenness, our sin, our shame, and our weakness; and He offers to bring restoration, forgiveness, grace, joy, strength, hope, etc. When God reviewed the terms of this agreement, He quickly declared, "Deal!" and then signed the agreement with His blood and sealed it by His Holy Spirit, binding it for all eternity.

Since that time, God has more than kept His side of the agreement, yet it's confusing to me as to why we haven't. Far too often we, as believers, put on this façade that we are good and that we don't struggle with sin. Somehow we have been misled to believe that if we admit what is really going on in our lives, we will be branded with a scarlet letter and deemed spiritually immature, lacking true faith. But what we are really saying when we live our lives in this manner is that we don't need the cross, effectively breaking our agreement with the Lord.

The repercussions of this prideful mindset has damaged the church to the point where many people are now afraid to ask for help and believe that they cannot come to church until they clean themselves up. In essence, our pride in hiding our own frailty has made the cross of no effect to many people as we have taken the message of the cross and made it foolishness to those who are even being saved by it.

OCTOBER 9th

Numbers 32:23: "and be sure your sin will find you out."

Your sin will find you out. My sin will find me out. Why do we not believe this to be true? Is it because we sin and there are seemingly no tangible consequences afterward, so we just keep on sinning? Sure we might feel bad, and we may even swear off that sin promising to never do it again, but by doing this all we have done is appeased our conscience and made room for that sin to lie comfortably dormant in our lives until the next time it calls our name.

Achan thought he could hide his sin; yet it found him out, and it cost him and his family everything, including their lives (Joshua 7). David thought he could hide his sin and it cost him dearly, as the Lord promised that the sword would never leave his family (2 Samuel 12:10). The lie that sin does not hurt is only equaled by the lie that sin does not hurt anyone else—yet time and time again we see that sin destroys lives, families, and ministries.

The Lord told Israel, "you cannot stand before your enemies until you take away the accursed thing from among you" (Joshua 7:13). Why would it be any different for us today? How can we expect to stand against the wiles of the enemy when we have sin hidden in our camp? The truth is that we will forever be in bondage to a particular sin until we do as James instructed us to do in James 5:16, "Confess your trespasses to one another, and pray for one another, that you may be healed." Because it's not that sin *might* find you out; it is, "be sure your sin will find you out."

I have been meditating a lot on what Jesus told Thomas in John 20:29, "Blessed are those who have not seen and yet have believed." In context, Jesus was speaking of us having faith in Him as Messiah. But over the last weekend, this truth took on a whole new perspective for me: Blessed are those who believe His Word and instructions, even though we might not see the consequences of them. The horrifying truth for us is that by the time we see the consequences of sin in our lives, it is too late for us to change anything we have done, and we must now face the cold reality of those trespasses. Yes, God will forgive us when we confess our sin to Him (1 John 1:9), but the tangible consequences of those choices still remain.

So, believer, do not believe the lie that we can hide our sin, or that sin does not have a hold on us. Trust in the Word of the Lord which is perfect and true . . . our sin will find us out.

OCTOBER 10th

> Isaiah 28:26: "For [God] instructs [the farmer] in right judgment, His God teaches him."

Before our daughter Kate was born, I had envisioned what she would be like in appearance, personality, and temperament. Imagine my surprise when I learned that she was nothing like what I had anticipated her to be; rather, she was more than I ever could have imagined. Michelle and I often sit and marvel at just how unique our daughter is, as we naturally assumed she would be a little Michelle clone. But God does not make clones; He creates matchless masterpieces, none like another. His perfect law of design ensures that we are not simply cardboard cutouts of some default template, nor blunders or slip-ups because He had an off day. Rather, we are living revelations of God's perfect vision for beauty and holiness that comes from the depths of His heart.

As Matthew Henry explained, we can surmise that because God created each one of us so differently, He must also handle each one of us differently as well. "Does [the farmer] not sow the black cummin and scatter the cummin, plant the wheat in rows, the barley in the appointed place, and the spelt in its place?" (Isaiah 28:25). Notice that some seed is sown, some is scattered, and some is positioned in rows; but ultimately, all are planted in their appropriate place. Just as the farmer knows how to handle each seed, and which soil type is best suited for each seed to flourish and grow in, God knows exactly how and where to place us that we might flourish and grow as well, for "God teaches him." It is easy to feel misplaced or miscast sometimes in this life, but rest assured, God knows you and He has you right where you need to be so that you might produce according to your designed purpose.[139]

Likewise, "The black cummin is not threshed with a threshing sledge, nor is a cartwheel rolled over the cummin; but the black cummin is beaten out with a stick, and the cummin with a rod. Bread flour must be ground; therefore he does not thresh it forever, break it with his cartwheel, or crush it with his horsemen"

(Isaiah 28:27–28). Notice that the cummin is easily separated with a stick and a rod, whereas the bread flour requires much more force. Just as the farmer knows which tool to use for each type of seed, he also knows the physical limits of each seed in that he will never thresh it too much, break it, or crush it to where the harvest is damaged and useless.[140]

Similarly, God knows exactly which methods to use with each one of us in order to refine us from that which corrupts His precious creation. Though it might feel like God gives us more than we can handle at times, we can rest assured knowing that God will never thresh us too much, break us, or crush us to where we are damaged and useless for His kingdom. On the contrary, the Lord uses the exact amount of threshing and grinding to perfect us more and more into His image, so that we might have the mind and heart of Christ and produce thirty, sixty, even one hundredfold (Mark 4:20).

OCTOBER 11th

Zechariah 4:6: "'Not by might, nor by power, but by My Spirit,' says the LORD of hosts."

Last Friday night at our annual men's conference, the speaker focused on Zechariah 4:6: "'Not by might, nor by power, but by My Spirit,' says the LORD of hosts." What he did not realize was that he would be a living example of that very verse coming to fruition as the night went on. Let me explain.

From a "Public Speaking 101" standpoint, there are certain things you should never do when addressing an audience. From that perspective, our speaker that night failed miserably. He continually slapped his fist into his hand, making this loud popping sound; he was sucking on some kind of throat lozenge or cough drop; and he seemed unprepared, even lost at times. Yet as he continued sharing, man's forbidden practices of public speaking slowly faded into the background and the power behind the message came forth, compelling many men to respond to its challenge.

Afterward, as I sat and reflected on the night's events, I said to the Lord, "He did everything wrong that you could do as a public speaker, and yet look at the response from his message . . . how is that possible?" That is when the Lord responded and said, it is "not by might, nor by power, but by My Spirit." The Lord graciously reminded me that when we rely on our ability, strength, or ingenuity in any work or ministry, we are restricting ourselves from fully receiving the power of the Holy

Spirit, because what we are essentially saying to God when we do this is, "I've got this, Lord." Whereas when we come to the Lord with a humble heart and realize we have nothing of eternal value to offer anyone—when we know that change only comes through the working of the Holy Spirit—then we are ready to be used.

I find it very comforting that it is never going to be about our ability to do what the Lord calls us to do, but rather our availability to do what He calls us to do, "For the eyes of the LORD run to and fro throughout the whole earth, to show Himself strong on behalf of those whose heart is loyal to Him" (2 Chronicles 16:9).

OCTOBER 12th

> Mark 8:4: "Then His disciples answered Him, 'How can one satisfy these people with bread here in the wilderness?'"

Even though Jesus' disciples had witnessed Him feed more than five thousand people with five loaves of bread and two fish just a few days earlier, the "that was then, this is now" brand of faith that is so common in all of us reared its ugly head once again. Jesus desired to feed the masses, and His disciples responded by saying, "How can one satisfy these people with bread here in the wilderness?" What the disciples were really asking Jesus was, "Lord, how can You possibly provide in this place? How can You possibly provide what is needed in this situation, Lord? Look at where we are, look at what we need . . . how can You satisfy us here, in this wilderness?"

I find it interesting that we recall God's great faithfulness and provision as stepping stones of faith, and yet we use those very things as stumbling blocks as to why He won't provide for us now. We say to ourselves, "Yeah, He provided in that situation, but this situation is completely different. Yeah, He provided for those needs, but this need is greater. Yeah, He provided for them, but He won't do it for me because they are [more special, more spiritual, more favored]."

To all those lies, I give you the big secret as to why He provided for all of those in the past. On the day Jesus provided for more than five thousand people on the grassy hills, to the day He provided for more than four thousand people in the desert wilderness, and everyone before, after, and in between, I want you to notice that the sole reason why Jesus provided for them was simply because they came to Him. That was the criteria for receiving provision from Jesus—the standard that needed to be met as to why people were satisfied in the wilderness. They went to Jesus. It didn't matter what the situation was, or how great the need was, or who they were; Jesus provided for every single person, simply because they made the choice to come to Him and receive.

So why would it be any different for us today? He is the same God today that He was yesterday, that He will be tomorrow. And just like those in the past, Jesus invites all of us today, "Come to Me . . . and I will give you . . ." (Matthew 11:28).

OCTOBER 13th

Ephesians 4:27: "nor give place to the devil."

Do we believe that by sinning, sin will actually become weaker in our lives? That's the lie, isn't it—that if we just give into that temptation it will go away and become a lesser evil to us? The truth is, although giving into temptation might temporarily silence the call, though it might lessen the struggle for that moment, what we've really done is given that sin an opportunity to grow and become more dominant within us. Think about it like this: If we allow Satan into our lives, will he really just leave us alone, or will he use that one little compromise to gain ground and continue taking more and more until he has all that we are?

After Jesus was arrested in the garden of Gethsemane to be questioned by the high priest, Peter was asked, "'You are not also one of this Man's disciples, are you?' He said, 'I am not'" (John 18:17). Peter bought into the lie that if he could just silence the fear this one time, if he could just avoid the confrontation of being Jesus' disciple in this moment, it would go away and he would be fine. But as we well know, that fear gained so much ground in Peter's life, and became so strong within him, that Peter would eventually profanely deny that He ever had anything to do with Christ.

The apostle Paul reminds us in Ephesians 4:27 that we should never "give place to the devil." Literally, we should never give Satan an opportunity to get even a little toe into our lives, because when we do, it will bring destruction (see David and Judas as examples). So what do we do when we sin? We deal with that sin right away before it can root and bear fruit.

Peter's ultimate failure was not that he denied Christ; it was that he did not properly deal with his sin right away, thus revoking its hold on his life. The mistake Peter made of thinking that his sin would go away was equaled by the mistake he made in thinking he could overcome that sin by himself. The same goes for us. When we sin, covering it up is never the answer, nor is trying to handle it on our own. Proverbs 28:13 reminds us that "He who covers his sins will not prosper, but whoever confesses and forsakes them will have mercy."

Believer, why would we ever want to hide our sin or try to handle it ourselves, when "The LORD will wait [for us], that He may be gracious to (us); and therefore He will be exalted, that He may have mercy on [us]" (Isaiah 30:18). In other words, God is ready to forgive; He is just waiting for us to return to Him.

OCTOBER 14ᵗʰ

1 John 4:17: "because as He is, so are we in this world."

A couple of weeks ago, Michelle asked me what God sees when He looks at her; in response I said, "He sees Jesus." In saying that, I did not mean that God literally sees His Son when He looks at my wife; rather, He sees the finished work of Jesus on the cross when He looks at her. I could confidently say this to my wife because ten years ago, I asked God if He would let me see myself through His eyes. He then gave me an incredible vision of the perfected me: no blemish, no wrinkle, no sin, just me with my arms stretched out wide completely overwhelmed with joy and peace. I often reflect on this vision because when I look at myself, I only see the sinner. Yet the Lord often reminds me, just "as [Jesus] is, so are [you] in this world."

This is a staggering concept to consider in light of who we are, what we say, what we do, what we think, how we act, etc. Yet none of these things truly define how God sees us "because as [Jesus] is, so are we in this world." When considering this, David Guzik posed the question, "How is Jesus now?" He is justified and righteous, forever glorified in the Father's presence.[141] And so if we are as He is, we should never be ashamed to come to our Father; we should never be fearful of standing before our God, regardless what we have done. This is what John reminds us of when he stated, "Love has been perfected among us in this: that we may have boldness in the day of judgment; because as He is, so are we in this world" (1 John 4:17). As believers in Jesus Christ, we can boldly stand before God on the day of judgment because of what Christ has done for us. There is nothing to fear, there is no hesitation, "because as He is, so are we in this world." Just as the Father received Jesus, He will also receive us.

OCTOBER 15th

Isaiah 30:18: "Therefore the Lord will wait, that He may be gracious to you."

When the impetuous son demanded his inheritance and left his father for the pleasures of the world, the father did not disown his son; rather, he gave his son what he asked for and diligently watched for his son every day, longing for his return. When his son finally did return, the father ran to him and lovingly embraced him, welcoming his son back as though he had never left (Luke 15). This is not just a parable that Jesus told His disciples one day; it is a never-ending theme we find throughout the Bible, of God's grace and mercy toward His children.

When the children of Israel blatantly told God that they wanted nothing to do with Him, the Lord allowed them to go their own way and fulfill their desires, yet He continually longed for their return—not so He could punish them or tell them, "I told you so!" No. This was His response to their rebellious wandering: "Therefore the Lord will wait, that He may be gracious to you; and therefore He will be exalted, that He may have mercy on you" (Isaiah 30:18). The Lord longed for their return so that He could show them mercy and grace.

For the last few months or so, Michelle and I have been teaching our twenty-month-old daughter Kate to come to us when we ask her to. Sure there are times we ask Kate to come to us because we need to correct her, but most often we ask Kate to come to us just so we might give her a hug, tell her we love her, or so that we might give her a special surprise. Well, why would it be any different with our Heavenly Father? What if our God calls us to draw near to Him just so He can hug us and tell us that He loves us? What if He wants to share with us the great mysteries of His Word? What if He wants to reveal His calling on our life that we have so longed for, or just wants to comfort us in our turmoil or prepare us for what lies ahead? The point is, our Father in heaven is waiting for us right now to draw near to Him, just so He might show us mercy and grace. What could we possibly be waiting for?

OCTOBER 16th

1 Timothy 4:1: "Now the Spirit expressly says that in latter times some will depart from the faith, giving heed to deceiving spirits and doctrines of demons."

I read an article recently about a pastor who decided that his church would not only allow those living in habitual unrepentant sin to serve in leadership, but that they would also look upon these sins as being permissible in the Lord's sight. The first question I had was, "How did this come about?" Apparently, some years earlier, the pastor noticed that people who were refusing to repent from habitual sin were leaving his church, so he decided to discuss with the church body whether or not they should accept these sins as being permissible in the Lord's estimation. The pastor stated that as he prayed about it, something that he described as a "divine wind" moved him to change the way his church was to look at these types of habitual sin. "Now the Spirit expressly says that in latter times some will depart from the faith, giving heed to deceiving spirits and doctrines of demons."

Before I go on, let me first say that God does not hate those who live in unrepentant, habitual sin, and the purpose of this devotion is not to bash the pastor nor those who struggle with these things. Rather it is a warning—a call to all believers to know what the Word of God says. I see Bible studies today that do not teach the Word of God accurately, comprehensively, or in context, and I ask the question, "How will that congregation of people defend themselves when the false teachers come, when the deceiving spirits attack their faith and their values? How will these people stand against the wiles of the enemy if they do not know what the Word of God truly says?"

It is said that if God were to speak audibly today, He would simply repeat what has already been written in the Bible. In other words, God would never contradict anything in the Bible, because He wrote it perfectly and completely. "The law of the LORD is perfect, converting the soul; the testimony of the LORD is sure, making wise the simple; the statutes of the LORD are right, rejoicing the heart; the commandment of the LORD is pure, enlightening the eyes" (Psalm 19:7–8).

For anyone to believe the deceiving spirit that promotes a demonic doctrine against the very Word of God is a sober reminder that this can happen to any one of us at any time if we turn our eyes from the Word of God. The warnings we are given in the Bible are real, and they are coming to fruition as we speak. Knowing this, the question that I pose here takes on an even greater sense of urgency. How will we ever be able to stand in the days of adversity if we do not know what the Word of God says? There is a reason the Word of God is called our sword—because we are in a very real battle and we need weapons to defend ourselves from all of the deceiving spirits and demonic doctrines that are coming, and that are already here right now (1 John 4:1–3). So believer, remember, it does absolutely no good for us to have a sword if we do not know how to use it.

OCTOBER 17th

Hosea 2:6: "I will hedge up your way with thorns, and wall her in, so that she cannot find her paths."

Before Kate was born, Michelle and I went through our entire house and baby-proofed our home as best we could. It's not that we didn't want our daughter to have freedom in our home; it's that we wanted to protect her from those things that would harm her. To allow her to just have free reign in our home without any limits would not only have been reckless; it would also have shown that we did not care about the wellbeing of our child.

In the book of Hosea, we see something very similar as we read about a time in Israel's history where God's people had "committed great harlotry by departing from the LORD" (Hosea 1:2). The love God had for His children never changed, even though Israel had rejected Him as their God and had chased after worldly things. So, to protect His children and to bring them back to repentance, the Lord decided to "hedge up your way with thorns, and wall her in, so that she cannot find her paths." By doing this, the Lord was essentially babyproofing His children's lives. It's not that God didn't want them to have freedom; it's that He wanted to protect them from those things that would eventually destroy them. To allow His children to have free reign in this world without any limits would not only have been reckless; it would also have shown that He did not care about their wellbeing.

Today, the amazing freedom that we have been given through Christ Jesus is often abused by Christians who want to justify their worldly behavior by proclaiming that we are no longer bound and are now free to do whatever it is *we* want to do. Whatever *we* want to do? Perish the thought! As Proverbs 14:12 reminds us, "There is a way that seems right to a man, but its end is the way of death." Even after walking with the Lord for nineteen years, I know not to trust myself to choose my own way in life because I recognize how deceitfully wicked my heart can be at times, and how I can justify just about any behavior in my mind. So when we begin chasing after worldly things that lead us away from the Lord, He will lovingly "hedge up [our] way with thorns, and wall [us] in, so that [we] cannot find [our] paths."

The problem we have when the Lord does this is that we often view His hedges as walls that confine us, instead of barriers that protect us. When this happens, and our ways are frustratingly and painfully cut off, we get angry and lash out against the Lord. It is in these times that we must remember that He does not do this to punish us, but rather to protect us from ourselves, because He loves us and He wants the very best for us.

OCTOBER 18th

Isaiah 32:15: "Until the Spirit is poured upon us from on high, and the wilderness becomes a fruitful field, and the fruitful field is counted as a forest."

When my parents were selling their home a couple years ago, my mom and I thought it would be fun to take a trip down memory lane and watch some home movies of when we first moved into our house. As the video started playing and I saw my unsaved self, my soul began to shudder and I was overcome with great sadness, because all I could see was death. There was no life in my eyes, no hope in my heart, and no substance to my being. I was an empty, depressed, suicidal, twenty-five-year-old who trusted in the world—until, that is, I gave my life to Jesus Christ and His Holy Spirit was poured out on me. Then, everything changed.

I was reminded of this when I was reading about how the children of Israel placed their trust in "Egypt for help, and rel[ied] on horses, who trust[ed] in chariots because they are many, and in horsemen because they are strong, but who do not look to the Holy One of Israel" (Isaiah 31:1). The end result of this misplaced trust was a land of desolation and ruin, as their fruitful fields and happy homes were overrun with thorns and briers and their bustling cities were deserted (Isaiah 32:12–14).

Isaiah stated that this would be Israel's lot in life, "Until the Spirit is poured upon us from on high, and the wilderness becomes a fruitful field, and the fruitful field is counted as a forest." Only the power of the Holy Spirit could bring richness and life to a deserted wasteland and transform it into a lush, fruitful field that is so abundant it must be considered a forest.[142] "Then justice will dwell in the wilderness and righteousness remain in the fruitful field" (Isaiah 32:16). Once the Holy Spirit is poured out, peace will reign in the land and He will bring quietness and assurance forever.

I cannot think of a greater description of how my life was so radically changed after I gave my life to Jesus Christ and His Holy Spirit was poured out upon me. The *Mad Max*-like wasteland of evil and chaos that was once my soul was transformed into a fruitful field of righteousness, as He brought quietness and assurance to my life. And even though trouble may come in this life, even "though hail comes down on the forest and the city is brought low in humiliation" (Isaiah 32:19), "My people will dwell in a peaceful habitation, in secure dwellings and in quiet resting places" (Isaiah 32:18). I can be at complete peace because though our country is failing, though the economy is tanking, though this world is perishing, and though sickness is spreading, I have a secure dwelling in a quiet and restful place that it is tethered to my Savior who lies behind the veil. Can you say the same? If not, let it be known, it is yours if you want it. Jesus Christ died for all of mankind, and desires to pour out His Holy Spirit on all who would ask.

OCTOBER 19th

> Genesis 18:33: "So the LORD went His way as soon as He had finished speaking with Abraham; and Abraham returned to his place."

A few years ago, a man walked up to me and another brother in the prayer room and asked if he could see a pastor because he needed prayer. We explained to him that there were no pastors in the prayer room, as they were all serving in their respective ministries at the time. He then looked at us and said with a very disappointed tone, "Well, I guess you'll do."

Why do we believe that one person's prayers are more powerful than another's? For some people it's because of a title or an ordination, but for most it's probably because at one point in time this particular person prayed for them and there was an immediate answer to that prayer. Thus, the natural assumption for us is that their prayers are more powerful than others.

But God is no respecter of persons (Acts 10:34)—meaning, He favors no one over another. So why do some prayers have immediate results and some take years before any fruit is seen? I believe the answer is found in Genesis 18 where Abraham was interceding for his nephew Lot. Over and over again Abraham prayed, appealing to God's merciful nature for Lot and his family. "So the LORD went His way as soon as He had finished speaking with Abraham; and Abraham returned to his place." Notice that the Lord went His way when He was done speaking with Abraham—not when Abraham was done speaking with God.

We gain some insight here from Revelation 5:8, where it states that there are golden bowls in heaven that "are full of incense, which are the prayers of the saints." The prevailing thought here is that different situations have different-sized containers that must be filled before that prayer will be answered. Some situations have small bowls to fill, and other situations have large bowls to fill. Regardless, every bowl is perfectly suited for every situation in width, depth, and volume. In Abraham's case, the vessel containing his prayers was now full, and there was nothing left for him to pray for. It was now on God to answer that prayer in His timing and in His way.

Our responsibility in all of this is to be diligent in prayer, just like Jacob was when he wrestled with God and refused to let Him go until He blessed Him (Genesis 32:22–32). Wisdom has it that if one person's prayers avail much (James 5:16), how much would ten, or twenty, or a hundred avail? Think of it like this: If I am trying to fill a swimming pool with a bucket, you can bet I am going to ask for as much help as I can get to help fill that thing up. The same logic can be said of prayer as well.

So, believer, though it can be very difficult to remain diligent in prayer as time goes on and despair begins to set in, remember, even though we live in an instant-gratification society today, God has a much different way of doing things—and oftentimes, waiting is a huge part of the answer to our prayers. As the Bible continually reminds us, "Blessed are all those who wait for Him" (Isaiah 30:18).

OCTOBER 20th

Isaiah 33:2: "We have waited for You."

"What is the key to waiting on the Lord?" This was the question I found myself wrestling with this morning as I was reading through the book of Isaiah. After thinking about it for a while, I decided to list out some of the things that we wait for in this life, hoping to find the answer. With that, I came up with two categories of things we wait for: 1) things by choice; and 2) things by circumstance.

I am always amazed at how many people line up at a theatre days before the release of a blockbuster movie; I am astonished by how many people camp out at a specific store weeks before a Black Friday sale. I myself have waited for hours in line just to ride the newest attraction at Magic Mountain. These are just a few of the things that we wait for by choice. Some of the things we wait for by circumstance would be things like the DMV, an urgent-care facility, and of course, traffic. Yet as different as each of these things are, they all have one common thread that answers our question: They have expectation.

Whether we are waiting in line for a movie, stuck in traffic, camping out at a store, or sitting at the DMV, we wait because we expect an end result. Well if we have this much faith in the things of this world, why do we lack such faith in the only One who is truly ever-faithful and never failing? Ultimately, we fail to wait on

God because we have no expectation of Him moving in that situation. Yet the Bible promises us over and over again that when we wait on the Lord, when we place our expectation in His hands, we are never ashamed:

> The LORD is good to those who wait for Him, to the soul who seeks Him. (Lamentations 3:25)

> For the vision is yet for an appointed time; but at the end it will speak, and it will not lie. Though it tarries, wait for it; because it will surely come, it will not tarry. (Habakkuk 2:3)

> And now, LORD, what do I wait for? My hope is in You. (Psalm 39:7)

When Michelle and I were waiting on the Lord to tell us if we should date, if we should get married, if we should have children, if we should buy a house, etc., the thing I always reminded her of was that if we wanted to get it right—if we wanted the Lord's perfect will in direction and in timing—all we had to do is pray and wait because the Lord would answer us. And He always has. So, believer, regardless what you are waiting for, do not give up; rather, place your expectation fully in the Lord, knowing that when you wait on Him you will be abundantly blessed.

OCTOBER 21ˢᵗ

> Isaiah 33:15: "who stops his ears from hearing of bloodshed, and shuts his eyes from seeing evil."

My mom was telling me the other day about how parents generally dealt with chicken pox when I was a kid. Rather than avoid the virus altogether, when a child would get infected, the mother of that child would let all of the other moms know and they would have a chicken-pox party so all of their kids would get infected. The theory here was that once you had chicken pox, you would be immune for the rest of your life and vaccinations would not be necessary.

Though this thinking might work for things such as chicken pox, it does not work in regard to sin. I hear many Christians today talking about how they need to expose their children to sin, so that they will be "immune" to it later in life. Michelle and I were reading a book in which the author stated that rated R movies, music, video games, media, are not sinful; it is the child who is sinful, and to keep your child from these things is being legalistic and controlling. It is true that children are sinners, but exposing them to such things would be like adding fuel to an already-lit fire. It doesn't put the fire out; it simply fuels it and makes it more powerful.

In the book of Isaiah, when the question was asked as to who can dwell with "the devouring fire?" (Isaiah 33:14), speaking of God's righteous judgment, the answer was, "He who walks righteously and speaks uprightly, he who despises the gain of oppressions, who gestures with his hands, refusing bribes, who stops his ears from hearing of bloodshed, and shuts his eyes from seeing evil: he will dwell on high; his place of defense will be the fortress of rocks; bread will be given him, his water will be sure" (Isaiah 33:15–16).

These verses do not speak of burying your head in the sand and ignoring the evils of society. Rather, they refer to making a stand against evil things, refusing to take part in them or even to be exposed to them.[143] David stated in Psalm 101:3, "I will set nothing wicked before my eyes." Solomon would later write in Proverbs 4:23, "Keep [guard] your heart with all diligence, for out of it spring the issues of life." The apostle Paul made it abundantly clear when he wrote in 1 Thessalonians 5:22, "Abstain from every form of evil." As graphic as the Bible can be at times, even the Bible abstains from describing certain evils so as to not expose the reader to those vile things.

The key to raising a child is found in Proverbs 22:6: "Train up a child in the way he should go." Read the Bible to your children; teach them what it says; expose them to the very Word of God because in this they will learn all about the evil things of this world. The difference is that they will learn about them through the eyes of God, not the eyes of the world.

OCTOBER 22nd

> Philippians 1:9: "And this I pray, that your love may abound still more and more in knowledge and discernment."

Contrary to what certain people might say today, true love is not blind; it is also not tolerant and accepting of all choices and behaviors. The Corinthian church prided themselves on their free love for all people and all things because they believed *that* was love; yet the apostle Paul strongly rebuked them for this practice, as they permitted a churchgoer to have sexual relations with his father's wife without consequence (1 Corinthians 5:1–7). It is true that we are to put on love above all other things (Colossians 3:14), as love fulfills both the law and the gospel. But love is never blind to ethical and moral correctness; rather, it abounds in both knowledge and discernment.

I find it perplexing that those who preach acceptance and tolerance of all things today (aka "love") spew venom on anyone who disagrees with their point of view. Herein lies the real problem with the world's practice of blind love: Without knowledge and discernment abounding in that love, it only leads to hate and contempt. The religious leaders in Jesus' day were very zealous for God, yet without knowledge and discernment, they were given to violence, rage, and even murder.[144]

But when love abounds in a "precise and correct knowledge of things ethical and divine,"[145] when it can perceive and discern social matters correctly, "not only by the senses but [also] by the intellect,"[146] through a relationship with Jesus Christ, then "you may approve of the things that are excellent . . . you may be sincere and without offense . . . filled with the fruits of righteousness which are by Jesus Christ, to the glory and praise of God" (Philippians 1:10–11). This is why the apostle Paul prayed for the Philippian church, "that your love may abound still more and more in knowledge and discernment"—so that even though they were sent out among the wolves, even though they would be hated and persecuted, they would be as wise as serpents and as harmless as doves in their witness to the world (Matthew 10:16).

OCTOBER 23rd

Isaiah 35:2: "They shall see the glory of the LORD, the excellency of our God."

When Israel refused to repent from their rebellion, they brought the Lord's judgment upon themselves and their land. The road to Jerusalem, which was once a highway of joy and celebration, would now lay waste as travelers would fear for their safety. Lebanon, which was famed for its cedars, Sharon for its roses, Bashan for its cattle, and Carmel for its corn, all lush with bountiful harvests of fruit and resources, would now be desolate wastelands (Isaiah 33). Until, that is, the Day of the Lord, for then, "A highway shall be there . . . and it shall be called the Highway of Holiness . . . the desert shall rejoice and blossom as the rose" (Isaiah 35:8). Furthermore, "It shall blossom abundantly and rejoice, even with joy and singing. The glory of Lebanon shall be given to it, the excellence of Carmel and Sharon. They shall see the glory of the LORD, the excellency of our God" (Isaiah 35:2).

I think it is very telling that the glory of the Lord, the excellency of our God, is seen in the restoration of those things that were once destroyed by sin and rebellion.

This is very important for us to understand, because too often we hide our brokenness from God and revert to the thinking that we must heal ourselves from the foolish decisions we have made. Yet how is that possible when God is the only source of restoration?

I remember hearing a story of a pastor who was challenged to a debate by an atheist. The pastor said he would agree to this debate if the atheist could provide witnesses of people who did not believe in God and yet were restored. He asked the atheist to bring a prostitute, a drug user, an adulterer, and a sexually immoral deviate who had been restored, renewed, or transformed by atheism and then he would have his debate. The atheist turned and walked away.

God desires to restore the brokenness that sin has brought. He longs to restore those things, those individuals like you and I, that have been devastated by the effects of sin. He loves to take that which is broken, empty, and useless—those things that the world has corrupted and discarded—and completely restore them into that which is whole, purposed, and effective. In fact, God restores so completely in Christ that we are brand-new creations; all things have passed away, behold, all things have been made new (2 Corinthians 5:17).

OCTOBER 24th

Isaiah 35:3: "Strengthen the weak hands, and make firm the feeble knees."

The most difficult part of the Christian walk is not the beginning (justification) or the end (coming glory), as both are jubilant times filled with celebration and joy. No, the most pressing time for the believer is what takes place in between these two points. Whether it is the trouble that life brings or the monotony of trudging through a barren landscape day after day, we struggle to endure in a society, and even in a church, that often leaves us feeling as though we are alone on a deserted island. This is why the Bible continually reminds us that our life here on Earth is not going to be a sprint, but rather a marathon, filled with hills and valleys, lush gardens and desert wastelands, in which we are to run with patience (Hebrews 12:1) pressing on toward the goal which God has called us to (Philippians 3:14). In other words, we are not to give up, but rather we are to rest in the Lord and have our strength renewed (Isaiah 40:31).

In Isaiah's day, the remnant of believers who still held true to God were struggling to press on because their nation was corrupt and perverse; their hearts were growing faint as their political and religious leaders were immoral idolaters who turned their backs on God, which in turn, was bringing the Lord's judgment in the form of a devastating Assyrian invasion. Knowing this, the Lord instructed Isaiah to "Strengthen the weak hands, and make firm the feeble knees. Say to those who are fearful-hearted, 'Be strong, do not fear! Behold, your God will come with vengeance, with the recompense of God; He will come and save you'" (Isaiah 35:3–4). Essentially, what the Lord was saying to His children was, "It is no time to have weak hands and feeble knees. This is when your nation needs you the most."

All of this begs the question, "Is our society as bad as it is today because the darkness is so great, or because the church has weak hands and feeble knees?" I fear it is the latter, as darkness is merely the absence of light; the only way for darkness to prevail is if light is not present—or in our case, not presently active in the battle. So where is the light today? Where is the power of the church? The Lord is saying the exact same thing to His church today that He said to Isaiah, "This is no time for you to stop working; this is no time for you to stop praying. This is when the world needs you the most, so strengthen those weak hands and make firm those feeble knees." May it be so today in each one of our lives.

OCTOBER 25th

Haggai 2:12: "[W]ill it become holy?"

As we enter cold and flu season, messages are going out all around the country telling us that we need to get flu shots so that we will prevent the spreading of the flu. But common sense tells us that the best way to avoid catching the flu is to simply avoid those who already have the flu. One of the ways we do this is by constantly washing our hands throughout the day.

I remember when our daughter was in NICU, Michelle and I had to wash from our hands all the way up to our elbows for three minutes, and then put on a gown over our clothes, so that we would not infect our baby girl with any harmful germs. After she was released from NICU four days later and we got her home, I caught a cold and was constantly washing my hands and wearing a breathing mask so that she would not be infected. What we learn from all of this is that a healthy person cannot make a sick person healthy, but a sick person can make a healthy person sick.

This is the same principle that the Lord spoke of in the book of Haggai when He asked, "If you are holy and you touch bread or water, does that make the bread or water holy? No. But, if you are unclean and you touch bread or water, does that make the bread or water unclean? Yes" (see Haggai 2:11–14). In other words, as Jon Courson well said, you who are "holy cannot make an unholy thing clean, but that which is unclean can make you that are holy, unholy."[147] Bottom line, impurity is contagious.

The Lord went into great detail about this in Leviticus 11 when He spoke about animal carcasses. There we are told that whatever touched the carcass of an animal was made unclean, not the other way around. But, if an animal carcass fell into a spring, it would not make the spring unclean, but rather the spring would make the carcass clean. What is so interesting about this statement is that springs were often referred to as "living water." And according to Jeremiah 2:13, the Lord is "the fountain of living waters." Thus, in a very real sense, Jesus Christ is the spring that cleanses us from all our sin.[148]

Remember, we are born into this world as sinners. We are not sinners because we sin; we sin because we are sinners. We are infected from birth—we are, in a sense, unclean, dead animal carcasses—and we need to be cleansed from our sin. Only Jesus Christ is able to do that, because only Jesus Christ defeated sin on the cross that day at Golgotha by the shedding of His blood.

But even after we have given our lives to Jesus and repented of our sin, we cannot just willingly expose ourselves to those things which are unclean, thinking that they will not defile us. No, we must avoid them, knowing that impurity is infectious. There is a reason why David stated he would set nothing evil before his eyes—because he recognized the danger it brings (Psalm 101:3). The Lord said it very clearly: "Be holy, for I am holy" (1 Peter 1:16). In other words, make the choice to be set apart and avoid those unclean things, so that we are not defiled.

OCTOBER 26th

Psalm 68:19: "Blessed be the Lord, who daily loads us with benefits."

How will you approach this day? For many, the thoughts of trouble, strife, and hopelessness come upon them the very moment they wake up. For them, it is sure to be a day littered with darkness and despair, as they are certain the day has set itself against them. For the believer, it should not be so. Instead, we should prepare ourselves every morning to run and meet God joyfully, full of thanksgiving and praise, knowing that He "daily loads us with benefits."

Even in the darkest of days, the full assurance of this hope remains because we are the heirs of His promise. The Lord loves to daily provide us with opportunities to praise Him, so He unwearyingly loads us up with the abundance of His graces—so much so that there is literally no room for us to receive anything further. The possibility of a child emptying the ocean with a bucket and a pail is more likely to come about than for us to ever exhaust the daily graces that God loads us with.

As orphans adopted by the One who conquered death and overcame the world, are we just victims helplessly living out our days in a violent and perverse world, eking by every day, or are we more than conquerors through Him who loves us (Romans 8:37)? To be a conqueror is to be someone who is victorious after a battle has taken place; the believer in Christ, who is more than a conqueror, is victorious before the battle even begins.

We have an unyielding hope set before us that is both sure and steadfast, because the Anchor of our soul is not still hanging on a cross, or buried in a tomb somewhere. No, our Living Hope, to whom we are tethered behind the veil, has risen from the dead and is sitting at the right hand of the Father, making intercession for each one of us right now. So, believer, how will you approach this day?

OCTOBER 27th

1 Peter 5:9: "Resist him, steadfast in the faith."

Last week a brother was telling me about a vision he was given of a loved one who was in bondage to drugs and alcohol. In the vision, this loved one was completely bound in a spider web, and a man dressed in armor with a giant broad sword was standing before her. At the time he received the vision, my friend wasn't sure if the man was there to kill or to protect the young woman. It was then that the Lord quickly reminded me that Satan does not have swords or knives or any other weapons of that nature; the weapons Satan wields against us are those of deception.

In 1 Peter 5:8, we are told that Satan "walks about like a roaring lion, seeking whom he may devour." Our minds read much into this upon first glance, as we quickly think Scripture is telling us that Satan is a ferocious beast with sharp claws and piercing fangs. As David Guzik pointed out, Colossians 2:15 reminds us that Satan was disarmed at the cross, meaning that Satan was declawed and defanged; all he can do now is walk around like a "roaring" lion, instilling fear into his prey.[149] This does not mean that he is harmless by any means, for deception is a very powerful weapon and he is a master craftsman at using it. Ask anyone who has ever considered suicide and they will tell you that they began believing the lie that everything was hopeless. Thankfully the Lord has given us a mighty weapon that shines light on and defeats Satan's lies. It is the Word of God.

When Jesus was led into the wilderness and was tempted by Satan, He defeated Satan by using the Word of God, not armies of angels and heavenly hosts. He simply stood on Scripture and defeated Satan's deception with God's truth. As the old adage goes, Satan does not have any new tricks, just new victims. Peter reminds us that we need to be watchful for these same kinds of deceptions, for they will come to us as well. Our defense against his attacks is simply this: "Resist him, steadfast in the faith." The word "resist" basically means "to stand firm" or "to stand against." Notice that we have the ability to stand against him and resist his lies when we place our faith in what God has said rather than in what our circumstances might tell us. It reminds us that Satan does not have the power to overtake us; the only way he wins in our lives is if we give in to his deception and believe his lies.

This is why it is so vitally important for every believer to know the Word of God for themselves, because this is ultimately how we will defeat the lies we are bombarded with every day. Whether it is lies about what beauty really is, about what will fulfill us, about sexual immorality not destroying, about the unexpected pregnancy ruining our lives, or lies about God's unconditional love and faithfulness for each one of us, they are all exposed, redefined, and defeated by the Word of God. It is here, in His Word, that we are "transformed by the renewing of [our] mind" (Romans 12:2).

OCTOBER 28th

2 Kings 18:4: "He removed the high places."

When Hezekiah became king over Judah, he made sweeping changes across the nation and did something that no other king before him had the courage to do: He "removed the high places" of worship. These were not solely idolatrous altars erected in the name of Baal or other idols of that day; they were also places of sacrifice that were performed in the name of the Lord our God. One of the problems was that the altars were built according to the desire of what the people wanted, not according to the desire of what God had instructed His children to do (Leviticus 17:1–4).

In effect, the high places were a direct reflection of the attitude and practice of the pagan worship in that day, in which it was common practice for people to offer sacrifices wherever and however they chose.[150] This was an offense to God, because He precisely instructed His children to bring their sacrifices to the tabernacle (and later the temple). But why? What's the big deal if people sacrificed how and where they wanted to, as long as it was directed to God? To answer that question, we only need look at the attitude and practice of our society today, in which people make up their own set of rules as to how they want to come to God (works, baptism, being a good person, etc.).[151] I believe God commanded His children to take their sacrifices to the tabernacle/temple as a foreshadowing truth to everyone that there would only be one name under heaven by which man could be saved, Jesus Christ (Acts 4:12).

God instituted an important principle that serves in direct contrast to the all the "high places" that exist today, such as: all roads lead to Heaven; we all worship the same God; we pray to men and women rather than Jesus; penance brings forgiveness; baptism, works, rituals, membership equal salvation, etc. God is reminding us that we cannot just pick and choose which parts of the Bible we want to follow; He is warning us that we cannot just make up our own religion and expect it to work out the way we want it to. The Lord, through His own desire and will, perfectly and painfully provided the way of salvation for all of mankind as only He could. To think that we can just add to, subtract from, or alter that path to suit our own desires is just foolishness. Jesus said it very plainly so that there would be no misunderstanding or misinterpretation, "I am the way, the truth and the life. No one comes to the Father except through Me" (John 14:6).

OCTOBER 29th

Proverbs 16:4: "The LORD has made all for Himself."

When Abraham was instructed to sacrifice his beloved son Isaac . . . when Shadrach, Meshach, and Abednego were being thrown into a fiery furnace . . . when it was revealed to Hezekiah that he was going to die . . . and when Mary was told she would be with child, they all placed their faith in the Lord because they all understood the underlying principle that the Lord has made all things for Himself. It doesn't mean they were happy about their situations, or even agreed with how the Lord was bringing them about. Yet, in spite of how they felt and what they thought, they still chose to deny themselves and place their trust in the Lord and His ways. Interestingly enough, the word "Himself" used here means an answer or response—a purpose. So the question we all must answer is, when the Lord chooses to use us for His purposes, when He allows things into our lives that we do not agree with, how will we respond?

Before we went to Israel in April of 2012, my wife and I prayed fervently that the Lord would heal me of my ongoing skin affliction. Months later, while we were in Israel, the Lord asked me, "Will you still love Me even if I don't heal you?" That is when I realized that I had placed my faith and hope in a healing, rather than in my God. When we returned home from our trip, I wrote a devotion about my affliction and the hope the Lord had given me through it. As I sat at my desk pondering exactly why the Lord wanted me to have this affliction, a response from one of our devotional readers came in saying, "You have no idea how much I needed to hear this today." It was then that I heard the Lord say, "That is why."

It was a great reminder of the fact that I was created for His purposes, not my own. I was also reminded of what I declared on April 22, 2000, "Lord, take my life, use it as You will, I am yours." Too often, we forget those words when we are faced with circumstances that do not align with our will, our timing, or what we want for our lives. How dare God take us at our word!

If there is one thing that the Lord has made abundantly clear to me over these last sixteen years of walking with Him, it is that His will, not mine, is not only best for me; it is also best for everyone who is in and around my life. This is why my wife and I diligently pray and wait for just about everything that we possibly can, because we want His perfect will for our lives, not ours. So, believer, how are you responding today to God's call on your life?

OCTOBER 30th

Matthew 10:16b: "Therefore be wise as serpents and harmless as doves."

When I was a kid, my dad often said to me, "Fool me once shame on you, fool me twice shame on me." I was reminded of this as I was meditating on Matthew 10:16, "Therefore be wise as serpents and harmless as doves." Over the last few months or so, I have probably quoted this verse about thirty times to myself, my wife, and many others whom I have spoken with. This was the counsel and direction that Jesus gave to His disciples when He sent them out as "sheep in the midst of wolves" (Matthew 10:16a).

Jesus is not telling us to be like a serpent or a dove; rather, He is telling us to adopt certain characteristics of a serpent and a dove as guidance in how we are to live in this fallen world. The first thing we notice is that we are to be wise as

320 Renovating Your Mind

serpents. When commenting on this verse, Matthew Henry explained that, unlike foxes who use their cunning "to deceive others," serpents use their cunning "to defend themselves." The lesson here is that even though we are called to be ministers to the people in this world, we are not called to recklessly expose ourselves to those who would do us harm over and over again. Rather, we are to make decisions that are fair and just regarding their best interests, but which also includes our own preservation as well.[152]

The second thing we notice is that we are to be as "harmless as doves." The interesting thing about doves is that by nature they do not provoke their enemies, nor are they provoked by them. This is a perfect description of the Holy Spirit, whom Jesus exhibited throughout His time here on Earth and especially at the cross. This Spirit, which curiously enough, we are told descended upon Him like a dove, is the same Spirit we are to exhibit to this world.[153]

The word "harmless" that is used here literally means to be unmixed and pure and refers to having no mixture of evil in our mind or our heart. Practically speaking, it means we are not to harm anyone nor are we to hold anything against them when they harm us. Showing others grace, however, does not mean that we are a punching bag for them to abuse whenever they so choose. Remember, we are not instructed to just be harmless; we are also instructed to be wise and to protect ourselves, for even Jesus warned His disciples to beware of men (Matthew 10:17).

A great example of the balance we are to have is found when Nehemiah instructed those under his care to rebuild the wall with one hand and hold a sword with the other (Nehemiah 4:17). The purpose of the sword was not to attack, as the order given was to defend themselves, their families, and their homes. We would be wise to receive this counsel as well.

OCTOBER 31st

John 17:17: "Sanctify them by Your truth. Your word is truth."

"Entertain me, I'm bored." This is seemingly the cry of many in our society today. No longer does man want to seek out and find truth for himself; he wants it given to him on a silver platter. No longer does he want to think for himself and determine what is right or wrong in a given situation; he wants to be told what to believe. Every morning we turn on our electronic devices searching for the *truth du jour*, just waiting to be fed whatever drivel may be out there. In a very real sense, our society has become the slothful man in Proverbs who buries his hand in his dish, and is too lazy to bring it back up to his mouth (Proverbs 26:15).

I often wonder how the love in a Christian's heart will grow cold in the last days (Matthew 24:12), how believers will be led astray by false teachers and false prophets, exchanging the pure devotion of Christ with a corrupt devotion for self (2 Corinthians 11:3). It's not hard to see how this will happen when you consider the fact that our attention spans are becoming that of a two-year-old child who can't sit still for more than a second because we are not being stimulated by our electronic addiction. We will set aside an inordinate amount of time to watch a video on just about anything under the sun, or scroll through and look at every picture that crosses our path, but when we happen upon any sort of written rhetoric—especially that which is of the Lord—we disregard it because *it takes too much time and effort* to read and comprehend what is being said.

I believe the Christian's heart will grow cold and believers will be led astray because they will stop reading the Bible and forsake seeking the truth for themselves. Everything they will base truth on will be what is given to them by someone else. Regardless of who it might be, if we do not know the truth for ourselves, how will we ever know if what others are telling us is actually truth? How will we ever change and grow and be transformed more and more into the image of Christ?

John 17:17 reminds us that it is the very truth contained in the Bible that sanctifies us as we read it, understand it, and apply it to our lives by the leading of the Holy Spirit. It is how we grow in faith, wisdom, and discernment. It is how we defend ourselves and our families from the deceptions of the world. It is how we stand firm and resist the enemy. And ultimately, it is how we know the Father and are able to glorify Him to this world. So, believer, pick up the Book, seek for yourself, and be sanctified by truth.

NOVEMBER 1st

> Isaiah 6:1: "In the year that King Uzziah died, I saw the Lord sitting on a throne, high and lifted up, and the train of His robe filled the temple."

For Isaiah, hopelessness was building: The much-loved king, Uzziah, was dead; chaos was mounting; Judah's enemies were stirring; and captivity was coming. It was then, in that moment, when all seemed darkest, when it seemed like the Lord was nowhere to be found, that Isaiah "saw the Lord sitting on a throne, high and lifted up, and the train of His robe filled the temple." Though it "seemed" like everything was out of control and was falling apart, the Lord made it abundantly clear to Isaiah that He was still on the throne and that He was still very much in control.

I had been thinking a lot about the perspective Isaiah was given as the 2016 presidential election approached. We must remember that regardless of how the election turned out, nothing has changed for the believer. Our hope has always been and always will be firmly secure in Jesus Christ, for we are tethered to the King of all kings who resides behind the veil and sits at the right hand of the Father. As Hebrews 6 reminds us, this unshakable hope that we have in Him is the anchor of our soul. Whereas if we were to anchor our hope to a person, party, or anything else for that matter, we will be hopeless indeed, for those things will always fail us.

To keep this perspective in place, we must adhere to the Lord's instructions and continue to pray for the leaders of this country, regardless who they might be, for the Bible says that when we make supplications, prayers, intercessions, and giving of thanks for those in authority, we will lead quiet and peaceable lives in all godliness and reverence (1 Timothy 2:2). The amazing benefit of praying and fasting for the 2016 election is that I have been changed. No longer is there worry or anxiety or fear about what may come, because my perspective has been placed exactly where it needs to be: on Jesus, sitting on the throne, high and lifted up.

NOVEMBER 2nd

John 14:27: "Peace I leave with you, My peace I give to you; not as the world gives do I give to you. Let your heart not be troubled, neither let it be afraid."

Last Monday night, Michelle and I gathered with many of our brethren to pray and intercede for the 2016 election. As we were enjoying fellowship with one another afterward, I noticed there was an excitement about the election that was not there beforehand. After mentioning it to several others, it was apparent to me that our excitement for the election had nothing at all to do with who would win. Rather, it was an excitement in what God was going to do because we knew that no matter what happened, He was on the throne and He was completely in control.

I think it is important to understand that the excitement we were feeling that night was an excitement that can only be born out of the peace that God gives us: "Peace I leave with you, My peace I give to you; not as the world gives do I give to you. Let your heart not be troubled, neither let it be afraid." Ray Stedman described this peace as "the ability to cope," meaning it is a peace that is not determined by situations, circumstances, or outcomes like the peace the world gives; rather it is a peace that overcomes situations, circumstances, and outcomes because it is a peace that can never be taken away from us.[154]

I was thinking a lot about this as I read certain posts on social media following the election. I completely understood why unbelievers reacted the way they did, because the only peace they have is founded in the world, and when that peace was taken away from them, they became scared and angry. What I did not understand were the posts I read from believers, who were lashing out and pointing fingers at others. It became clear to me that these believers were scared and angry because they were seeking their peace in the world rather than finding it in Christ; and because of that, they were unable to cope with what had happened.

Jesus reminds us that it is only when we seek the peace He gives, the peace that surpasses all understanding, the peace that cannot be taken away from us, that we can be in such a state that our hearts will not be troubled, nor will they be afraid regardless what might occur.

NOVEMBER 3rd

Philippians 1:27: "Only let your conduct be worthy of the gospel of Christ."

About ten years ago, one of our upper management presented a customer-service training program to every employee. The two-hour-long session focused on having the right attitude, being professional, nice, courteous, patient, etc. Strangely enough, though, this man also told us stories of his experiences at fast-food restaurants in which he would berate employees for taking too long or even for just working there. He then continued on this bizarre tirade by speaking down to people for not having college degrees as it made them inadequate. What this man did not understand was that customer service is not an attitude we are just to put on from 8–5; rather, it should be who we are 24/7, regardless if we are at work or not.

For many believers, this perfectly describes us spiritually as we have misinterpreted Scripture as saying "we are to witness," rather than "we are witnesses." We act like witnesses at specific times or at specific locations, but then we clock out and leave our Christianity behind us for the rest of the day. It is kind of like saying "amen" after a prayer and thinking that God is no longer around us because we have signed off with Him.

In Philippians 1:27, the apostle Paul exhorts us, "let your conduct be worthy of the gospel of Christ." The word "conduct" means to be a citizen, and specifically refers to our citizenship in Christ. Paul is reminding us that we are no longer citizens of this world; we are now citizens of heaven, and thus we should live in such a way that the gospel of Christ is magnified in and through our lives regardless where we may be or what we may be doing.

For example, when I travel abroad, it does not mean that I am no longer an American citizen; I am an American citizen no matter where I go or what I do. And I do not need to try to be an American citizen; it is simply who I am. In the same regard, as believers, we are witnesses for Christ no matter where we are or what we are doing. The only question is, what kind of witness are we presenting to others? Is it one that attracts people to Jesus, or one that repels them from Him?

The challenge Paul gives us here is to be citizens that are worthy of the gospel, who reflect the image of Christ to others regardless what the situation might be. W. Glyn Evans said, "The gospel is simply a collection of words, terms, and phrases, all of which are difficult to understand unless they are made clear by someone's life. Looking at us, the unsaved community should be able to see a connection between what we are and what the gospel is declaring."[155] In other words, our behavior should be suitable to the gospel so that we do not give man an excuse to blaspheme God, but rather a reason to praise Him. As Warren Wiersbe well said, "The most important weapon against the enemy is not a stirring sermon or a powerful book; it is the consistent life of believers."[156]

NOVEMBER 4th

Isaiah 40:1: "'Comfort, yes, comfort My people!' says your God."

The instruction the Lord gave to Isaiah thousands of years ago, to comfort His people, has as much relevance for us today as it did for Isaiah back in his day. In fact, I believe this instruction was not just given to Isaiah for that specific time, but was given to every prophet and minister for all time: "Comfort . . . My people!" We must read this charge as though the Lord has just spoken it into existence, and that He has spoken it directly to each one of us. Second Corinthians 1:3 (emphasis added) reminds us that our God is "the God of *all* comfort." Thus, as David Guzik reminded us, with every message that we deliver, regardless what it might be, comfort must be a part of it.[157]

The Lord instructed Isaiah to comfort His people by assuring them of three things: 1) Their warfare is ended; 2) their iniquity is forgiven; and 3) their Lord is coming (Isaiah 40:2–5). It might have seemed strange for Isaiah to tell God's people that their warfare had ended when the Babylonian invasion was still coming; yet even though the battle of life remained, the war itself was over.

The second thing Isaiah was to assure God's people of was that their iniquity was forgiven. The first thirty-nine chapters describe how Isaiah revealed Israel's sin and rebellion against the Lord, so the people knew of their transgression and the consequences that it would bring. To now hear that the Lord had pardoned all of their iniquity must have comforted them greatly. And lastly, the Lord told Isaiah to remind His people that He was coming for them. The language given to Isaiah was common language that was often used to make preparations for a triumphant king. The Lord wanted it to be made very clear to His people, "Be comforted, your King is coming."

The key to being comforted in the midst of this life and all of its raging is to set our hearts on what is true, not on what we see. "The grass withers, the flower fades, but the word of our God stands forever" (Isaiah 40:8). When I was promoted to a new position in a different department at the county, after I put in my two weeks' notice to my current supervisor, no matter how bad the job got, no matter how mistreated I was by my current supervisor, no matter how much warfare there was, I could easily look past it all and be comforted because I knew it was only temporary and that I would soon be leaving. The same goes for us today in Jesus Christ. This world is only temporary for us; soon, we will be leaving and heading to our true home in heaven. So, believer, be comforted. Your warfare has ended, your iniquity has been pardoned, and your King is coming for you.

NOVEMBER 5th

Mark 6:5: "Now He could do no mighty work there, except that He laid His hands on a few sick people and healed them."

I once read that faith and unbelief use the same key; the difference is that one way unlocks the door, and the other way locks it. When Jesus went back to His hometown of Nazareth, we are told that "He could do no mighty work there, except that He laid His hands on a few sick people and healed them." I find it amazing that

Jesus could raise the dead, cast out any demon, command any storm to be still, heal any sickness or handicap . . . but He could do nothing with unbelief.

Ron Daniel stated that it's not that "He physically couldn't," do miracles, but rather that "He morally couldn't."[158] Jesus still performed miracles in Nazareth as we are told that He laid His hands on a few sick people and healed them, but He couldn't morally perform miracles among the unbelieving Nazarenes. John 1:12 reminds us, "But as many as received Him, to them He gave the right to become children of God, to those who believe in His name." Think of it like this: If I am sick, and I do not go to the doctor, how can the doctor possibly help me?

The simple truth that we need to recognize here is that Jesus could do no mighty work among these people simply because they would not come to Him; they did not believe on Him as the Messiah and thus they had no expectation of receiving anything from Him. "And He marveled because of their unbelief" (Mark 6:6). What would it take to marvel the Creator of the universe, the God who created everything? Faith. Jesus marveled two times in the Bible—once because of the presence of faith (Luke 7:9), and once because of its absence.[159]

We often talk about the enemies that we face in this life . . . Satan, the world, our flesh; and yet our greatest enemy we often neglect and allow to fester within our heart. Remember, Satan has been defeated, the world has been overcome, and the flesh has been beaten down. Yet unbelief goes unchecked within us every day. We need to stop focusing on our defeated enemies and start focusing on the one enemy who truly defeats us, because "all things are possible to him who believes" (Mark 9:23).

NOVEMBER 6th

1 Corinthians 4:7: "And what do you have that you did not receive? Now if you did indeed receive it, why do you boast as if you had not received it?"

The Lord spoke to me this week about the proper function of the gifts He has given to each one of us through the coming upon of His Holy Spirit. Our role, as stated many times over, is simply to make ourselves available for that gift to be exercised; the management and empowerment of that gift is solely at the discretion of the Lord. He is the One who is responsible for the enabling of that gift, the path it is to follow, and the potency it is to carry as His purposes dictate for that situation. "So shall My word be that goes forth from My mouth; it shall not return to Me void, but it shall accomplish what I please, and it shall prosper in the thing for which I sent it" (Isaiah 55:11).

In a very real sense, we are merely a host to that gift, and in no way should the glory of that gift ever be a jewel placed in our crown. As my good friend Darrell often reminds us, "After a successful surgery, you don't hug the scalpel." So why would we ever take credit when the gifts of the Spirit are manifested through our lives? This was essentially the question that the Lord posed to me this week as I was preparing to teach: "Patrick, how can you take credit for a gift that was given to you?"

There is much freedom in what the Lord spoke to me about this week, for all the pressure of performance, production, results, reception, response, etc., were removed far from my reach as the Lord made it clear, "Patrick, you are not the Christ, I am" (John 1:20). The apostle Paul stated in Romans 1:14 that he was a debtor to all men. He recognized that the gifts he had been given from the Lord were meant to be used for the betterment of others, not the promotion of self. Thus he was in debt, obligated to use them for the Lord's glory and purpose.

As W. Glyn Evans pointed out, our gifts do not belong to us, but rather they belong "to the people for whom God intended [them]."[160] The only asset we can duly claim is the Lord's eternal promise of salvation through Christ Jesus our Lord.[161] So believer, "what do you have that you did not receive? Now if you did indeed receive it, why do you boast as if you had not received it?"

NOVEMBER 7th

Isaiah 42:1: "Behold! My Servant . . ."

What's the more powerful message: that you and I are sinners, or that you and I have a God who willingly died for our sin? That you and I deserve death, or that you and I are offered grace? That you and I are not worthy of love, or that you and I are unconditionally loved? It is interesting how we so easily grasp and hold onto the negative aspect of our carnal nature; all the while we ignore and reject the positive counterparts that completely mitigate and overcome those things for us in Jesus Christ.

The reason we, as believers, are failing to walk in the power and victory of our Lord and Savior today is because we spend too much time focusing on the problem, us, instead of rejoicing in the solution, Jesus. We know that we are bruised reeds and smoking flax, but we mistakenly allow those things to define us, our character, our attitude, our perspective, and our spiritual inheritance because we fail to appre-hend the rest of the verse in which the Lord says to us, "A bruised reed [I] will not break, and smoking flax [I] will not quench" (Isaiah 42:3).

The Lord assures each one of us that even if we have been bruised, crushed, bent, and shattered by this life, He will gently and tenderly mend and restore us into something that will be stronger, more beautiful, and more useful than before. Even if our spiritual walk produces more smoke than fire, and our hope and faith in the Lord is weak and waning, the Lord says He will take that smoldering wick and fan it into a flame that will burn brightly for His kingdom.[162]

Believer, the Father is imploring all of us today, "Stop focusing on your weak-nesses and 'Behold! My Servant. . . .' Study Him; set your focus upon Him, My chosen One, My Son, Jesus Christ. He is a covenant to all mankind of My love and grace; He is the light to the lost and will open the eyes of the blind; He will bring out the prisoners from the prison, all of those who sit in darkness and despair." So which message will we grasp and hold onto today: that we often stumble, or that we will never fall for He upholds us with His mighty right hand?

NOVEMBER 8th

Joshua 1:5: "[A]s I was with Moses, so I will be with you."

One of the hardest things to endure is when a season with someone dear to you comes to an end. I have faced many such seasons since I gave my life to Christ—spiritual fathers for a specific time of growth, dear brothers and sisters who have gone home to be with the Lord, and incredibly close friends who have been called by God to leave our church, the state, and even the country for a greater purpose. It's at these times that we can often feel sadness and maybe even fear because of the void that has been left behind by those people. Yet at the same time, we must recognize that these are also very rare opportunities afforded to us to mature in the Lord, and to examine exactly where our faith and hope is placed.

In Joshua 1, Joshua faced an end to a season similar to ours, but with a mag-nitude we cannot fathom. After the death of Moses—the leader of the children of Israel, Joshua's spiritual father, counselor, and dear friend—God called Joshua to take over his position of leadership. Joshua struggled mightily with this calling, as the thought of replacing a national icon like Moses seemed impossible. God addressed Joshua's fear and doubt by promising him, "as I was with Moses, so I will be with you."

The Lord knew that Joshua had witnessed all of the incredible things that He had done through Moses, and so God made it very clear to Joshua, "Just as I was strong and faithful on Moses' behalf, so I will be strong and faithful on your behalf as well." God was essentially refocusing Joshua's faith to where it needed to be: on the Lord Almighty, not on His servant Moses. God reminded Joshua that victory was never dependent on Moses' abilities, just as it would never be dependent on his abilities. Victory only came about because of the Lord's great faithfulness to those who respond to His calling and are obedient to His instructions.

The Lord then reinforced the weight of this promise to Joshua and the children of Israel by the first miracle He performed under Joshua's leadership. It is no coincidence that the Lord chose to part the Jordan River; it was a testimony that it was in fact He, not Moses, who had parted the Red Sea. For Joshua and the children of Israel to witness this miracle before they entered the Promised Land, it assured them that just "as I was with Moses, so I will be with you."

NOVEMBER 9th

Exodus 20:23: "You shall not make anything to be with Me."

After I surrendered my life to Jesus Christ, I wanted to do something that would honor Him as my Lord and Savior, so I decided to wear a gold cross around my neck. About a year later, as I was getting ready for work one morning, the chain for my cross broke and I began to panic. "What do I do now?" It was as if my only avenue to God was gone and I was completely separated from Him. That is when the Lord spoke to me and said, "Patrick, you do not need that cross; you have Me."

I find so much peace in the fact that though God is a very complex being, the relationship that He desires to have with us is a very simple one. When the Lord spoke to the children of Israel in Exodus 20 regarding the relationship they were to have with Him, He told them, "You have seen that I have talked with you from heaven. You shall not make anything to be with Me; gods of silver or gods of gold you shall not make for yourselves" (Exodus 20:22–23). Simply put, God was saying: You do not need anything else; you have Me, and I am always with you. He further reinforced this point when He gave His children instructions on building altars for sacrifices:

> An altar of earth you shall make for Me, and you shall sacrifice on it. . . .
> In every place where I record My name I will come to you, and I will bless

you. And if you make me an altar of stone, you shall not build it of hewn stone; for if you use your tool on it, you have profaned it. Nor shall you go up by steps to My altar. (Exodus 20:24–26)

Essentially, God was telling His children, "Keep it simple, and you will keep it about Me." He didn't care where they built the altar: "In every place where I record My name I will come to you, and I will bless you." He didn't care how lavish the materials used for the altar were: "An altar of earth you shall make for Me . . . you shall not build it of hewn stone." And He didn't care how small the altar was: "Nor shall you go up by steps to My altar . . ." He just wanted His children's focus to be on Him.

A few years ago, while visiting some dear friends who are missionaries in Cabo San Lucas, Michelle and I visited a church that was being built in a local colony (barrio). It had a concrete floor, cinder-block walls, and a roof made out of a couple pieces of thin metal siding. As I stood there looking at this building, I turned to the pastor of the church and said to him, "This is the most beautiful church I have ever seen." And it was. The beauty of that church was in the simplicity of it all. There was no altar, no giant stage, no colored lights, no big screens . . . nothing that would get in the way of worshiping God and teaching His Word. There was only an incredible sense of purity and freedom from the business that has become corporate church today. This is the type of simplicity that God had in mind when He was speaking to His children in Exodus 20.

Too often today our worship and devotion fails to be a pleasing fragrance to the Lord because it has become far too complicated. We put such a huge burden on ourselves to hewn the stones of our altars through legalistic, material-driven devotion times, and compact, overregulated, overscheduled church services that we entirely miss out on the One we are supposed to be worshiping. I believe God is still having to remind His children today, "You shall not make anything to be with Me." So, believer, stop making it so complicated and burdensome; just keep it simple, and you will keep it about God.

NOVEMBER 10th

Isaiah 43:1: "Fear not, for I have redeemed you; I have called you by your name; you are Mine."

It is easy to believe that as we grow and mature in the Lord, the list of our short-comings will decrease. Yet the more we are transformed into the image of Jesus, the more we will find that the list actually increases. And as we experience this continual pulling back of the veil of our fallen nature, we begin to pose many different heartfelt questions to our Father in heaven. "Lord, You examine and know my heart, my thoughts, my intentions; nothing escapes Your sight; so how can You still love me, Lord? How are You not done with Me when I fall so short of Your glorious standard?" To that the Lord reassuringly answers us, "Fear not, for I have redeemed you; I have called you by your name; you are Mine." We find in this amazing promise that not only has God paid the price for our sin, "I have redeemed you," but that His ownership of us is both personal, "I have called you by your name," and eternal, "you are Mine."[163]

In the closing verses of the previous chapter, Isaiah 42, we are told that the children of Israel refused to walk in God's ways even while He was correcting them for their disobedience. They remained steadfast and stubborn in their rebellion to God. As Matthew Henry pointed out, one would naturally assume that God would just discard and abandon them; yet in the opening of Isaiah 43, we see God's amazing response to their stubbornness, "But now, thus says the LORD, who created you, O Jacob, and He who formed you, O Israel; 'Fear not, for I have redeemed you; I have called you by your name; you are Mine.'" God's unfathomable goodness takes occasion from Israel's ugly heart to give greater glory to His mercy and grace.[164]

The truth is that as we grow and mature in the Lord, we will learn just how bankrupt we truly are without Him; and yet with that revelation, we are also afforded the opportunity to apprehend just how great His grace and mercy are toward us when we consider His promises of forgiveness and justification in spite of our fallen nature. We fail to stand on His promises when the depths of our flawed nature and wickedness are revealed to us because we think that they are also being revealed to the Lord, as if He did not know about them. Yet when Christ was sent by the Father, when Jesus climbed up on the cross, our sin, everything that we would ever think and do was in full view for Him to see. And yet even with that knowledge, our loving Father still assures us, "Fear not, for I have redeemed you; I have called you by your name; you are Mine."

NOVEMBER 11th

Isaiah 43:2: "I will be with you."

I believe the greatest fear we have when facing a difficulty is the fear that we are all alone in that situation. So it stands to reason that our greatest comfort when facing a difficulty should be the fact that God is with us through it all. David said as much in Psalm 23:4 when he wrote "Yea, though I walk through the valley of the shadow of death, I will fear no evil; for You are with me." David confessed that he could only walk through the valley of the shadow of death and fear no evil because he knew that God was with him.

When Joshua was leading the children of Israel into the Promised Land, and was very afraid, the Lord promised him that "as I was with Moses, so I will be with you" (Joshua 1:5). When the Babylonian captivity was awaiting Israel, the Lord promised them, "When you pass through the waters, I will be with you; and through the rivers, they shall not overflow you. When you walk through the fire, you shall not be burned, nor shall flame scorch you. For I am the LORD your God, the Holy One of Israel, your Savior" (Isaiah 43:2–3).

When we make God our refuge in times of difficulty, and trust in the fact that He is with us in that situation, we will not be compelled to run, frantically trying to escape the trial as if it will overcome us. Rather, we will casually and peacefully "walk through the fire," knowing that we will not be burned by the flames because our Savior is with us, watching over and protecting us at all times.[165]

It reminds me of a story I once heard about how some early Native American trained their young men to be braves. It is said that on the boy's thirteenth birthday, the boy's father would blindfold his son and lead him deep into the forest, where the young man would stay for the entire night. You can imagine how scary this must have been for the young man, as every time there was a sound, his mind would imagine the worst. When morning finally came, the boy would remove his blindfold—and to his great delight, he would see that his father was sitting across from him all night long, watching over and protecting him. How true this is with our Father as well.

So, believer, even though we might not see our Father in our trials, there is nothing for us to fear because we are never alone. The Lord promises each one of us, no matter where you are or what you are facing, "I will be with you."

NOVEMBER 12th

Matthew 15:6: "Thus you have made the commandment of God of no effect by your tradition."

Traditions, in themselves, are not necessarily a bad thing. We all have them, and they can be very useful if they are properly managed and applied. But when tradition becomes law, we then have a problem, because it is there that we stop testing tradition with Scripture, and we start testing Scripture with tradition.

So even though the religious leaders were experts in God's law, they were clueless in regard to God's heart because they lacked the proper understanding of the purpose of the law. More damaging to them though was that their faith was firmly placed in the traditions of the religious system rather than in the God they professed to be worshiping by those traditions.

The root of the problem was that these men were committed to following the letter of the law instead of allowing themselves to be led by the spirit of the law. In Hosea 6:6 (NLT) the Lord said to His people, "I want you to show love, not offer sacrifices. I want you to know me more than I want burnt offerings."

The religious leaders were never able to truly grasp the heart of God because they were too occupied with keeping, enforcing, and imposing the law. And anytime this happens, whether it is in church, in a Bible study, in our family, or even with holiday celebrations . . . tradition becomes enthroned as our lord and master and we lose all of the necessary attributes of God such as compassion, grace, mercy, and love. Essentially, we lose the very heart of God, and in its place we take on the attributes of the law: death, condemnation, rigidness, and rejection.

Jesus said in Matthew 15:6, "Thus you have made the commandment of God of no effect by your tradition." I believe He was referring to the two greatest commandments here: "'You shall love the LORD your God with all your heart, with all your soul, and with all your mind.'. . . And the second is like it, 'You shall love your neighbor as yourself'" (Matthew 22:37, 39). Tradition makes these commandments of no effect, Jesus said, as it rejects the true intent of the Lord's heart and only adheres to the requirements of the Law.

NOVEMBER 13th

Acts 15:10: "Now therefore, why do you test God by putting a yoke on the neck of the disciples which neither our fathers nor we were able to bear?"

I was sharing with a brother last week about how often I have found myself being critical of others lately. The more we talked about it, the more I began asking questions like, "How did this happen? When did I become so critical? What is the source of this criticism?" The answer came a few days later through two of our best friends, Mark and Jen, who reminded me that oftentimes we hold others to standards that are not of the Lord—standards of salvation, teaching, worship, marriage, raising children, politics, decision making, cultural issues, family values, etc. What I found is that the manmade standards that I hold others to are those very things which cause me to be critical.

We see a great example of this in Acts 15, when certain men came down from Judea and were telling new Gentile believers that they had to be circumcised in order to be saved. When this argument was taken before the council in Jerusalem, Peter stood up and said, "Now therefore, why do you test God by putting a yoke on the neck of the disciples which neither our fathers nor we were able to bear?" Essentially, Peter was asking these men why they were putting a standard on new believers that God did not require—a standard that even they, themselves, could not meet.

I think it is very telling that Peter used the word "yoke" to describe what these men were doing. A yoke is something placed around the neck of an animal in order to control it. So when we expect others to live by our standards, we are essentially trying to control them by having them live the way we believe is best. Yet what I have come to realize through all of this is that we cannot expect others to live by our standards. When we hold others prisoner to our standards, trying to control what they do and how they do it, strife and conflict arise within our hearts when they fail to live up to those standards. Essentially, what we are doing is loading them down with a yoke that they were never meant to carry—a yoke that is heavy and burdensome in bondage, as opposed to that of Christ which is easy and light in freedom.

NOVEMBER 14th

> Romans 11:6: "And if by grace, then it is no longer of works; otherwise grace is no longer grace. But if it is works, it is no longer grace; otherwise work is no longer work."

Last weekend, as Michelle and I were furniture shopping with our twenty-three-month-old daughter Kate, we came across an escalator in one of the stores we visited. For my wife and I, this was no big deal, as we have ridden escalators hundreds of times before; but for Kate, this was her first time seeing one, and so she was very excited to ride on it. During one of the many trips up the escalator, Kate began climbing the stairs, to which Michelle quickly responded, "Kate, you don't need to do anything; the escalator will automatically carry you to the top." It was then that the Lord spoke to my wife and said, "This is exactly the way it is with grace."

Paul said something very similar to this in Romans 11 when he wrote, "But if it is of works, it is no longer grace." I think this is the perfect explanation of grace: If you have to do anything at all to receive grace, then it is no longer grace, because "if by grace, then it is no longer of works; otherwise grace is no longer grace." David Guzik explained that grace, by definition, is "the free gift of God." It is not given based on performance or the potential to perform; rather, it is based solely on the kindness of the One giving the grace.[166]

One of my favorite stories in the Bible is when Jesus raised Lazarus from the dead. If you read this story in John 11, you will notice that Lazarus did nothing to earn Jesus' favor. I mean, honestly, how could he? He was dead. Jesus raised Lazarus of His own volition. That is grace. Too often people pervert the whole premise of what grace is when they force us to earn their forgiveness, when they refuse to let go of misdeeds by continually bringing them up over and over again, when they love us only when we do good things or only when we are in line with their standards. Again, "if it is of works, it is no longer grace." So, believer, make this the standard as to how you receive grace from God, and how you show grace to others.

NOVEMBER 15th

Exodus 14:14: "The LORD will fight for you, and you shall hold your peace."

As my good friend Darrell often reminds us, the Lord will never allow us to escape the need for faith. Thus, in order for us to endure the trials of this life and grow in faith, we must continually exercise our faith like we would if we were building muscle. The problem is that we believe faith has only one defining characteristic to it and that is, "we must do something in order to exercise it." Yet more often than not, the greater exercise of faith is not to do something per se, but rather to do nothing and allow God to work things out in His time and in His way, as we commit that situation to Him through prayer.

When the children of Israel were trapped between the sea, the mountains, and the Egyptian army, they were not instructed to do something; rather, they were told to do nothing: "Stand still, and see the salvation of the LORD, which He will accomplish for you today. . . . The LORD will fight for you, and you shall hold your peace" (Exodus 14:13–14). Why was it so important for the children of Israel to stand still and do nothing? A couple of reasons: first, so they would not make the situation worse. Too often we fail to trust in the Lord by taking matters into our own hands thus reaping the consequences—not of the original problem, but from the chaos we created when we began doing things in our own strength and wisdom (see Abram and Sarai in Genesis 16 as an example). Second, it was important for them to do nothing so they would know without a doubt that it was only God who delivered them that day—not some foreign god, and not themselves.

This is one of the more vital aspects in our walk with the Lord because it is here "that you may know and believe Me, and understand that I am He . . . [that] besides Me there is no Savior. I have declared and saved, I have proclaimed, and there was no foreign god among you; therefore, you are My witnesses . . . that I am God'" (Isaiah 43:10–12). The Lord reminds us here that we are His witnesses to the world that He alone is God and that there are no others. And many times, our witness is only perfected and established by us standing still in a difficult situation and allowing Him to fight for us. It makes sense if you really think about it, because how can we rightly proclaim to others that He alone is God—that He alone delivers, defends, heals, saves, etc.—if we ourselves do not first believe it and live it out first? The simple truth is that before we can ever move out in faith, we must first be able to stand still in faith, knowing that He alone is our salvation.

NOVEMBER 16th

Isaiah 43:16: "Thus says the LORD, who makes a way in the sea and a path through the mighty waters . . ."

A mighty power was growing against the children of Israel in the form of Babylon, and soon Israel would be taken captive by them . . . but only for a season as the Lord quickly reminded them: I am "your Redeemer" (Isaiah 43:14); and no matter what may happen, no matter what might come against you, self-inflicted or not, that will never change, for "I am the LORD, your Holy One, the Creator of Israel, your King" (Isaiah 43:15). Though Israel had desired many earthly kings rather than the Lord their God, they truly only had One King—the Holy One—and that would never change.

How could Israel be sure, though? How could they find peace in the midst of their tribulation, and be assured that the Lord would eventually deliver them? Sure, the Lord had done mighty acts of deliverance in the past—more specifically, the deliverance of the children of Israel from the woeful bondage of Egypt—but that situation was different than the one they were facing now. Sure He did it then, but what about now? This enemy was bigger, stronger, more powerful . . . how could they be sure the Lord would deliver them this time? "Thus says the Lord, who makes a way in the sea and a path through the mighty waters. . . ."

Notice that the Lord reassured His children by stating: I am He "who makes a way in the sea and a path through the mighty waters. . . ." The Lord is not speaking in the past tense here, referring to a onetime event that had previously occurred; no, He is speaking in the present continual sense ("makes") and is referring to what He will continue to do throughout the ages. He is their King and their God, and that will never change. The Lord promises His children that He is still making ways through the seas for them in their day; He is still creating paths through the mighty waters to deliver them in this day, for this time, against this power. Nothing has changed with God. Unfortunately, nothing has changed with His people either.

We often fall into the same cycle of fear and doubt when we face the powers that rise up against us. We anxiously say to ourselves, "Sure, He did it for them, back then, but what about for me now? How do I know that He will deliver me in this situation?" Believer, we can know, we can be certain, we can rest assured, because He is our Redeemer, our King, and our God, and He still makes ways in the seas and paths through mighty waters for us today, for this time, against this power, and in this situation. Nothing has changed. God is still the same today, that He was then, that He will be tomorrow. So "Fear not, for I have redeemed you; I have called you by your name; you are Mine" (Isaiah 43:1).

NOVEMBER 17th

Matthew 6:22: "If therefore your eye is good, your whole body will be full of light."

Last Saturday morning, Michelle and I were having pictures taken of our daughter Kate, as she will be turning two years old on July 26th. During the photo shoot, we tried all sorts of things to get Kate to look at the camera and sit still for more than a minute, but keeping the focus of a two-year-old can be a very difficult thing to do. The one thing that worked really well was when I took that which was her focus, like a bottle of bubbles or her baby doll, and held it up while standing behind the photographer. It was then that her focus was locked into where it needed to be, and we were able to get some really good pictures of her.

There will be many times in our lives when the Lord has to do this very thing with us as well. We can become so distracted with the things of this life, and all of its shiny little treasures, that we often fail to make time to just sit at the feet of our

Lord and focus on Him for more than a minute. So to get our focus back to where it needs to be, the Lord will oftentimes take away from us that which is our focus. He will remove that which we desire, or even allow a sickness or a trial into our lives, just so we will place our focus back to where it really needs to be, on Him.

Jesus warned His disciples about the danger of having a misplaced focus in Matthew 6:22–23, when He stated, "The lamp of the body is the eye. If therefore your eye is good, your whole body will be full of light. But if your eye is bad, your whole body will be full of darkness. If therefore the light that is in you is darkness, how great is that darkness!"

We somehow believe that we can live in both worlds and be OK—that we can have two separate and completely contradictory focuses and not drift away from the Lord. Yet the Lord makes it clear that this is impossible for "No one can serve two masters" (Matthew 6:24). As David Guzik explained, if our focus is on Him and on heavenly things, our whole body will be full of light; if our focus is on self and on worldly things, our whole body will be full of darkness.[167] And if darkness is the only light we have, "how great is that darkness?" For us to think that light and darkness can coexist in anything, especially within us, is foolishness. Darkness is simply the absence of light; therefore, there can only be one dominant force within us at a time—it's either light or darkness. So, believer, where is your focus today?

NOVEMBER 18th

Isaiah 44:3: "I will pour water on him who is thirsty."

A brother was sharing with me last week about how dry he was spiritually. Apparently he had become so busy with all of the things that life throws at us that he hadn't spent any time with the Lord in quite a while. So he asked me to pray for him, that he would "get back" into fellowship with the Lord. I quickly reminded him, "Getting back in fellowship with the Lord takes as long as it does for your knees to hit the ground. You don't need to pray about it; you just need to do it. It's not a long, drawn-out process; it's a simple act of petition that takes about a second. Bro, the Lord is just waiting for you to come to Him so that He can pour out His Living Water on you. All you need to do is ask."

We find a great picture of this in the book of Isaiah. The promise of the coming judgment to the children of Israel at the end of Isaiah 43 was quickly replaced with the promise of complete restoration at the beginning of Isaiah 44. The Lord assured His children, "Fear not, O Jacob My servant; and you, Jeshurun, whom I have chosen" (Isaiah 44:2). Interestingly enough, the name Jeshurun means "the upright one"; by that definition alone, we should pause and consider the magnitude of what is being stated here. Even in their purposed rebellion and blatant sin toward the Lord, God still called His children beloved and upright.

"Fear not . . . for I will pour water on him who is thirsty, and floods on the dry ground; I will pour My Spirit on your descendants, and my blessing on your offspring" (Isaiah 44:2–3). Notice that the Lord's desire is to restore and bless His children, not curse and crush them because of their sin. God has proven again and again that He is ready, willing, and able to restore us at any time—with one condition: We must desire to receive that restoration. "I will pour water on him who is thirsty." To all who are thirsty, the Lord says, floods of Living Water, My Holy Spirit, will not be rationed to you, not just be given to you, but rather will be poured out upon you like floods of water on dry ground. As David Guzik well said, "God is looking for 'dry ground' to pour out floods upon!"[168] Are you dry? Do you lack? Good, because the Lord is looking for dry ground to pour out upon. The imagery here speaks not of a two-and-a-half-gallon bucket of water being poured out and exhausted in a moment's time; but rather a never-ending gushing torrent like Niagara Falls sweeping across the desert.

The thing that really convicted me about this great promise is that, if the Lord is ready, willing, and able to pour out an abundance of His Spirit and Power on all of those who are thirsty . . . why is the church so weak and powerless today? Why is there such a lack of the moving of the Holy Spirit in and through our lives? Believer, if we thirst, if we want more of Him, the Lord will gladly pour out floods of His Living Water on us in abundance. The question we have to ask ourselves is, "What are we really thirsting for?"

"If you then, being evil, know how to give good gifts to your children, how much more will your Heavenly Father give the Holy Spirit to those who ask Him!" (Luke 11:13).

NOVEMBER 19th

Mark 8:23: "So He took the blind man by the hand and led him out of the town."

Shortly after I got saved, I went through about a twelve-month purging process from the world. My friends, my girlfriend, my old habits, the way I used to deal with problems, the way I thought, the way I spoke, etc., were all being purged from my life—and it really, really hurt. It was by far the hardest time of my life as I sought the Lord, prayed, and cried just about every single day.

Yet when I look back on that time now, I do not look back with disdain or with sorrow; in fact, I look back on it very fondly because it was in that time that I was closer to the Lord than I ever have been in my life. I can honestly see now that He had taken me by the hand and led me out of the town that I once lived in when I was blind and corrupt, and healed me of those infirmities just like He did with the blind man in Mark 8. But, just as the blind man let go of Jesus' hand once he was healed, so did I.

It is an interesting dilemma we face in our relationship with the Lord. When we find ourselves in the midst of life's most difficult times, we spend the whole time trying to get out of those difficulties; yet it is there, in the fire, that we are closest to our Savior. So, is it better to be in the fire and have the Creator of the universe holding our hand, leading us to the place where we will be healed of those things that hinder us by refining us and purging away the dross . . . or to be free of the fire and not have that level of intimacy and transformation that so enriches our souls?

I am not saying that we should look forward to the fire and trials of life because they can be very painful; but, with that, we should learn to embrace those times when they do come because we know that our Savior is with us, holding our hand, and leading us through them. And truth be told, we should never fear the Lord's fire because it will never burn us; rather, His fire burns away the dross and the chaff by refining that which is precious: us. And it is here, in this tempering process, that the Father eventually sees His reflection in the finished product.

NOVEMBER 20th

2 Peter 1:5–7: "But also for this very reason, giving all diligence, add to your faith virtue, to virtue knowledge, to knowledge self-control, to self-control perseverance, to perseverance godliness, to godliness brotherly kindness, and to brotherly kindness love."

Life is a continual progression of growth and maturity. This is not only true physically and mentally, but even more so spiritually. Mushrooms can shoot up overnight, but they only last for a few days; oak trees, on the other hand, can take years to grow, but they last for centuries. Spiritually speaking, mature, strong believers don't just shoot up overnight. It would be great if on the day we were saved, we were at the level of Spurgeon or Moody when they were at their peak, but that just doesn't happen; there are no shortcuts to spiritual growth. The walk with Jesus is a continual progression of growth and maturity that takes place over time. It's not a sprint; it's a marathon. Too often we forget this and become consumed with anxiety, because we try to live in the future with the person we are today.

For example, when Michelle first got pregnant with our daughter Kate, in October of 2013, we began looking at the due date, wondering, "How in the world are we going to do this? We know absolutely nothing about labor and delivery, parenting, training up a child, etc. How is this ever going to happen?" What the Lord quickly reminded us of was that we were only the Patrick and Michelle of that day in October 2013; in nine months, when Kate would be born, we would be different people than we were that day. By the time Kate was to come, we would be ready for her arrival. That doesn't mean we would have all the answers, but maturity-wise, we would be ready to be the parents that she would need us to be on that day.

Too often we try to imagine the October 2013 version of ourselves having a baby when it's not the October 2013 version of ourselves that is going to have a baby; it is the July 26, 2014 version of ourselves that will be having a baby. They will be ready, they will be prepared; we are not, because we are not there yet. With that being said, though, we cannot just sit around and do nothing and expect ourselves to magically be ready. We must diligently redeem the time by learning and growing and preparing for that day.

In 2 Peter 1:5–7, Peter reminds us of this very thing: "But also for this very reason, giving all diligence, add to your faith virtue, to virtue knowledge, to knowledge self-control, to self-control perseverance, to perseverance godliness, to godliness brotherly kindness, and to brotherly kindness love." This kind of transformation doesn't happen overnight; it is a measured progression that takes place over time as we seek to grow and mature in the Lord.

And as we see these things being added to our own lives through a purposed, diligent walk with Jesus, our nature becomes more and more like His, and less and less like the world's. Essentially, we are progressing away from who we once were, and gradually moving more toward who He is. It is proof to us, and to all those around us who are watching, that we are being "conformed into the image of His Son" (Romans 8:29), and that we are being "transformed by the renewing of [our] mind" (Romans 12:2).

342   Renovating Your Mind

NOVEMBER 21ˢᵗ

> John 7:38: "He who believes in Me, as the Scripture has said, out of his
> heart will flow rivers of living water."

I was watching a documentary the other day about planet Earth, and it was amazing to witness how water can transform a lifeless, barren desert into a life-filled,
lush oasis. The transformation is so radical, so monumental, that it can only be
described as a miracle.

Reflect on this thought as you consider what Jesus stated about believers in
John 7:38: "He who believes in Me, as the Scripture has said, out of his heart will
flow rivers of living water." The thought here is that Jesus has empowered each one
of us to such a degree that wherever we go, whatever we do, we should bring change
to that environment. Life should spring forth, regardless of how lifeless or barren
or hostile that environment is. We see a symbolic picture of this in Psalm 84:6,
where the psalmist wrote, "As they pass through the Valley of Baca [Weeping], they
make it a spring." The Valley of Baca was a lifeless, barren desert, and yet as Jews
passed through it with their hearts set on the pilgrimage, they made it a spring that
brought forth much life.

Should it be any different with the environments we find ourselves in today?
Too often we yield to our environment and allow it to change us, instead of allowing
the power of the Holy Spirit to change that environment through us. As Michelle
and I often pray for ourselves and for our children, "Lord, let us be thermostats,
not thermometers." Thermostats change the environment, whereas as thermometers just measure it.

This principle is reflected in the fact that God did not use definitions to describe
things such as love, faith, grace, and the power of prayer; no, He used people to
define them for us as they lived them out in the sight of others. Jesus laying down
His life for us is how God defined love; faith is defined by those like Abraham and
Noah; grace is defined by those like David, Rahab, and the apostle Paul; and the
power of prayer is seen in the lives of Moses and Elijah. The people in and around
our lives will understand what love, faith, and grace are as we live those things out
in front of them; they will see the power of prayer as we pray for them and with
them. This is how we change our environments just as lifeless, barren deserts are
made into life-filled, lush springs.

NOVEMBER 22nd

Psalm 62:5: "[F]or my expectation is from Him."

After my dad had given his life to Jesus, I placed an unfair expectation on him of how he should live now that he was saved. I expected an immediate and radical transformation, one in which he would be fervent for the Lord in both word and deed. Basically, I expected him to be like me, because that is what happened when I got saved. And when those behaviors did not come to fruition, and my expectation of him was left unmet, I found myself angry, discouraged, and fearful because I began to doubt if my dad was even saved.

Yet when I look at the Bible and read what it says about bearing the fruit of salvation, it says some will bear fruit "a hundredfold, some sixty, some thirty" (Matthew 13:8). So if my dad only ever bore one piece of fruit, if only one behavior in his life had changed, isn't that still bearing fruit? Isn't he still saved? The problem was that my dad's salvation was not enough for me; I needed more from him simply because I had placed an unfair, unbiblical expectation on him that he was never meant to fulfill.

We see this very thing lived out in the lives of the disciples after Jesus had died on the cross. Though Jesus told them time and time again that He would die and be raised up three days later, their expectation that the coming Messiah would establish an earthly kingdom and free Israel from Roman oppression clouded their minds and deafened their ears to everything Jesus had said about His kingdom. And because their expectations of the Messiah were left unfulfilled, they became angry, despondent, and fearful.

We are no different, though. How many times has our faith in the Lord been fractured simply because we projected our unbiblical expectations onto Him? How many times have we turned our hearts away from Him because we expected Him to do something in a certain way at a certain time, and it did not come to pass as we desired? We must remember that whenever we place unbiblical expectations on anyone, regardless who it might be, we are going to find ourselves angry, disappointed, and discouraged. So, believer, take a minute and consider what expectations you have placed on Jesus . . . on your parents . . . your spouse . . . your children . . . your brethren. Are they expectations of what you desire, or are they expectations that line up with what the Bible says?

NOVEMBER 23rd

> 1 John 2:3: "Now by this we know that we know Him, if we keep His commandments."

It is very easy to get discouraged when we read a verse like this because we generally focus on the obedience aspect of the verse; and being that we are not always obedient to God, we might begin questioning if we even truly know God. It's at this point that we need to ask ourselves: does obedience bring knowledge of God, or does the knowledge of God bring obedience? If you read this verse again, you will see that the focus is not on obedience per se; rather, it is on knowing God.

The word "know" that John uses here is the Greek word *ginosko*. It means to gain knowledge through experience. So, to know God, we must first experience God. Notice that John wrote in the perfect active indicative tense, so you could translate it this way, "by this we can know right now that we have known and continue to know Him."[169] Knowing God in this sense refers to a present, continual, ongoing knowledge of God that keeps progressing as we spend time with Him. It is not a one-time experience of knowing God, such as on the day we were saved; it is a continual act of knowing God more and more each day.

The point that John is making to us is that the more we get to know God, the more we will want to be obedient to Him. David Guzik said, "The evidence of someone knowing God and fellowship with Him is that they keep His commandments—a simple, loving obedience is a natural result of fellowship with God."[170] So we can surmise that this passage is more a barometer of where we are in our walk with God than anything else. When we find it difficult to obey God and follow His instructions, it should be a warning to us that we are not spending enough time getting to know Him.

I once heard a story from a pastor about a man who went on a trip and brought his wife back a box of glow-in-the-dark matches. When they turned the lights off, they couldn't see the matches, and he just figured he had been cheated. Soon after, the wife noticed some writing on the side of the box: "If you want me to shine in the night, keep me in the light." The same can be said about us.

NOVEMBER 24th

> Isaiah 45:19 (NLT1996): "I did not tell the people of Israel to ask Me for something I did not plan to give."

God does not tell us to ask for things that He does not plan to give us. He does not stir our hearts into action just to leave those desires wanting. He does not lead us down paths that will just end in failure. And He does not speak in such a way that we cannot understand what He is saying. In fact, the Lord declares to all of us, "I publicly proclaim bold promises. I do not whisper obscurities in some dark corner so no one can understand what I mean. And I did not tell the people of Israel to ask Me for something I did not plan to give. I, the LORD, speak only what is true and right" (Isaiah 45:19, NLT1996).

God openly proclaims bold promises to all of mankind because He intends to keep them. Essentially, He is challenging each one of us to stand on His Word and see if they come to pass just as He has promised. Do you need wisdom? Ask for it (James 1:5). Are you spiritually dry? Ask for the Holy Spirit to refresh you (Luke 11:13). Do you need help in your time of need? Come boldly to His throne of grace and ask for help (Hebrews 4:16). The psalmist caught on to this remarkable aspect of faith as he issued to us the very same challenge in Psalm 34:8: "taste and see that the LORD is good."

I am convinced that the lack of power and strength in the church today derives specifically from a lack of knowing and believing in God's promises. I mean, how can we ever be expected to pray for the miraculous if we do not have His promises as the fuel for our petitions? How can we ever stand in the storms of life if we do not have His promises as the anchor of our hope?

Believer, understand that God desires for us to hold Him to His promises. He longs for His children to exercise their faith so much so that He has not only spoken them through the prophets of old, but He has also thoroughly documented them in the Bible so that we can stand on them whenever we are in need. Knowing this, believing this, trusting in this, we will be emboldened to pray the very promises of God with absolute expectation of them coming to pass, and we will walk confidently through the valley of the shadow of death fearing no evil, because we know that He is with us (Psalm 23).

NOVEMBER 25th

Matthew 10:16a: "Behold, I send you out as sheep in the midst of wolves."

The hardest part of growing up in a military family for me was the constant moving from place to place. It seemed like just about every other year I was the new kid at school. To counteract all of the difficulty I faced with this kind of life, I developed a defense mechanism that helped me quickly adapt to the ever changing environments I found myself in—I became whoever the other kids wanted me to be. This way I was welcomed in right away, I was well liked, and I avoided as much awkwardness and conflict as possible.

The problem with doing this though was that somewhere along the line I lost my own identity. I had no idea who I really was because I was too busy trying to be who everyone else wanted me to be. It was not until I gave my life to Christ at the age of twenty-nine that the Lord began to unearth who I really was—but even that brought on a whole new set of challenges as I was now a believer and follower of Jesus Christ in a world full of unbelievers.

Jesus made it very clear to His disciples about who they were in comparison to the world, and what they would experience as believers, "I send you out as sheep in the midst of wolves. . . . But when they deliver you up . . . you will be hated . . . they [will] persecute you" (Matthew 10:16, 19, 22-23). Christ never told us to worry about the wolves or be afraid of the wolves; rather, He said "beware" of them, meaning, be attentive to their behaviors and addictions as to avoid them. That's why I think it is interesting that we often warn of wolves in sheep's clothing, yet the greater danger to the church and the body of Christ today are the sheep in wolves' clothing, because it is there that we compromise our faith and lose our identity as to who we truly are in Christ.

The apostle Paul warned us in Romans 12:2 to "not be conformed to this world," because although they might seem like small, insignificant compromises when we decide to hide who we are in order to avoid conflict and fit in—though they might seem like good intentioned choices when we adopt the world's behaviors so that we can "minister" to others on their ground, by doing this we will ultimately lose our identity in Christ and forget that we are the salt and the light. As Jesus well said:

> You are the salt of the earth; but if the salt loses its flavor, how shall it be seasoned? It is then good for nothing but to be thrown out and trampled underfoot by men.

> You are the light of the world. A city that is set on a hill cannot be hidden. Nor do they light a lamp and put it under a basket, but on a lampstand, and it gives light to all who are in the house. Let your light so shine before men, that they may see your good works and glorify your Father in heaven. (Matthew 5:13-16)

NOVEMBER 26ᵗʰ

Isaiah 48:18: "Oh, that you had heeded My commandments!"

There is a fine line between legalism and diligence. Legalism says I have to follow God's instructions or else I will be punished—i.e., I will not be loved, I will not be forgiven, I will not be saved, etc. This outlook generally leads to discouragement and depression. Diligence says, I am already loved, I am already forgiven, I am already saved, and yet I still want to follow God's instructions because I recognize the benefits that come from them. This outlook leads to peace and joy.

The Lord has reasoned with man about this very thing for thousands of years. He has tried to get us to realize that His instructions are for our betterment, not our punishment:

> Oh, that they had such a heart in them that they would fear Me and always keep all My commandments, that it might be well with them and with their children forever. (Deuteronomy 5:29)

> Oh, that you had heeded My commandments! Then your peace would have been like a river, and your righteousness like the waves of the sea. (Isaiah 48:18)

Yet for whatever reason, we still do not fully trust God and what His Word says. So, as Matthew Henry pointed out, to help us understand why we should trust Him and heed His instruction, let us consider three things about the Lord as stated in Isaiah 48:17-18. The first thing the Lord reminds us of is that He is our Redeemer. "Thus says the LORD, your Redeemer, the Holy One of Israel. . . ." He was the One who willingly died on the cross for us so that we would be free from sin and death. Second, He is our instructor: "I am the LORD your God, who teaches you to profit." He instructs us in those things that are profitable for us and that make up for our peace. And lastly, He is our guide, "who leads you by the way you should go." He not only enlightens our eyes to see clearly in which way to go, He also directs our steps so that we might not stumble and fall.[171]

After careful consideration of these things, why should we not follow His counsel and instruction? Sadly, there are many times that we blame God for allowing difficult things into our lives when clearly it was our disobedience to God's instructions that caused us to reap those consequences. It makes me wonder about my own life and how much difficulty would be eliminated if I just followed His counsel and walked in His righteousness. Solomon spoke of this in the Book of Proverbs, "He who walks with integrity walks securely. . . . The integrity of the upright will guide them" (Proverbs 10:9, 11:3).

As the Lord reminded His people, "I publicly proclaim bold promises. I do not whisper obscurities in some dark corner so no one can understand what I mean. And I did not tell the people of Israel to ask Me for something I did not plan to give. I, the Lord, speak only what is true and right" (Isaiah 45:19, NLT1996). As we mature and grow in the Lord, we will find that the wise thing to do in a situation is simply the right thing to do in a situation as stated in the Word of God—not out of legality because we will be punished, nor because we will fall out of favor with God if we don't, but rather because we recognize the benefits and blessings that come from following His instructions.

NOVEMBER 27th

Isaiah 49:4: "Then I said, 'I have labored in vain, I have spent my strength for nothing and in vain.'"

It is very easy to believe that the kingdom work in which we labor is all in vain. We fervently, passionately, painstakingly pray for others, witness to others, serve others, etc., and more often than not it's as if we are not making any difference in their lives whatsoever. It can be very discouraging.

Thankfully, we have a High Priest who can fully relate to this. In Isaiah 49:4, though it was Isaiah speaking, we can rightly assign this verse to our Messiah who would surely be tempted with the same type of discouragement we often experience: "Then I said, 'I have labored in vain, I have spent my strength for nothing and in vain.'" I am sure that Jesus was tempted by the thought that all His work, all His sacrifice, was merely in vain as He was rejected over and over again by mankind ("To Him who man despises . . ."; Isaiah 49:7)

Yet Jesus did not allow that discouragement to take root, as He quickly rebuked it by putting it all into perspective: "Yet surely my just reward is with the LORD, and my work with my God" (Isaiah 49:4). Matthew Henry reminds us, "Though the labor be in vain as to those that are labored with, yet not as to the laborer himself, if he be faithful: his judgment is with the Lord."[172] Jesus knew very well that His only concern was to be obedient to the Father's instructions—as it is obedience, not results, that are our just reward. He overcame the temptation to be discouraged by placing His trust firmly with the Father, and not with the results of that labor.

We must have this same perspective when following the Lord's calling in our own lives. Far too often we allow the tangible results of our service dictate to us whether we are to be joyful or discouraged, yet this is merely a carnal view rooted in our flesh and pride of a spiritual work that we cannot truly see nor fathom. We must find our joy in the fact that we do our work unto the Lord as He instructs—because, after all, our labor is for His great purposes, not for our ego, our pride, or our reputation.

NOVEMBER 28th

Isaiah 49:9: "That You may say to the prisoners, 'Go forth.'"

I have noticed a fatal flaw in our faith: We often take God's complete, infinite, all-encompassing work and redefine its boundaries, shrinking it down to a selective, finite, and limited work. We do this based on feeling, sin, sight, and circumstance. So, to refresh our perspective on how complete, infinite, and all-encompassing His works really are, let us consider His plan of salvation.

"It is too small a thing that You should be My Servant to raise up the tribes of Jacob, and to restore the preserved ones of Israel; I will also give You as a light to the Gentiles, that You should be My salvation to the ends of the earth" (Isaiah 49:6). It was not enough for Jesus to just come and save Israel, for that was a small, limited work in the eyes of the Lord. No, the Lord desired for all men to be saved; thus, Jesus came for all mankind, making it a complete and all-encompassing work.

But salvation is only the beginning of His work in our lives, not the end. "They shall feed along the roads . . . they shall neither hunger nor thirst, neither heat nor sun shall strike them" (Isaiah 49:9–10). Salvation should not be limited to a "Get out of hell free" card; it is life, it is freedom, it is provision, it is power, it is purpose, and much, much more. For many Christians, salvation is thought of as our end; and yet the Lord says to all of us, there is so much more for you. I liken it to going to Hawaii and then sitting in your hotel room the entire time. Sure, you are there, but there is so much more to Hawaii than just being there.

One of the more powerful works that salvation brings is a complete freedom from all things: "That You may say to the prisoners, 'Go forth.'" Jesus has boldly, publicly proclaimed to all that would receive Him as Lord and Savior that we are free from the world and everything in it, for He has overcome the world (John 16:33). Yet we continue to sit in our cells as though we are still prisoners—even though the door is open and the chains have fallen off. Consider the time when

Peter was in prison and the door opened and the chains fell off; Peter still had to make the choice to get up and walk out (Acts 12:5–10). The same goes for us. Jesus has proclaimed to each one of us, "Go forth" from that cell, for you are free indeed.

So, believer, do not limit the work of complete and total freedom that Jesus has performed in your life. Get up and walk out, for the door is opened wide and the chains have fallen off.

NOVEMBER 29th

> Isaiah 51:2: "For I called him alone, and blessed him and increased him."

There are many levels of dissatisfaction in this life, but none greater than to not be doing what the Lord has specifically made us to do. Understand that the Lord has a very specific purpose and calling for every single one of us, as He has created and gifted us in such ways that we will flourish and will be fulfilled in ways that we cannot know apart from that calling. But it's important to remember that oftentimes, when that call comes, it will not be easy for us to answer it—because that calling will take a great measure of faith to step out and be obedient.

As I was praying to the Lord about the purpose and calling on my own life, I came across this passage in Isaiah 51:2, in which the Lord told His children, "For I called him [Abraham] alone, and blessed him and increased him." We read of this great calling in Genesis 12:1–2: "Now the Lord had said to Abram, 'Get out of your country, from your family, and from your father's house, to a land that I will show you. I will make you a great nation; I will bless you and make your name great; and you shall be a blessing.'"

Notice that this was not an easy call to answer, as Abram was not only called to leave everything that was familiar and comfortable to him (his country and his family), but also had to forsake his obligation as the new leader of his father's house and head out to a land that he did not know. This calling took a great measure of faith to answer, and I am sure that Abram heard from all sides about why he should not do this. It is also important to understand that there was nothing special or unique about Abram; he was an ordinary man who came from an ordinary family, yet the Lord made him with a very specific purpose in mind, and only in answering that call and fulfilling his purpose would Abram ever become the man Abraham.

This should greatly encourage all of us to answer the call when it comes, because though we may be called to leave everything comfortable and familiar, the Lord's promise remains, regardless of the situation or the calling. Even though He "called him alone, [He] blessed him and increased him." The Lord met all of Abram's needs and fulfilled that calling on his life, just as He had promised.

NOVEMBER 30th

Deuteronomy 17:16–17: "But he shall not . . . lest his heart turn away."

On Tuesday morning, Michelle took our two children, Kate (two years old) and Joel (six weeks old), to the park just behind our house. Surrounding the playground at this particular park is a concrete sidewalk with about a two-foot dropoff onto the playground floor. So while Michelle was playing with Kate on the playground, Joel was safely parked in the stroller on top of the sidewalk right behind them.

At some point while Michelle was speaking with another mom, Kate decided that Joel needed to be closer to where they were standing, and so she began pushing the stroller toward the playground. As Michelle turned to see what Kate was doing, she knew right away what was going to happen and quickly called out for Kate to stop. But Kate did not listen, and both she and Joel tumbled head over heels onto the playground floor; thankfully, neither of them was hurt. The blessing in all of this is that it afforded us a great opportunity to teach Kate about listening and obeying.

Later, as Michelle and I were talking about the day's adventures, we recognized the spiritual lesson that was given to us about obedience and trusting in God's Word. Kate did not obey Michelle's command to stop because she could not see the danger in what she was doing. Michelle, on the other hand, could see exactly what was going to happen and thus she called out for Kate to stop.

This is how it is with us and God. We choose to ignore His instructions because we cannot see anything wrong with what we are doing. But God can see the danger in all of it; that is why He has given us instructions on what not to do. Unfortunately for us, we too often view God's Word as a barrier from good things, when in reality it is a guardrail that protects us from harm.

Take Solomon, for example. Here is arguably the wisest man who ever lived, and yet his heart turned away from God simply because of his failure to trust in what God's Word said. In Deuteronomy 17:16–17, the Lord gave three commands to those who would be king: "But he [the king] shall not multiply horses for himself, nor cause the people to return to Egypt to multiply horses. . . . Neither shall he multiply wives for himself lest his heart turn away; nor shall he greatly multiply silver and gold for himself." Though these commands might seem insignificant and harmless, the warnings were very clear: If you do these things, your heart will turn away from the Lord. Solomon chose to ignore these commands, and sure enough, his heart turned away from the Lord just as God said it would.

"Oh, that you had heeded My commandments! Then your peace would have been like a river, and your righteousness like the waves of the sea" (Isaiah 48:18). Believer, we would be wise to take God at His Word and trust in what it says, because when we obey His instructions, peace and righteousness will continually reign in our lives.

DECEMBER 1ˢᵗ

> Isaiah 53:2: "He has no form or comeliness; and when we see Him, there is no beauty that we should desire Him."

After Michelle and I met and became friends, she would often send me pictures of God's creation while she was out running. One picture that really caught my eye was a picture of a red rose. Now, I am not really a flower guy, so I was not sure why it stood out to me so much at the time or why I even decided to save the picture. But months later, the Lord moved my heart to write a letter to Michelle that was focused around that picture.

The premise of the letter was this: Though the rose is beautiful in appearance and is what initially attracts people to it, it's the fragrance of the rose that keeps people captivated. If the rose smelled like a skunk, for example, there would not be a lasting attraction, no matter how physically beautiful it was. The thing the Lord wanted me to share with Michelle was that though she was physically beautiful, it is the fragrance of Christ within her that truly makes her beautiful and attractive. "You should clothe yourselves instead with the beauty that comes from within, the unfading beauty of a gentle and quiet spirit, which is so precious to God" (1 Peter 3:4, NLT). I learned many years ago that the initial attraction we have for someone is determined by the eyes; but once you get to know that person, the attraction will either grow or fade depending on who that person is inside.

There is no greater example of this than our Lord Jesus Christ who, as Isaiah tells us, had "no form or comeliness; and when we see Him, there is no beauty that we should desire Him." There was nothing majestic about Jesus' appearance; He was just an average-looking guy. You could walk right by Him and not even remember Him five seconds later. Yet I think each one of us who knows Him could rightly say without hesitation, He is the most beautiful person we have ever met, even though we have no idea what He looks like. Simply put, we are attracted to Jesus—not because of what He looks like, but rather because of who He is. Jesus was more focused on being fit for the cross than being "cross-fit." And so should we. So, believer, where is your focus right now—on shaping your body, or shaping your character?

DECEMBER 2nd

Isaiah 53:3: "He is despised and rejected by men; a man of sorrows, and acquainted with grief."

In Isaiah 53:3, we are told that Jesus was "despised and rejected by men; a man of sorrows, and acquainted with grief." In a very real sense, Jesus was despised and rejected partly *because* He was a man of sorrows who was acquainted with great grief. In fact, we are told that men hid their faces from Him; they turned their backs on Him and looked the other way because of His sorrow and grief, which they believed were self-inflicted consequences through sin and rebellion: "we esteemed Him stricken, smitten by God, and afflicted" (Isaiah 53:4).

Isaiah reminds us that Jesus was smitten and afflicted because "He has borne our griefs and carried our sorrows" (Isaiah 53:4). Jesus did not have pity parties; He did not feel sorry for Himself or grieve over His lot in life.[173] No, the sorrows and griefs that He carried were not His, but rather were ours. All the sufferings of the body, mind, and soul that we will ever face in this life, Jesus carried so that we would be free.

The image here is that Jesus loaded up all of our sorrow and grief onto His back and carried them for us so that we wouldn't have to. And yet, for some strange reason, we still carry around our sorrow and grief as though we have no other choice. Each day we wake up, load it all up onto our backs like good little soldiers, and then we try to live life—all the while crumpling under its enormous weight. We desperately seek complete freedom in Christ, yet it continually escapes our grasp because we forget that even though Jesus took our sorrow and grief for us, it does us absolutely no good if we don't release those things into His hands.[174]

In Hebrews 4:15 we are told, "For we do not have a High Priest who cannot sympathize with our weaknesses." Jesus took our sorrow and grief upon Himself so that we could have a High Priest who could sympathize with our plight; who could comfort us in our sorrow and relieve us in our grief; who would understand exactly what we are going through and provide us with exactly what we need. So the question for us is not, "Can Jesus help us?" but rather, "Will we allow Him to help us?" Believer, victory and freedom are yours if you so choose.

DECEMBER 3rd

> Isaiah 53:10: "Yet it pleased the LORD to bruise Him; He has put Him to grief."

Isaiah 53 is often titled "The Suffering Servant," as it gives us general details about the suffering that Jesus endured spiritually, physically, mentally, and emotionally. In this chapter we read that He was despised, smitten, afflicted, wounded, bruised, chastised, oppressed, taken, and cut off, just to name a few. But then, in the midst of this very somber passage, we read something seemingly out of place: "Yet it pleased the LORD to bruise Him; He has put Him to grief." Come again?

Please understand, though the Father orchestrated this from the very beginning, the pleasure He received was not from Jesus suffering; rather, it was from the *result* of Jesus' suffering . . . salvation for all mankind: "The pleasure of the LORD shall prosper in His hand" (v. 10). God does not enjoy seeing anyone suffer; but with God, the ends always justify the means—not just for Him, but for the one suffering as well. "[Jesus] shall see the labor of His soul and be satisfied" (v. 11). Honestly, would Jesus have been satisfied if He had yielded to Satan during the temptation in the wilderness and avoided all the pain and suffering that He would eventually encounter? Would He really have been satisfied if He had not taken the cross? No. Jesus' satisfaction was tied directly to the fruit of His suffering, not the avoidance of it. The same goes for us.

I remember when Michelle was in labor with our first child, Kate; after about twenty-six hours of extremely painful labor, she grabbed my arm and told me that we were never having another child. Yet two years later, we had our second child, Joel. The key for Michelle was that she did not focus on the pain and suffering of labor and delivery; rather, she looked forward to what that pain and suffering would produce. Romans 5:3–4 reminds us of this very thing (emphasis added): "[W]e also glory in tribulations, *knowing* that tribulation produces perseverance; and perseverance, character; and character, hope." Notice that we are not to glory in the suffering; rather, we are to glory in knowing what the suffering will produce: perseverance, character, and hope. For it is in this, the fruit of the labor of our soul, that we shall be satisfied.

DECEMBER 4th

Isaiah 40:8: "The word of our God stands forever."

It is unfortunate how we naturally add conditions to the Word of God and change the Lord's promises from being received to being achieved. It's as if we read between the lines of what He has said, rather than believe what He really means. For example, the Lord promised His people in Jeremiah 29:13, "And you will seek Me and find Me, when you search for Me with all your heart." In Matthew 7:7–8, Jesus affirmed this same promise during the Sermon on the Mount: "Ask, and it will be given to you; seek, and you will find; knock, and it will be opened to you. For everyone who asks receives, and he who seeks finds, and to him who knocks it will be opened."

Yet my interpretation of what the Lord really means is that I have to labor in prayer for at least a week, if not more; I must continually make good choices, deny self, and avoid anything that is not "holy" because if I don't, I must start over, for it's only when I meet these conditions that will I find the Lord. But that is not what the Lord promised, nor is it what He said. He clearly stated, "you will seek Me and find Me, when you search for Me with all your heart . . . Ask, and it will be given to you; seek, and you will find; knock, and it will be opened to you. For everyone who asks receives, and he who seeks finds, and to him who knocks it will be opened." So, having done nothing else, if I were to earnestly seek the Lord, even if it was just for one minute, wouldn't I find Him? Yes, I would.

This type of dysfunction extends well beyond prayer as well. The Lord says that He loves us, yet we continually believe that we must earn His love; He says that we are forgiven by grace, through faith, yet we continually try to earn His forgiveness through works and deeds, etc. Isaiah 40:8 reminds us that "The word of our God stands forever," meaning His truths will endure every persecution and opposition that comes against it. It will be confirmed to be steadfast and true, for it has been established by God Himself. So, believer, take God at His word, trust in it, stand upon it, and find the freedom, victory, hope, and joy that we are promised with it.

DECEMBER 5th

Isaiah 7:14: "Behold, the virgin shall conceive and bear a Son, and shall call His name Immanuel."

After our daughter Kate was born, Michelle and I really began praying about starting our own family traditions during the holidays. It was during this process that
we realized just how crazy this time of year has become. Stress, busyness, sadness,
depression, guilt, loneliness . . . these were just some of the things we noticed in
our lives and in the lives of those we spoke to about the Christmas season. I think
Michelle summed it up best when she said, "There is no 'Silent Night' anymore. No
peace. No rest. No joy." It was eye-opening for us, to say the least, because it stood
in direct contrast to the whole meaning of Christmas.

The Immanuel prophecy was given to Israel in the midst of one of its darkest periods of sin and rebellion, "For everyone is a hypocrite and an evildoer, and
every mouth speaks folly" (Isaiah 9:17). It was a promise of hope, that the coming
"trouble and darkness, [and] gloom of anguish" (Isaiah 8:22) of Assyria's bondage
would not last forever, "For unto us a Child is born, unto us a Son is given" (Isaiah
9:6). This was not just a promise of salvation for Israel, but for all of mankind, "The
people who walk in darkness will see a great light. For those who live in a land of
deep darkness, a light will shine" (Isaiah 9:2, NLT).

What I have noticed is that the "trouble and darkness, [and] gloom of anguish"
that people experience during the Christmas season comes only when we "look to
the earth" and make Christmas about everything other than Jesus Christ. If we were
to place our focus on celebrating the birth of our Savior, the Hope of coming glory,
the Light who shines in the darkness, and realize that God is with us, we would be
delivered from the bondage and darkness that stress, busyness, sadness, depression,
guilt, and loneliness brings.

DECEMBER 6th

Isaiah 8:22: "Then they will look to the earth, and see trouble and darkness, gloom of anguish; and they will be driven into darkness."

On December 2, 2015, there was a mass shooting in the city of San Bernardino
in which many people were killed and injured. Right away people began searching
for answers: "Why did they do it? What was the motive behind it all?" Once more
information came to light about who these people were and how the shooting took
place, people began pointing fingers and expressing their opinions as to how to prevent this from ever happening again. Some stated that we have a Muslim problem;
others stated that we have a gun-control problem. Now, I am all for protecting our

borders from those who threaten to kill us, absolutely, but even if there were no Muslims in our country, and even if we controlled the sale of all firearms, would the shootings really stop?

The truth of the matter is that anytime we "look to the earth" for answers, we will only "see trouble and darkness, [and] gloom of anguish"; and rather than be lifted up, we "will be driven into darkness." There is no motive that will ever explain or justify what happened that day, because it is just pure evil. It is proof that Satan is alive and well and is still deceiving people into believing his lies of hate and anger. We live in a dark and fallen world that is ruled by the great deceiver; and any time we look to his world for answers, we will get worldly answers that fuel his agenda of fear and hate and will drive us further into hopelessness and despair. So rather than look to the world for answers, "should not a people seek their God?" (Isaiah 8:19).

I once read that when we look to the world for answers, we only focus on the motive behind the act, the people who committed the act, and the means to perform the act—all earthly things. Yet when we look to God for answers, we focus on the true nature behind it all. We see that the motive, the people, and the means are not the reasons behind that which took place; they are merely symptoms of a greater problem that we all have: a fallen sinful nature. We see that our enemy is not flesh and blood, but rather spiritual in nature. Our battle is not a physical one, but rather a spiritual one (Ephesians 6:12). We see that the solution is not of this world, but rather is in Jesus Christ, the only name under heaven by which we are saved (Acts 4:12). Only He can change the heart of man and overcome the sinful nature, through the power and working of the Holy Spirit.

So, believer, do not look to the world for answers, because it will only cause you to think and act like the world. Rather look to God for answers, so that you might have His heart and mind in all things and toward every person.

DECEMBER 7th

Acts 8:4: "Therefore those who were scattered went everywhere preaching the word."

After the attack on Pearl Harbor on December 7, 1941, it is recorded that Japanese Admiral Isoroku Yamamoto stated, "I fear all we have done is to awaken a sleeping giant and fill him with a terrible resolve."[175] Understand that up to that point in time, the United States had not gotten involved in World War II and had actually hoped to stay out of it altogether. But once Japan attacked Pearl Harbor, the United States had no choice but to engage in war.

We see something very similar in Acts 1:8, when Jesus had instructed His disciples to go out and share the gospel with the whole world; yet the church did not go. They were, in a sense, a sleeping giant that was just content to exist within its own comfortable boundaries. But when Stephen was martyred for his faith, and persecution came to the church, it was then that believers scattered into the surrounding regions and began sharing the gospel. "Therefore those who were scattered went everywhere preaching the word." The church, though reluctant, was finally awake and moving as Christ had instructed.

I was thinking about all of this when reflecting on some of the recent decisions made by the Supreme Court. Upon first glance, they seem like huge victories for the ruler of this world. Yet upon further review, all Satan did was disturb a sleeping giant. I am not speaking of God here, but rather am referring to the church in the United States. Far too long we have stood idly by, not getting involved in the warfare all around us because we were too comfortable within our own boundaries.

Well, the war is now at our doorsteps and there is nowhere left for us to go. With this, I believe each Christian will have one of two reactions as the days continue to draw near: 1) We will be emboldened in our faith as we are resolved to engage in this war and fulfill the ministry Christ has given us; or 2) we will shrink from the persecution, abandon our faith, and conform to the world's ideology. In other words, there will be a separating of the wheat and the chaff.

Believer, I have read the Bible and I know how it all ends: Christ wins, and it's not even close. But there are still battles that must take place. We can no longer afford to be a sleeping giant that is just content within our own comfortable boundaries. We must engage in these battles as there is no power on Earth as great as the church when it uses the spiritual weapons our Father has gifted us with.

DECEMBER 8th

Deuteronomy 32:18: "Of the Rock who begot you, you are unmindful, and have forgotten the God who fathered you."

There is nothing worse for a believer than to lose the presence of Christ. This is not speaking of salvation; rather, it is speaking toward the loss of fellowship with

Him. Generally when we sense the loss of His presence, we automatically assume it is because of sin. Though it is true that sin separates us from God, there are also times that the Lord will withdraw from us in order to stir a greater hunger for Him within us.

But probably the most overlooked reason for the loss of His presence is when we neglect our relationship with Him. We are told in Deuteronomy 32:18 that even though the Lord chose Israel to be His people, even though He provided for their every need and defended and delivered them from their all of their enemies, "Of the Rock who begot you, you are unmindful, and have forgotten the God who fathered you." The children of Israel began neglecting the relationship they had with their Father, because they had become lazy in that relationship and had taken it for granted.

The danger that neglect poses to us is that it is not an obvious or intentional act that we would quickly recognize; rather, it is a slow, clouded process that leads us to be unmindful. I think we find a great analogy of this very thing in Proverbs 24:30–31 where Solomon wrote, "I went by the field of a lazy man, and by the vineyard of the man devoid of understanding; and there it was, all overgrown with thorns; its surface was covered with nettles; its stone wall was broken down." This man's vineyard did not all of the sudden become barren and dilapidated in one day; no, it slowly died over time as he continually neglected to care for it. Likewise, our relationship with Christ must be tended to and cultivated in order to thrive and bear fruit. But if we neglect that relationship and become unmindful of it, it too will become broken down and fruitless just like this vineyard.

So, believer, how is your relationship with Christ right now? Is it a fresh, lively garden that is bearing fruit; or is it a broken-down, fruitless orchard, overgrown with thorns and weeds?

DECEMBER 9th

Acts 4:13: "And they realized that they had been with Jesus."

When Peter and John were arrested and brought before the religious leaders for carrying on the ministry of Christ, they were asked, "'By what power or by what name, have you done this?' . . . Now when they saw the boldness of Peter and John . . . they realized that they had been with Jesus" (Acts 4:7, 13). I find it interesting that it was not what Peter and John specifically said that caused the religious leaders to realize they had been with Jesus; it was how they displayed the heart of Christ that led them to this conclusion.

I was reminded of this when Michelle and I attended a funeral a couple of weeks ago. As the pastor got up and shared the gospel, I was taken by the genuineness of this man in how he shared Christ. It was not a plastic sales pitch on salvation, steeped with theological references displaying a thorough head knowledge of the God of the Bible. No, this was a humble, heartfelt, Spirit-led eyewitness account of someone who knew Jesus personally. I honestly do not remember one thing the pastor said, but I do remember that when he spoke, I saw a man who had been with Jesus.

Oh, how we need to know Jesus more. Too often I have been guilty of living by the letter of the law instead of being moved by the heart of Christ and following the spirit of the law. Too often I have come across believers who display an impressive head knowledge of the Bible, and yet completely lack the heart of Christ. Too often I have heard sermons that are so steeped in theological doctrine that the heart of God is nowhere to be found in them. Oh, how we need to know Jesus more.

The purpose of studying the Bible is not for us to find a method in life or to establish a relationship with doctrine. No, it is a time that is to be set aside so that we might get to know the Father, the Son, and the Holy Spirit more personally. It is when we seek to know the heart of God that we are transformed more into His image. And it is here, in this personal relationship with Christ, that others will realize that we too have been with Jesus.

DECEMBER 10th

> 2 Chronicles 7:14: "[I]f My people who are called by My name will humble themselves, and pray and seek My face, and turn from their wicked ways, then I will hear from Heaven, and will forgive their sin and heal their land."

It is easy to blame the state of our country on the divisive, the corrupt, the perverse, etc. Yet when I consider the brokenness of our country in view of 2 Chronicles 7:14, the blame falls squarely upon the shoulders of the believer, not the heathen. For the Lord has said, "if My people who are called by My name will humble themselves, and pray and seek My face, and turn from their wicked ways, then I will hear from Heaven, and will forgive their sin and heal their land." God was directly speaking to the nation of Israel here, yet the underlying truth that we need to intercede on behalf of our nation applies to all believers of all countries.

Notice the Lord specifically said "if *My people.*" He is speaking to the believer here, not to the carnal man. The truth the church does not want to hear is that our country is falling apart because *we* lack the proper conviction to humble ourselves, pray, and turn from our sin. We fail to adhere to the Lord's prescription for healing because we are too concerned with our own personal self-satisfaction and lot in life. We have essentially become the wheat that is being choked out by the thorns of this life, failing to mature because we are too focused on the world's riches and treasures.

When proclaiming the need for a national day of fasting and prayer, Abraham Lincoln said, "Intoxicated with unbroken success, we have become too self-sufficient to feel the necessity of redeeming and preserving grace, too proud to pray to the God that made us."[176] A people absorbed with satisfying self will never be a people of great faith, for it is only when we are distressed by our lack—only when we have true, honest self-examination—will we realize our sin and emptiness. Having this type of transparency and focus is what will compel us to plead with God to fill our need, and this is what will ultimately lead us to humbly seek His face, repent of our sin, and fulfill God's desire to heal our land.

DECEMBER 11th

> Matthew 16:24: "If anyone desires to come after Me, let Him deny Himself, and take up his cross, and follow Me."

As I was praying to the Lord this morning while getting ready for work, out came, "Lord, drive me." I was caught by that prayer, "Lord, drive me." I wasn't sure where it came from or why I even said it, but the more I meditated on it, the more I realized that this was a weak prayer from a weak man who did not want to endure the battle of the day. It was as if to say, "Lord, I want to walk in Your Spirit, I want to make good decisions, I want to stand against the stream, but only if You do it for me. I don't want to face this world, I don't want to stand firm and make the tough choices myself; I want You to carry me and do it all for me so that I don't have to."

Yet throughout the New Testament we hear Jesus calling to all of us, "Follow Me." Make the choice to deny yourself, take up your cross, and follow Me

(Matthew 16:24). The Lord will not drive us, because He does not want to develop weak-minded individuals who will eventually be driven by whatever the most popular agenda might be for that season. No, the Lord wants to develop men and women of great courage who have the strength of mind in Christ Jesus, who will follow Him by faith because they trust in Him and in His Word and choose to do so at their own peril. He wants soldiers who will make the right decisions no matter how hard they might be, how insignificant they might seem, or how many people they might offend—soldiers who will not cower in the day of adversity.

Believer, there is a reason why we are not raptured up to heaven the moment we surrender our lives to Jesus Christ: because there is work for us to do. We often get discouraged and refuse to stand because we say there are too many against us—that we won't make a difference in the grand scheme of things. And so we yield and withdraw, doing nothing. But our individual mission is not to make sweeping changes across the state, country, or world, for that would overwhelm any one of us. No, we as individuals are just to go and make changes across the place and path the Lord has for us today, following Him as He leads us.

So regardless if it is one or one hundred, regardless if no one is around, we choose to do that which He would have us do because we have answered the call to follow Him in all things. This is how we mature, this is how we are strengthened, this is how we are sanctified, and ultimately, this how we are transformed by the renewing of our mind so that we might prove what is good and acceptable and the perfect will of God (Romans 12:2).

DECEMBER 12th

> Philippians 3:12: "[B]ut I press on, that I may lay hold of that for which Christ Jesus has also laid hold of me."

I read something interesting about when Spain was at the height of their power in the fifteenth century. They had the motto *Ne Plus Ultra* imprinted on their coins, which means "Nothing further." Spain had mistakenly believed that they had already arrived, and that there was nothing more for them to achieve. Yet once the New World was discovered, they quickly changed their coins to read *Plus Ultra*, which means, "More beyond."[177]

This is essentially what the apostle Paul was telling the Philippians in his letter to them regarding his walk with the Lord: "Not that I have already attained, or am already perfected; but I press on, that I may lay hold of that for which Christ Jesus has also laid hold of me" (Philippians 3:12). Paul desperately wanted the purpose which Jesus laid hold of him for, the "upward call of God in Christ Jesus" (v. 14). This is why Paul could gladly "count all things loss for the excellence of the knowledge of Christ Jesus my Lord" (v. 8) because in that loss Paul would "know Him . . . the power of His resurrection, and the fellowship of His sufferings" (v. 10).

Essentially, Paul was saying that there was nothing more important than to know Christ and to be known by Him. For many, though, we take on the perspective after being saved that there is nothing more for us; we have arrived, and so we will just sit and wait for the rapture to come. Yet Paul implores us to press on, because there is so much more beyond the honeymoon of the salvation experience.

I was talking with a brother on Sunday and he was telling me of his desire to know God more. While speaking with him, I noticed that he was upset and was viewing this desire as a problem because he did not have enough time to spend with God. I quickly asked him, "How much time would be enough to do that?" I then shared with him that the desire to know God should never be looked upon as a problem, because it is a hunger that should never be quenched. In fact, having that desire is proof that we are growing and maturing in the Lord and ultimately is what compels us to press on toward the upward call of God in Christ. It's this constant desire that changes us to look upon all things as loss for the excellence of the knowledge of Christ Jesus. It's only when we lose that desire and feel satisfied with our knowledge of God that we should be worried. So, believer, how would you describe your spiritual life right now? Is there nothing further, or is there more beyond?

DECEMBER 13th

Isaiah 55:11: "[S]o shall My word be that goes forth from My mouth; it shall not return to Me void, but it shall accomplish what I please, and it shall prosper in the thing for which I sent it."

Just a little more than three years ago, when Michelle and I found out that she was pregnant with our first child Kate, we immediately ran out and bought an iPad and a pair of headphones. Why, you ask? Because we fully believe what Isaiah 55:10–11 says:

> For as the rain comes down, and the snow from Heaven, and do not return there, but water the earth, and make it bring forth and bud, that it may give seed to the sower and bread to the eater, so shall My word be that goes forth from My mouth; it shall not return to Me void, but it shall accomplish what I please, and it shall prosper in the thing for which I sent it.

Even though doctors will tell you that a baby cannot hear sounds in the womb until weeks twenty-nine through thirty-three, we believe what God's Word says, that His Word does not return void, but rather will always prosper and produce fruit. So by faith, we installed a Bible app on our iPad, plugged in the headphones, placed the headphones on Michelle's stomach, and let God's Word be spoken to our five-week-old child. As we continued to do this, the Lord gave us the most amazing picture of what was happening inside the womb; as Kate was being knit together, the Word of God was being woven into the very fabric of her being, spiritually, physically, mentally, and emotionally. From that point on, our continued prayer for her was that His Word would be the foundation of who she would be.

The question we must ask ourselves is, how much do we really believe what God's Word says? When we believe it as truth, we begin to stand on it and apply it in ways that we never considered before. Second Timothy 3:16–17 reminds us that "All Scripture is given by inspiration of God, and is profitable for doctrine, for reproof, for correction, for instruction in righteousness, that the man of God may be complete, thoroughly equipped for every good work." These verses have compelled Michelle and I to continually expose our children to the Word of God as much as we possibly can. Even though my son Joel was eight weeks old when we started, I have really enjoyed leading him through the book of Proverbs, because I fully believe that we are both growing in faith from it (Romans 10:17). People might say, "He's not going to understand. You are wasting your time." But what does God say about that? Again, what do you believe?

DECEMBER 14th

> Isaiah 55:7: "Let the wicked forsake his way, and the unrighteous man his thoughts; let him return to the Lord, and He will have mercy on him; and to our God, for He will abundantly pardon."

Michelle and I have always emphasized forgiveness with our two-year-old daughter Kate. We continually talk to her and teach her about how completely and abundantly Jesus forgives us of our sin when we turn to Him and seek forgiveness. So after Kate makes a bad choice and is disciplined for that choice, we hug her, tell her how much we love her, explain to her why she was disciplined, pray for her, and then we say, "It's all gone!" and we never bring up what she did again.

Well, the other day, as we were playing with Kate at home, she made a couple bad choices which led to her being disciplined. After I hugged her, told her how much I loved her, explained to her why she was disciplined and prayed for her, I said to her, "It's all gone!" She immediately ran out of her bedroom with her arms stretched high into the air yelling, "I'm forgiven! I'm forgiven!" It was an awesome moment to experience, because our daughter knew without a doubt that she was completely forgiven. Oh, how we need to have this same perspective today.

Proverbs 29:6 (NLT) says, "Evil people are trapped by sin, but the righteous escape, shouting for joy." When did we, as believers, become so somber and stoic about the Lord's promises? Have we taken for granted the amazing grace that has been afforded to us through Christ our Lord, or do we just not believe it to be true? The Lord promised us in Isaiah 55:7, "Let the wicked forsake his way, and the unrighteous man his thoughts; let him return to the LORD, and He will have mercy on him; and to our God, for He will abundantly pardon."

When we turn to the Lord for forgiveness, regardless if it's for the first time or the thousandth time, He does not reject us; He does not institute a penance for our sin where we have to work our way back into His good graces. Rather, He has mercy on us and abundantly pardons us regardless of who we are or what we have done. Is it not astounding to consider the fact that, in light of all we have said and done, we are completely and abundantly forgiven of our sin? Should we not be joyfully running around with our arms stretched high in the air, yelling, "I am forgiven! I am forgiven!"?

The greatest aspect of God's forgiveness to me is that He never brings up our sin again. Once it is forgiven, it is gone, never to resurface. We are reminded of this in Psalm 103:12, as the psalmist states that our sin has been removed as far away from us as the east is from the west. Yet this is the part of forgiveness that we often struggle with the most, because even though the Lord moves on from our sin, we often do not; we still dwell on it, bringing it up over and over again in our minds. The key to receiving and believing this amazing promise is to put sin in its proper perspective: When we sin, we sin against the Lord; so if He can forgive us and move on from it, why can't we? First John 1:9 promises us that "If we confess our sins, He is faithful and just to forgive us our sins and to cleanse us from all unrighteousness." So, believer, remember and believe that in Christ, you are forgiven!

DECEMBER 15th

> 1 Peter 5:6–7: "Therefore humble yourselves under the mighty hand of God, that He may exalt you in due time, casting all your care upon Him, for He cares for you."

Have you ever rolled something away, just to have it roll right back on you? That is essentially what 1 Peter 5:7 is referring to when Peter wrote, "casting all your care upon Him." Jon Courson said that this phrase means "to roll something [away] that will most likely roll back upon you."[178] That is why Peter wrote this in the present continual sense, because "casting" is not a onetime action we perform; it's something that we must continually do over and over again until we are delivered from that situation.

But before we can truly cast our cares on the Lord, we must humble ourselves, "for 'God resists the proud, but gives grace to the humble.' Therefore [because God resists the proud and gives grace to the humble] humble yourselves under the mighty hand of God, that He may exalt you in due time, casting all your care upon Him, for He cares for you" (1 Peter 5:5–7). To properly understand what this verse is telling us, we should read it in this manner: "Therefore humble yourselves under the mighty hand of God by casting all your care upon Him; He will exalt you in due time because He cares for you."

There is an order of events that takes place here that we would be wise to note. When we continually cast our cares on the Lord, we are in fact rebuking the temptation of pride and unbelief by taking all of the control of that situation out of our hands. In turn, we are humbling ourselves under the Lord's mighty hand by saying, "I trust You to handle this Lord, in Your way and in Your time." Again, this is not something we do one time; it's something we continually do until He lifts us out of that situation. When will that happen? "In due time," Peter says—more specifically, in the Lord's time. This is what faith in action looks like, because waiting for the Lord to deliver us in His perfect timing is an extremely difficult thing to do. Proverbs 13:12 reminds us of this: "Hope deferred makes the heart sick."

So how do we trust that God will exalt us when our cares keep rolling back on us? By continually reminding ourselves that "He cares for us." Most religions, at their very best, are lucky if they can find a time when their god is good.[179] Our God, the one true God, is not only good all the time, but He is also a God who cares for His children. I think it's interesting that we use this characteristic of God very casually as we quote it to other people all of the time, but do we really believe it to be true?

When I was sixteen years old, I totaled my parents' car. I was so afraid to tell my parents what had happened that I asked my friend to call my dad for me and tell him we were in an accident. When my dad arrived at the scene, my friend asked me, "Do you want me to stand in between you and your dad?" Now, my dad is not a mean man in any sense of the word, but because of my lack of trust in my dad's love for me, I painted an awful picture of who he was to my friend. Well, my dad being my dad, he walked right past what was left of their car, didn't even look at it, and came directly to me to make sure I was OK. His only concern was for my wellbeing.

As believers, when we fail to humble ourselves and trust in God, and we allow worry and unbelief to come in and change who God is in our minds and hearts, the world is given a picture of a God who does not care for His children. But, when we stand in faith, continually casting our cares upon Him because we know our God loves and cares for us, the world will see God for who He truly is.

DECEMBER 16th

> Hebrews 11:5: "By faith Enoch was taken away so that he did not see death, 'and was not found because God had taken him'; for before he was taken he had this testimony, that he pleased God."

It can be very humbling to read Hebrews 11 and learn of the men and women who performed incredible acts of faith in the most adverse of times. It is very easy to come away from this chapter comparing ourselves to them, asking, "What have I ever done?" But then we read about this man named Enoch: "By faith Enoch was taken away so that he did not see death, 'and was not found because God had taken him'; for before he was taken he had this testimony, that he pleased God."

So what do we know about Enoch? In Genesis 5 we are told that he lived sixty-five years, begot Methuselah, and then "walked with God for three hundred years and had sons and daughters" (Genesis 5:22). Yet nothing is said about any amazing acts of faith he might have performed. So why was Enoch listed in the "Hall of Faith"? Simple, he walked with God. Wait, what?

Could the Christian life really be that simple? Could our lives in Jesus really boil down to just walking with God? Not works or deeds or achievements, or how many people we lead to Christ . . . but simply walking with God? I think we can get so caught up in how others are radically serving the Lord that we belittle ourselves and our calling, because we are not doing the same things they are doing. But what if we are not called to do those things? What if we are called to simply pray and intercede for others in the quiet of our home? What if we are called to just walk with God in the shadows of the spiritual giants of our day—will we be content with that? Will we be obedient to that calling, even if we get no recognition from man?

Michelle shared with me something she read in Psalm 64 a while back, and it begged the question, what is God's expectation of us? The question we should be examining ourselves with is, "What is God's expectation for my life?" Not, "What is my pastor's, or my friend's, or my parents' expectation for my life?" When we place our focus on what man expects of us instead of what God expects of us, we are led astray and distracted with works and deeds that just complicate and busy our lives. All the while, we miss out on the beautiful simplicity of just walking with God and knowing Him more intimately.

Enoch's testimony to all of mankind was simply this: "he pleased God." And as Hebrews 11:6 reminds us, without faith it is impossible to please God. So we see that Enoch was a great man of faith simply because he walked with God. Could there be a greater testimony than this? So, believer, what will your testimony be when all is said and done?

DECEMBER 17th

Isaiah 63:9: "In all their affliction He was afflicted."

If we were to consider the immense magnitude that is God—discounting the sufferings of Jesus Christ while He was here on Earth—we would quickly be reminded that God cannot suffer injury, He cannot be diminished, and He can never, ever, be afflicted. Yet in a time of public declaration to the children of Israel, remembering the Lord's mercies toward His beloved people throughout their history, the prophet Isaiah stated, "In all their affliction He was afflicted."

Regardless what the Israelites would face or feel or deduce in their coming season of captivity and suffering, Isaiah reminded his brethren that their devoted Father was not a dispassionate God or a hardhearted bystander. Rather, He suffers when they suffer; He grieves when they grieve; and He is pained when they are pained, because He loves and cares for them the way a Father would his own child.[180] We catch a glimpse of this during a time of rebellion and suffering where we are told about God, "His soul could no longer endure the misery of Israel" (Judges 10:16). God is forever connected to Israel as their Father, and nothing will ever change that.

It is also important to note that the Father always sympathized with His people, as He would take what was done to them as a direct attack on Himself. We see evidence of this when Saul was fervently persecuting Christians. It was at the peak of that persecution that Jesus appeared to Saul and asked him, "Saul, Saul, why are you persecuting Me?" (Acts 9:4).

Matthew Henry found an even more interesting Hebrew translation of Isaiah 63:9, which states, "In all their affliction there was no affliction." The thought here is that though God's children were suffering under intense affliction, His grace transformed that affliction into something good; the severity of that affliction was lessened by God's mercies to the point that they were sustained and comforted through it all. The time of distress that was so intense, turned out to be so brief, "and ended so well," that it was in effect no affliction at all for God's children. Unlike the others in their day, the difficulties that God's children encountered were not afflictions per se, but rather remedies for what truly ailed them.[181]

It's hard to look at this and not be comforted and assured in our times of difficulty, because even though God was referring to the Israelites in this passage of Isaiah, we have been grafted into the kingdom of God through the blood of Jesus Christ; thus, we are now spiritual children of Israel. So, believer, remember in your times of difficulty that in all your affliction, you are not alone, for He too is afflicted; and that with Him, by His grace and mercy, when all is said and done, it will be as if there was no affliction.

DECEMBER 18th

Isaiah 64:7: "And there is no one who calls on Your name, who stirs himself up to take hold of You."

What is the greater threat to us: that we sin, or that we do not seek forgiveness? This is the question I asked myself as I was reading Isaiah 64.

The children of Israel were lamenting the absence of God's divine intervention in their lives due their ongoing sin and rebellion, "But you have been very angry with us, for we are not godly. We are constant sinners; how can people like us be saved? We are all infected and impure with sin. When we display our righteous deeds, they are but filthy rags. Like autumn leaves, we wither and fall, and our sins sweep us away like the wind" (Isaiah 64:5–6, NLT). Does this sound familiar to you? I know that I have spoken these very things to God many times in my walk. The thing we must understand is that it's not just you and me; this is the state of the entire human race from the moment we are born. But is this the real issue?

"Yet no one calls on Your name or pleads with You for mercy. Therefore, you have turned away from us and turned us over to our sins" (Isaiah 64:7, NLT). It's important to remember that though sin separates us from God, unrepentance is what eventually turns Him away from us. As evil as sin is—and it is evil—the issue here was not that they sinned, but rather that no one called upon God. No one pleaded for mercy; no one sought out His grace through repentance. The children of Israel just continued on in their sin.

The difference between a believer and an unbeliever is not whether we sin or not, for all men have sinned and all men fall short of God's glorious standard (Romans 3:23). No, the difference is that those who call on His name, who plead for His mercy, who seek His grace and repent of their sin, to these shall be the kingdom of God; to these shall be forgiveness and eternal life.

It is true, the Lord meets those who rejoice and carry on in righteousness (Isaiah 64:5), and so we should abstain from sin with all our heart, soul, mind, and strength. But with that, when we do sin, we should never allow our sin to keep us from seeking His mercy and grace, for that is the very reason why Jesus Christ came.

My good friend Bill Hanley wrote the following concerning this very subject: "Are you able to see your faults, your flesh, getting in the way of grace and mercy? Call sin by its name and take it to the cross. Do you hate the sin enough to ask, 'What has this done to a loving God who came in the flesh, died for me, and now continues to pray for me?' Do you view your sins like Christ did when He suffered and took all your sins to hell? Recognize what Christ did at the cross. Nothing is as valuable as seeing your sin in light of what Christ did at the cross."[182]

DECEMBER 19th

John 3:30: "He must increase, but I must decrease."

In 1 Corinthians 7, the apostle Paul spoke about both the benefits and challenges of being single and married. One of the more important points that Paul made was that "He who is unmarried cares for the things of the Lord—how he may please the Lord. But he who is married cares about the things of the world—how he may please his wife" (1 Corinthians 7:32–33). His point was that the single person does not have the responsibilities that go along with having a family; thus, they are more available to spend time serving and getting to know the Lord; the married person must divide his or her time between the Lord, their family, and themselves.

So, how should that time be divided? This subject came up last weekend as Michelle and I were fellowshipping with some dear friends of ours, and I was explaining to them the mistake we often make when transitioning from being single to being married. When I was single, my time was divided up into two categories: time for myself and time for God. So for the sake of argument, let's just say it was 50% for me and 50% for God. When I got married, it became 50% for me, 25% for God and 25% for Michelle. Then our daughter Kate was born, and it became 50% for me, 17% for God, 17% for Michelle, and 16% for Kate. Then our son Joel was born, and it became 50% for me, 12.5% for God, 12.5% for Michelle, 12.5% for Kate, and 12.5% for Joel.

Do you see the problem here? Rather than my time remaining constant and God's time dwindling, it should have been that God's time was left untouched and my time that was lessened. The sheer number of complications that arise from this self-first system of living are too numerous to count, simply because if I am investing 50% of my time in me, and only 12.5% in God (if that), I will be the more dominant influence in my life, and that is never a good thing as my thoughts will always lead to my way of living, not His.

John Ruskin once said, "When a man is wrapped up in himself, he makes a pretty small package."[183] W. Glyn Evans echoed this sentiment, "I will never amount to anything for Christ until I attend my own funeral."[184] Believer, we must rally behind what John the Baptist rightly declared to his disciples when they were concerned with Jesus' growing popularity among the people, "He [Jesus] must increase, but I must decrease" (John 3:30). We must remember that spiritual growth and maturity are predicated on us denying self. Oh, how we need to get out of the way and allow the Holy Spirit to possess more of our being. What can we possibly bring that would best the authority, power, and saving grace of Jesus Christ? In Him we have all things; apart from Him, we have nothing.

DECEMBER 20th

> Genesis 22:2: "Take now your son . . . and offer him there as a burnt offering."

When I study for a message and I come across a command from God, I always like to attach to it the consequence of following or not following that command, because more often than not it seems like that is what is needed in order for us to be obedient. Well recently, as I was preparing for an upcoming teaching, I kept encountering verses that instructed believers to be about the Father's business and to do the work He has left for us to do. And so, like I always have done in the past, I kept searching for the consequence of what would happen if we are not about His work, but rather are preoccupied with the cares of this life.

It was then that God gave me a revelation about this. He reminded me that it shouldn't matter what the consequence to a command is, because that should never be our call to arms. We should be obedient to His instructions simply because that is what He has instructed us to do. Nothing further should be required from the God who willingly died to save us from our sin.

But it begs the question, "Have we become such a people that we will only obey God's commands if the consequence is severe enough, or the blessing rich enough?" Our obedience to Christ should never be based on the consequence of obeying or disobeying that command; we shouldn't need to be threatened or bribed in order to be obedient. We should be obedient because He is our Lord and Savior and because we trust Him to be faithful and His Word to be true. At some point in time, we placed our faith in Him, gave Him our life, and said, "Lord, I trust You with my eternal destiny." Were those merely empty words?

I think back to the test of all tests of faith, when God told Abraham to sacrifice his son, Isaac, whom Abraham loved more than anything else (apart from God, that is). If you were to read this section of verses, you would see that God never gave Abraham a consequence to His command, yet Abraham fully obeyed God. He did not need to be bribed or threatened in order to obey; he simply needed God's Word. That is the example that we should follow, for Abraham was never more Christ-like than he was in that moment, because He obeyed God's Word without consequence. I pray it will be so with us as well.

DECEMBER 21ˢᵗ

Mark 14:47: "And one of those who stood by drew his sword and struck
the servant of the high priest, and cut off his ear."

Peter found himself engaged in a war that he was neither prepared nor equipped
for. He could draw a sword on a great multitude of soldiers, but he could not sit
down and pray with Jesus for an hour.[185] He had mistakenly placed his faith in his
strength and in the weapons of this world, rather than in the Almighty God and
the weapons He has given us.

But are we any different? How quickly we reach for the wrong weapons when
we are engaged in battle. We see a situation and we react in the flesh rather than
reflect in the Spirit. For us to be successful in battle, we have to change our thinking
from the carnal to the spiritual, as our battle is not a physical one, but a spiritual
one. Our weapons of warfare are not of this world; they are prayer and the preaching of God's Word.

We need to stop swinging for the head, and start focusing on the heart. You
want to change your family, your workplace, your community, this world . . . you
want to turn it upside down and wreck it for Jesus . . . then get on your knees and
pray so that you will be prepared for every good work. Study the Word of God,
know it, apply it, preach it, so that you will be equipped for every good work.

The truth is that when we lose confidence in the weapons that Christ has given
us, we lose all effective power for change and victory. When that happens, we pick
up the weapons of this world, which only maim and bludgeon. How many ears
have we cut off by trying to wage war in our own strength? Too many to count, I
fear.

The failure of the disciples in the garden was not in their intent or their
fervor, for they loved Jesus incredibly. No, their failure was in their preparation
as they did not watch and pray. Though we too love Jesus, we often reject the
instructions to watch and pray because we see no peril on the horizon; we see
no reason to watch and pray as we mistakenly place our confidence in our own
strength and abilities by proclaiming, "I will be ready." And yet we are neither
prepared nor equipped for the coming battle, all because we lack faith in the
weapons He has given us.

The question we have to ask ourselves is, how will we ever stand in the day
of adversity if we are not a people who faithfully pray and skillfully wield the
Word of God? An even better question is, when *is* the day of adversity? Do we

know? When are we going to get that phone call, that diagnosis? When will the persecution of Christians come to our doorstep? The mistake we often make is that we wait to prepare ourselves until a situation has come upon us; but by that time, it is already too late and we are found to be lacking. So, believer, don't be caught unprepared or unequipped for the day's battle, because every day could be the day of adversity.

DECEMBER 22nd

Luke 5:17: "And the power of the Lord was present to heal them."

One day, four men brought a paralytic man to Jesus. Unable to reach Jesus because of the crowd, these four men tore open the roof of the house where Jesus was teaching and lowered the paralytic man down to Him. "When [Jesus] saw their faith, He said to [the paralytic man] 'Man, your sins are forgiven you'" (Luke 5:20). I have always wondered why Jesus said this first, and didn't just heal the paralytic right away. Many expositors have offered up their thoughts as to why Jesus did this, but just recently the Lord showed me that the answer lies in the sections prior to this verse.

"Now it happened on a certain day, as He was teaching, that there were Pharisees and teachers of the law sitting by, who had come out of every town of Galilee, Judea, and Jerusalem. And the power of the Lord was present to heal them" (Luke 5:17). The "them" that Dr. Luke is referring to here were the Pharisees and the teachers of the law. Rich Cathers stated that the word "heal" not only means "to cure or heal," but it also means "to free from error and sins; to bring about ones salvation."[186] It was then, at that time, that the four men brought the paralytic man to Jesus.

All of this was set up by God so that the Pharisees and the teachers of the law could see that the power to forgive them of their sins was in their midst. This is why Jesus said to the paralytic, "Man, your sins are forgiven you." Jesus wanted everyone to see that He was the Messiah. The power to heal them was present; they could be forgiven; they could receive salvation and be free from the condemnation of the law.

Naturally, upon hearing Jesus say this, the Pharisees and the teachers of the law questioned this in their hearts:

"Who is this who speaks blasphemies? Who can forgive sins but God?"

But when Jesus perceived their thoughts, He answered and said to them, "Which is easier to say, 'Your sins are forgiven you' [which requires no proof], or to say, 'Rise up and walk [which requires much proof]?' But that you may know that the Son of Man has power on earth to forgive sins—" He said to the man who was paralyzed, "I say to you, arise, take up your bed, and go to your house."

Immediately he rose up before them, took up what he had been lying on, and departed to his own house, glorifying God. (Luke 5:21–25)

It is at this time of year that we are reminded that the power to forgive is present and is with us. That is what the angels proclaimed when Jesus was born: "For there is born to you this day in the city of David a Savior, who is Christ the Lord" (Luke 2:11). After all, Jesus' very name means "God with us." So believer, rejoice, for He is with us, and the power to forgive all sin is present, ready, and willing.

DECEMBER 23rd

Mark 14:49: "But the Scriptures must be fulfilled."

The immense regard Jesus had for Scripture is simply incredible to me. As Matthew Henry commented, "He would bear anything," even death on the cross, rather than have "the least jot or tittle" of God's Word "fall to the ground" and be trampled upon.[187] With that thought in mind, we should rejoice in the fact that just as Jesus fulfilled all Scripture regarding His suffering, He also fulfilled all Scripture regarding His glory—and He will fulfill all Scripture regarding those who call upon Him as Lord and Savior as well.

If we surrender our lives to Christ, we will live with Him for all eternity; if we endure and abide in Him, we shall also reign with Him; if we deny Him, He will also deny us; if we are faithless, He remains faithful because He cannot deny Himself (2 Timothy 2:13). This is the song that the early church would sing as they faced incredible pressure and persecution. We must remind ourselves, as they did, that Jesus cannot deny who He is; He cannot retract any word He has spoken or any promise that He has made, for He is the Yes and Amen, the faithful and true witness (Revelation 3:14).

We often fail to stand, not because we lack faith in Him, not because He has failed us, and not because we have a weak faith, but simply because we are not intimately familiar with the promises He has given us. And because we lack the knowledge of His mighty assurances, His deliverances, and His provisions, we have nothing to stand on, nothing to place our hope in when we face adversity. And it is there, in those moments of unsupported faith, that fear is empowered, causing us to crumble under even the slightest of pressures. So, believer, get to know the Word of God, for it is trustworthy, complete, authoritative, sufficient, and it will always accomplish what it says.

DECEMBER 24th

Luke 5:17: "And the power of the Lord was present to heal them."

I woke up one Christmas Eve morning in excruciating pain. My neck had somehow gotten wrenched while I was sleeping and I could barely turn my head in either direction. Immediately, I started praying that God would heal me as it was Christmas Eve and Michelle and I had a lot of plans. I began to get a little frustrated as I tried to figure out what I had done that caused my neck to be so out of whack, but I refused to allow it to get me down and I just kept praying.

As I thought about the best course of action, it came to mind that I should call my old chiropractor, whom I had not seen in about four years. But then I thought, "It's Christmas Eve; he is not going to be working." But I felt led to call his office anyway. Coincidently, he "just happened" to be there seeing one of his patients. We had a quick conversation about what was going on with my neck, and he said he could see me quickly before he left town that morning.

After I got off of the phone with him, I felt the Lord say to me, "Patrick, maybe this appointment has nothing to do with you at all; maybe this appointment has to do with him." The more I thought about this, the more I had peace about what was going on. On my way to his office, I prayed, "Father, please impress on my heart whatever it is that You want me to say to him and I will say it."

Once I got there, we caught up a little bit, and then he began working on my neck and shoulder. As he was doing this, I shared with him what the Lord had impressed on my heart that morning—that all of this had nothing to do with me, but everything to do with him.

He was kind of startled by what I said, and I began to sense that there was something going on in his life that was troubling him. We began to talk about prayer, God, church, and the Bible, and eventually I asked him if I could pray for him. He gladly agreed, and I prayed what I believed the Lord wanted me to pray. When I had finished praying, he grabbed me and gave me a big hug as if to say, "I really needed that." It was in that moment that I felt the Lord say to me, "It's not enough to pray for him, Patrick; ask him if he will receive me as His Lord and Savior."

So I explained to him what I believed the Lord had said to me while we were hugging, and I asked him if he wanted to surrender his life to Jesus Christ. He said yes. After he gave his life to Christ, I prayed for him again, and I remember thanking God so much for wrecking my neck so that I could be a part of this incredible moment. It was then that I became overwhelmed by what was transpiring before me. I got to watch this man go from death to life in a matter of seconds.

As I was leaving his office, I looked back at him to say goodbye one last time, and I will never forget the smile he had on his face as he was saying to himself, "I am a new creation." Truly the power of the Lord is present today to forgive men of their sin. So believer, be ready; divine appointments abound because today is the day of salvation, and the power of the Lord is present to forgive.

DECEMBER 25th

> Titus 1:2: "in hope of eternal life which God, who cannot lie, promised before time began . . ."

Unmet expectations will always lead to unbelief—and unbelief, at its very core, is everything that is opposite of God, for without faith it is impossible to please God (Hebrews 11:6). So how do we defeat unbelief, you ask? By trusting in the fact that God cannot lie. It's not that God won't lie, or that God doesn't desire to lie, it is that God *cannot* lie. Just as you and I cannot be anything other than human, God cannot lie. It's impossible for Him to ever do so because He is truth, and there is no shadow of turning within Him (James 1:17). This truth should be the first thing we say to ourselves every time we read the Bible, every time we face a difficulty, and every time we are tempted with unbelief. God cannot lie.

Consider this as you read John 14:1–3: "Let not your heart be troubled; you believe in God, believe also in Me [Jesus]. In My Father's house are many mansions; if it were not so, I would have told you. I go to prepare a place for you. And if I go and prepare a place for you, I will come again and receive you to Myself; that where I am, there you may be also."

If you have never studied the traditional Hebrew marriage sequence of events, it is quite fascinating. It begins with the betrothal, in which the prospective bridegroom would travel from his father's house to the home of his prospective bride. He would then pay the purchase price for her, thus establishing the marriage covenant with her. The bridegroom would then return to his father's house (which meant being separated from his bride for a short period), during which time he would prepare the living accommodations for his wife in his father's house. The bridegroom would then return for his bride, but at a time that she did not know; thus, she would always have to be prepared. They would then return to his father's house to consummate the marriage and celebrate the wedding feast for the next seven days.[188]

The parallelism we find with the promise that our Bridegroom, Christ, has given to us, His bride, cannot be missed. Jesus left His Father's house to come to our home so that He might pay our purchase price and establish a covenant with us. He ascended into heaven and returned to His Father, so that He might prepare a place for us in His Father's house. He will return for us at a time that we do not know; thus, we must always be prepared. We will then be with Him, where He is, and will celebrate the Wedding Feast of the Lamb for all eternity.

So believer, remember, God cannot lie—"if it were not so, I would have told you." The expectation of Christ's return should be where our hope is firmly placed; this should be the expectation that is at the forefront of our mind and thoughts throughout the rest of our days because "everyone who has this hope in Him purifies himself, just as He is pure" (1 John 3:3). Having this hope will weaken the desire for this world and its ways, keep our focus on that which is true, and always ensure that we will be ready at His return.

DECEMBER 26th

Philippians 4:4: "Rejoice in the Lord always. Again I will say, rejoice!"

The basic theme of the letter to the Philippians is joy. But the obvious question is, "How do we rejoice always and in every circumstance?" We do it by thinking rightly, Paul says, because how we think ultimately determines how we feel.[189] Joy is such a powerful theme throughout this letter; because of that, what is often missed is the fact that the apostle Paul exhorted the church in Philippi to think rightly, as he specifically referred to our thought lives more than twenty times in this letter. In other words, Paul instructs us to put on the mind of Christ, because when we do this, we will be joyful.

When considering Philippians 1, Jon Courson said that we can't change our hearts; but we can change our minds. We can't change how we feel, but we can change how we think. This is a very important concept for us to understand because even though God can change our heart, He will never change our mind. God has given mankind the freedom to think and choose as we please, and He will never take away or infringe upon that freedom. But if we change our minds, God will then change our hearts.[190]

Proverbs 23:7 states, "For as [a man] thinks in his heart, so is he." The word "heart" used here refers to the place where one thinks and reflects, not the center of emotions and feelings. How else can we explain how Paul—sitting in a Roman prison, knowing that he could die at any moment—could write a letter that is not only full of joy, but also instructs *us* to rejoice always?

The point is that we cannot just stand idly by and expect joy to just miraculously come to us. Choices have to be made—tough choices. There has to be an effort on our part to change how we think, regardless of how we feel or what situation we find ourselves in. When we put on the mind of Christ, and change our thinking from what we feel is true to what Christ says is true, our behavior will change and we will bring glory to God. This is how we mature; this is how we are strengthened; this is how we are sanctified; and ultimately, this how we are transformed by the renewing of our mind so that we might prove what is good and acceptable and the perfect will of God (Romans 12:2).

DECEMBER 27th

Romans 5:20: "But where sin abounded, grace abounded much more."

The promise of what sin brings into our lives is a very sobering message, to say the least. It reminds us that sin destroys, condemns, and ultimately separates us from God. As sinners, we know this to be true, as we have all experienced firsthand the destruction, condemnation, and separation that sin brings. But is this the entire message that we are to receive in regard to sin?

Forever coupled with the promise of what sin brings is the greater promise that there is grace and forgiveness through Christ Jesus our Lord: "where sin abounded, grace abounded much more" (Romans 5:20). This divine marriage of curse and redemption is clearly seen throughout the Bible, as the Lord continually promised what would happen if His people turned away from Him. Yet along with that promise, the Lord also vowed that forgiveness was readily available for them if they so desired it (Psalm 86:5).

It is vitally important for us to remember that the promise of what sin brings against us is not the full message God has given us; rather, it is simply the precursor to a greater message: that in Christ there is abundant forgiveness (1 John 1:9). Too often we only embrace the first half of this message—that sin destroys, condemns, and separates us from God—and we forget that "as through one man's offense judgment came to all men . . . even so through one Man's righteous act the free gift came to all men, resulting in justification of life" (Romans 5:18). If we receive the truth regarding our sin, we must also receive the truth regarding Christ's forgiveness. You cannot have one without the other.

As David Guzik pointed out, when Nathan the prophet told David that his sin had been put away by the Lord; the only reason why David could believe that he was forgiven for committing adultery with Bathsheba, and murdering Uriah, was because he could believe that he had sinned.[191] Realizing and confessing our sin is not a curse by any means; rather, it is the steppingstone to seeking and receiving God's great forgiveness. So, believer, even as "our heart condemns us" when we come face to face with our sinful nature, remember, "God is greater than our heart" and is ready and willing to forgive (1 John 3:20).

DECEMBER 28th

> 2 Chronicles 30:18a: "[Y]et they ate the Passover contrary to what was written."

We exercise wisdom when we implement structure for a church service, Bible study, or prayer meeting, as all things should be done decently and in order (1 Corinthians 14:40). But with that, we must also use caution when keeping that agenda, as there is a fine line between having structure and being legalistic. The problem of legalism generally arises when we have structure without deviation; it is there that the Spirit is quenched and the structure quickly becomes law.

In 2 Chronicles 30, we read about a time in Israel's history when King Hezekiah cleansed, established, and restored worship at the temple. He then called on all of Israel to travel to Jerusalem and celebrate the Passover feast. Unfortunately, most people did not know how to properly prepare for Passover because it had not been celebrated in many years. "For a multitude of the people . . . had not cleansed themselves, yet they ate the Passover contrary to what was written" (2 Chronicles 30:18a). Yet the Lord did not strike them down. He did not condemn them or punish them for breaking the Law. Rather, He had mercy on their souls and "listened to Hezekiah" (2 Chronicles 30:20), who had prayed for them saying, "May the good Lord provide atonement for everyone who prepares his heart to seek God" (2 Chronicles 30:18b).

If you were to read this entire chapter, you would find that just about every law regarding the Passover celebration was broken; yet the Lord blessed the people and forgave them of their sin because the attitude of their heart prevailed over their outward activity.[192] We have to remember that it will always be about the heart with the Lord. Though these people were ignorant of the law, though they did just about everything wrong, their hearts truly sought the Lord, and that is what mattered most. The Lord does not want ritual; He wants intimacy. F. B. Meyer once said, "You may not understand doctrine, creed, or rite; but be sure to seek God. No splendid ceremonial nor rigorous etiquette can intercept the seeking soul."[193]

I fear that we too often fail in this area, as we intercept the seeking soul by holding them to our structured religion. We turn away those that walk into church still reeking of the world; we rebuke those who are ignorant of our laws, or who do not look or act the part of the Christian. We send them away bruised and rejected by our religiosity, when all they desired was to come and worship the Lord. We must remember, as Grotius well said, "Ritual institutions must give way, not only to a public necessity, but to a public benefit and advantage."[194]

Mahatma Gandhi wrote in his autobiography that when he was seeking to heal his country from the division that the caste system had created, he sought to convert to Christianity. But as he walked into the church one Sunday morning to speak with the minister about Christ and salvation, the ushers refused to allow him to be seated and told him to go and worship with his own people. Oh, how we need to deviate from our religious structure and remember that Jesus did not come to create division, establish rituals, and enforce the law. No, He came to save the sick and to break down every barrier so that all men could come to Him and be saved.

DECEMBER 29th

> Romans 1:16: "I am not ashamed of the gospel of Christ, for it is the power of God to salvation."

I once heard a pastor give an entire message about the founding father of his church. From a public speaking standpoint, this man nailed it as the message was well thought-out, engaging, humorous, and eloquently spoken. From a biblical standpoint, this man failed miserably, as he never once mentioned the name of Jesus Christ. Though this man delivered a good message that tickled the ears of man, the truth is that it was a powerless message that changed no one, saved no one, and ultimately bore no fruit of eternal value.

The apostle Paul came across something very similar when he shared the message of the cross with the Jews and the Greeks. The Jews rejected this message because they were looking for a powerful sign; the Greeks rejected it because they were looking for logical wisdom. In the eyes of the Jews and Greeks, the message about a Messiah who was crucified to save man from his sin was neither powerful nor logical; it was just foolishness.

The temptation for Paul would have been to come up with a message that was attractive to both the Jews and the Greeks, one that would tickle their ears, but as Paul wrote to the Romans, "I am not ashamed of the gospel of Christ, for it is the power of God to salvation." Paul clearly understood that there was only one message that would truly change lives and cultures, and that was the message of the cross.

Prior to Christmas Eve 2003, the culture in my family was very different than it is now. We did not hug; we did not say "I love you"; we did not show emotion; and we never shared anything personal. This was not my parents' fault, mind you; it was how they were raised, and how their parents were raised, and how their parents' parents were raised. For more than one hundred years the culture in my family remained the same until Christmas Eve 2003. That was the night that I shared the gospel of Jesus Christ with my family.

To my knowledge, no one received salvation that night; but as time progressed, the culture in my family slowly began to change. We soon began hugging one another and telling each other "I love you"; we began sharing what was going on in our lives and even started showing emotion. As time went on, we started praying together and eventually had a family Bible study on Sunday afternoons. The most important thing that came out of that night, though, was the fact that over time, each member of my family gave their life to Jesus Christ.

It truly is an amazing thing, when you consider the fact that more than one hundred years of conditioned behavior was radically changed when the gospel of Jesus Christ was shared. So, believer, if you want to change the lives and the culture of your family, your coworkers, and your community, preach Christ crucified (1 Corinthians 1:21). Only the message of the cross has the power to change and transform, because only the gospel of Jesus Christ is the power of God to salvation.

DECEMBER 30th

Deuteronomy 7:6 (NLT): "For you are . . . a special treasure."

One of Kate's favorite books is *Benjamin's Box* by Melody Carson. It is the story of a boy named Benjamin who lived in Jerusalem during the days of Jesus' earthly ministry. As the story goes, Benjamin's grandfather gave him a treasure box containing only some ordinary straw. When Benjamin's friend Eli asked him about the straw, Benjamin explained that the "straw came from the bed of a baby who was born in a stable. My grandfather was a shepherd then, and he said the baby would grow up to be king."[195] Eli laughed as he questioned the significance of the straw and the baby. This sets the stage for the rest of the book, in which Benjamin would go on and collect more treasures that are significant to the week of Jesus' crucifixion such as fur from the donkey Jesus rode in on, a broken cup from the Last Supper, a gambling stone from the guards at the crucifixion, etc.

This inspired my four-year-old daughter to do something very similar. Much like the reaction Eli had to the straw in Benjamin's box, many people look at the treasures Kate has collected and dismiss them as being insignificant. In the world's eyes, daisies from the field she plays in at church, sticks from the park behind our house, rocks and dead leaves along the sidewalk, discarded pieces of paper, used scotch tape, broken rubber bands . . . they are all worthless and should be thrown away. In the world's estimation, these things have no value or significance because there is nothing special about them. But in Kate's eyes, they are all treasures.

I was thinking about this as I was placing a detached cotton-swab head in her treasure box as she requested. I realized that though I may consider these things to be irrelevant and unimportant, to her they are all very special and significant—just as each one of us is very special and significant to God. The world will often label us as useless, worthless, insignificant, and damaged. It will discard us and toss us aside because we have no value in the world's system. Yet the Lord says to each one of us—yes, even you: You are special, you are significant, you have a great purpose, you are a new creation, you have been fully restored; in My eyes, you are priceless, and I love you, [insert your name here].

The thing we must remember is that we are not to conform to the world's value system, which says we have to be [fill in the blank] in order to be special. Contrary to what the world says, our value is not measured by how we look, how much money we have, our marital status, our job, our clothes, our car, our education, or our past. Our value is not even determined by what we think of ourselves because of what we have or have not done in our lives. Our value is only determined by who we are in God's eyes, and He says we are His beloved masterpieces, His precious treasures, His eternal inheritance . . . quite simply, we are the apple of His eye. In the Lord's value system, we are defined by who we are in Jesus Christ, not who we are in the world. So, believer, remember, you "belong to the LORD your God. . . . [He] has chosen you to be his own special treasure" (Deuteronomy 7:6, NLT).

DECEMBER 31st

> Psalm 37:25: "I have been young, and now am old; yet I have not seen the righteous forsaken, nor his descendants begging bread."

One New Year's Eve, Michelle and I thought it would be a good idea to look back on the previous year, month by month, and give thanks to the Lord for all of the blessings He had poured out on us. We reflected on all the things that God had done for us, the lessons we learned, the doors that He closed, the trials and difficulties that grew us, etc. We reflected on the birthdays and anniversaries we celebrated, and we thanked God for all of the people He had brought into our lives.

It was then, in that time of prayer, that I was reminded of the fears we faced and the situations of hopelessness that had come up throughout the year—and it hit me that not once did any of those fears ever come to fruition. Not once were we overtaken by that hopeless situation; not once did we ever lack for that which we needed; not once were we forsaken; not once were we cast out because of our sin; not once did God fail us in any way, shape, or form. And I bet that if we looked back on all the years before that, we would all say the same exact thing that David said here: "I have been young, and now am old; yet I have not seen the righteous forsaken, nor his descendants begging bread."

The coming year, without a doubt, is going to have challenges for us. It is going to have difficulties. We will find ourselves discouraged, fearful, and facing seemingly impossible situations. Maybe you are even experiencing some of these things right now. Believer, do not fear; do not be anxious; do not worry or fret about these things, for our God is a good God. He is faithful, and He is the One who is in control of all things. He has never failed us, He has never forsaken us, and He never will. He will see us through all things for our God has overcome the world, and in Him, we are more than conquerors. So "give thanks to the LORD, for He is good! For His mercy endures forever" (Psalm 136:1).

ENDNOTES

1. Francis of Assisi, The Little Flowers of St. Francis Assisi, Goodreads, https://www.goodreads.com/quotes/4342-all-the-darkness-in-the-world-cannot-extinguish-the-light (accessed March 18, 2019).

2. David Guzik, "Acts 5—The Church Grows Despite Opposition," Enduring Word, 2018, https://enduringword.com/bible-commentary/acts-5.

3. Ibid.

4. Guzik, "James 5—The Life of a Living Faith," Enduring Word, 2018, https://enduringword.com/bible-commentary/james-5/.

5. Ibid.

6. Guzik, "Acts 14—The Conclusion of the First Missionary Journey," Enduring Word, 2018, https://enduringword.com/bible-commentary/acts-14.

7. Jim Cymbala, You Were Made for More (Grand Rapids, MI: Zondervan, 2008), 193–194.

8. Ibid.

9. Jon Courson, Jon Courson's Application Commentary: New Testament (Nashville, TN: Thomas Nelson, 2003), James 5:15, 1531

10. Guzik, "James 5—The Life of a Living Faith."

11. Chuck Smith, Living Water (Santa Ana, CA: The Word for Today, 1996), 38.

12. Guzik, "Genesis 28—Jacob Flees from Esau," Enduring Word, 2018, https://enduringword.com/bible-commentary/genesis-28/.

13. Quoted by Guzik, "Isaiah 40—Comfort and Strength for God's People," Enduring Word, 2018, https://enduringword.com/bible-commentary/isaiah-40/.

14. Quoted by Ed Rea, "Daily Devotions with Pastor Ed Rea," Packinghouse Christian Fellowship, November 1, 2012, http://packinghouseredlands.org/devotional.

15. Quoted by Erwin W. Lutzer, "Get the Right Start Every Day," Moody Church Media, https://www.moodymedia.org/articles/get-right-start-every-day (accessed July 21, 2017).

16. Charles Swindoll, *The Christian Life* (Berlin, MD: Vision House, 1994), 94

17. John MacArthur, *The MacArthur Study Bible* (Dallas: Word, 1997), James 3:6, 1931.

18. Ron Daniel, "Study Notes for James 3:1–12," Ron Daniel . . . a renaissance kinda guy, 1998–2019, http://www.rondaniel.com/library/59-James/James0301.php.

19. Guzik, "James 3—Warnings and Words to Teachers," Enduring Word, 2018, https://enduringword.com/bible-commentary/james-3.

20. Jim Cymbala, *Spirit Rising* (Grand Rapids, MI: Zondervan, 2012), 36–37.

21. Guzik, "Exodus 31—The Call of Bezaleel and Aholiab," Enduring Word, 2018, https://enduringword.com/bible-commentary/exodus-31.

22. Ibid.

23. Ray Stedman, "Things That Don't Work: The Search for Meaning," Ray Stedman Authentic Christianity, September 19, 1982, https://www.raystedman.org/old-testament/ecclesiastes/the-search-for-meaning.

24. Guzik, "Exodus 33—Israel's Path of Restored Fellowship," Enduring Word, 2018, https://enduringword.com/bible-commentary/exodus-33.

25. Ibid.

26. Daniel, "Study Notes Hosea 11:1–14:9," Ron Daniel . . . a renaissance kinda guy, 1998-2019, http://www.rondaniel.com/library/28-Hosea/Hosea1101.php.

27. Charles Spurgeon, *Morning and Evening*, January 14 a.m., Blue Letter Bible, https://www.blueletterbible.org/devotionals/me/view.cfm?Date=01/14&Time=both&body=1.

28. Quoted in Rea, "Daily Devotions with Pastor Ed Rea," Packinghouse Christian Fellowship, April 3, 2012, http://packinghouseredlands.org/devotional.

29. Guzik, "Exodus 32—The Golden Calf," Enduring Word, 2018, https://enduringword.com/bible-commentary/exodus-32.

30. Guzik, "Isaiah 6—Isaiah's Conviction, Cleansing and Call," Enduring Word, 2018, https://enduringword.com/bible-commentary/Isaiah-6.

31. Ibid.

32. Spurgeon, *Morning and Evening*, January 14 p.m., https://www.blueletterbible. org/devotionals/me/view.cfm?Date=01/14&Time=both&body=1.

33. MacArthur, *MacArthur Study Bible*, Daniel 1:8, 1227.

34. Chuck Smith, *Living Water* (Santa Ana, CA: The Word for Today, 1996), 38.

35. John MacArthur, *The MacArthur New Testament Commentary: Revelation 1–11* (Chicago: Moody Press, 1999), 129.

36. Guzik, "1 John 2—Hindrances to Fellowship with God," Enduring Word, 2018, https://enduringword.com/bible-commentary/1John-2.

37. Guzik, "Hebrews 6—A Warning to Discouraged Believers," Enduring Word, 2018, https://enduringword.com/bible-commentary/Hebrews-6.

38. Guzik, "Isaiah 26—Judah's Kingdom of God Song," Enduring Word, 2018, https://enduringword.com/bible-commentary/Isaiah-26.

39. Matthew Henry, *Matthew Henry's Commentary on the Whole Bible*, Proverbs 2, Blue Letter Bible, https://www.blueletterbible.org/Comm/mhc/Pro/Pro_002. cfm?a=630001.

40. Guzik, "Galatians 5—Standing Fast in the Liberty of Jesus," Enduring Word, 2018, https://enduringword.com/bible-commentary/Galatians-5.

41. W. E. Vine, "Vine's Expository Dictionary of NT Words," StudyLight, https:// www.studylight.org/dictionaries/ved/l/love.html.

42. Guzik, "Romans 5—Benefits of Being Justified through Faith," Enduring Word, 2018, https://enduringword.com/bible-commentary/Romans-5.

43. MacArthur, *The MacArthur New Testament Commentary: Acts* (Chicago, IL.: Moody Press, 1996), 326.

44. Stedman, "Maintaining Love: Love Made Visible," Ray Stedman Authentic Christianity, June 11, 1967, https://www.raystedman.org/new-testament/1-john/love-made-visible.

45. Ibid.

46. Guzik, "Genesis 3—Man's Temptation and Fall," Enduring Word, 2018, https://enduringword.com/bible-commentary/Genesis-3.

47. Brian and Cheryl Broderson, Packinghouse Couples' Retreat, personal communication, July 23, 2013.

48. MacArthur, *MacArthur Study Bible*, Romans 6:4, 1703.

49. Alistair Begg, "They Crucified Him: Mark 15:16-32," Truth for Life: The Bible Teaching Ministry of Alistair Begg, March 18, 2013, https://www.truthforlife. org/resources/sermon/they-crucified-him.

50. Ibid.

51. Guzik, "Matthew 17—Jesus Transfigured, Triumphant, and Taxed," Enduring Word, 2018, https://enduringword.com/bible-commentary/Matthew-17.

52. Justin Alfred, Packinghouse Men's Retreat, personal communication.

53. Guzik, "Matthew 4—The Temptation of Jesus and His First Galilean Ministry," Enduring Word, 2018, https://enduringword.com/bible-commentary/ Matthew-4.

54. Ibid.

55. W. Glyn Evans, *Daily with the King* (Chicago: Moody Publishers, 1979), January 31.

56. MacArthur, *MacArthur Study Bible*, Psalm 84:6, 817.

57. Ibid., Proverbs 24:27, 912.

58. *Star Wars: Episode V, The Empire Strikes Back,* directed by Irvin Kershner (1980; Los Angeles: Twentieth Century Fox Home Entertainment, 2004), DVD.

59. Evans, *Daily with the King*, December 15.

60. MacArthur, *MacArthur Study Bible*, Proverbs 10:20, 890.

61. Ibid., Isaiah 50:4–11, 1033.

62. Evans, *Daily with the King*, December 7.

63. Henry, *Matthew Henry's Commentary*, Proverbs 10:20, https://www.blueletter-bible.org/Comm/mhc/Pro/Pro_010.cfm?a=638001.

64. Ibid., Psalm 51:6, https://www.blueletterbible.org/Comm/mhc/Psa/Psa_051. cfm?a=529001.

65. MacArthur, *MacArthur Study Bible*, Proverbs 11:24, 892.

66. Guzik, "Matthew 13—The Kingdom Parables," Enduring Word, 2018, https:// enduringword.com/bible-commentary/Matthew-13.

67. Ibid.

68. Guzik, "Romans 7—Exposing the Weakness of the Law," Enduring Word, 2018, https://enduringword.com/bible-commentary/Romans-7.

69. Henry, *Matthew Henry's Commentary*, Proverbs 13:2-3, https://www.blueletter-bible.org/Comm/mhc/Pro/Pro_013.cfm?a=641001.

70. Ibid., Proverbs 13:4, https://www.blueletterbible.org/Comm/mhc/Pro/Pro_013.cfm?a=641001.

71. Ibid.

72. Cathers, "Acts 1:6–8: Sunday Morning Bible Study," Calvary Chapel Fullerton, May 11, 1997, http://calvaryfullerton.org/Bstudy/44%20Act/1997/44act01b.htm.

73. Ibid.

74. MacArthur, *MacArthur Study Bible*, Proverbs 3:18, 880.

75. Ibid., Luke 22:10, 1559.

76. Guzik, "Romans 12—Living the Christian Life," Enduring Word, 2018, https://enduringword.com/bible-commentary/Romans-12.

77. Cathers, "Isaiah 40:12–31: Sunday Morning Bible Study," Calvary Chapel Fullerton, December 26, 1999, http://calvaryfullerton.org/Bstudy/23%20Isa/1999/23Isa40b.htm.

78. Guzik, "Joshua 9—The Gibeonite Deception," Enduring Word, 2018, https://enduringword.com/bible-commentary/Joshua-9.

79. MacArthur, *MacArthur Study Bible*, Psalm 67:1, 800.

80. Guzik, "1 Corinthians 13—Agape Love," Enduring Word, 2018, https://enduringword.com/bible-commentary/1Corinthians-13/.

81. Daniel, "Study Notes: 1 Samuel 13:1–14:52," Ron Daniel . . . a renaissance kinda guy, 1998-2019, http://www.rondaniel.com/library/09-1Samuel/1Samuel1301.php.

82. Nancie Carmichael and William Carmichael, *Lord Bless My Child* (Sisters, OR: Deep River Books, 2011), xxv.

83. MacArthur, *MacArthur Study Bible*, 1 Peter 4:7, 1947.

84. Stedman, "Let God be God: The Test," Ray Stedman Authentic Christianity, September 4, 1977, https://www.raystedman.org/old-testament/job/the-test.

85. Ibid.

86. Courson, "Daily Devotional with Pastor Jon Courson: Exodus 27:16," https://www.joncourson.com.

87. Ibid.

88. Evans, *Daily with the King*, November 4.

89. Courson, "The Law of the Leper Part 2: Leviticus 13–14," Searchlight with Pastor Jon Courson, January 29, 2012, https://www.joncourson.com/teaching/teachingsplay.asp?teaching=S7011.

90. Evans, *Daily with the King*, December 4.

91. Ibid.

92. Ibid., December 11.

93. Ibid.

94. MacArthur, *MacArthur Study Bible,* Philippians 2:12, 1823.

95. Courson, "Leviticus 15:1–17:10," Searchlight with Pastor Jon Courson, February 1, 2012, https://www.joncourson.com/teaching/teachingsplay.asp?teaching=W7021.

96. Ibid.

97. Henry, *Matthew Henry's Commentary*, Psalm 9:10, https://www.blueletterbible.org/Comm/mhc/Psa/Psa_009.cfm?a=487001.

98. Guzik, "1 Corinthians 6—Lawsuits and Loose Living," Enduring Word, 2018, https://enduringword.com/bible-commentary/1Corinthians-6.

99. Guzik, "Genesis 17—God Reaffirms the Covenant," Enduring Word, 2018, https://enduringword.com/bible-commentary/Genesis-17.

100. Evans, *Daily with the King*, March 11.

101. Ibid.

102. Stedman, "John: Who is This Man? – That Other Helper," Ray Stedman Authentic Christianity, March 24, 1985, https://www.raystedman.org/new-testament/john/that-other-helper.

103. Ibid.

104. Henry, *Matthew Henry's Commentary*, Proverbs 19, https://www.blueletterbible.org/Comm/mhc/Pro/Pro_019.cfm?a=647001.

105. Courson, "Leviticus 21–24," Searchlight with Pastor Jon Courson, February 15, 2012, https://www.joncourson.com/teaching/teachingsplay.asp?teaching=W7023.

106. Gene Pensiero, "2 Corinthians 1:1–11," Calvary Hanford, November 11, 2009, http://media.calvaryhanford.com/2corinthians/Chapter01a.pdf.

107. Guzik, "2 Corinthians 1—The God of All Comfort," Enduring Word, 2018, https://enduringword.com/bible-commentary/2Corinthians-1.

108. Pensiero, "2 Corinthians 1:1–11," Calvary Hanford, November 11, 2009, http://media.calvaryhanford.com/2corinthians/Chapter01a.pdf.

109. Guzik, "Romans 12—Living the Christian Life," Enduring Word, 2018, https://enduringword.com/bible-commentary/Romans-12.

110. Guzik, "James 4—The Humble Dependence of a True Faith," Enduring Word, 2018, https://enduringword.com/bible-commentary/James-4.

111. *The NKJV Study Bible*, second edition (Nashville: Thomas Nelson, 2007), Understanding the Bible, xvi.

112. *NKJV Study Bible*, 2 Timothy 3:16–17, 1929.

113. Guzik, "2 Corinthians 6—Paul's Resume," Enduring Word, 2018, https://enduringword.com/bible-commentary/2Corinthians-6.

114. Guzik, "2 Corinthians 10—How to Judge and Apostle," Enduring Word, 2018, https://enduringword.com/bible-commentary/2Corinthians-10.

115. Stedman, "John: Who Is This Man? The Testing of Faith," Ray Stedman Authentic Christianity, November 13, 1983, https://www.raystedman.org/new-testament/john/the-testing-of-faith.

116. Ibid.

117. Courson, *Jon Courson's Application Commentary: New Testament*, John 15:3, 563.

118. Guzik, "1 John 2—Hindrances to Fellowship with God," Enduring Word, 2018, https://enduringword.com/bible-commentary/1John-2.

119. Stedman, "1 John 1: The Fruit of Fellowship with Christ—The Man Who Rationalizes Sin," Ray Stedman Authentic Christianity, October 9, 1966, https://www.raystedman.org/new-testament/1-john/the-man-who-rationalizes-sin.

120. Ibid.

121. Stedman, "Leviticus: The Way to Wholeness—Power to Do," Ray Stedman Authentic Christianity, September 5, 1971, https://www.raystedman.org/old-testament/leviticus/power-to-do.

122. Ibid.

123. Guzik, "John 13—Jesus, the Loving Servant," Enduring Word, 2018, https://enduringword.com/bible-commentary/John-13.

124. *NKJV Study Bible*, John 13:1, 1686.

125. *NKJV Study Bible*, John 13:37, 1688.

126. G. Campbell Morgan, *The Westminster Pulpit*, Volume IX (Grand Rapids, MI: Baker, 2012), 318–323.

127. Daniel, "Study Notes: Philippians 1:1–2," Ron Daniel . . . a renaissance kinda guy, 1998–2019, http://www.rondaniel.com/library/50-Philippians/Philippians0101.php.

128. *NKJV Study Bible*, Acts 1:14, 1707

129. Henry, *Matthew Henry's Commentary*, Acts 2, https://www.blueletterbible.org/Comm/mhc/Act/Act_002.cfm?a=1020001.

130. *NKJV Study Bible*, Acts 1:14, 1040.

131. *NKJV Study Bible*, Acts 1:2, 1040.

132. David Guzik, "Isaiah 7—Shear-Jashub and Immanuel," Enduring Word, 2018, https://enduringword.com/bible-commentary/Isaiah-7.

133. *NKJV Study Bible*, Isaiah 7:9, 1051.

134. Stedman, "Isaiah: The Salvation of the Lord—O Come Immanuel," Ray Stedman Authentic Christianity, December 22, 1985, https://www.raystedman.org/old-testament/isaiah/o-come-immanuel.

135. Guzik, "Isaiah 12—Words from a Worshipper," Enduring Word, 2018, https://enduringword.com/bible-commentary/Isaiah-12.

136. Ibid.

137. Pensiero, "Ephesians 4:1–16," Calvary Hanford, October 29, 2008, http://media.calvaryhanford.com/ephesians/Chapter4a.pdf

138. Guzik, "Isaiah 26—Judah's Kingdom of God Song," Enduring Word, 2018, https://enduringword.com/bible-commentary/Isaiah-26.

139. Henry, *Matthew Henry's Commentary*, Isaiah 28, https://www.blueletterbible. org/Comm/mhc/Isa/Isa_028.cfm?a=707001.

140. Ibid.

141. Guzik, "1 John 4—Abiding in God and His Love," Enduring Word, 2018, https://enduringword.com/bible-commentary/1John-4.

142. Guzik, "Isaiah 32—A King's Reign of Righteousness," Enduring Word, 2018, https://enduringword.com/bible-commentary/Isaiah-32.

143. *NKJV Study Bible*, Isaiah 33:15, Page 1088.

144. Henry, *Matthew Henry's Commentary*, Philippians 1, https://www.blueletter-bible.org/Comm/mhc/Phl/Phl_001.cfm?a=1104001.

145. Strong's Greek Lexicon, G1922, *epignosis*, Blue Letter Bible, https://www. blueletterbible.org/lang/lexicon/lexicon.cfm?Strongs=G1922&t=KJV.

146. Ibid., *aesthesis*, https://www.blueletterbible.org/lang/lexicon/lexicon. cfm?Strongs=G144&t=KJV.

147. Courson, "Leviticus 11–14," Searchlight with Pastor Jon Courson, January 25, 2012, https://www.joncourson.com/teaching/teachingsplay. asp?teaching=W7020.

148. Ibid.

149. Guzik, "1 Peter 5—For Shepherds and Sheep," Enduring Word, 2018, https://enduringword.com/bible-commentary/1Peter-/.

150. Guzik, "Leviticus 17—The Sanctity of Blood," Enduring Word, 2018, https://enduringword.com/bible-commentary/Leviticus-17.

151. Ibid.

152. Henry, *Matthew Henry's Commentary*, Matthew 10, https://www.blueletterbi-ble.org/Comm/mhc/Mat/Mat_010.cfm?a=939001.

153. Ibid.

154. Stedman, "John: Who Is This Man? That Other Helper," Ray Stedman Authentic Christianity, March 24, 1985, https://www.raystedman.org/new-testament/john/that-other-helper.

155. Evans, *Daily with the King*, August 9.

156. Warren Wiersbe, *Be Joyful: Even When Things Go Wrong, You Can Have Joy— NT Commentary Philippians* (Colorado Springs: David C. Cook, 2008), 52

157.   Guzik, "Isaiah 40—Comfort and Strength for God's People," Enduring Word, 2018, https://enduringword.com/bible-commentary/Isaiah-40.

158.   Daniel, "Study Notes: Mark 6:1-56," Ron Daniel . . . a renaissance kinda guy, 1998–2019, http://www.rondaniel.com/library/41-Mark/Mark0601.php.

159.   Guzik, "Mark 6—Rejection, Opinions and Miracles," Enduring Word, 2018, https://enduringword.com/bible-commentary/Mark-6.

160.   Evans, *Daily with the King*, May 18.

161.   Ibid.

162.   Quoted by Guzik, "Isaiah 42—The Servant's Song," Enduring Word, 2018, https://enduringword.com/bible-commentary/Isaiah-42.

163.   Guzik, "Isaiah 43—Fear Not," Enduring Word, 2018, https://enduringword.com/bible-commentary/Isaiah-43.

164.   Henry, *Matthew Henry's Commentary*, Isaiah 43, https://www.blueletterbible.org/Comm/mhc/Isa/Isa_043.cfm?a=722001.

165.   Guzik, "Isaiah 43—Fear Not."

166.   Guzik, "Romans 11—The Restoration of Israel," Enduring Word, 2018, https://enduringword.com/bible-commentary/Romans-11.

167.   Guzik, "Matthew 6—The Sermon on the Mount," Enduring Word, 2018, https://enduringword.com/bible-commentary/Matthew-6.

168.   Guzik, "Isaiah 44—The LORD, Your Redeemer," Enduring Word, 2018, https://enduringword.com/bible-commentary/Isaiah-44.

169.   Rich Cathers, "1 John 1–2: Sunday Evening Bible Study," Calvary Chapel Fullerton, April 1, 2001, http://calvaryfullerton.org/Bstudy/62%20 1Jo/2001/621Jo01-02.htm.

170.   Guzik, "1 John 2—Hindrances to Fellowship with God," Enduring Word, 2018, https://enduringword.com/bible-commentary/1John-2.

171.   Henry, *Matthew Henry's Commentary*, Isaiah 48, https://www.blueletterbible.org/Comm/mhc/Isa/Isa_048.cfm?a=727001.

172.   Henry, *Matthew Henry's Commentary*, Isaiah 49, https://www.blueletterbible.org/Comm/mhc/Isa/Isa_049.cfm?a=728001.

173.   Guzik, "Isaiah 53—The Atoning Suffering and Victory of the Messiah," Enduring Word, 2018, https://enduringword.com/bible-commentary/Isaiah-53.

174. Ibid.

175. "Isoroku Yamamoto Quotes," BrainyQuote.com, https://www.brainyquote. com/quotes/isoroku_yamamoto_224334 (accessed August 11, 2018).

176. Abraham Lincoln, "Proclamation Appointing a National Fast Day, March 30, 1863," *The Collected Works of Abraham Lincoln,* ed. Roy P. Basler, vol. 6 (New Haven, CT: Yale Law Journal Company, 1954), 156.

177. Guzik, "Philippians 3—Leaving Law and Pressing on to Jesus," Enduring Word, 2018, https://enduringword.com/bible-commentary/Philippians-3.

178. Courson, *Jon Courson's Application Commentary: New Testament,* 1 Peter 5:7, 1577.

179. Guzik, "1 Peter 5—For Shepherds and Sheep," Enduring Word, 2018, https:// enduringword.com/bible-commentary/1Peter-5.

180. Guzik, "Isaiah 63—Prayer from Captivity," Enduring Word, 2018, https:// enduringword.com/bible-commentary/Isaiah-63.

181. Henry, *Matthew Henry's Commentary,* Isaiah 63, https://www.blueletterbible. org/Comm/mhc/Isa/Isa_063.cfm?a=742001.

182. Bill Hanley, personal communication, February 6, 2017.

183. "John Ruskin Quotes," BrainyQuote.com, https://www.brainyquote.com/ quotes/quotes/j/johnruskin143120.html (accessed June 17, 2017).

184. Evans, *Daily with the King,* February 16.

185. Guzik, "Matthew 26—Jesus' Betrayal and Arrest," Enduring Word, 2018, https://enduringword.com/bible-commentary/Matthew-26.

186. Cathers, "Luke 5:17–26—Wednesday Evening Bible Study," Calvary Chapel Fullerton, April 5, 2000, http://calvaryfullerton.org/Bstudy/42%20 Luk/2000/42Luk05b.htm.

187. Henry, *Matthew Henry's Commentary,* Mark 14, https://www.blueletterbible. org/Comm/mhc/Mar/Mar_014.cfm?a=971001.

188. Chuck Missler, "The Wedding Model, Pattern Is Prologue: The Rapture, Part 2," Koinonia House, January 1, 2003, http://www.khouse.org/articles/2003/449.

189. Courson, "Philippians 1," Searchlight with Pastor Jon Courson, March 8, 1995, https://www.joncourson.com/teaching/teachingsplay.asp?teaching=W689.

190. Ibid.

191.   Guzik, "2 Samuel 12—Nathan Confronts David," Enduring Word, 2018, https://enduringword.com/bible-commentary/2Samuel-12.

192.   MacArthur, *MacArthur Study Bible,* 2 Chronicles 3:18–20, 628.

193.   F. B. Meyer, "Our Daily Homily: 2 Chronicles," GototheBible.com, http://www.gotothebible.com/Meyer/dailyhomily2chronicles.html.

194.   Quoted by Henry, *Matthew Henry's Commentary,* 2 Chronicles 30:20, https://www.blueletterbible.org/Comm/mhc/2Ch/2Ch_030.cfm?a=397001.

195.   Melody Carson, *Benjamin's Box* (Grand Rapids, MI: Zondervan, 1997), 10.